BTEC
Level 3

edexcel
advancing learning, changing lives

SPORT LEVEL 3

Book 2 BTEC National

Mark Adams | Ray Barker | Wendy Davies
Adam Gledhill | Chris Lydon | Chris Mulligan
Alex Sergison | Louise Sutton | Nick Wilmot

Published by Pearson Education Limited, a company incorporated in England and Wales, having its registered office at Edinburgh Gate, Harlow, Essex, CM20 2JE. Registered company number: 872828

www.pearsonschoolsandfecolleges.co.uk

Edexcel is a registered trademark of Edexcel Limited
Text © Pearson Education Limited 2010

First published 2010

16
10 9

British Library Cataloguing in Publication Data
A catalogue record for this book is available from the British Library.

ISBN 978 1 846906 50 3

Edited by Liz Cartmell
Designed by Wooden Ark
Typeset by Tek-Art
Original illustrations © Pearson Education Limited and Vicky Woodgate 2010
Cover design by Visual Philosophy, created by eMC Design
Cover photo/illustration © Masterfile
Back cover photos © Shutterstock/Danny Warren, Shutterstock/Jonathan Larsen
Printed in China by Golden Cup

Websites
The websites used in this book were correct and up to date at the time of publication. It is essential for tutors to preview each website before using it in class so as to ensure that the URL is still accurate, relevant and appropriate. We suggest that tutors bookmark useful websites and consider enabling learners to access them through the school/college intranet.

Disclaimer
This material has been published on behalf of Edexcel and offers high-quality support for the delivery of Edexcel qualifications.
This does not mean that the material is essential to achieve any Edexcel qualification, nor does it mean that it is the only suitable material available to support any Edexcel qualification. Edexcel material will not be used verbatim in setting any Edexcel examination or assessment. Any resource lists produced by Edexcel shall include this and other appropriate resources.

Copies of official specifications for all Edexcel qualifications may be found on the Edexcel website: www.edexcel.com

Contents

Also available

There are many different optional units in your BTEC Level 3 National Sport qualification, which you may use to form specialist pathways or to build a broader programme of learning. This student book covers a huge choice of optional units for the Edexcel BTEC Level 3 National Extended Diploma in Sport across the two main pathways and some support for the Outdoor Adventure Pathway, but if you want all the mandatory units for the two main pathways and some mandatory units for the Outdoor Adventure Pathway you may be interested in Student Book 1.

Written in the same accessible style with the same useful features to support you through your learning and assessment, *BTEC Level 3 National Sport Student Book 1* (ISBN: 9781846906510) covers the following units:

Unit number	Credit value	Unit name
1	5	Principles of anatomy and physiology in sport
2	5	The physiology of fitness
3	10	Assessing risk in sport
4	10	Fitness training and programming
5	10	Sports coaching
6	10	Sports development
7	10	Fitness testing for sport and exercise
8 & 9	10	Practical team sports and Practical individual sports
11	10	Sports nutrition
17	10	Psychology for sports performance
27	10	Technical and tactical skills in sport
28	10	The athlete's lifestyle

BTEC Level 3 National Sport Student Book 1, ISBN: 9781846906510

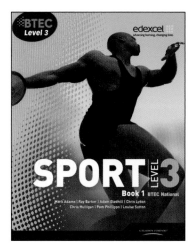

Available direct from www.pearsonfe.co.uk/btec2010 and can be ordered from all good bookshops.

About the authors

Mark Adams is a Senior Verifier for Sport Levels 1 to 3 and has worked with Edexcel for seven years. He has taught for ten years at schools and colleges across all qualifications. Mark is a consultant with the Premier League education and learning team. He is the series editor for our BTEC Level 3 National Sport and BTEC Level 3 National Sport and Exercise Science resources and has written for our BTEC Level 2 First Sport books.

Ray Barker has worked as sports manager and lecturer in a number of contexts for 30 years for companies and colleges in Scotland, Wales, the USA and France. He has written extensively on Sport topics and has assisted in the development of awards for Edexcel and other exam boards. He currently lectures at the University of Hull and is external examiner at Loughborough College and Cardiff School of Sport.

Wendy Davies has been a lecturer for the past 14 years after a varied career in the sport and leisure industry. She initially trained as a PE teacher and has worked in leisure management, sports development, coaching and lecturing. She is now on the management team in a busy department of a large FE college teaching a range of units and levels.

Adam Gledhill has nine years experience teaching throughout Further and Higher education, has been involved with Edexcel's qualification development for five years and external verification for three years and was a co-author of the previous editions of this book for Heinemann. Alongside teaching, Adam is currently working towards a PhD in Sport Psychology around the area of talent development in football at Loughborough University and provides sport science support to youth athletes in a range of sports.

Chris Lydon is a department manager and senior sports lecturer currently teaching BTEC courses at a Further Education college. In this role he is involved in the professional development of new staff and introduces them to BTEC assessment and verification. He has wide-ranging experience of teaching Further Education and Higher Education programmes and has contributed to a number of BTEC Sport textbooks published by Heinemann.

Chris Mulligan has been teaching BTEC qualifications for the last ten years and has taught across all levels. He has worked for Edexcel for the last five years as an external verifier and has written unit specifications for the new First and National Diplomas in Sport. Chris was also an author of the previous BTEC National Sport student book as well as the BTEC Level 3 National Sport Teaching Resource Pack.

Alex Sergison has spent 12 years instructing and lecturing at all levels. He specialises in outdoor education and has provided management and advice for a number of outdoor activity centres including the Weymouth and Portland National Sailing Academy's water sport school. Alex is responsible for outdoor education course development for Weymouth College and has been working with Edexcel developing new watersports qualifications.

Louise Sutton is a principal lecturer in sport and exercise nutrition at Leeds Metropolitan University and currently manages the Carnegie Centre for Sports Performance and Wellbeing. She is a member of the Health and Fitness Technical Expert Group of SkillsActive, the Sector Skills Council for Active Leisure and Learning in the UK. In 2005 Louise was awarded the Re-Energise Fitness Professional of the Year award for her commitment and contribution to raising standards in nutrition training and education in the health and fitness industry.

Nick Wilmot has worked in education for 9 years and has experience of teaching a range of FE and HE courses. Nick has experience of writing high level curriculum and has also contributed to previous editions of this book, BTEC National Sport Student Book 2 published by Heinemann. Nick has an MSc Applied Sport and Exercise Science and specialises in the physiological assessment of athletes and sports psychology.

Credits

The authors and publisher would like to thank the following individuals and organisations for permission to reproduce photographs:

p1 Imagestate. John Foxx Collection; **p3** Pearson Education Ltd. Jules Selmes; **p5** Shutterstock/Joe Gough; **p7** Shutterstock/Diego Cervo; **p10** Shutterstock/Darin Echelberger; **p12** Shutterstock/Tusia,; **p14** Shutterstock/Robert Fullerton; **p16** Shutterstock/Whitechild; **p18** Shutterstock/sculpies; **p23** Shutterstock/James Peragine; **p25** Shutterstock/Steve Broer; **p27** Pearson Education Ltd/Jules Selmes; **p28** Getty Images/Hulton Archive; **p40** Press Association Images/AP/Gerry Broome; **p41** Getty Images/Sports Illustrated; **p47** Shutterstock/Wolfgang Amri; **p49** Matthew Lewis/Stringer/Getty Images; **p51** Shutterstock/Karin Lau; **p53** iStockPhoto/TommL; **p55** Pearson Education Ltd. Gareth Boden; **p57** Shutterstock/iofoto; **p64** Shutterstock/Benis Arapovic; **p65** Jamie McDonald/Staff/Getty Images; **p77** Shutterstock/Apollofoto; **p79** iStockPhoto/skynesher; **p81** Pearson Education Ltd. Jules Selmes; **p91** Shutterstock/Monkey Business Images; **p97** Shutterstock/Poleze; **p102** Shutterstock/Danny Warren; **p105** Pearson Education Ltd. Studio 8. Clark Wiseman; **p107** © Ariel Skelley/Blend Images/Corbis; **p109** Pearson Education Ltd. Jules Selmes; **p111** Shutterstock/Tonobalaguerf; **p117** Shutterstock/Frank Herzog; **p123** Shutterstock/Dusan Zidar; **p124** Getty Images/Jamie MacDonald; **p126** Shutterstock/Monkey Business Images; **p137** Yuri Arcurs/shutterstock; **p139** iStockPhoto/skynesher; **p141** Pearson Education Ltd. Jules Selmes; **p142** Shutterstock/Rene Jansa; **p143** Shutterstock/Morgan Lane; **p145** Pearson Education Ltd/MindStudio; **p150** Masterfile/Jerzyworks; **p150** Shutterstock/Monkey Business Imagery; **p152** Lucas Dawson/Stringer/Getty Images; **p154** Shutterstock/Prism68; **p157** Getty Images/Superstudio; **p158** Alamy/Chris Rout; **p163** Shutterstock/John Lumb; **p167** Pearson Education Ltd. Gareth Boden; **p169** © Inspirestock/Corbis; **p171** © 2010 Photos.com; **p175** Hamish Blair/Staff/Getty images; **p177** David Scharf/Science Photo Library; **p193** Shutterstock/Patrizia Tilly; **p195** Shutterstock/Eoghan McNally; **p197** Pearson Education Ltd. Jules Selmes; **p199** Shutterstock/Sportlibrary; **p204** Shutterstock/Sportsphotographer.eu; **p220** Alamy/Adrian Sherratt; **p221** © 2010 Photos.com; **p223** Jamie McDonald/Staff/Getty Images **p225** © 2010 Photos.com; **p226** Shutterstock/Andreas Gradin; **p231** Getty Images/Staff; **p239** Shutterstock/Jonathon Larsen; **p247** Shutterstock/Antonio Jorge Nunes; **p249** Pearson Education Ltd. Gareth Boden; **p251** Pearson Education Ltd. Studio 8. Clark Wiseman; **p268** Pearson Education Ltd. Gareth Boden; **p268** Pearson Education Ltd. Gareth Boden; **p269** Pearson Education Ltd. Gareth Boden; **p274** Pearson Education Ltd. Gareth Boden; **p277** Shutterstock/Yuri Arcurs; **p279** David Madison/Getty, Adam Pretty/Getty; **p281** Pearson Education Ltd. Studio 8. Clark Wiseman; **p285** Adam Pretty/Staff/Getty Images; **p287** Shutterstock/afaizal; **p293** Bryn Lennon/Staff/Getty Images; **p295** Julian Finney/Staff/Getty Images; **p303** Shutterstock/Ajay Bhaskar; **p305** iStockPhoto/ictor; **p307** Pearson Education Ltd. Jules Selmes; **p308** Shutterstock/Chris Mole; **p327** Shutterstock/Karen Struthers; **p329** iStockPhoto/pixdeluxe; **p331** Pearson Education Ltd. Gareth Boden; **p343** Shutterstock/Dragan Trifunovic; **p345** Shutterstock/sonya etchison; **p352** Getty Images/Dan Kenyon; **p355** Shutterstock/Yuri Arcurs; **p357** © David Durochik/Corbis; **p359** Shutterstock/Tracy Whiteside; **p378** Pearson Education Ltd. Arnos Design; **p379** Photodisc. Photolink; **p381** Getty Images/Colorblind; **p383** Shutterstock/ImageryMajestic; **p385** iStockPhoto/Andresr; **p387** Shutterstock/Andrey Shadrin; **p390** Shutterstock/Tyler Olson; **p391** Imagestate. John Foxx Collection; **p397** Getty Images/Hill Creek Pictures; **p405** Pearson Education Ltd. Jules Selmes.

The authors and publisher would like to thank the following individuals and organisations for permission to adapt or reproduce diagrams and tables:

p233 Talent Identification Template courtesy of The Youth Sport Trust.

p337 Towards five hours of PE and sport for all young people, adapted from *The PE and Sport Strategy for Young People: A guide to delivering the five hour offer*, courtesy of Sport England

p347 'Rough & Ready Reckoner', adapted from the Brainboxx www.brainboxx.co.uk

About your BTEC Level 3 National Sport book

Every year the Sport and active leisure sector outperforms the rest of the UK economy and with the approach of the London 2012 Olympic and Paralympics Games the opportunities available within this sector are more varied than ever before. BTEC Level 3 National Sport will help you succeed in your future career within the sport and active leisure sector. It's designed to give you plenty of flexibility in selecting optional units so you can meet your interests and career aspirations. The principles of sport that you will learn here underpin many aspects of professional life within the sector and reflect the enormous breadth and depth of the subject – from principles of anatomy and physiology to talent identification and development, organising sports events and fitness testing for sport and exercise.

Your BTEC Level 3 National in Sport is a **vocational** or **work-related** qualification. This doesn't mean that it will give you *all* the skills you need to do a job, but it does mean that you'll have the opportunity to gain specific knowledge, understanding and skills that are relevant to your chosen subject or area of work.

What will you be doing?

The qualification is structured into **mandatory units** (M) (ones you must do) and **optional units** (O) (ones you can choose to do). How many units you do and which ones you cover depend upon the type of qualification you are working towards.

- BTEC Level 3 National Certificate in Sport: three mandatory units plus one optional unit to provide a total of 30 credits
- BTEC Level 3 National Subsidiary Diploma in Sport: three mandatory units plus one mandatory specialist unit plus optional units to provide a total of 60 credits
- BTEC Level 3 National Diploma in Sport (Performance and Excellence – **PE**): nine mandatory units plus optional units to provide a total of 120 credits
- BTEC Level 3 National Diploma in Sport (Development, Coaching and Fitness – **DCF**): eight mandatory units plus optional units to provide a total of 120 credits
- BTEC Level 3 National Diploma in Sport (Outdoor Adventure – **OA**): seven mandatory units plus optional units to provide a total of 120 credits
- BTEC Level 3 National Extended Diploma in Sport (Performance and Excellence – **PE**): nine mandatory units plus optional units to provide a total of 180 credits.
- BTEC Level 3 National Extended Diploma in Sport (Development, Coaching and Fitness – **DCF**): eight mandatory units plus optional units to provide a total of 180 credits.
- BTEC Level 3 National Extended Diploma in Sport (Outdoor Adventure – **OA**): seven mandatory units plus optional units to provide a total of 180 credits.

The table below shows how the units covered by the books in this series cover the different types of BTEC qualifications.

Unit no.	Credit value	Unit name	Cert	Sub Dip	Dip (PE)	Dip (DCF)	Dip (OA)	Ext Dip (PE)	Ext Dip (DCF)	Ext Dip (OA)
1	5	Principles of anatomy and physiology in sport	M	M	M	M	M	M	M	M
2	5	The physiology of fitness	M	M	M	M	M	M	M	M
3	10	Assessing risk in sport	M	M	M	M	M	M	M	M
4	10	Fitness training and programming		O	M	M	M	M	M	M
5	10	Sports coaching		O	O	M		O	M	O
6	10	Sports development		O		M			M	
7	10	Fitness testing for sport and exercise	O	M+	M	M		M	M	
8	10	Practical team sports		O	O	M*		O	M†	
9	10	Practical individual sports		O		M*			M†	
10	10	Outdoor and adventurous activities		O		O*			O	
11	10	Sports nutrition		O	M	O		M	O	O
12	10	Current issues in sport		O	O	O	O	O	O	O
13	10	Leadership in sport		O		O	M		O	M
14	10	Exercise, health and lifestyle		O		O			O	O
15	10	Instructing physical activity and exercise		O	O	O		O	O	
16	10	Exercise for specific groups							O	
17	10	Psychology for sports performance		O	M	O		M	O	
18	10	Sports Injuries			O	O	O	O	O	O
19	10	Analysis of sports performance			O			O	O	
20	10	Talent identification and development in sport						O	O	
21	10	Sport and exercise massage			O	O		O	O	
22	10	Rules, regulations and officiating In sport			O	O		O	O	
23	10	Organising sports events				O	O	O	O	O
24	10	Physical education and the care of children and young people		O		O	O	O	O	O
25	10	Sport as a business				O	O	O	O	O
26	10	Work experience in sport		O	O	O	O	O	O	O
27	10	Technical and tactical skills in sport		O	M				M	
28	10	The athlete's lifestyle		O	M				M	

Units in yellow are covered in this book. Units in green are covered in *BTEC Level 3 National Sport Student Book 1* (ISBN: 9781846906510).

* Learners **must select either** Unit 8 or Unit 9 as a mandatory unit.

* Learners **may select**, as an optional unit, whichever of Unit 8 or Unit 9 that was not taken as a mandatory unit, **or** alternatively may select Unit 10.

* Learners **must not** select all three of Unit 8, Unit 9 and Unit 10.

+ One unit must be taken from each of these units.

† Learners must select **one** of these units (Unit 8 or Unit 9) as a mandatory unit, and may select the other as an optional unit.

How to use this book

This book is designed to help you through your BTEC Level 3 National Sport course.

It contains many features that will help you develop and apply your skills and knowledge in work-related situations and assist you in getting the most from your course.

Introduction

These introductions give you a snapshot of what to expect from each unit – and what you should be aiming for by the time you finish it!

Assessment and grading criteria

This table explains what you must do in order to achieve each of the assessment criteria for each unit. For each assessment criterion, shown by the grade button **P**, **M**, **D** there is an assessment activity.

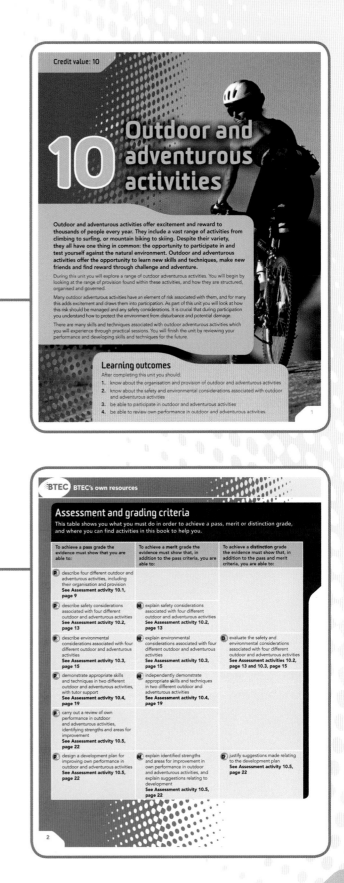

Assessment

Your tutor will set **assignments** throughout your course for you to complete. These may take a number of forms. The important thing is that you evidence your skills and knowledge to date.

Stuck for ideas? Daunted by your first assignment? These students have all been through it before…

Unit 10 Outdoor and adventurous activities

How you will be assessed

This unit will be assessed by an internal assignment that will be designed and marked by staff at your centre. Your assessment could be in the form of:
- presentations
- case studies
- practical tasks
- written assignments.

Rebecca, 17-year-old passionate climber

Studying this unit convinced me that I should pursue a career in outdoor adventurous activity. I can't imagine being stuck behind a desk; I need to be outside finding a challenge every day. Although I have been climbing for years, this unit made me look again at what I was doing and consider the safety and the environmental implications of my participation and how I could better protect myself and the natural environment.

It was interesting to investigate and participate in other activities as well as see how they are organised and governed as well as learn plenty of new skills.

The practical instruction that I received in all the activities was brilliant. The instructors were motivational. They helped me learn new skills and techniques and improve existing ones. I really enjoyed examining how I could review sessions for myself and create development plans for the future to ensure I keep improving. This unit was a great opportunity. I hope that one day it could be me teaching outdoor activity and inspiring more people to give it a go.

Over to you!

1. Rebecca clearly loves being outside. What appeals to you about outdoor and adventurous activity?
2. Which part of this unit do you think you will find the most interesting?

Activities

There are different types of activities for you to do: **Assessment activities** are suggestions for tasks that you might do as part of your assignment and will help you develop your knowledge, skills and understanding. **Grading tips** clearly explain what you need to do in order to achieve a pass, merit or distinction grade.

Assessment activity 10.2   P2 M1 D1   BTEC

1. Participate in a range of outdoor adventurous activities making observations as well as conducting individual research. Now imagine that you are training potential instructors and create a presentation, using a program such as PowerPoint® describing the safety considerations associated with four different outdoor and adventurous activities. **P2**

2. During the presentation ensure that you explain the safety considerations associated with four different outdoor and adventurous activities. **M1**

3. Finally, include in the presentation an evaluation of the safety considerations associated with four different outdoor and adventurous activities. **D1**

Grading tips

Structure your PowerPoint clearly and use a new slide for each point you make.
- To attain **P2** you must consider both your own and others' safety.
- To attain **M1** you must show why each safety precaution must be taken.
- To attain **D1** you must reflect upon the effectiveness of each safety consideration.

There are also suggestions for activities that will give you a broader grasp of the Sport sector, stretch your understanding and deepen your skills.

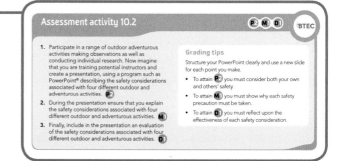

Activity: Emergency action plans

Imagine that you were in charge of organising an outdoor adventurous activity. Think about the flow diagram in Figure 10.1 and describe how you would go about dealing with an accident resulting in a possible back injury.

Personal, learning and thinking skills

Throughout your BTEC Level 3 National Sport course, there are lots of opportunities to develop your personal, learning and thinking skills. Look out for these as you progress.

Functional skills

It's important that you have good English, Mathematics and ICT skills – you never know when you'll need them, and employers will be looking for evidence that you've got these skills too.

Key terms

Technical words and phrases are easy to spot. You can also use the glossary at the back of the book.

WorkSpace

Case studies provide snapshots of real workplace issues, and show how the skills and knowledge you develop during your course can help you in your career.

There are also mini-case studies throughout the book to help you focus on your own projects.

WorkSpace

George Denzel
Windsurf instructor

George works for a small windsurfing company that hires out equipment and gives instruction at all levels. The centre is recognised by the RYA as an approved training provider. George's responsibilities include:

- taking bookings for tuition and equipment hire
- welcoming and briefing new arrivals to the centre
- providing safety cover from a rescue craft for those hiring windsurf equipment
- providing tuition to both groups and individuals
- ensuring the centre maintains standards set out by the RYA.

'Most days I arrive at 9 a.m. There are three other people working at the centre, including Mark the centre manager. Every morning we start with a meeting to discuss the day ahead. We check the forecast and assign roles for the day.

Next I will help set up. The rescue craft must be fuelled and warmed up, boards and sails unlocked and welcome signs put out. We always make sure that the site is really tidy as first impressions count for a lot.

During the day I may be instructing beginners or coaching more advanced students. Sometimes I am in charge of providing rescue cover for all those on the water and at other times maintaining any equipment. My day finishes at about 5 p.m. and then I often head out onto the water.

The best thing about my job is spending so much time outdoors on the water. Every day presents me with new challenges and I get lots of satisfaction from inspiring new windsurfers and teaching them new skills. It is fantastic being able to earn a wage doing something that you enjoy. I intend to gain more experience and eventually hope to manage a centre myself.

In terms of skills, I have to communicate with other members of the team and clients every day so this is certainly at the top of the list. The practical skills I practised during my Sport BTEC, I now use every day to demonstrate techniques to other windsurfers. I worked hard at developing my balance and coordination so that now I feel confident when teaching.'

Think about it!

- What activities might you like to instruct in the future?
- What skills might you need to develop to help you?
- In small groups discuss what skills are most important for someone who wants to start a career in the outdoor adventurous activity industry.

23

Just checking

When you see this sort of activity, take stock! These quick activities and questions are there to check your knowledge. You can use them to see how much progress you've made.

Edexcel's assignment tips

At the end of each unit, you'll find hints and tips to help you get the best mark you can, such as the best websites to go to, checklists to help you remember processes and useful reminders to avoid common mistakes.

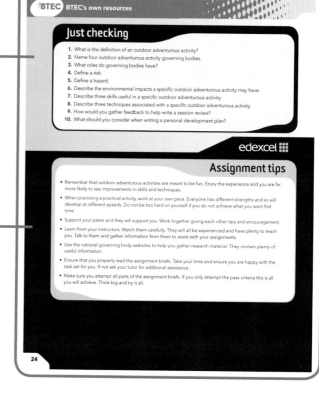

Don't miss out on these resources to help you!

Have you read your **BTEC Level 3 National Study Skills Guide**? It's full of advice on study skills, putting your assignments together and making the most of being a BTEC Sport student.

Ask your tutor about extra materials to help you through the course. The **Teaching Resource Pack** which accompanies this book contains interesting videos featuring Tottenham Hotspur, activities, presentations, a Podcast and information about the Sport sector.

Visit www.pearsonfe.co.uk/videopodcast to view or download a free video podcast that you can use at home or on the go via your mobile phone, MP3 player or laptop. Wherever you see the podcast icon in the book you'll know that the podcast will help you get to grips with the content. You can also access this podcast for free on the internet www.edexcel.com/ BTEC or via the iTunes store.

Your book is just part of the exciting resources from Edexcel to help you succeed in your BTEC course.
Visit www.edexcel.com/BTEC or www.pearsonfe.co.uk/BTEC2010 for more details.

Credit value: 10

10 Outdoor and adventurous activities

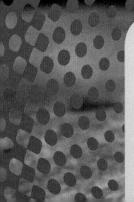

Outdoor and adventurous activities offer excitement and reward to thousands of people every year. They include a vast range of activities from climbing to surfing, or mountain biking to skiing. Despite their variety, they all have one thing in common: the opportunity to participate in and test yourself against the natural environment. Outdoor and adventurous activities offer the opportunity to learn new skills and techniques, make new friends and find reward through challenge and adventure.

During this unit you will explore a range of outdoor adventurous activities. You will begin by looking at the range of provision found within these activities, and how they are structured, organised and governed.

Many outdoor adventurous activities have an element of risk associated with them, and for many this adds excitement and draws them into participation. As part of this unit you will look at how this risk should be managed and any safety considerations. It is crucial that during participation you understand how to protect the environment from disturbance and potential damage.

There are many skills and techniques associated with outdoor adventurous activities which you will experience through practical sessions. You will finish the unit by reviewing your performance and developing skills and techniques for the future.

Learning outcomes

After completing this unit you should:

1. know about the organisation and provision of outdoor and adventurous activities
2. know about the safety and environmental considerations associated with outdoor and adventurous activities
3. be able to participate in outdoor and adventurous activities
4. be able to review own performance in outdoor and adventurous activities.

Assessment and grading criteria

This table shows you what you must do in order to achieve a pass, merit or distinction grade, and where you can find activities in this book to help you.

To achieve a **pass** grade the evidence must show that you are able to:	To achieve a **merit** grade the evidence must show that, in addition to the pass criteria, you are able to:	To achieve a **distinction** grade the evidence must show that, in addition to the pass and merit criteria, you are able to:
P1 describe four different outdoor and adventurous activities, including their organisation and provision **See Assessment activity 10.1, page 9**		
P2 describe safety considerations associated with four different outdoor and adventurous activities **See Assessment activity 10.2, page 13**	**M1** explain safety considerations associated with four different outdoor and adventurous activities **See Assessment activity 10.2, page 13**	
P3 describe environmental considerations associated with four different outdoor and adventurous activities **See Assessment activity 10.3, page 15**	**M2** explain environmental considerations associated with four different outdoor and adventurous activities **See Assessment activity 10.3, page 15**	**D1** evaluate the safety and environmental considerations associated with four different outdoor and adventurous activities **See Assessment activities 10.2, page 13 and 10.3, page 15**
P4 demonstrate appropriate skills and techniques in two different outdoor and adventurous activities, with tutor support **See Assessment activity 10.4, page 19**	**M3** independently demonstrate appropriate skills and techniques in two different outdoor and adventurous activities **See Assessment activity 10.4, page 19**	
P5 carry out a review of own performance in outdoor and adventurous activities, identifying strengths and areas for improvement **See Assessment activity 10.5, page 22**		
P6 design a development plan for improving own performance in outdoor and adventurous activities **See Assessment activity 10.5, page 22**	**M4** explain identified strengths and areas for improvement in own performance in outdoor and adventurous activities, and explain suggestions relating to development **See Assessment activity 10.5, page 22**	**D2** justify suggestions made relating to the development plan **See Assessment activity 10.5, page 22**

How you will be assessed

This unit will be assessed by an internal assignment that will be designed and marked by staff at your centre. Your assessment could be in the form of:

- presentations
- case studies
- practical tasks
- written assignments.

Rebecca, 17-year-old passionate climber

Studying this unit convinced me that I should pursue a career in outdoor adventurous activity. I can't imagine being stuck behind a desk; I need to be outside finding a challenge every day. Although I have been climbing for years, this unit made me look again at what I was doing and consider the safety and the environmental implications of my participation and how I could better protect myself and the natural environment.

It was interesting to investigate and participate in other activities and see how they are organised and governed as well as learn plenty of new skills.

The practical instruction that I received in all the activities was brilliant. The instructors were motivational. They helped me learn new skills and techniques and improve existing ones. I really enjoyed examining how I could review sessions for myself and create development plans for the future to ensure I keep improving. This unit was a great opportunity. I hope that one day it could be me teaching outdoor activity and inspiring more people to give it a go.

Over to you!

1. Rebecca clearly loves being outside. What appeals to you about outdoor and adventurous activity?
2. Which part of this unit do you think you will find the most interesting?

1. Know about the organisation and provision of outdoor and adventurous activities

Outdoor and adventurous activity encompasses a huge range of activities. Some are described below.

Key term

Outdoor and adventurous activity – physical activity that stimulates and challenges participants and is done outside, often in a hostile environment.

1.1 Types of activities

Land based activities

Snow skiing – skiing is predominantly a mountain sport that involves the use of a ski for each foot. This is a long flat device designed to allow the user to slide over the ground. Skis are used in conjunction with bindings that connect them to boots. Poles are held in each hand to aid balance. Skiing has many disciplines such as downhill racing, cross-country, free style or ski jumping. It appeals to a range of participants.

Mountain biking – this involves the use of a bicycle that has been developed to cope with rough terrain and continuous punishment. The bikes are reinforced, use thicker tyres than road bikes to allow extra grip and utilise suspension to soften impacts. They have a large number of gears that can be selected to allow efficient performance up and down hills.

Orienteering – the aim of this sport is to navigate between a sequence of control points marked on a map in the quickest time possible. Competitors must decide upon the most efficient route and at what pace to progress. Orienteering can be done in a wide range of terrains from mountainside to beach sand dunes.

Climbing – this is the ascent of an incline or steep face normally using both hands and feet to aid progress. Climbing is usually done with the aid of specialised equipment such as ropes, harnesses and technical shoes and normally involves two people working together to support one another. Climbing is often done on rock faces; however there are other disciplines such as ice climbing. Over the last few years deep water soloing has become popular. This is climbing over water without ropes or support equipment and relying on the water to break your fall should you lose contact with the rock face.

Caving – this is exploration or travelling through cave systems. Due to the lack of light, caving relies on torches and lamps. Caves come in all shapes and sizes and offer a variety of challenges from basic navigation, to squeezing through tiny nooks and crannies. Although most caving is done in dry caves, you can explore flooded caves. One of the most extreme forms is cave diving with the aid of specialist breathing apparatus.

Water based activities

Windsurfing – this is a water sport that involves the use of a board with a sail attached and relies on wind for propulsion. Windsurfing can be done in a range of conditions from waves to dead flat lakes. When a participant is travelling at speed you will normally find that they are attached to the board with foot straps and the sail with a harness. This helps them control the large forces acting on the equipment in windy conditions.

This kayaker is out in challenging conditions. What skills would he need to perform at this level?

Kayaking – this is the propulsion of a water craft with a deck by one or more individuals using a double ended paddle. Kayaking is popular and accessible to a wide range of people. Kayaking can be done on the sea or lakes and rivers. Kayaks vary in design to increase efficiency in different conditions. For example, a sea kayak designed for long journeys will be long and pointed to allow it to cut through the water and travel at speed whereas a kayak for rapids may be shorter and wider to increase manoeuvrability and stability.

Sailing – this is the propulsion of an on-water craft or vessel using the wind harnessed by sails. The craft can vary in size from dinghies no more than 2 metres in length to yachts over 20 metres long. Sailing can take place on lakes, coastal waters or wild oceans. Due to the variety of vessels and venues, sailing is a popular sport.

Air based activities

Paragliding – this involves flying under a canopy that was originally developed from a parachute design. The canopy is lightweight but highly efficient at catching and holding gentle currents in the air which are essential to provide and maintain lift. As the canopy has no solid skeletal system it is easy to transport. Although most paragliders use hills and mountainsides as launch sites, it is possible to launch by being towed by a powerful winch system. Paragliding provides participants with huge freedom once airborne. Flights of over 150 km have been made within the UK.

Hang gliding – this utilises a sophisticated yet simple wing-like framework consisting of carbon fibre and aluminium struts giving high tech sail fabrics a shape. The hang glider is launched into the wind on a hillside or can be towed aloft by an aircraft. The idea is to stay airborne for as long as possible and this can mean long journeys over many miles.

Take it further

More outdoor activities

Carry out some research to find other activities that fit into the categories of land, water or air based outdoor activity.

1.2 Organisation of outdoor and adventurous activities

Most established outdoor and adventurous activities have a national governing body which provides structure and organisation. Additionally, there are statutory bodies and voluntary bodies that affect both participation in and organisation of an activity. Despite many of these activities being governed individually or in small groups, there are many similarities in the way they are organised.

National governing bodies

These governing bodies have various roles and responsibilities which benefit the activities' current and future participation levels. They employ staff to organise and perform different jobs. Examples of national governing bodies and associated websites are listed in Table 10.1 below.

Although each governing body manages itself individually, many of their roles and responsibilities are similar. These could be:

- regulating safety and standards
- designing training schemes
- promoting the activity

- organising competitions and events
- providing grass roots opportunities.

Regulating safety and standards

In any activity safety must be paramount. Governing bodies are particularly interested in safety issues as incidents involving injury or death can have a hugely detrimental effect on the participant levels of any sport. A sport that is deemed to be too high risk is unlikely to see as much take-up as one in which the risk seems to be managed. Governing bodies regulate safety and standards in two ways:

- They design training schemes for participants and instructors. The instructor training ensures that anyone teaching a particular activity has had appropriate experience and training. During an instructor training course potential instructors will be assessed practically, coached intensively in instructional techniques and trained in depth in appropriate precautions that should be taken before and during a session. Consequently anyone being trained by a recognised instructor can do so with the confidence of knowing they are adequately qualified.

Table 10.1: National governing bodies for outdoor and adventurous activities. Why not visit some of these websites and find out more about sports you might be interested in trying?

Sport	Water, air or land based	National governing body	Website
Kayaking and canoeing	Water based	British Canoe Union	www.bcu.org.uk
Sailing, windsurfing and power boating	Water based	Royal Yachting Association	www.rya.org.uk
Surfing	Water based	British Surfing Association	www.britsurf.co.uk
Paragliding and hang gliding	Air based	British Gliding Association	www.gliding.co.uk
Skiing and snowboarding	Land based	British Association of Snowsport Instructors	www.basi.org.uk
Orienteering	Land based	British Orienteering Federation	www.britishorienteering.org.uk
Climbing and mountaineering	Land based	British Mountaineering Council	www.thebmc.co.uk
Caving	Land based	British Caving Association	www.british-caving.org.uk

- Many governing bodies implement regular inspections of training facilities providing instruction in the relevant activity. On-site inspectors vigilantly monitor levels of tuition, safety standards and procedures as well as the quality of resources and equipment. This ensures that participants can take part in activities at centres with confidence.

Designing training schemes

Training schemes give you confidence in the organisation of an activity. There is another very positive reason for governing bodies to design structured training schemes: they ensure that there is a route for progression for those participating in an activity at any level. Once participants have had a taste of an activity they should have adequate opportunity and support to continue. If an early interest is not quickly followed up on, many potential new participants are likely to be lost.

A good training scheme will allow progression from grass roots instruction to elite training, and be clear for participants to understand. On completion of courses, certification is normally awarded. This acts as a motivational tool and provides evidence of competency that takes you to the next level of instruction.

Promoting the activity

To generate interest in an activity it should be promoted efficiently. Many outdoor adventurous activities are not mainstream and to encourage new participation strong national governing bodies will be proactive in promoting their activity. Many governing bodies have visually stimulating websites, publish books and manuals, and provide regular magazines or flyers to advertise current developments and news. These are all fantastic ways of promoting an activity; however, they are no competition for live demonstrations and people actually having a go.

Competitions and events

Competition is vital to promote a sport. It provides a visual spectacle that may inspire those watching to participate in the activity. Competition takes place at all levels from junior amateur events to professional well funded championships. This progression gives competitors experience and coaches the opportunity to spot those with potential to compete at an elite level. When a country has athletes competing at an activity at a high level you are more likely to see press coverage, which helps promote the activity and inspire new recruits.

National governing bodies have a vital role in supporting and organising events. They coordinate entries, arrange venues and ensure that competition is fair. They make sure that all aspects of the competitions are provided safely. During world class events the national governing bodies may not have complete responsibility for the delivery but they are likely to provide support and advice and maintain a strong presence.

These inexperienced young skiers are lucky enough to be getting great instruction. What training scheme are they likely to be taking part in?

Grass roots opportunities

Grass roots are the first rung on the ladder for participation in an activity and the most important. Grass roots training is about inspiring a new generation to participate in an activity. If an activity is to maintain popularity, national governing bodies must push grass roots training at every opportunity. Taster days are one of the best tools of any governing body to encourage grass roots participation. These are one-off sessions where the priority is to promote the activity and inspire future participation rather than learning skills and techniques.

Statutory bodies

Statutory bodies such as the Countryside Agency or the Civil Aviation Authority enforce government legislation designed to protect the public and the environment. They often work with, and provide advice for, activity governing bodies on developments within their activities or the law. The statutory bodies clamp down on offenders breaking any laws and pursue convictions.

Voluntary bodies

Voluntary bodies include clubs and associations or local education outdoor centres. In general these are designed to help people to access affordable opportunities within an activity.

Clubs are common within many activities such as sailing, climbing and walking. They rely upon volunteer (unpaid) staff to organise them and aim to provide a safe and social way to experience an activity. Although some do, many clubs do not offer training; instead they focus on providing a clear way for people to regularly participate. Local education outdoor centres offer free or subsidised activities through schools and community groups. Their focus is on providing opportunity for all, irrespective of economic or social background.

1.3 Provision of outdoor and adventurous activities

The provision of outdoor and adventurous activities determines how easy it is for people to participate. Thus provision locally and nationally can determine a sport's popularity. Without demand for a sport, provision is unlikely to be developed and fewer opportunities created for participation.

Local provision

Centres and clubs have a huge responsibility for providing local opportunity in an activity. Grass roots sessions are vital for encouraging initial participation in a sport. Clubs and centres should work hand in hand with local councils and schools to promote and provide opportunities within their activity.

Case study: The Royal Yachting Association (RYA)

The RYA is the national governing body for all forms of boating. This includes dinghy sailing, yacht sailing, motor yachting, RIBs and sports boats, personal water craft, cruising and narrow boats and windsurfing. The RYA is a world leader in what it does. Some of its roles include:

- lobbying to protect the interests of boaters
- providing expert advice for its members and affiliated centres
- organising racing events
- designing first class training schemes and providing world renowned professional qualifications

- nurturing and supporting Britain's sailing talent
- encouraging sailing for people with a disability
- growing the sport through events and initiatives designed to make boating as accessible as possible.

The RYA has worked hard to become the driving force behind boating in Britain. They communicate with their members with an organised website and regular magazine.

1. **Which other activities have large governing bodies to support and grow them?**
2. **Could any other governing bodies learn from the RYA's example?**

'Have a go' or taster days are a fantastic way to get people involved. However, as already stated, it's vital that there is a strategy to follow up on an enjoyable experience to encourage take-up. Schemes such as youth clubs and structured courses must be available and easily accessible.

Unfortunately, many outdoor adventurous activities are expensive. In order that activities are available for all, centres and clubs often apply for subsidies, grants and sponsorship.

National provision

National frameworks usually rely on governing bodies to maintain them. Thanks to governing body certification and standardisation of teaching it should be relatively easy for participants to move between training centres and clubs. As participants reach higher levels, and elite athletes begin to emerge, training often takes place at national camps and academies. Camps may move between venues; academies tend to be at a fixed location. Both require participants to travel to attend them.

Influences upon provision

There are many things that can affect the numbers participating in an activity and provision:

- Media portrayal – how much coverage an activity is given and if it is portrayed in a positive way.
- Location – outdoor adventurous activities rely on the environment. It is often not possible to participate in an activity locally if the environment does not allow it. Even with suitable venues available, they are not always accessible for local people. Public transport may not be in place to provide a suitable service.
- Finance – many outdoor and adventurous activities are expensive. Those with a lower income are less likely to spend money on expensive equipment vital for participation. This is when clubs can play an invaluable role by offering an affordable way of taking part. Some regions are lucky enough to have educational centres that have support to enable them to offer affordable activities. These often come in the form of local authority centres supported by local government. These centres may be multi-discipline or focused on one or a small number of activities. However, they will be focused upon providing opportunity in activities appropriate to the region.

Assessment activity 10.1   P1   BTEC

Imagine that you work for a government initiative created to promote outdoor adventurous activity. Design a poster that describes four different outdoor and adventurous activities, including their organisation and provision. P1

Grading tips

To attain P1:

- choose the types of outdoor adventurous activities that interest you
- use the websites for the governing bodies listed earlier in the unit when conducting research
- consider: providers, participants, training opportunities, roles of national governing bodies, equipment, financial implications, competitive opportunity.

PLTS

When conducting research you will be using your skills as an **independent enquirer**. If you design a poster that promotes outdoor and adventurous thinking you can develop your skills in **creative thinking**.

Functional skills

By creating this poster you are providing evidence towards skills in **English**.

2. Know about the safety and environmental considerations associated with outdoor and adventurous activities

Many people are drawn towards outdoor and adventurous activities because of the potential excitement they offer and the opportunity they present to spend time out of doors in the natural environment. Unfortunately, where there is excitement and the potential for people to spend time outside, there is also often an element of risk to both the participants and the environment.

2.1 Safety considerations

When thinking about the associated dangers attached to an activity you need to consider **hazards** and **risks**.

Key terms

Hazard – anything that has the potential to cause a person harm.

Risk – the chance that a hazard may cause harm to someone.

The Health and Safety Executive, the government body responsible for controlling and monitoring hazards and risks, categorises hazards in the following way:

- **Mechanical** – this can be any moving equipment or machinery, e.g. the propeller on a ski boat or the gears on a mountain bike.

- **Physical** – this incorporates slips, trips and falls, e.g. slipping on ice while mountain walking or falling from a harbour wall while mooring a boat.

- **Chemical** – this is most likely to be fuel, cleaning products or maintenance equipment, e.g. the fuel for a motor boat or lubricant for a mountain bike.

- **Environmental** – this is from either weather or terrain, e.g. lightning while windsurfing or a blizzard while skiing.

- **Biological** – this could be any bacteria or microorganisms that may cause infection, e.g. polluted water while kayaking.

- **Organisational** – this could be things such as poor planning, rushing to complete a job or participating in an activity without relevant training or experience.

Lightning is dangerous to be out in no matter what activity you are doing. What other types of weather could be hazardous to various activities?

Activity: Hazards associated with an activity

Think about a specific activity. In small groups, identify as many hazards as you can that may affect participation in this activity. Now, as a whole group, compile all your thoughts and explain how these hazards may jeopardise the safety of a group or individual.

Risk assessments

When considering hazards and their associated risks one of the most useful tools you possess is risk assessment. Risk assessment allows you to identify and manage risk effectively. Each time you participate in an activity you probably subconsciously assess the associated risks. This may be looking around at uneven ground, keeping an eye on the weather or ensuring you pack up before dark.

A risk assessment is a way of formalising this process and it allows you to create a working document that encourages continual management of hazards and risks (see Table 10.2). Written risk assessments come in many formats and may vary in design between activity and venue.

However, the following process should still remain the same:

1. Identify the hazard – the categories discussed on page 10 should help in identifying potential hazards. Hazards vary between activities and venues. You should be aware that hazards are not always easy to spot. Sometimes they appear during a session when you thought you had prepared for all eventualities. You should consider a risk assessment a working document and be prepared to add or amend hazards where necessary.

2. Decide who may be affected – participants, staff and bystanders. Some hazards may affect everyone in the area and some only an individual. For example, smoking near a fuel can could cause an explosion and harm anyone nearby, but a climber not wearing their helmet will only harm themselves.

3. State any existing control measures – these include protective equipment, providing an adequate briefing and training or only taking part in suitable conditions. If no control measures are in place this should be documented.

4. Rate the risk – be able to grade any risks clearly and logically. A simple way of grading risks is as follows:
   - Give the risk a severity rating between 1 and 5.
     1 is the lowest risk – where the outcome would be only minor, easily treatable, injury.
     5 is the highest risk – where the outcome may be serious injury or death.
   - Give the risk a probability rating between 1 and 5.
     1 is the lowest probability – where the incident is highly unlikely to happen.
     5 is the highest probability – where the incident is very likely to happen.
   - Now multiply the severity by the probability. This gives you a figure between 1 and 25 to rate the risk as follows:
     Very low (1–5) – a risk that is highly unlikely to affect a session.
     Low (5–10) – a risk that is unlikely to affect a session as long as suitable precautions are taken.
     Medium (10–15) – a risk that will need strict management but may allow an activity to go ahead.
     High (15–20) – a risk that is likely to make an activity unviable without further precautions being implemented.
     Severe (20–25) – a risk that would certainly make an activity unviable.

5. Suggested measures for development – finally, identify and record any further actions that may be taken to minimise a risk. On implementation of these further actions the risk assessment may be amended and risk rating altered to reflect ongoing development.

For a full exploration of risk assessment, refer to Student Book 1 Unit 3 Assessing risk.

Table 10.2: An example of a risk assessment.

Identify the hazard	Who may be affected?	Existing control measures	Risk rating = severity × probability	Suggested measures for development
Uneven terrain at bottom of sailing slipway	Instructor and clients	Everyone must wear appropriate footwear and instructors should warn clients of hazard	Severity: 2 Probability: 3 Risk = 6 = low	Area at bottom of slipway to be cleared of all moveable debris

Basic precautions

Writing a risk assessment helps to identify a number of precautions that should be taken before, during and after an activity.

- **Before** – planning an activity session is crucial to its smooth running and the safety of the group. A session should be planned for the ability of the group and choosing a suitable venue is important. To ensure adequate amounts of equipment are taken you must know participant numbers. As all these activities are outside a weather forecast is essential to ensure suitable conditions. Finally, before departing you should tell someone where you are going and what time you will return so if you get into difficulties the alarm will be raised.

- **During** – during the session be vigilant of potential hazards. Adequate rests should be taken and both water and food taken on board regularly. Protective equipment should be worn at all times.

- **After** – on completion of a session you should ensure that everyone is accounted for. Report your return to the person you spoke to before leaving. Any equipment should be checked and necessary maintenance performed to ensure it is ready for next time.

Personal protective equipment (PPE)

Participants in outdoor adventurous activity should wear appropriate personal protective equipment (PPE). PPE is developed to protect you from the prevailing conditions and many injuries directly resulting from participation in various activities. The following are a few examples of PPE that may be used for various activities.

- **Buoyancy aid** – this is a flotation device which is used in sports such as sailing, windsurfing and kayaking. It is worn over the body like a jacket, and should fit snugly to ensure it does not ride up in the event of the participant entering the water. A buoyancy aid will not keep a victim's head clear of the water in the event of them being knocked unconscious.

- **Climbing helmet** – protection of the head is essential for the climber in the event of a fall and for the belayer to protect them from falling rock. A climbing helmet is lightweight and should fit tightly but comfortably and not obscure a climber's vision.

A buoyancy aid is essential for many water sports. What other PPE may be used in water sports?

- **Walking boots** – specialised walking boots offer good grip over different terrains. They support the ankle when a participant is travelling over difficult terrain. Many walking boots are water resistant. Walking boots should be fitted accurately before purchase to prevent rubbing blisters.

Emergency procedures

Despite your best intentions, occasionally something will go wrong during an outdoor adventurous session. Knowing how to deal with an incident ensures that a situation does not get out of hand. Figure 10.1, a simple flow diagram, can be used to help plan for an emergency.

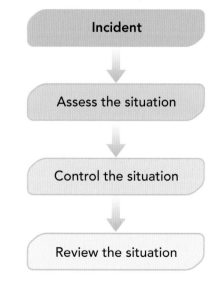

Figure 10.1: Planning in an emergency. How do you think you would handle an emergency situation?

- **Incident** – examples of the many incidents that could occur during an outdoor adventurous activity session include: a fall while climbing resulting in a broken leg; an unexpected change in the weather while sailing; getting lost while mountain walking.

- **Assess the situation** – when assessing the situation consider the safety of: the victim, anyone else in the group and yourself. You are no good to anyone if you become a victim yourself and allowing anyone else in the group to put themselves at risk could potentially escalate a situation to the point where it is beyond your control. Additionally you should be considering whether you need any support from friends, colleagues or the emergency services.

- **Control the situation** – put into practice any procedures necessary to control the incident. This may range from applying simple first aid to finding shelter and calling the emergency services. You must not take action that could put your own, or another member of the group's, safety at risk. If you doubt your own ability to deal with a situation then call for assistance as soon as possible. Keep the entire group together, keep them safe and wait for professional help.

- **Review the situation** – learn from the incident. Use your experience to help you plan for the next session and avoid the incident happening again.

Activity: Emergency action plans

Imagine that you were in charge of organising an outdoor adventurous activity. Think about the flow diagram in Figure 10.1 and describe how you would go about dealing with an accident resulting in a possible back injury.

Assessment activity 10.2

P2 M1 D1

BTEC

1. Participate in a range of outdoor adventurous activities making observations as well as conducting individual research. Now imagine that you are training potential instructors and create a presentation, using a program such as PowerPoint® describing the safety considerations associated with four different outdoor and adventurous activities. **P2**

2. During the presentation ensure that you explain the safety considerations associated with four different outdoor and adventurous activities. **M1**

3. Finally, include in the presentation an evaluation of the safety considerations associated with four different outdoor and adventurous activities. **D1**

Grading tips

Structure your presentation clearly and use a new slide for each point you make.

- To attain **P2** you must consider both your own and others' safety.

- To attain **M1** you must show why each safety precaution must be taken.

- To attain **D1** you must reflect upon the effectiveness of each safety consideration.

PLTS

When participating in activities you will be showing skills as a **self manager**. When conducting research you will be displaying your skills as an **independent enquirer**. When creating a presentation you will be developing your skills as a **reflective learner**.

Functional skills

When creating a presentation you will be providing evidence towards both your **English** and **ICT** skills.

2.2 Environmental considerations

The nature of participation in outdoor adventurous activity means that there is some impact on the environment – some common ways are listed below. Participants should always limit this impact to preserve the environment for others in the future.

Erosion

Erosion is the gradual destruction or reduction of something through continued wear and tear. Any terrain that humans come into contact with is eroded over time. The speed of erosion is determined by the number of people participating and the type of terrain and its resilience. For example, a path that goes over rock is likely to erode more slowly than one that goes over soft peat marshland. Unfortunately, human erosion often exposes the terrain to other forms of erosion. For example, paths that are regularly used may be worn away to the point where they form small gullies. These new gullies allow a route for water to flow down and this water causes its own erosion thus aggravating the situation. Much erosion can be slowed or stopped with simple precautions. Paths can be reinforced by laying gravel or having a raised wooden walkway built over them.

Disturbance of flora and fauna

Wildlife of all sorts is affected by human activity although often disturbance is unintentional. It may occur through walking over plant life or disturbing nesting birds while climbing. A little common sense goes a long way to protecting wildlife. Think before you take part in an activity. Are you going to cause disturbance and if so could you come back at another time when this may be reduced, for example, after birds have finished nesting? You will find warning signs in place when rare and protected plants and animals are present. Pay attention to these signs and always try to keep to marked paths and trails.

Pollution

As the number of people taking part in outdoor adventurous activities has increased, so has the amount of pollution caused. Pollution is caused in three ways:

- **Air pollution** – this is caused by vehicles used to access areas suitable for activity. Participants should

Which other sports and outdoor activities can cause soil erosion?

consider using other forms of transport such as bicycles wherever possible. Air pollution is also caused by some forms of activity themselves such as motocross. When taking part in activities such as this, participants must consider others. Some areas have banned activities like motocross because of complaints made about participants who, through their reckless behaviour, show no respect for the environment or local people.

- **Rubbish** – it is impractical to have bins in some places so all rubbish should be removed on departure. Rubbish ruins the environment visually and can be very dangerous for animals and birds who may become entangled in it or eat it.

- **Chemical products** – these may be in the form of cleaning products used to protect equipment after use, lubricants designed to aid performance or specialist repair materials such as fibreglass used to fix sailing craft. All should be used with caution and none should be allowed to drain into the ground or water where they could potentially poison both plants and animals.

Construction of facilities

Facilities are needed to store equipment and provide a sheltered place to give training and feedback. Facilities must be sited with respect to the environment and where possible avoid disturbing plant and wildlife. Facilities need access in the form of a road or track, as well as the use of electricity, water and drainage.

2.3 Guidelines and legislation

If you are unsure about appropriate behaviour while participating in outdoor adventurous activities there are a number of sources of information which clearly set out guidelines and legislation.

The Countryside Code

This is available at www.naturalengland.org.uk. This document explains the public's responsibilities and land owners' responsibilities in caring for the countryside.

Countryside Rights Of Way Act (2000)

This is the legislation that can be used to enforce the law protecting the countryside. It deals with access, rights of way, conservation and areas of outstanding natural beauty. Those people ignoring guidelines and legislation laid out in the Countryside Code and Countryside Rights Of Way Act (2000) could face large fines or even prison sentences.

Take it further

Explore the Act

What are the five areas that the Countryside Rights Of Way Act covers and why are these areas relevant to outdoor adventurous activity?

Assessment activity 10.3

P3 M2 D1   :BTEC

1. Imagine that you work for an environmental group looking at the effects outdoor adventurous activities have on the environment. Write a letter to the council that describes the environmental considerations associated with four different outdoor adventurous activities. **P3**

2. In the letter explain these environmental considerations associated with four different outdoor and adventurous activities. **M2**

3. Finally, in the letter evaluate the environmental considerations associated with four different outdoor and adventurous activities. **D1**

Grading tips

When considering environmental issues talk to your instructors to gather first hand research into how they feel their activities affect the environment.

- To attain **P3** for each activity consider points under pollution, erosion, disturbance and building of facilities.

- To attain **M2** you must show the importance of each of the points you have made.

- To attain **D1** you must use personal experience and research to show the level at which each activity affects the environment.

PLTS

When considering a letter you will be developing skills as an **independent enquirer** and **reflective learner**.

Functional skills

When writing a letter you are working on skills in **English**. If you word process the letter you will be demonstrating evidence of **ICT** skills.

3. Be able to participate in outdoor and adventurous activities

Participation in outdoor adventurous activities relies on the use of specific skills and techniques. These may be quite different between activities and may differ within an activity itself as you move across disciplines.

3.1 Skills

Skills are categorised as hard or soft. Hard skills are sometimes known as physical skills, such as power, speed or endurance. Soft skills are social, emotional or intellectual skills, such as teamwork, planning or communication.

> **Key term**
>
> **Skill** – an ability that can be learned or developed to allow an activity to be completed.

Hard/physical skills

- **Cardiovascular endurance** – the ability of the body to deliver oxygen where needed. This is essential in any activity that requires prolonged exertion such as a long walk up a mountain or a lengthy kayak journey.
- **Muscular endurance** – the ability of the body to process energy efficiently. This may be required when rock climbing on a steep face or paddling a surfboard through big waves.
- **Strength** – the ability of the body to apply force in any given direction (strength may be required to drag a sailing dinghy clear of the water at the end of a session).
- **Flexibility** – the ability of the body to move around any joint. This could be useful when performing a trick on a windsurfer, or a tight turn on skis.
- **Speed** – the ability of the body to perform a movement rapidly. This could be vital when running during an orienteering competition or sprinting on a mountain bike.
- **Power** – the ability of the body to exert force in any given direction in a limited time. This may be vital for some difficult moves when climbing or when pulling a sail up while racing a dinghy.

Landing a paraglider takes quite a lot of coordination. Can you name some other airborne sports that require coordination?

- **Coordination** – the ability to make several movements at once to achieve a single objective. This could be useful when turning a windsurf board or when landing a paraglider.
- **Accuracy** – the ability to precisely control movement in any given direction. This is vital when performing a technical climbing move.
- **Agility** – the ability to move from one movement type to another quickly and efficiently. This could be useful when moving while performing a high speed turn.
- **Balance** – the ability to keep the body over its own centre of gravity. This would certainly be needed when walking along an uneven path or standing on a surfboard.

Different activities require a range of hard skills in different quantities. Some may rely upon one skill heavily but barely require another. Even within a sport there may be times when you rely upon one skill for one move and another for a different move.

Case study: Surfing hard skills

Jason has just started surfing and has had some basic lessons which he found really useful. He has just invested in his first board. At present he is struggling to paddle out through the breaking waves. Once out and in position he is able to catch a wave but often finds that as soon as he stands he falls straight off.

1. **Which hard skills would you suggest Jason needs to work on?**

2. **Can you think of any activities or exercises he could do that may help him improve these hard skills?**

Soft skills

- **Communication** – the ability to relay a message clearly and efficiently between two or more people. The message may need a reply that is well communicated. The communication between climber and belayer must be excellent to ensure safe climbing.

- **Leadership** – the ability to take control of a situation. This could be useful when deciding which route to take to leave a mountainside before dark.

- **Patience** – the ability to take the time to complete a task without allowing a delay to cause anxiety. This could be useful when going mountain bike riding with someone less able than yourself.

Case study: Mountain biking soft skills

Samantha has been mountain biking for five years and is now very proficient. She loves the sport and is always trying to encourage others to give it a go. The local Youth Mountain Biking Club is looking for volunteers to lead sessions for young novice mountain bikers. Volunteers would be responsible for organising trips and routes and ensuring the safety of the youngsters, while also promoting the benefits of the sport.

1. **What soft skills would benefit Samantha in helping with the club?**

2. **How might the soft skills she would need at the club differ from those she might need when riding with her friends?**

- **Organisation** – the ability to ensure that a task is prepared for and carried out in an efficient manner. This would be useful when packing kit to take to the beach to go windsurfing.

- **Teamwork** – the ability to work well within a group. This would be essential for a group ascent of a long, steep rock face.

- **Problem solving** – the ability to find solutions to an issue. This may be useful in the event of a kayaker damaging their boat while a long way from home.

- **Risk awareness** – the ability to spot potential risks and respond as necessary to avoid an incident. This would be vital when setting out on a sailing trip when a storm appears suddenly on the horizon.

- **Negotiation** – the ability to work together and find a compromise to a situation. This is vital to avoid arguments when deciding upon a route to mountain bike.

- **Motivation** – the ability to push yourself or others beyond the point where some may give in. This is essential when tiredness sets in during a long cross-country skiing session.

As with hard skills some activities rely upon different soft skills, in various amounts at different times.

Activity: Skills

Think about various hard and soft skills. Which ones do you feel you are strong at and which ones do you feel you need to develop?

3.2 Techniques

Techniques may rely upon multiple skills to complete them. For example, the technique of turning at speed on skis requires balance, coordination and flexibility.

Key term

Technique – techniques are always specific to an activity. They are how we perform movements, use equipment and ensure we get the best out of ourselves and our team.

Examples of climbing techniques

Belaying – this is when you support the climber by controlling the rope. Good belaying relies upon being able to support the climber in the event of a fall at all times and so one hand should always remain upon the dead end of the rope. During a climber-led ascent, a belayer will find they must play the rope out and pull it back in several times to ensure the climber is adequately protected.

Crimping – a way of grasping a small hold on a rock face precisely and powerfully. Crimping involves hyperextending the first finger joint and usually half extending the second. For additional grip the thumb can then be placed over the top of the fingers. Crimping can place a large amount of strain on fingers so should be done with caution.

Smearing – this is when a climber relies upon using the bottom of their shoe to create friction against the rock face rather than using any recognisable foot hold. Increasing the amount of shoe in contact with the rock face can be achieved by bending the ankles and allowing the heel to drop below the toes.

Bridging – when a climber finds themselves in a position where they can apply opposing pressure to a rock face on either side of themselves. By pushing in opposite directions additional grip is often found.

Examples of windsurfing techniques

Tacking – when the windsurf board turns through 180° with the nose passing through the wind. During the turn the windsurfer must angle the sail towards the back of the board, keep their arms as straight as possible and move around the front of the board. The windsurfer's feet must be placed accurately to prevent the board tipping and throwing them off.

Beach starting – when a windsurfer steps straight up onto the board with the sail ready in their hands to go. A good beach start involves keeping the board pointing across the wind, drawing the board into the body with the back foot, extending the arms and stepping up and forward onto the board.

Harnessing – when a windsurfer uses a harness to help them take the power of the sail. When harnessing, a windsurfer should commit their body weight to the harness loops, and ensure that their arms remain as straight as possible. In the event of a turn the windsurfer must release the harness from one side of the sail, complete the turn and reattach the harness on the other side.

Jumping – when a windsurfer becomes airborne. To jump, a windsurfer must travel at speed, spot a large piece of chop or a wave and time a sharp upwards motion with their legs with a sudden pull upon the sail for power. On landing the windsurfer must flex their knees to absorb the impact.

For proficient windsurfers, jumping is exhilarating and enjoyable. What other outdoor adventurous activities may involve jumping?

Assessment activity 10.4

P4 M3   **BTEC**

1. Participate in two different outdoor adventurous activities. Demonstrate appropriate skills and techniques in two different outdoor and adventurous activities with tutor support. Record demonstrations of skills and techniques with video footage. **P4**

2. Independently demonstrate appropriate skills and techniques in two different outdoor and adventurous activities, once again recording demonstrations with video footage. **M3**

Grading tips

To aid the development of skills and techniques, watch any instructor demonstrations closely as they will show the most efficient way of completing a task. Ask someone to video you and watch this footage to try to identify areas for improvement.

- To attain **P4** consider ways in which you can develop skills and techniques in your own time.
- To attain **M3** you must be self-reliant so consider what will allow you to participate in the activity safely without support.

PLTS

When demonstrating skills and techniques you will be developing skills as a **self manager** and **effective participator**.

Functional skills

When reviewing and presenting your video evidence you will demonstrate functional skills in **ICT**.

4. Be able to review own performance in outdoor and adventurous activities

No matter what activity you are participating in and at what level, an ability to review performance is invaluable to ensure continued development. For those aspiring to instruct or coach activities, reviewing is an essential skill to develop as it allows you to pinpoint and communicate areas for improvement which can be worked on in subsequent sessions.

4.1 Gathering feedback

Useful reviewing relies upon good feedback from the session. Feedback can be obtained from:

- you, the participant
- your peers
- your instructor, coach or tutor.

Feedback should be seen as an opportunity for development. It is a positive part of the learning process and when acted upon correctly can be invaluable for a performer's development. Feedback can be:

- verbal – during participation or in a debrief situation
- written – in reports, feedback sheets or observation checklists
- visual – with video or photographic evidence.

Feedback should be given as close to a session as possible, when the activity is fresh in the mind of both the participant and the person giving feedback. Feedback can be given during or after a session. However, if given during, care must be taken to ensure it is not a distraction from the task in hand. A session may incorporate a few short breaks to award feedback. Alternatively, a session may end with a debrief which includes giving feedback. A well-planned session will often utilise both these methods.

Self evaluation

When collecting feedback remember that your own opinions and judgements are as important as other people's. Record your own evaluation of personal performance on review sheets or in a diary. When recording your own performance remember to consider both strengths and areas for improvement. Consider the skills and techniques necessary and how you intend to develop them.

Positive feedback and areas for improvement

Feedback should be a positive experience; it is meant to be beneficial to your development. When giving feedback, and reviewing a session, emphasis should be placed on positive achievements as well as areas for improvement. Although focusing on areas for improvement is essential for you to understand how to improve performance, examining what went well is good for motivation and helps progress.

4.2 Reviewing performance

Review sheets are an invaluable tool for recording strengths and areas for improvement identified during a session. They mean that you can recap the last session before taking part in a new one and make any necessary preparations to help you improve. They can also act as a great motivational tool when you look back through them after a number of sessions and can clearly see your own progression.

4.3 Development plans

After completing a series of reviews of sessions it may be worth designing a development plan to aid with continued improvement. When thinking about development plans you should consider the following three stages:

Figure 10.2: A development plan. How could putting one together help you to improve your performance?

Where am I now?

When considering this, be honest and realistic. This is where first class feedback is invaluable. Be accurate in your own assessment of your current ability in order to set sensible goals for the future. A good way to assess your present position is by using a SWOT analysis:

Strengths — What do I do well? What am I good at?

Weaknesses — What do I need to improve? What prevents me from performing at my best?

Opportunities — What resources do I have available to me that could assist my development?

Threats — What could prevent me developing?

The following is a simple SWOT analysis written by an intermediate surfer:

Strengths – I am physically fit and very motivated. I consistently stand up and have caught a number of lengthy waves. I am confident in the water and not afraid to take a fall.

Weaknesses – I sometimes get frustrated when I have a poor session. I sometimes misjudge where I need to place myself in relation to the approaching wave and I need to improve my foot positioning once standing.

Opportunities – I live very close to the beach and have my own surfboard and wetsuit. There is a surf school in the local town.

Threats – I am very busy with work at present so I don't get as much time on the water as I'd like. I have a recurring shoulder injury that can slow me down.

Where do I want to get to?

When setting personal targets you may choose to set them in relation to a peer's performance or against the next step on a pre-designed training scheme or on aspirations to perform a specific manoeuvre. For a target to be achievable you must want to reach it. Consider you own aims and objectives. These will always be unique. Remember that everyone develops at different speeds and has different goals. For example, one person may aim to get to the top of a climbing route and overcome their fears while another may aim to lead climb the same route. Although both objectives are to succeed on the same route, they are very different. When setting goals a simple and useful tool is writing SMART targets.

Specific

Measurable

Achievable

Realistic

Timed

It is possible to set more than one SMART target at any given time and be working on them all simultaneously. The following is a SMART target written by a climber:

Specific – I would like to be able to climb a route called Consommé on Portland in Dorset.

Measurable – this is a route graded at 6a+.

Achievable – I have managed to climb a 6a currently and so feel this is a good progression.

Realistic – I have good strength and fitness and seem to be improving rapidly. I live within walking distance of the climb so should have plenty of opportunity to practise.

Timed – I aim to complete this climb within four weeks.

How can I get there?

When considering how to achieve a goal you should think about the following points:

- **Training** – associated with learning new techniques. This can be done individually or with help from instructors or friends. This may be in the form of recognised qualifications or more specific individual delivery.
- **Resources** – essential to the activity, some resources may be borrowed or hired whereas you may need to buy others.
- **Support** – many activities rely upon individuals working together to achieve a goal. Without the required support a goal may simply not be achievable.
- **Accessibility** – different activities rely on different terrain and conditions. The distance that someone lives from a venue can help or hinder the completion of a target.
- **Diet** – performance in many activities may be improved by making adjustments to diet. This can range from losing excess weight to increasing the amount of energy absorbed in any given day.
- **Training** – associated with improving physical fitness. All types of fitness can be developed. It may be necessary to consider using a gym or an exercise routine to improve this.

Remember

Taking part in outdoor adventurous activities is meant to be enjoyable. Although setting targets is extremely useful for aiding performance it is important not to let targets get in the way of having a great experience. If you are not enjoying an experience you can lose your motivation and therefore targets will become unachievable.

Assessment activity 10.5

P5 P6 M4 D2 BTEC

1. After each session complete a review sheet to consider own performance identifying strengths and areas for improvement. **P5**

2. Design a development plan for improving own performance in outdoor and adventurous activities. **P6**

3. From the review sheets and development plan explain identified strengths and areas for improvement in own performance in outdoor and adventurous activities, and explain suggestions relating to development. Present this in a clear written essay. **M4**

4. In the written essay additionally justify suggestions made relating to the development plan. **D2**

Grading tips

- To attain **P5** and **P6**:
  - gather feedback from as many sources as possible
  - consider skills and techniques that you already possess but need to develop, as well as ones you need to learn.
- To attain **M4** show the relevance of the points and suggestions you have already made to your own personal development in a specific activity.
- To attain **D2** show your reasoning behind making points and suggestions. Look at other performers for inspiration. Why do they train in the way they do?

PLTS

By reviewing skills and techniques and creating a development plan appropriate to outdoor and adventurous activities you will be developing your skills as a **reflective learner**.

Functional skills

When reviewing skills and techniques and creating a development plan you will be working towards skills in **English**. If you design the review sheets yourself you will be showing skills in **ICT**.

George Denzel
Windsurf instructor

George works for a small windsurfing company that hires out equipment and gives instruction at all levels. The centre is recognised by the RYA as an approved training provider. George's responsibilities include:

- taking bookings for tuition and equipment hire
- welcoming and briefing new arrivals to the centre
- providing safety cover from a rescue craft for those hiring windsurf equipment
- providing tuition to both groups and individuals
- ensuring the centre maintains standards set out by the RYA.

'Most days I arrive at 9 a.m. There are three other people working at the centre, including Mark the centre manager. Every morning we start with a meeting to discuss the day ahead. We check the forecast and assign roles for the day.

Next I will help set up. The rescue craft must be fuelled and warmed up, boards and sails unlocked and welcome signs put out. We always make sure that the site is really tidy as first impressions count for a lot.

During the day I may be instructing beginners or coaching more advanced students. Sometimes I am in charge of providing rescue cover for all those on the water and at other times maintaining any equipment.

My day finishes at about 5 p.m. and then I often head out onto the water.

The best thing about my job is spending so much time outdoors on the water. Every day presents me with new challenges and I get lots of satisfaction from inspiring new windsurfers and teaching them new skills. It is fantastic being able to earn a wage doing something that you enjoy. I intend to gain more experience and eventually hope to manage a centre myself.

In terms of skills, I have to communicate with other members of the team and clients every day so this is certainly at the top of the list. The practical skills I practised during my Sport BTEC, I now use every day to demonstrate techniques to other windsurfers. I worked hard at developing my balance and coordination so that now I feel confident when teaching.'

Think about it!

- What activities might you like to instruct in the future?
- What skills might you need to develop to help you?
- In small groups discuss what skills are most important for someone who wants to start a career in the outdoor adventurous activity industry.

Just checking

1. What is the definition of an outdoor adventurous activity?
2. Name four outdoor adventurous activity governing bodies.
3. What roles do governing bodies have?
4. Define a risk.
5. Define a hazard.
6. Describe the environmental impacts a specific outdoor adventurous activity may have.
7. Describe three skills useful in a specific outdoor adventurous activity.
8. Describe three techniques associated with a specific outdoor adventurous activity.
9. How would you gather feedback to help write a session review?
10. What should you consider when writing a personal development plan?

edexcel

Assignment tips

- Remember that outdoor adventurous activities are meant to be fun. Enjoy the experience and you are far more likely to see improvements in skills and techniques.

- When practising a practical activity, work at your own pace. Everyone has different strengths and so will develop at different speeds. Do not be too hard on yourself if you do not achieve what you want first time.

- Support your peers and they will support you. Work together giving each other tips and encouragement.

- Learn from your instructors. Watch them carefully. They will all be experienced and have plenty to teach you. Talk to them and gather information from them to assist with your assignments.

- Use the national governing body websites to help you gather research material. They contain plenty of useful information.

- Ensure that you properly read the assignment briefs. Take your time and ensure you are happy with the task set for you. If not ask your tutor for additional assistance.

- Make sure you attempt all parts of the assignment briefs. If you only attempt the pass criteria this is all you will achieve. Think big and try it all.

12 Current issues in sport

Sport contributes to society in many ways; it provides jobs, entertainment, opportunities for endeavour, and improves our health, fitness and well-being. Sport does not exist in a vacuum. It impacts on society and is itself influenced by society; for example, sport is affected by sport in schools, racism, sexism, corruption, drugs, inequality and commercialism. Sport is often used to try and solve social problems, for instance helping deprived children improve their health, and to improve social inclusion.

The media influence on modern-day sport is covered in this unit along with commercialisation and the use of technology.

This unit explores the development of sport from the pre-industrial era to the present day. The UK sports industry is examined in detail and it is related to broader international influences. Sports participation is explored, along with barriers to participation and cultural factors that affect participation.

Learning outcomes

After completing this unit you should:

1. know how sport has developed in the UK
2. know how media and technology influence modern sport
3. know how contemporary issues affect sport
4. understand the cultural influences and barriers that affect participation in sports activities.

25

Assessment and grading criteria

This table shows you what you must do in order to achieve a pass, merit or distinction grade, and where you can find activities in this book to help you.

To achieve a **pass** grade the evidence must show that you are able to:	To achieve a **merit** grade the evidence must show that, in addition to the pass criteria, you are able to:	To achieve a **distinction** grade the evidence must show that, in addition to the pass and merit criteria, you are able to:
P1 describe the development and organisation of a selected sport in the UK **See Assessment activity 12.1, page 35**	**M1** explain the development and organisation of a selected sport in the UK **See Assessment activity 12.1, page 35**	
P2 describe the influence of the media on a selected sport in the UK **See Assessment activity 12.2, page 39**	**M2** explain the influence of the media on a selected sport in the UK **See Assessment activity 12.2, page 39**	
P3 describe the effect that technology has on a selected sport **See Assessment activity 12.3, page 41**	**M3** explain the effect that technology has on a selected sport **See Assessment activity 12.3, page 41**	
P4 describe the effects of four contemporary issues on a selected sport **See Assessment activity 12.4, page 45**	**M4** explain the effects of four contemporary issues on a selected sport **See Assessment activity 12.4, page 45**	**D1** evaluate the effects of four contemporary issues on a selected sport **See Assessment activity 12.4, page 45**
P5 explain the barriers to sports participation **See Assessment activity 12.5, page 50**		
P6 explain three cultural influences on sports participation **See Assessment activity 12.5, page 50**		
P7 describe three strategies or initiatives which relate to sports participation **See Assessment activity 12.5, page 50**	**M5** explain three strategies or initiatives which relate to sports participation **See Assessment activity 12.5, page 50**	**D2** evaluate three strategies or initiatives which relate to sports participation **See Assessment activity 12.5, page 50**

How you will be assessed

Assessment of this unit can take a varied approach to allow customisation and reflect the nature of current thinking in sport, particularly when applied to the areas of media and technology. Assessments could be in the form of:

- a written report
- a series of leaflets or presentations
- a multimedia presentation
- a web-based article
- witness statements and observation records might also apply.

James McCartney, 16-year-old footballer

When I started this unit and saw how diverse the assessments were I thought this would be a challenge. However, after talking with my tutor it was clear I would have to be careful to select a sport which would cover all the issues asked for in the assessments and there had to be lots of information available about that sport. Being a keen football player I chose the FA.

I chose a sports governing body with a good website and made sure that it was a sport often covered in the media, that technology had changed it and several issues surrounded it. I used our school library to research books on barriers to participation and cultural influences. I also arranged a meeting with a sports development officer from our local leisure department to find out about strategies and initiatives running to help participation locally.

I enjoyed talking with the sports development officer as I might do that for a career. The FA website had plenty of detail for me to study. I learned that there is so much more to providing sporting opportunities than I had thought before.

Over to you!

- **As you have to carry out a similar assessment task to James, what can you learn from his method of approaching this task?**
- **Which parts of this unit do you think you will find especially challenging?**
- **How might you prepare for tackling this unit?**

1. Know how sport has developed in the UK

1.1 Development

Early British sport

Early British sport rose out of activities born in countryside leisure, education and military activities. In this section you will investigate different historical periods and social developments that played a role in forming sport in our society today. (See Figure 12.1)

Agricultural society

In the agricultural society of medieval and early modern Britain and Ireland, existence was mainly subsistence – living off the land to survive. There would not be time to take part in leisure activities on a day to day basis. Hard physical work was the norm for many, including children. On market days, or at fairs, there would be an opportunity to pursue leisure activities like drinking, dancing, cock-fighting, bear-baiting, dog-fighting, gambling and bare-fist fighting. The local hostelry would be the focus for village life, and often the place where people might take part in more gentle pursuits such as billiards, bowls and skittles.

The rich were able to travel and hunted on neighbouring estates or went to the coast to sail. They also played real tennis. Ordinary people were prevented from hunting by game laws which made poaching a crime. For the poorer peasants there were sports like mob football and demonstrations of skill in pursuits such as archery.

Much physical activity had traditionally been for military purposes – getting fit to fight, and building strength to wield swords, pikes and axes. Sport was represented by fencing, archery and sparring.

How does this equipment differ from the modern Olympians' archery?

During the Puritan period of Cromwell's protectorate, there was pressure on any kind of sport as the authorities and church preferred people to worship rather than play.

After the restoration of the monarchy in 1660, King Charles II resurrected sports, and tennis, yachting and hunting grew in popularity. Other sports, such as early forms of cricket, skating and fishing, were followed by the rich. Some traditional events that took place are still represented today by surviving country shows and county fairs like the Great Yorkshire show.

Cricket was born around the early 1700s and by the mid century county matches were not uncommon.

Activity: Through the centuries

Identify and discuss other agricultural or animal-based sports and military activities that have carried on through the centuries.

Case study: The Great Yorkshire Show

One example of these traditions is the Great Yorkshire Show, held in Harrogate every July at the agricultural showground. In 2011 the 153rd show will take place, demonstrating how popular this type of show still is. You can still see some traditional sports and pastimes in the country pursuits and forestry events arenas, such as pole-climbing, show jumping, scurry racing, dog handling and falconry.

1. **Visit the website at www.greatyorkshireshow.com.**

2. **Why do you think there are still some enduring country sports?**

Effects of the Industrial Revolution

In the 19th century cities grew, but life was hard – conditions were often cramped and unsanitary. Work was physically demanding (mining, weaving and other factory work or labouring on building sites) and there was little time off, and no additional earnings available for sport and leisure activities. Despite mechanisation, children were still being put to work to increase family income. Not until the Education Act of 1870 was it compulsory for them to go to school instead.

In cities, sport and leisure opportunities were fewer, and different from country sports, with activities for the working classes being spectator sports such as boxing, wrestling and rowing. Many activities had a gambling dimension and were blood sports brought in from historical country pursuits, such as dog-fighting.

Aristocratic sports flourished among the richer classes, who were benefitting from trade and land ownership. They had leisure time and were able to follow interests such as dancing and stage plays, and to continue their country pursuits such as hunting, riding and shooting.

Britain's trading empire had grown around the world; this meant that many British sports were exported with traders and colonists. For example, the origins of cricket in places like the Caribbean, India and Australia can be traced back to its roots in the days of Britain's imperial rule.

Influence of public schools

'Public' schools were so called because they were originally founded to provide an education outside the houses of the rich. However, the schools and their endowments increasingly became used by the nobility turning the public school system into the one we know today (i.e. independent fee paying schools). This system grew in the early nineteenth century and sports flourished within the walls of the public schools, especially rugby, cricket, tennis and soccer, for the schools were wealthy and had extensive playing fields. Rules were made to help structure sports, and these form the basis of rules and regulations today. Public schools made a great contribution to sport with old boys carrying British sporting traditions and values around the globe.

In the poorer Victorian slums, factory workers and their children had little leisure to speak of other than street and pub games. Their working week would be close to 70 hours. However, there were many more public holidays than now. Bills went through Parliament in the late 1800s which gave us the bank holidays we have today. The Victorians were also very generous, creating parks and gardens in many cities along with libraries, theatres and playing fields and of course Victorian baths.

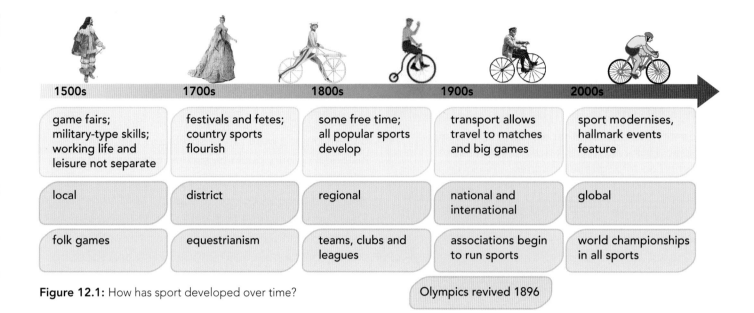

1500s	1700s	1800s	1900s	2000s
game fairs; military-type skills; working life and leisure not separate	festivals and fetes; country sports flourish	some free time; all popular sports develop	transport allows travel to matches and big games	sport modernises, hallmark events feature
local	district	regional	national and international	global
folk games	equestrianism	teams, clubs and leagues	associations begin to run sports	world championships in all sports

Olympics revived 1896

Figure 12.1: How has sport developed over time?

Rationalisation

More general affluence spread and the middle class emerged. They wanted to adopt sports previously only in the realm of the rich. They promoted **rationalisation** of sport and leisure to encourage more organised, structured and 'wholesome' recreation – sports and games with a healthy purpose (like swimming, athletics, lawn tennis and cycling). This was in sharp opposition to the drinking, gambling and blood sports, such as bare-knuckle fights, of the working classes. There are several motives for the 'rational recreation' philosophy:

- Making people healthier – both physically and spiritually.
- Giving them sport and leisure activities to help them forget the drudgery of work.
- Compensating them for hard physical labour.
- Helping them to get fresh air and escape poor working conditions.

Regulation

At this time, the influence of the public schools created a general trend towards the **regulation** of how sports were played – this was called codification. For example, boxing adopted the Queensberry rules in 1867. Sports associations, leagues and clubs began to form too, many being 'works teams' such as Arsenal, the football team formed in 1886 by workers at the Woolwich Arsenal Armaments Factory.

Development in this period gave much more structure and fabric to sport, laying down the modern foundations. City councils also played an active role in providing sports venues for their communities. The beginnings of professionalism were laid down too. The Olympic Games were reintroduced by Baron de Coubertin in 1896.

Key terms

Rationalisation – more organised and structured sport.
Regulation – following rules.

20th century

The start of the last century saw a period of great flux in Britain, with the First World War, then the depression, followed by the Second World War. Between the wars, people were determined to enjoy themselves. There were big sporting events such as the FA Cup Finals, the Oxford and Cambridge Boat Race, the Derbies and Wimbledon, which gave sport and leisure a chance to flourish.

Better working conditions

After the Second World War, the hours of work shortened, giving more leisure time, and wages increased, giving some disposable income. The new-found leisure time of the working classes was

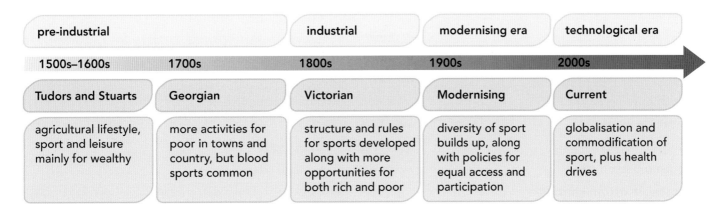

pre-industrial		industrial	modernising era	technological era
1500s–1600s	1700s	1800s	1900s	2000s
Tudors and Stuarts	Georgian	Victorian	Modernising	Current
agricultural lifestyle, sport and leisure mainly for wealthy	more activities for poor in towns and country, but blood sports common	structure and rules for sports developed along with more opportunities for both rich and poor	diversity of sport builds up, along with policies for equal access and participation	globalisation and commodification of sport, plus health drives

Figure 12.2: Can you describe the growth of sports and leisure?

quickly filled with amusements and entertainment, but also with some sports matches taking on the more commercial approach that we see today. Opportunities to play and watch football, cricket and golf grew as stadiums and grounds were built.

Activity: Origins

Investigate your favourite football team – when was it formed and what were its origins?

Influence of war

War has a profound effect on society and this was true for Britain after a series of wars. However, war did bring some benefits for sport and leisure:

- New technology was created.
- People were motivated to compensate themselves after the austerity of war and enjoy and value their leisure time more.
- Sport provided a form of safe, shared competition.
- It provided a bridge to rebuild relationships.
- Sport could carry great national pride, just as armies did.

Women had proved themselves in the war effort, in both world wars, so opportunities began to open up for their participation in sport (although equality was some way off, with most sports being male-dominated).

Outdoor activities

In contrast to urban sport and leisure, interest grew in the outdoors; as transport improved people could get to the coast or into the hills. Some richer people made the 'grand tour' of spas and resorts in Europe, spreading sports and health interests such as skiing, climbing and simply 'taking the waters'. There was sufficient interest in winter sports activities for the Winter Olympics to be created in 1924.

1.2 Key national organisations

In the late 1890s sports governing bodies were set up to organise, control and develop individual sports – including the Rugby Football Union (RFU), the Football Association (FA) and the Lawn Tennis Association (LTA). In the 1990s some new bodies were set up to control and develop sport in a more strategic way (including the English Institute for Sport, UK Sport and Sports Coach UK). This move was designed to help sports governing bodies who had tended to do their own thing and lacked a joined-up strategy. After some poor Olympic performances, the government was keen to change this. Some key organisations and their websites are shown in Table 12.1.

Table 12.1: Key organisations. Add their year of origin to complete your time frame of sports organisation developments.

Sports governing bodies	
Rugby Football Union	www.rfu.com
Football Association	www.thefa.com
Lawn Tennis Association	www.lta.org.uk
Irish Football Association	www.irishfa.com
Welsh Bowling Association	www.welshbowlingassociation.co.uk
British Canoe Union	www.bcu.org.uk
Scottish Hockey Union	www.scottish-hockey.org.uk
England Basketball	www.englandbasketball.co.uk
Strategic organisations	
Department for Culture, Media and Sport	www.culture.gov.uk
Central Council of Physical Recreation	www.ccpr.org.uk
UK Sport	www.uksport.gov.uk
Sport England	www.sportengland.org
Sport Scotland	www.sportscotland.org.uk
Sports Council Wales	www.sports-council-wales.org.uk
Sport Northern Ireland	www.sportni.net
English Institute for Sport	www.eis2win.co.uk
Sports Coach UK	www.sportscoachuk.org
English Federation of Disability Sport	ww.efds.net
Women's Sports Foundation	www.womenssportsfoundation.org

Department for Culture, Media and Sport (DCMS)

The DCMS covers a broad range of sectors under its wing, including the arts, the National Lottery, tourism, libraries, museums and galleries, as well as sport. It has a specific Sport and Recreation division with a Director who briefs the Minister for Sport. The DCMS funds Sport England and supports UK Sport, along with the National Lottery. For example, in 2009 the DCMS committed over £36 million to a scheme called Sports Unlimited, an innovative scheme to try and attract 900,000 youngsters to taster sessions in sport before 2011. In addition, it has supported the new Wembley Stadium project, and the Olympic builds. In June 2008 the DCMS published 'Playing to win – a new era for sport' which sets out the Government's ambition to become a truly world leading sporting nation.

Central Council of Physical Recreation (CCPR)

The CCPR is the oldest sporting body (other than governing bodies). It was formed in 1935 in response to a concern that PE was a low priority and children were not healthy enough. At that time, few young people stayed on at school after 14.

Take it further

Inspect the CCPR

Visit the website of CCPR at www.ccpr.org.uk. How is it structured? Identify its divisions and assess what role they play in delivering sport in this country.

UK Sport

This is one of the UK's newest sports organisations, formed in 1997. UK Sport aims to work in partnership with the home-country sports councils (Scotland, England, Wales and Northern Ireland) and with other agencies to try and attain world-class success. It is responsible for managing and distributing public investment, and is a distributor of funds raised by the National Lottery through the DCMS.

UK Sport's mission is: 'to work in partnership to lead sport in the UK to world-class success'. Its goals can be summed up as to:

- encourage world class performance and to develop home-grown expertise to support our athletes for the London Olympiad
- have an international programme that has a worldwide impact to bring best practice in other sporting nations to the UK
- promote world class standards of sporting conduct and give a strategic lead
- lead a world-class anti-doping programme for the UK and improve the education and promotion of ethically fair and drug-free sport.

UK Sport guides the overall strategy for the whole of the UK. Each country has a sports organisation (previously called a sports council) that is responsible for implementing plans, funding development and supporting all kinds of sports initiatives.

Sport England

Sport England's focus is hinged around three outcomes:

1. Growing the numbers of people taking part in sport.
2. Sustaining these numbers.
3. Improving talent development to help more people excel.

To achieve its aims Sport England has set the following the targets:

- One million people taking part in more sport.
- More children and young people taking part in five hours of PE and sport a week.
- More people satisfied with their sporting experience.
- 25 per cent fewer 16–18 year olds dropping out of at least five sports.
- Improved talent development in at least 25 sports.

Sport Scotland

Sport Scotland's mission is 'to encourage everyone in Scotland to discover and develop their own sporting experience, helping to increase participation (60 per cent by 2020) and improve performances in Scottish sport'. As well as running the Scottish Institute of Sport (www.sisport.com) to support the development of high-performance sport in Scotland, Sport Scotland runs three national centres: Inverclyde (sport), Cumbrae (watersports) and Glenmore Lodge (Europe's leading outdoor centre). It also distributes National Lottery and government money for sports development, makes awards to create links between schools and communities, and supports areas and groups deprived of sporting opportunities.

Sports Council Wales

Sports Council Wales is the national organisation responsible for developing and promoting sport and recreation. It was set up in 1972, and is the main advisor to the Welsh Assembly Government on all sporting matters. It is also responsible for distributing lottery funds to sport in Wales. Its main focus is to increase the frequency of participation by persuading those who are currently sedentary to become more active and to encourage people, young and old, to develop a range of activities through which to achieve healthy levels of activity.

Take it further

Sports Council Wales

Evaluate Sports Council Wales' strategic plan 'Climbing Higher' and its shift in plans for children, women and girls, by visiting its website at www.sports-council-wales.co.uk.

Sport Northern Ireland

Sport Northern Ireland describes itself as the lead facilitator for sport in Northern Ireland. It aims to increase and sustain its commitment to participation in the province, and to:

- raise the standards of sporting excellence
- promote the good reputation and efficient administration of sport
- increase and sustain committed participation, especially among young people

It has a strong drive to improve leadership skills among coaches and helpers so that they can work more effectively in the community. Performance-level athletes are given a range of support and advice.

Activity: Sports councils' goals

Using material from the text and your own research, identify and describe the main similarities and differences of the strategies and goals of the four sports councils.

1.3 National governing bodies

These organisations aim to promote and develop a particular sport. Almost all types of sport have a national governing body. A few examples include:

Basketball

Each country in the UK has its own basketball association. Collectively, they make up the British Basketball Federation (www.british-basketball.co.uk), and from this the Great Britain team is chosen.

Hockey

The Irish Hockey Association (www.hockey.ie) was formed in 2000, as a result of the merger of the two pre-existing unions which governed men's and women's hockey separately. The origins of both the pre-existing unions date back to the late 19th century, when they were formed. Typical work for this association includes their hockey camps.

Canoeing

The British Canoe Union (www.bcu.org.uk) is the governing body of paddlesport and was set up in 1936 to send a team to the Berlin Olympics. It is the lead body for canoeing and kayaking in the UK. It has divisions in all four countries of the UK. An estimated 2 million people take to the water in a canoe or kayak each year.

Cricket

The England & Wales Cricket Board (ECB) state its development aims as increasing:

- participation
- club membership and affiliations
- coaching and volunteering roles
- funding
- equity
- relationships with all counties.

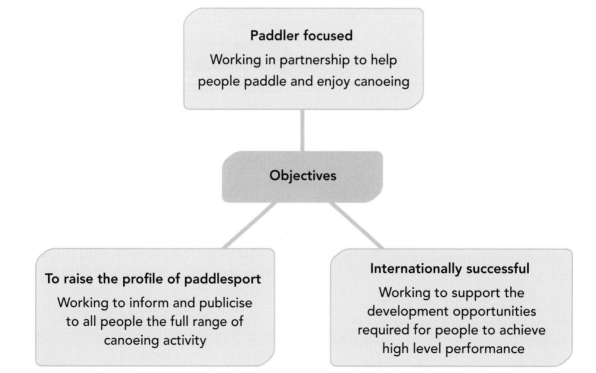

Paddler focused
Working in partnership to help people paddle and enjoy canoeing

Objectives

To raise the profile of paddlesport
Working to inform and publicise to all people the full range of canoeing activity

Internationally successful
Working to support the development opportunities required for people to achieve high level performance

Figure 12.3: Objectives of the British Canoe Union. What issues could prevent the British Canoe Union from achieving its objectives?

Take it further

ECB funding

In 2008, ECB announced a £30 million investment in facilities and in club cricket, the most significant injection of funding ever in cricket in England and Wales. Visit their website at www.ecb.co.uk to learn more or choose them as one of your case studies.

Assessment activity 12.1

P1 M1   **BTEC**

Using material from the text and your own research, prepare a presentation using a program such as PowerPoint® to describe or explain the development and organisation of a selected sport in the UK. **P1 M1**

Grading tips

- To attain **P1** link your description to some of the national bodies and show how it works with others and what issues it might be currently tackling. You might cover scale, structure and provision.

- To attain **M1** clearly explain how the sport you have selected has been developed and is now organised. You might make some historical notes and show links to other agencies.

PLTS

When describing or explaining the development of a selected sport you will be using your skills as an **independent enquirer**. This will also be the case when you describe or explain its organisation.

Functional skills

By researching online and creating this presentation you are providing evidence towards skills in **ICT**. Evidence for **English** could be generated through discussion on what to include.

2. Know how media and technology influence modern sport

2.1 Media

There are several different forms of media and each raises issues for sport, some positive and others negative. The ability of people and organisations to communicate received a massive boost in the late 20th and early 21st centuries, with mobile phones, iPods, satellite television, Xbox Live, Wiis and the Internet. This new technology has brought with it issues for sport as it draws young people away from physical activity.

Television

This has had a huge impact and brings with it considerations of commercialisation, good and bad presentation, reporting and journalism. Satellite television can beam in sport 24 hours a day from all around the globe. The running of many sports events has been geared up to suit television audiences.

Participation might be increased as a result of young people watching a great performance on television and being inspired to take up a sport. This happened with cycling after the Beijing Olympics. Or you might watch a charity run and decide to have a go to raise money for a good cause. On the downside, the increase in childhood obesity through lack of activity might well be linked to computer games and television viewing. People watch television for an average of just over 26 hours per week. Other figures show that commercial television accounts for 64 per cent of total broadcast viewing, with the BBC taking the remaining share. Sports events are an important portion of this.

Sponsorship

Sponsorship is said to have a symbiotic relationship with sport – one can't live without the other. Sponsorship does bring in much-needed cash to a club. However, in football, for example, there never seems to be enough sponsorship money filtering down to lower league sides to help them survive or develop new talent.

Businesses are keen to be sponsors as they will gain media exposure if their event or team is reported. However teams have to be winners to retain their sponsorship and in the credit crunch of 2009 many sponsors withdrew to save on costs.

Advertising

Advertising is a necessity for many professional sports – without it they would not exist. It brings in cash to pay players and to run clubs and stadiums. Television cameras pick up and highlight sponsors' logos. Some of these logos appear in 3D on the pitch.

Spectatorism

The increased coverage of sport means that fewer people will be playing. They might be considered consumers rather than supporters. Many big match crowds are dominated by corporate spectators looking

Activity: Broadcasting rights for national events

Consider these news stories:

- Sky Sports won the exclusive UK rights to screen the Ryder Cup in 2010 and 2012 and extended its coverage of the PGA European Tour for a further four years as the battle for the subscription fees of the UK's golf fans takes another turn.

- Setanta Sports acquired the UK television rights for the Indian Premier League's (IPL) Twenty20 cricket competition in a five year deal with the IPL.

- The International Olympic Committee and the European Broadcasting Union announced that the BBC won the UK television, radio and online rights to cover the 2010 Winter Olympics from Vancouver and 2012 Games.

What issues can you see coming out of these reports under the following headings: access, costs, control, market share/profits, impact on the sport?

for entertainment, leading to fewer true fans in the crowd. Football hooliganism still surfaces to spoil some matches. Test match crowds really do differ from those at football matches. Why do you think this is?

Television offers ways of watching events that would be impossible to attend otherwise, and reaches a far larger audience than could ever fit into a stadium.

Because of the entry fees paid by spectators, plus sponsorship and **broadcasting rights**, players can now be paid more, facilitating the growth of the professional player in sports other than football.

Punditry

Television uses sports **pundits** (an Indian word for an expert) – former players or athletes who give their analysis and opinions on matches. Notable ones might be Alan Hanson or John McEnroe. It is possible that you might have a favourite pundit or commentator.

Narrative technique

Narrative technique is how a commentator describes a sequence of events or paints the picture of the sporting scene on television or radio. This can influence our opinion of an incident. It helps us to imagine how an athlete might be thinking or feeling, capturing the moment, the drama, in words.

> ### Remember
>
> Narrative technique can bias your interpretation of events.

Key terms

Broadcasting rights – having the contract to televise an event.

Spectatorism – watching sport.

Punditry – so called expert opinion.

Narrative technique – the style of making a commentary.

Rule changes

Media demands have had an impact on the rules of some sports, for example, the third umpire in cricket or the video referee in rugby whose decision can overturn that of the match official. Hawkeye (invented by Dr Paul Hawkins) has been developed by Roke systems for sports applications. It is used in tennis for decisions on serving and challenges.

In the US, American football and basketball are so reliant on television coverage for their funding that they have adapted and changed their rules and competitions in order to suit television scheduling. In both sports, time-outs and official game stoppages have been built in to allow the television companies to show advertisements.

> ### Take it further
>
> **Video replay debate**
>
> Debate in groups whether video replays should be used in football to decide penalties, offsides, handball and bookable offences.

Local and national press

Local newspapers are very good at reporting the progress of local teams. Read any local or regional newspaper and you will find reports and scores for everything that happens locally, from under-11s football and cricket, to the achievements of individuals in cross-country or swimming. These stories and photos are essential to sell local newspapers.

The national press has a strong influence, including the power to damage individuals' careers when journalists comment on performances which are circulated to millions of people. Examples include the departure of the England Rugby Union coach Andy Robinson, or the negative press received by England's cricketers in Australia while trying to defend the Ashes (Figure 12.4).

Magazines

Sport-related magazines cover health, fitness, exercise, diet and the body (see Figure 12.5). They can have a positive influence, with good guidance and interesting articles or programmes to follow. However, many images of slim, fit people puts pressure on others to attain an ideal and this can cause dietary and emotional problems.

Abject England rolls over

FRIDAY JANUARY 5, 2007

The inevitable happened 12 minutes before lunch this morning when Matthew Hayden hit the run that gave Australia victory by 10 wickets in the final test and the 5–0 whitewash they have craved for the last 16 months. Set to score 46, Justin Langer and Hayden took just one ball shy of 11 overs to complete England's biggest humiliation in 86 years....

Figure 12.4: How can the press influence how we think about sport?

Figure 12.5: How might people feel pressured by the images in magazines?

Sensationalism

Many journalists who work for the tabloid press have been accused of sensationalising the news that they report. That is, blowing it up out of proportion or even, in some cases, making it up. This obviously helps them sell more newspapers, but the downside is that athletes and players can receive 'negative' press, which may affect them personally or may deter a sponsor. Many famous sports stars are pursued by the paparazzi so that they can be caught on camera unexpectedly.

Gender imbalance

The media has a habit of giving male sports much more attention than female sports. This creates a gender imbalance with female sports losing out, not just on publicity, but also on sponsorship as they cannot command the same space in newspapers and on television. When women's sports are reported they will have fewer column inches or maybe just a glamorous photo. In 2009 England's women's teams won the cricket world cup and got through to the final of the European football cup – little was seen in the press but there was some television coverage. Think about why this might be the case.

Jingoism

This term means extreme chauvinism or nationalism. We can identify examples of this in the media when sports programmes focus exclusively on male athletes or on only one country's athletes.

The Internet

The Internet has a huge influence, attracting young people away from active sports to sedentary solo activities. This may be why we have such low levels of participation in sports in the UK. However, it does offer real-time viewing of sport and global coverage, making events more accessible to more people. Plus, the arrival of broadband means that people have faster access to more information than ever before, and are able to catch up with TV programmes they've missed.

Chat rooms give people the chance to communicate over great distances with lots of people. This can spread information and gossip about sports stars. However, despite the opportunity to interact with many people remotely, chat rooms can encourage a sedentary and lonely lifestyle.

On fan sites, people who are keen to follow a sport or club can sign up and receive news of their favourite team or player. A fan site means teams and individuals can have a global presence, for example, the Spurs Singapore fan site. The sites carry advertisements which provide revenue. The typical contents of a fan site include:

- a forum to discuss the team
- blogs from players or fans
- surveys and match analysis
- deals on supporters' kit
- travel and accommodation for away matches
- competitions
- downloadable clips of action
- player profiles.

Merchandising

An important function of the Internet is merchandising. This has boomed in recent years. Almost every kind of sports goods is for sale online, from team kit to specialist footwear or equipment. This has led to the demise of some high street chains and smaller sports shops. All large club stadiums have merchandising shops and these are mirrored with online sales.

Assessment activity 12.2

P2 **M2** **BTEC**

Using material from the text and your own research, prepare a report which describes and explains:

- the positive influence that the media has had on a selected sport in the UK
- some negative impacts of the media. **P2** **M2**

Grading tips

- To attain **P2** link your description to real examples you have researched and found. Create a logical set of headings for your report. Make sure you choose an appropriate sport that has plenty of examples.

- To attain **M2** you must clearly explain both the positive and negatives influences, using clear subheadings and real examples. Make sure you choose an appropriate sport that has plenty of examples.

PLTS

When describing or explaining the influences of the media you will be using your **independent enquirer** skills. If you work in a group you can develop your **effective participator** skills.

Functional skills

By word processing your report you are providing evidence towards skills in **English**. If you use the Internet for research, you are using your **ICT** skills and may also do so if your report includes graphics or multimedia content.

2.2 Technology

We live in a technological age – the era of gadgets and instant communication. Many of the devices invented have been sport specific or adapted to be sports' aids.

Clothing

A range of thermally efficient and breathable types of material have been developed for outdoor activities. Other examples are spin-offs from space technology such as waterproof Teflon-coated jackets. Gloves with a 'thinsulate' layer to help insulation from the cold are also available.

Fluorescent garments are often worn by sportsmen and women to improve visibility and safety. Some rugby players use special gloves with a 'grippy' surface to increase their catching ability; climbers wear sticky boots to aid their friction footholds.

Some controversy has also arisen over the buoyancy and slipperiness of some swimsuits, with a call to ban them and revert all records to 2007 levels before they were approved.

Personal equipment

Outdoor sports participants can use a range of devices including hand-held satellite navigation aids and pedometers. Pagers and mobile phones might come into this category as well as personal organisers and notepads. Ski poles have been adapted for older walkers and reaction sunglasses help provide increased protection from the sun. Home-based exercise has improved with the production of modern gym equipment. You can also consider the level of technology that goes into our sports shoes. Lightweight personal protection for high impact sports has been created, including body armour for American football players, padding for cricketers and protection for hockey goalkeepers, and helmets for all.

How do you feel about clothing technology that improves performance?

Cameras

Digitisation has allowed camera technology to move forward massively. The benefits to sport are very obvious, from movement analysis to image creation and the capturing of sporting moments by nano-photography which freezes the action in great detail.

By using camera replay systems, critical incidents can be analysed to give the 'correct' decision or help the referee or umpire to make their decision, for example, rugby tries, cricket shots and run outs. The third eye principle can capture and retain the moment which the human eye and brain cannot achieve in quite the same way. In the 2010 Winter Olympics the use of 'super slo-motion camera work' allowed us to watch the 'aerials' in fine detail so that we could better appreciate their technique and complexity.

Analysis

Analysis in sport has benefited from new technology. Drug testing capabilities have been enhanced in the race to analyse and identify the drug-takers in sport. The world anti-doping agency has benefited as 80 per cent of tests are random and can now be done outside the laboratory. Lord Coe commented that an Olympics in London without drug cheats looks impossible, but added: 'We are winning the battle, the technology is much better, and we will present the best possible environment for a drug-free Games in London.'

Computer and video analysis means that athletes' techniques can be studied carefully, while biomechanics are much more easily understood for those studying in this area. One such system is Dartfish.

You are probably most familiar with Computer Games Applications of new technology. Many are sports-based and interactive giving everyone, even the couch-bound, the chance to take some exercise. Examples include Wii Fit and Wii Sports.

Lactate threshold measurement is another technological advance which helps with training. A small hand-held kit is now available to help measure the maximal lactate steady state (MLSS) that an athlete can continue at for an extended period of time without slowing. Lactate threshold is the best known indicator of endurance performance.

Hyperbaric chambers are available in portable form so that users can breathe higher levels of oxygen. Hyperbaric Oxygen Therapy (HBOT) is a painless procedure in which a person is exposed to increased pressure, thus allowing greater absorption of oxygen throughout the body tissues. This increased pressure allows more oxygen to reach the cells within the body leading to many healing and therapeutic benefits.

Computer software programmes now allow us to transfer data to and from our personal devices or the Internet. This has many applications for sports management such as equipment and facility management, maintenance scheduling and diagnostic tests. There are also secure line options and encryption services to ensure safety and privacy of data.

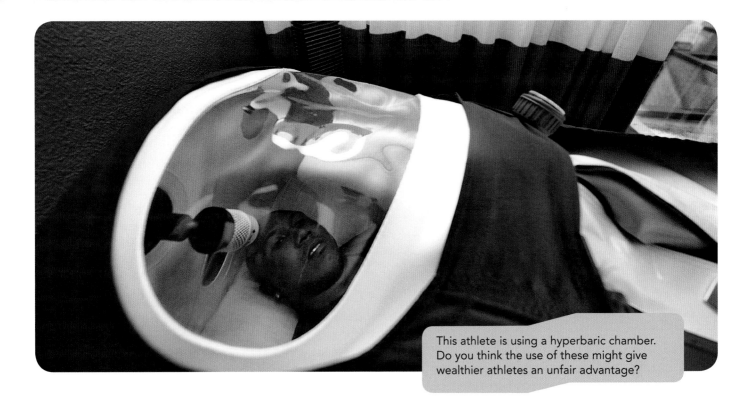

This athlete is using a hyperbaric chamber. Do you think the use of these might give wealthier athletes an unfair advantage?

Assessment activity 12.3

P3 M3 BTEC

Using material from the text and your own research, prepare a magazine article which describes or explains the effects of technology on a selected sport in the UK. P3 M3

Grading tips

- To attain P3 you might use some pictures, i.e. photos of technology being used by an athlete to help them analyse or improve their performance. Choose an appropriate sport that has plenty of examples.

- To attain M3 make clear explanations in your article (look at some real ones for guidance). Try to use several technological dimensions.

PLTS

When describing and explaining you will be using your **independent enquirer** skills. If you discuss effects with others, you can develop your **effective participator** skills.

Functional skills

By carrying out research and writing your magazine article you are providing evidence towards skills in **English**. If you use the Internet for research and photographs to illustrate it you are showing evidence of your **ICT** skills. You may also do this by using an electronic medium to support your presentation.

3. Know how contemporary issues affect sport

Sport in society has transformed since the 18th century. But it still carries issues and some are as old as sport itself (racism and sexism to name two); others reflect our technological age (for example, the media and globalisation) and materialism.

3.1 What are contemporary issues?

Contemporary means 'current' and an issue can be described as 'a topic of discussion about which people have different views'. Some of the issues affecting sport our explored below.

Deviance

Deviant behaviour is a recognised violation of social norms – such as hooliganism, violence or verbal abuse. For some people, sport can provide a potential solution, or at least a pathway, to conformity and good citizenship. Many sport development schemes have been used to try and help change negative behaviour. **Deviance** can also be demonstrated in the desire to win or succeed at all costs – some athletes will cheat or use drugs to enhance their performance.

Playing sport is a good way to help with anti-crime initiatives. Sport can help people understand discipline and rules, and may help to build confidence and other social skills. Sports development schemes often adopt an anti-crime agenda – crime rates drop when more constructive sports are available, especially in deprived areas of major cities. Voluntary organisations and police forces have been using this tool for inclusion for many years.

Sport can help tackle **social exclusion**. It has been used successfully to draw people back into normal, healthy habits and give them opportunities to improve their lives.

Remember

The social and economic cost of crime to the nation is enormous – over a quarter of the working age population has a previous conviction, and the annual cost of crime is over £50 billion.

Gamesmanship is the cynical side of sport. With the pressure to win in many sports, gamesmanship has become all too frequent. Can you think of an example?

Case study: Crime reduction through sport

One specific project typifies many others – a partnership scheme between Nacro, the national crime reduction charity, Chelmsford Borough Council, Chelmsford College and other community-based organisations. An extract in 2009 shows some of its aims which again typify many others:

- To provide holiday sports courses for young people during the Easter holiday period.
- To provide sporting activities for young people during the summer holiday period in conjunction with our partners.

- Deliver one-off events throughout the year including an Extreme Sports Day at Essex University and an Anti-Racism Event as part of the FA's initiative to 'Kick racism out of football'.

Source: www.chelmsford.gov.uk

1. **What do you think are the main reasons for young people turning to crime and vandalism in the first place, and why do you think sport is seen as such a good solution?**

2. **What other benefits to society will there be if more people are involved, and have better access, to sport?**

Key terms

Deviance – cheating or bad behaviour.

Social exclusion – feeling as though you are outside normal society.

Gamesmanship – when dubious tactics are employed in a sport to gain an advantage over the opposition, e.g. intimidation (this can be psychological and/or physical) or an attempt to disrupt concentration.

When it comes to taking drugs to enhance sporting performance, we tend to think of the high-level athletes who have been caught, but there are many other players who just want to build strength or body mass. There are many issues here:

- It is unethical to enhance performance using drugs.
- It breaks rules and codes of conduct.
- There could be long-term effects on health.
- The costs of policing it.

Can you think of other doping issues? The list of banned drug classes is shown in Table 12.2.

Some supplements and medicines contain banned substances and this has caught out athletes who have tested positive after taking medication, for example, the Olympic skier Alain Baxter who claimed that a tiny trace of methamphetamine had originated from a Vicks inhaler. Further information can be obtained from the World Anti-Doping Agency (WADA).

Education and sport in schools

Physical education (PE) and sport in schools has become a key issue for everyone involved in education. Targets have been set for schools to create more time for PE (75–90 minutes per week in primary schools). For secondary schools, the amount of time and range of activities are more flexible but most aim for a minimum of two hours of PE per week. The standard types of PE and sport on offer are:

- gymnastics
- invasion games
- swimming
- outdoor activities
- net and wall games
- striking and fielding games.

Table 12.2: Consider the underlying risks for drug takers shown by the side effects.

Drugs/banned substance	Taken to:	Side effects
Stimulants	<ul><li>increase alertness</li><li>improve concentration</li><li>increase aggressiveness</li><li>decrease fatigue</li><li>shorten reaction time</li></ul>	<ul><li>Increased cholesterol level</li><li>Increased risk of heart attack, hypertension, stroke, liver and kidney damage, jaundice, depression, aggression, mood swings, acne and skin disease</li></ul>
Peptide hormones and growth factors	<ul><li>stimulate growth and cell reproduction and regeneration</li><li>increase muscle mass</li><li>increase energy levels</li></ul>	<ul><li>Increased risk of diabetes</li><li>Joint swelling</li><li>Joint pain</li><li>Carpal tunnel syndrome</li></ul>
Anabolic agents	<ul><li>create lean body mass</li></ul>	<ul><li>Nausea and dizziness</li><li>Headaches</li><li>Muscle cramps</li><li>Heart flutters</li></ul>
Diuretics	<ul><li>reduce weight</li><li>draw off water to mask other drugs in the body</li></ul>	<ul><li>Dehydration and cramps</li><li>Dizziness</li><li>Heart damage</li><li>Kidney failure</li></ul>

These activities aim to:

- give pupils skills and confidence
- create a lifelong learning attitude/interest in sport
- give regular activity and exercise sessions
- help pupils to work in a team
- help pupils to learn to follow rules and play fair
- give pupils a chance to take part in activities away from home and outdoors.

Child protection

The safety and security of children has become a major issue for our society. Legislation under the Child Protection Act of 1999 was brought in to give guidance on this. Sports governing bodies and clubs are among the most proactive in terms of child protection. Most clubs must now have a child protection policy in place before they can become affiliated.

Sport England and the National Society for the Prevention of Cruelty to Children (NSPCC) have guidelines for clubs to follow. Every person working with children in a sports context must undergo a Criminal Records Bureau check to determine whether they have a criminal past or record that would make them unsuitable to work with children. Each school or club needs to have a procedure to follow if anything suspicious happens.

Health initiatives

Recently, much attention has been paid to the health risks associated with obesity in young people. Television programmes such as Jamie's School Dinners have highlighted bad eating habits and a lack of exercise as the main causes of obesity. As a result, there have been campaigns to try and encourage young people to eat healthier school meals and take more exercise. Change4Life is one example.

Racism

According to the Commission for Racial Equality, **racism** means 'holding biased or unfair views about other nationalities or ethnically different people, and treating them as inferior'. Unfortunately, incidents of racism in sport and our modern multicultural society are still common – for example, racist comments at football matches directed at non-white or non-UK players. The Football Association has been running a strong campaign for several years called 'Let's Kick

Racism Out of Football' (www.kickitout.org) and in 2000 a Racial Equality Charter for Sport was launched (www.sportingequals.com).

Commercialisation

Commercialisation means making sports into a more marketable 'commodity' that can be sold to audiences, spectators or participants, usually for a profit. Examples include:

- selling the television rights to a big match, e.g. the UEFA Champions League
- selling official team strips and other merchandising
- package deals to travel to a big event, e.g. the Winter Olympics
- the chance to gamble, e.g. online betting.

Sport as a global spectacle

Globalisation is a result of a number of factors – commercialisation, global communications, travel and also professionalism, which allows players to compete around the world in their sport or to play for teams in any country. The sports landscape, takes in the whole globe, and we are now able to watch sport 24/7 from around the world – its big business.

Take it further

Global sport – who wins?

Discuss with a partner, then in a group of three or four, and then as a class:

- Who receives the profits from global sports events? Does globalisation mean that we need huge international federations to run our sports?
- Do the television channels show us everything we want to see – or just what they want us to see?
- Are sport's interests really at the heart of it all?

Politics

In the present sports climate, politics is having an impact in several ways. In a positive way, the support of the UK government has helped to win the bid for the London Olympics. This support continues with funding. In a negative way, governments and human rights campaigners have not always been in favour of athletes competing against other countries which have a poor human rights or safety record, for example, South Africa, China, Uganda and North Korea. You will probably recall the protest about China's human rights record when the Olympic flag was carried through London in 2008. Consider also the withdrawal of the Tongan Football team by their President after the shooting at the African Cup of Nations in Angola in January 2010.

At regional and local levels the evidence of 'political positivism' can be seen by the funding for regeneration schemes that are driven by sport aims, for example, Leigh sports village. However, was this a vote catcher?

Religion and culture

The UK is a multicultural society. Religious and other cultural issues present challenges for sport.

- Muslim women have to wear full body coverage to play and compete and no bodily contact is allowed.
- Other religions may not wish followers to play during specific fasting or prayer periods.
- Many sports facilities now provide prayer rooms.
- Other cultural barriers might be language, lack of education and little or no knowledge of British sports.

Some specific associations have been set up to try and overcome cultural barriers such as the British Asian Rugby Association (BARA) and The Women's Sport and Fitness Foundation (WSFA).

Gender issues

Gender differences in sport have a long history – sport was a male-dominated sector (and some would argue it still is). Women have had to fight to compete in many sports. Men held the opinion that women were too weak or frail to compete in men's sports – or should be looking after the home and children. The Victorians saw women as objects of beauty that should not expose flesh, perspire or be exposed to contact sports.

Participation rates in sport among women and girls are much lower than for men. Reasons for this gender gap can be grouped as practical, personal and social and cultural.

Minorities can face high levels of stigma from their own communities, as well as the wider population. This is particularly so for the lesbian, gay, bisexual and transgender (LGBT) community.

Assessment activity 12.4   P4 M4 D1   BTEC

Imagine you are a trainee sports reporter for a local newspaper, eager to make a splash with a series of articles over the next few weeks. You have chosen four main areas you will write about to investigate and expose underlying issues.

1. Select from the topic headings in this outcome (see pages 42–45). You should also select one sport to focus on.

2. Prepare four articles for your paper, including the main issues, research undertaken and giving your views on what should be done. P4 M4 D1

Grading tips

- To attain P4 you could use previous newspaper articles to help you. But ensure you show the effects and don't just describe the source. Focus on impacts.

- To attain M4 give good detail and show your understanding of the issues on your selected sport and its effects.

- To attain D1 evaluate the issues with examples and go on to show the effects clearly and in depth.

PLTS

When you analyse what issues you will focus on you are likely to produce evidence of your **independent enquirer** skills. You will be using your **creative thinker** skills when you review contemporary issues. If you work in a group you can develop your **effective participator** and **team worker** skills. Working independently will produce evidence that you are a **self-manager**.

Functional skills

By describing explaining or evaluating these selected issues and writing these articles you are providing evidence towards skills in **English**. If you use a computer or software to produce your articles and to help you research, you will improve your **ICT** skills.

4. Understand the cultural influences and barriers that affect participation in sports activities

Over the centuries, differences in culture have influenced what, how and why sport is played. There are many barriers which prevent people from playing, some personal, some material, and some cultural. Many agencies have derived strategies and initiatives to help encourage and give access to sporting opportunities in our society.

4.1 Barriers to participation

Time

Lack of time is the most frequently cited reason for not participating or taking exercise. To take part in sport, people may have to juggle priorities such as work, parenting and domestic duties. This creates a spectrum with dedicated people at one end and non-participants at the other – all may wish to participate but some have no free time.

Resources

Resources fall into three main groups: financial, physical and people. The two ends of the resource spectrum show the divide that has always existed in sport and leisure participation (Figure 12.6).

Fitness

Lack of fitness is often the excuse given by people who say they cannot take part in sport. They probably need to build up their fitness to help them participate. Initially, the problem is finding the motivation to do so. This needs to be tackled with a positive mindset and a gradual approach.

Ability

Lack of ability can prevent someone from taking part at a higher level, but it should not prevent them from finding a sport that they can enjoy. Getting some coaching to improve ability, or joining a class with a friend, is a good strategy.

Lifestyle

A busy lifestyle is often a reason for not participating in exercise or sport. We have a culture of long work hours in the UK, where people who are eager to impress colleagues, or get promoted, stay late at work. This eats into their leisure time. Prioritising areas other than work might help them to achieve a better work–life balance. On the other side of the argument, some people will choose certain sports because of their status, for example, golf or sailing. Conversely, this might put others off joining.

Medical conditions

People with genuine medical conditions need to take exercise under supervision or guidance. Many do so under GP referral schemes, where a trained instructor looks after their needs, perhaps at a local gym, after being referred by their doctor. For those recovering from an operation, exercise can be of help, for example, the Walk to Health campaign.

Few resources	Abundance of resources
Little money Few or poor facilities Lack of team mates	Lots of money Many, high quality facilities A range of play mates

Figure 12.6: How is a lack of resources a barrier to participation in sport?

Walking is Britain's most popular physical activity – which do you think is the next most popular?

4.2 Cultural influences

The influences and differences in our society relating to sports participation stem from four main areas.

Gender difference

This has produced inequality in terms of access to and participation in sport. In the past, and still to an extent today, many women have been stereotyped into domestic roles, leaving fewer opportunities or activities suitable for them to participate in. During the 1980s a more enlightened and equal approach began to emerge, allowing women's participation in sports to blossom in the UK. This may have been spurred on by the equal pay act, feminist activists and the formation of women's only sports federations.

Ethnicity

Ethnicity refers to a population whose members identify with each other, usually on the basis of a common genealogy or ancestry, and who are united by common cultural, linguistic or religious traits. It can influence what or whether we play or succeed in sport, other people's attitudes and progress.

Age

In 2006 new legislation was passed making it illegal to discriminate against anyone on the basis of age. For older people in the sports industry, this means they should be able to continue working for longer if they wish, be just as eligible for promotion as a younger candidate, and have the same terms and conditions of contract.

In terms of participation, as people age they take less exercise so greater encouragement is needed here.

Socio-economic groups

Socio-economic groups are a concept created in the 20th century to help classify society into different types. This is basically a crude measure, based on income and job type, which produces the categories in Table 12.3. These groups can be useful in considering participation rates and reasons for non-participation.

Key terms

Ethnicity – belonging to a group of people who identify themselves as from one nationality or culture.

Socio-economic groups – ways of grouping people according to income and job.

Table 12.3: Socio-economic groups. Discuss which categories are most likely to participate in sport and why.

Classification	Type of job
1.1	Employers in industry, commerce, etc. (large establishments)
1.2	Managers in local and central government, industry, commerce, etc. (large establishments)
2.1	Employers in industry, commerce, etc. (small establishments)
2.2	Managers in industry, commerce, etc. (small establishments)
3	Professional workers – self-employed
4	Professional workers – employees
5.1	Intermediate non-manual workers – ancillary workers and artists
5.2	Intermediate non-manual workers – foremen and supervisors non-manual
6	Junior non-manual workers
7	Personal service workers
8	Foremen and supervisors – manual
9	Skilled manual workers
10	Semi-skilled manual workers
11	Unskilled manual workers
12	Own account workers (other than professional)
13	Farmers – employers and managers
14	Farmers – own account
15	Agricultural workers
16	Members of armed forces
(17)	Inadequately described and not stated occupations

Source: www.gov.statistics.uk

4.3 Strategies and initiatives

A number of sports-related agencies have designed a range of strategies (plans) and initiatives to help people participate.

National

Game Plan was a national government plan for sport, created in 2002. It detailed the government's vision and strategy for sport from a mass participation and a performance perspective up until 2020 (note that it was published before the awarding of the 2012 Olympic Games to London). To research Game Plan, see www.culture.gov.uk. Try to identify whether a new strategy has been put in place after the 2010 election.

Every Child Matters is a government strategy which proposes a range of measures to reform and improve children's care nationally. The aim is to protect children and to maximise opportunities open to young people to improve their life chances and fulfil their potential, particularly through sport and out-of-school activities.

Sporting Equals is a national initiative which is working towards creating a society where:

- people from ethnic minorities can influence and participate equally in sport
- understanding of racial equality issues that impact on sport is high
- providers of sport work towards a fully integrated and inclusive society
- cultural diversity is recognised and celebrated.

The Talented Athlete Scholarship Scheme (TASS) is a national DCMS (government)-funded programme that is a partnership between sport and higher and further education. The programme distributes awards to talented athletes who are committed to combining sport and education.

Plan for Sport 2001 was the 2001 action plan based on the document *A Sporting Future For All*, published by the government in 2000. It was followed by Game Plan and Playing to Win in 2008. These action plans deal with initiatives to develop sport in education, community and the modernisation of organisations involved in sport. This is an ongoing strategy, and the DCMS website gives regular updates on its progress and the Olympics.

Coaching Task Force 2002 was set up by the DCMS to look at ways of improving coaching. It published a report in July 2002, with the following targets:

- to implement a UK Coaching Certificate by January 2007
- to have 45 Coach Development Officers in post by April 2005
- to get 3000 Community Sports Coaches in post by the end of 2006
- research to be produced on 'Sports Coaching in the UK'.

Check their website (www.sportscoachuk.org) to see what was achieved.

Local

Girls First was a scheme run locally in secondary schools in Wales, giving £1000 to each qualifying school to provide after-school activities, specifically targeting girls' participation. It was hoped that by providing enjoyable activities on a regular basis, more girls would be encouraged to form positive habits about exercising and keeping healthy.

TOP Programmes was probably the best known scheme to help develop sport across England. The initiative, led by the Youth Sports Trust, aimed to supply schools with a sports bag and trained leaders, giving them ready access to resources for sport.

Active Sports is an ongoing national development programme, supported by Sport England, that aims to help young people get more from their participation in sport – from grassroots to high-level young performers. The programme is based around targeted sports,

Kiran Matharu is not just unusual for a golfer; she is the first female British Asian sports champion. Which other top sports people come from an Asian background?

including basketball, cricket, girls' football, hockey, netball and rugby union. Each local area is encouraged to devise its own content to suit local needs and facilities. This programme is now coming to an end and being replaced by funding for Whole Sports Plans involving schools and clubs.

Sportsmark is an award made to outstanding schools for sports provision. Derived from the success of Sportsmark, there are several others in operation now too: Activemark for primary schools, Sportsmark for secondary schools and Sports Partnership Mark for independent schools. Schools will receive the award if at least 90 per cent of pupils across the school are doing at least two hours of sport.

Assessment activity 12.5

(P5) (P6) (P7) (M5) (D2) **BTEC**

Imagine you have recently been employed as a sports development officer for a local authority. You have been asked to put together a plan for the multicultural borough that you look after. Carry out the following tasks:

1. Explain the full range of barriers to participation in sports that people of all abilities, age groups, income groups, genders and ethnic types experience. **P5**

2. Explain three cultural influences that have an impact on sports participation. **P6**

3. Describe, explain and evaluate three strategies or initiatives which relate to sports participation. **P7** **M5** **D2**

Grading tips

- To attain **P5** you need to cover a good range of examples in your description, perhaps using case studies to illustrate or support your point.

- To attain **P6** your descriptions of three cultural influences can be drawn from a range. Make sure you are thorough and clear when you present your evidence.

- To attain **P7** there are many strategies and initiatives currently available for you to use. Perhaps try some contrasting ones. Keep your description clear.

- To attain **M5** good explanations will be needed and clear links to participation established.

- To attain **D2** an in-depth analysis will be important. Evaluation means you need to do some analysis and get your facts right.

PLTS

Working independently will produce evidence of your **self-manager** skills. Evidence of your **independent enquirer** skills will come through as you prepare your material explaining the influences and barriers. **Creative thinker** evidence could be found as you explain influences and barriers clearly, maybe making contrasts. If group work is involved that should produce evidence of your **effective participator** skills and some **team worker** evidence too.

Functional skills

By presenting or writing and discussing your plan, you are providing evidence towards skills in **English**. If you use a computer to produce your plan and to help you research, e.g. to produce tables or images, you will provide evidence of **ICT** skills.

Matt Ison
Sports development officer

Matt Ison works for a northern council's sport development department. The district he is responsible for has some rundown estates, but there are a few success stories about professional athletes from his patch who have done well. With the increase in immigration to the area, he has been faced with some new challenges in the last year.

To do his job effectively Matt needs a range of knowledge at his fingertips and lots of contacts.

Matt is regularly in touch with Sport England and local schools' sports partnerships to see where funding might be found or what their development plans are. He also uses the media to help him publicise programmes and events in the borough. He is regularly on the radio on Fridays and often appears in the Saturday sport pages attending these events.

He has had two big challenges recently:

- First of all, he has had to find ways to help new immigrants integrate with local communities. Some football games have helped with this which Matt managed to get sponsored by a local firm.

- The second challenge sees him trying get more kids into clubs to keep them active, but as many of them come from poorer families this has not been easy. He has been able to test their fitness levels before and after playing using some new gadgets – this has helped to keep them interested.

Local politicians have supported Matt in these initiatives and one or two former local players have come back to visit and to help with publicity.

Think about it!

- What other programmes do you think Matt could try for his area?
- Which governing bodies might help him?
- What sort of training do you think Matt went through to get where he is today?

Just checking

1. What was sport in pre-industrial society generally like?
2. How important were the public schools in helping to develop sport for society?
3. Can you explain 'rationalisation' and 'regulation' developments in sport?
4. Give names in full for the following – DCMS, CCPR and NGB.
5. Give reasons why sport is often called 'big business' these days.
6. Name the three main sectors in the sports industry.
7. Give two examples of new technology helping sport to develop
8. Give four ways in which the media can affect sports.
9. Explain how 'racism' and 'sexism' can affect participation in sports, giving examples of each.
10. List five barriers to participation in sports.

edexcel

Assignment tips

- Some of the issues that affect sport come from society, for example, participation (an example would be that of more children playing on computers and playing less sport).

- Some issues in society are fostered by sport, for example, gambling. Be clear which is which.

- Whichever direction or source the issue comes from there might be positive and negative outcomes – explore both in your work, for example, when considering issues connected to the media.

- There is a government drive to improve social issues through sport. These issues are often deeply embedded – try to uncover them.

- The sporting framework of the UK has grown up in a piecemeal way over centuries so we are left with a fragmented patchwork of provision – that should come across in your work.

- Our multicultural society presents new challenges, especially in city areas. Try to identify and assess these to add value to your work.

- Overall your work will be improved if you: ask questions of your tutor; discuss ideas with others before you begin; read the briefs carefully; carry out thorough research. The information is out there so find it!

13 Leadership in sport

A sports leader is often the unsung hero or heroine who never gets a medal, payment or a media interview. The sports leader is the person who introduces individuals to sport and supports their development. Being a sports leader requires having knowledge about everything from the skills, techniques or tactics which they must deliver to the methods which motivate performers. The more experience a sports leader has, the better their ability to develop sports performers' ability and achievement.

Sports participation levels in the UK are continually increasing. As more people participate in sport, more people are required to lead sport and physical activity. To ensure that sports leaders deliver appropriate activity sessions, they need to be properly qualified with a specific level of experience. This increase in demand of qualified and experienced sports leaders has created a skills shortage in the industry.

This unit will introduce you to the responsibilities, qualities, characteristics and roles of effective sports leaders. You will also examine the importance of psychological factors in leading sports activity sessions including motivation, personality, cohesion and the formulation of groups. You will plan, deliver and review a sport activity session for a group of sports performers.

Learning outcomes

After completing this unit you should:

1. know the qualities, characteristics and roles of effective sports leaders
2. know the importance of psychological factors in leading sports activities
3. be able to plan a sports activity
4. be able to lead a sports activity.

Assessment and grading criteria

This table shows you what you must do in order to achieve a pass, merit or distinction grade, and where you can find activities in this book to help you.

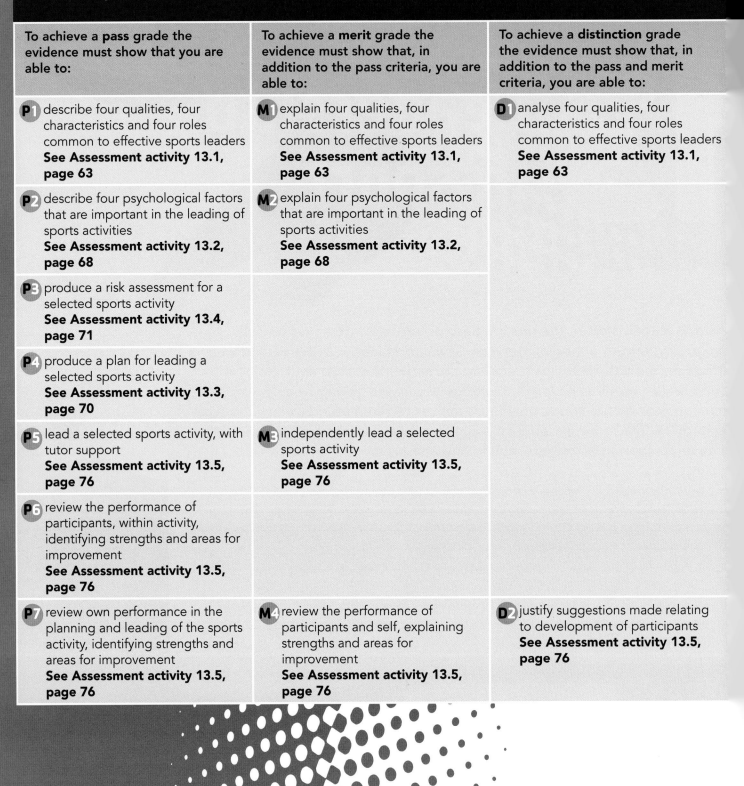

To achieve a **pass** grade the evidence must show that you are able to:	To achieve a **merit** grade the evidence must show that, in addition to the pass criteria, you are able to:	To achieve a **distinction** grade the evidence must show that, in addition to the pass and merit criteria, you are able to:
P1 describe four qualities, four characteristics and four roles common to effective sports leaders **See Assessment activity 13.1, page 63**	**M1** explain four qualities, four characteristics and four roles common to effective sports leaders **See Assessment activity 13.1, page 63**	**D1** analyse four qualities, four characteristics and four roles common to effective sports leaders **See Assessment activity 13.1, page 63**
P2 describe four psychological factors that are important in the leading of sports activities **See Assessment activity 13.2, page 68**	**M2** explain four psychological factors that are important in the leading of sports activities **See Assessment activity 13.2, page 68**	
P3 produce a risk assessment for a selected sports activity **See Assessment activity 13.4, page 71**		
P4 produce a plan for leading a selected sports activity **See Assessment activity 13.3, page 70**		
P5 lead a selected sports activity, with tutor support **See Assessment activity 13.5, page 76**	**M3** independently lead a selected sports activity **See Assessment activity 13.5, page 76**	
P6 review the performance of participants, within activity, identifying strengths and areas for improvement **See Assessment activity 13.5, page 76**		
P7 review own performance in the planning and leading of the sports activity, identifying strengths and areas for improvement **See Assessment activity 13.5, page 76**	**M4** review the performance of participants and self, explaining strengths and areas for improvement **See Assessment activity 13.5, page 76**	**D2** justify suggestions made relating to development of participants **See Assessment activity 13.5, page 76**

How you will be assessed

Your assessment could be in the form of:

- video recorded presentations of you describing the qualities, characteristics and roles of effective sports leaders
- a written report of the psychological factors that are important in the leading of sports activities
- session plans completed for a sports activity session
- observation records of your performance while leading the sports leadership session
- video recordings of you delivering the sports leadership session
- assessment of your own performance while delivering the session
- a development plan which identifies and describes methods for improving performance.

Gill Cook, 21-year-old Sports Development Officer

This unit gave me a great deal of knowledge about the theory behind delivering sports leadership sessions, as well as the practical ability to plan, prepare and deliver sessions to a variety of different sports performers. I always enjoyed sports coaching and wanted to be a netball coach and this course, and particularly this unit, really motivated me. I realised that if I wanted to be a sports coach I would have more of a chance of realising my goal by gaining the knowledge and ability to lead sessions for a variety of sports and physical activity sessions rather than just one. I was introduced to a variety of different sports and different methods of delivering sessions. I enjoyed learning about the psychological factors involved in leading activity sessions and I am using the appropriate teaching style to support the formulation of groups right now.

Over to you!

1. Why do you think a sports leader is more employable if they can coach more than one sport?
2. What is a sports development officer?
3. Provide examples of when knowledge of groups is required as a sports leader.

1. Know the qualities, characteristics and roles of effective sports leaders

What are the most important characteristics a sports leader needs?
Whenever we participate in or observe sport we see a variety of sports performers, coaches and managers who take on the vital role of leader. It is the leader who supports the development of other sports performers. Provide five examples of sports leaders from the world of sport. For each identify why you think they are effective.

1.1 Qualities

In order for someone to be a successful sports leader, it is important that he or she has a number of qualities (Figure 13.1).

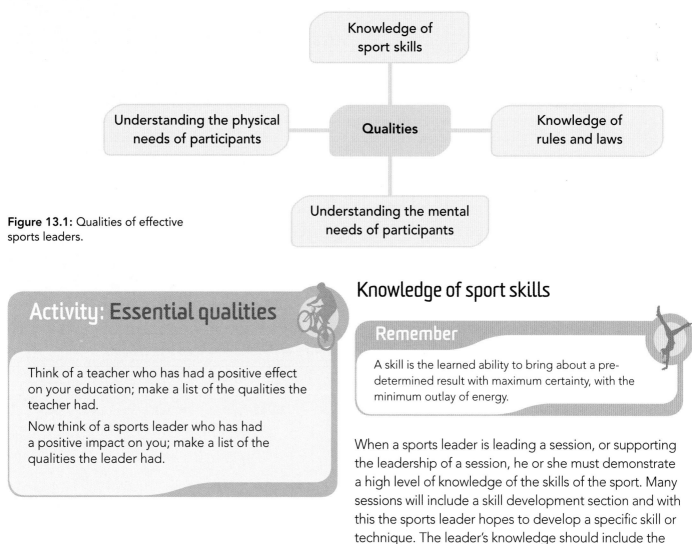

Figure 13.1: Qualities of effective sports leaders.

Activity: Essential qualities

Think of a teacher who has had a positive effect on your education; make a list of the qualities the teacher had.

Now think of a sports leader who has had a positive impact on you; make a list of the qualities the leader had.

Knowledge of sport skills

Remember

A skill is the learned ability to bring about a pre-determined result with maximum certainty, with the minimum outlay of energy.

When a sports leader is leading a session, or supporting the leadership of a session, he or she must demonstrate a high level of knowledge of the skills of the sport. Many sessions will include a skill development section and with this the sports leader hopes to develop a specific skill or technique. The leader's knowledge should include the techniques that are required to apply the skill.

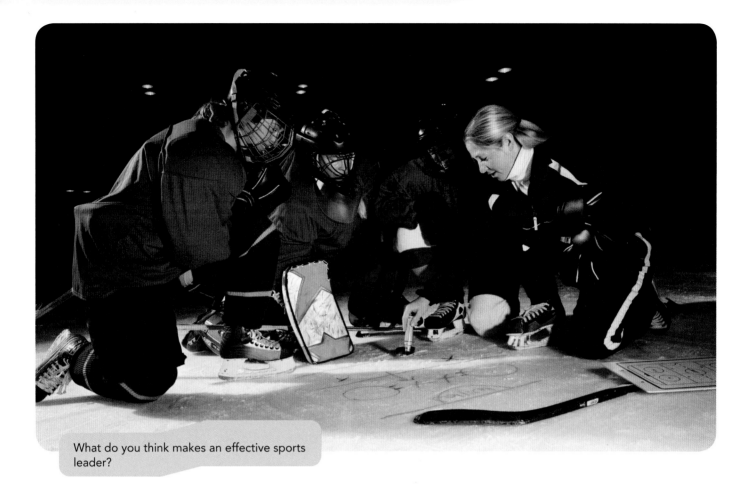

What do you think makes an effective sports leader?

To lead a session effectively, and to gain respect, the leader must have equal if not better knowledge of the sport than the participants. If, for example, a sports leader delivered a session of cricket to an advanced group of performers and only had limited knowledge of the sport, the participants could become frustrated, their performance could be hindered and the fun and excitement of the session could be spoiled.

Knowledge of rules and laws

Remember

Rules and laws are what govern sports and games.

A good sports leader needs to demonstrate a sound knowledge and understanding of the rules and laws of the sports that they are leading. They must be a role model to the athletes in their sessions. Passing on knowledge of the rules and regulations to athletes inculcates them with the laws of the sport.

Understanding the mental needs of participants

Participating in sport and physical activity is as much about developing the mind as the body. Many studies have shown that participating in physical activity can raise your mood and improve mental health. Many medical professionals actually prescribe exercise to people who are depressed and stressed. However, there are other reasons why people participate in exercise and a sports leader should understand these.

A sports leader will deliver sessions to different groups, each with their own set of needs and motivations, and the leader needs to understand what these are. For example, some people may wish to participate in sport and physical activity for social needs, whereas other people may wish to participate because they need to achieve a goal. In each of these instances, a sports leader must consider the content of the session, including the types of activities that will be most appropriate for the mental needs of the group.

Understanding the physical needs of participants

Sports leaders need an awareness and understanding of the different physical needs of different client groups. For example, a group of older women will have different physical needs to those of a group of young children. A sports leader may deliver sessions with similar aims but very different activities. In some instances activities have to be adapted within a session because not all situations will enable sports leaders to separate individuals with different physical needs. Inclusivity is an important quality of a sports leader.

1.2 Characteristics

A characteristic is a distinguishable feature or trait that sets one person apart from another. There are a number of key characteristics of good sports leaders (Figure 13.2).

Objectivity

Sports leaders have to demonstrate objectivity – judgement that is not affected by emotions and is disinterested, factual and based on observation. Sports leaders need to exercise this characteristic in a number of settings including:

- amongst mixed ability levels of performers
- when there is conflict within the group
- when leading sessions with people from different races and religions.

A sports leader should demonstrate objectivity in all sessions by being fair and equal to all. They should never show favouritism towards individuals.

Patience

A sports leader should be patient in all sessions. It is vital at all times to have a calm persona and never show anger towards sports performers and to always endeavour to develop everyone within each session. This may include differentiating activities as appropriate (ensuring people of lesser abilities achieve a goal within the session as well as those with high ability levels). As a sports leader you should not rush sports activity sessions. You may have to coach sessions to individuals of different abilities and disruptive individuals. You must manage these people appropriately.

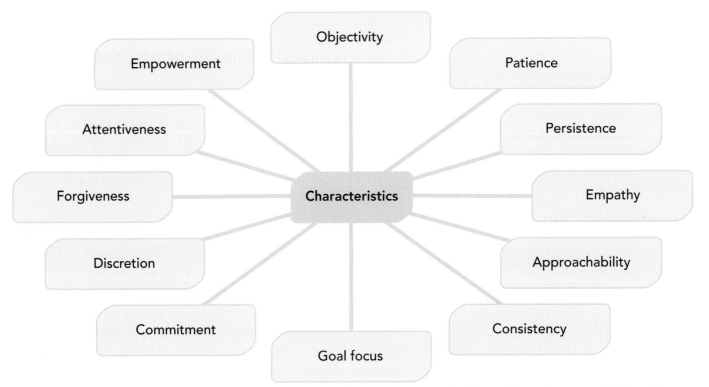

Figure 13.2: Characteristics of effective sports leaders – why are these important in developing the performance of athletes?

Persistence

Persistence is perseverance and dogged determination! You need to be persistent when leading sports and physical activity sessions to ensure that you continue to develop your athletes, even if you believe they can't improve further. Persistence requires sports leaders to review and reassess their aims and objectives. For example, if during a sports activity session the sports performers fail to achieve the desired goals due to a lack of ability, you must not give up but continue to try and encourage them. The participants may not have developed technically in a session but they will have enjoyed themselves.

Empathy

Empathy is the ability to appreciate and understand the needs of others. A sports leader must demonstrate empathy in all sessions towards a wide range of performers. Each session that you deliver may include people of different abilities and from different cultures and religions. You must take into account the needs of each individual within the session and ensure that everyone meets a specific target or goal. It is possible to have different aims and objectives for each sports performer within a session. Setting different targets for people with different needs and requirements is called differentiation.

Approachability

A sports leader should be approachable and everyone should find it easy to discuss with them any issues they might have. A sports performer who may want to discuss methods of developing their performance must not feel intimidated or overawed. Sports leaders need to be friendly with the athletes they work with but maintain a professional relationship and at times this may include criticising performance and providing feedback for development. This can make the relationship very challenging.

A sports leader is the main point of contact for many people as well as the performers whom they are coaching including parents, other sports leaders, officials, teachers, etc. You should consider your characteristics and how you conduct yourself.

Consistency

Consistency means reliability, conformity and coherency. A sports leader should demonstrate consistency in each session that they deliver by always displaying the same behaviour and characteristics. This will make the participants feel comfortable and at ease. Activities within sessions need to consistently develop and challenge the sports performers and must be easy to reproduce.

Goal focus

Goals or targets can be:

- short-term
- medium-term
- long-term.

A sports leader will set and share goals with many people including sports performers, other leaders, parents and teachers. For every session that a sports leader delivers they should set targets to achieve by the end of the session (these can also be called aims and objectives). When a goal has been set and agreed you need to strive towards achieving it.

In order to remain on target you must be motivated and determined. Until goals have been met you should be focused on them. This may include generating training sessions around supporting the achievement of the goal and ensuring that sports performers are regularly updated. The goal is not just a measurement of the sports performer; the goal and its achievement is also the target and achievement of the sports leader.

Commitment

Commitment is an essential characteristic of a sports leader. A committed leader will apply lots of time and effort in order to develop the participants of the sports sessions that they deliver. You should have excellent attendance and put a lot of effort into succeeding in every session.

A sports leader may be subject to some very difficult situations including:

- bad weather
- challenging sports performers
- low ability performers.

Sports leaders should demonstrate their commitment by consistently attending every sports activity session whatever the weather, the number of people present, the result or behaviour of participants.

Discretion

A sports leader will demonstrate discretion by ensuring that any information they learn through their role remains confidential. A sports leader may be privy to personal information which must be kept private from others. This information could include:

- a particular injury or illness the sports performer has or has had
- personal problems
- issues with other members of the session
- issues with other sports leaders.

At times, sports performers may disclose information which you need to share with people of authority in the club or school and sometimes with the police. If a child discloses something worrying you must be aware of the correct procedures to follow regarding child protection and disclosure. (For more information regarding child protection see Unit 5 Sports coaching book 1 page 122 and Unit 24 Physical education and the care of children and young people.)

Forgiveness

When leading sports and physical activity sessions you need broad shoulders. At times you may observe unacceptable behaviour and attitudes amongst athletes and spectators – people may even direct their frustrations towards you. You must not take this personally and you must show forgiveness towards all. It is also important you never react inappropriately towards athletes or spectators. A sports leader should always demonstrate behaviour that they would expect to receive.

Attentive

A sports leader must pay great care and attention to every last detail of the session they plan and deliver, ensuring that the performers carry out each activity planned within the session appropriately following clear instructions and technical guidance. You, as a leader, should show due care and attention to each of the athletes for whom you are responsible and should demonstrate attentiveness when observing the application of each skill, technique or activity. If you spot any discrepancies in the application, then you should stop the sports performer and try and develop their skill or technique. Some sports performers may require more attention than others and you must not make these people feel inadequate and incompetent.

Empowerment

In order to ensure that every sports performer in their session develops, a sports leader must motivate, encourage and inspire. If they can successfully engage everyone who participates within their session, then they will develop their ability to empower them.

Activity: Sports leaders – the good and the bad

From your own experiences, think of a sports leader who has demonstrated each of the characteristics described above in a good way and provide examples of how they did this. Now think of a sports leader who has failed to demonstrate each characteristic and explain how they did this. Discuss your findings with your group.

1.3 Roles

To be a successful sports leader you must develop your sessions and methods of delivery to encourage performers to learn. You also need to fulfil each of the following roles (see Figure 13.3) but it takes time to become an effective leader and plenty of dedication and practice.

Organiser

As a sports leader you have to be organised and prepared. Organisation starts prior to the delivery of a session. Meticulous planning is essential and may begin weeks in advance of a session. If you are planning a session for a group of sports performers whom you have never met before, then you might want to find out some important information about them. This includes gathering health screening questionnaires, consent forms and details of the performers' levels of experience within the sport or physical activity. This will help you to consider which activities you may deliver as part of your session.

When a session is planned you should carry out a risk assessment well in advance. A well-prepared session plan should be used although, at times, you will have to deliver activities that are not pre-prepared. You need contingency plans in the event of a variety of scenarios including:

- bad weather
- lack of equipment

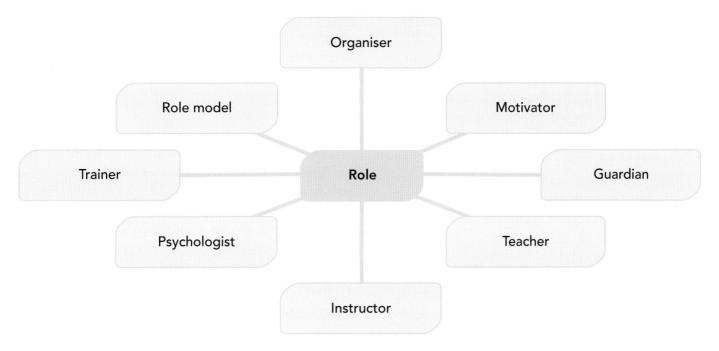

Figure 13.3: Do you think you will be able to fulfil all the roles of a successful sports leader?

- unavailability of the facility
- too many people attending the session

As well as preparing the equipment for the sports session, you should ensure that it is in full working order and that you know how to use it safely and effectively. All of these checks should take place before the session. You should also be insured to use the equipment (see the information about insurance in Unit 25).

By completing all of the appropriate preparation for the delivery of a sports session you will demonstrate effective organisation and professionalism.

Motivator

When leading sessions you must be a motivator. For a complete novice to a sport, the first session is often the most important and the one that will affect future participation. Experienced sports performers also require motivation to ensure that they remain engaged in the session at all times.

As a motivator you have to maintain the interest and application of each sports performer. In order to understand how someone is motivated, you must learn about their personality. There are two major types of motivation: intrinsic and extrinsic – these are explored in more detail in this unit on page 66. (See also the

motivation section on page 286–290 in Student Book 1, Unit 17 Psychology for sports performance) You must include appropriate rewards for each participant within your session to ensure that they remain motivated.

Guardian

A guardian is someone with the duty to care for and protect others. When a sports leader delivers training sessions to sports performers, he or she must care for, and is responsible for the welfare of, each of the participants for the duration of the activity.

Teacher

As a sports leader you must teach each participant so that they can develop as a performer in the sport. When delivering sports and psychical activity sessions to young children and beginners, you will often start by using teaching techniques to support them so they can learn the basic skills. As a performer develops in these skills you will then provide further support to enhance their efficiency and effectiveness at applying a skill. When educating sports performers you have to understand how people learn. Sports performers learn best when they:

- are actively involved in sports coaching sessions, rather than passively listening and watching the coach

- recognise how, when and where new techniques, skills or tactics can be used within the sport
- are encouraged to build on previous experiences and skills learned, or from another sport (some skills can be transferred from sport to sport, e.g. catching in cricket could be transferred to develop the skill of receiving in basketball, netball or rugby)
- are interested, enjoying themselves and motivated by the session
- can see or feel that improvements in their performance are being made.

The sports leader will need to be aware that some sports performers will develop differently and may require a mixture of teaching styles, whereas some will develop following just one style. Effective sports leaders develop a range of styles to deal with a wide variety of learning needs.

Instructor

An instructor is someone who leads and develops learning through instruction. A sports leader will take the role of an instructor when leading sports activity sessions. They must demonstrate effective verbal and non-verbal communication.

Psychologist

Key term

Psychologist – an expert in the field of psychology (the science of mental life).

A sports leader needs to understand how minds work as well as how bodies function. You must be aware of the personality of sports performers, what motivates them and how they interact with each other. The more knowledge you have about each of these factors, the more you can ensure your athletes will develop and meet their own goals as well as those you have set them.

Trainer

In their role as trainer, the sports leader must be aware of the physical, technical and tactical demands of the specific sport. He or she should have a bank of

specific activities that can be drawn upon to develop the participant's ability to perform to their optimum in competitive situations. The most common trainer in the world of sport is probably the fitness trainer who develops the physical and skill-related components of fitness for the sports performer.

To support the development of sports performers, coaches need a sound knowledge of health and fitness and training principles. As a trainer you should be able to design and implement programmes that are appropriate for the sports performers and which reflect the sports in which they compete. When planning fitness development sessions, you need to consider:

- age
- ability
- interests
- experience.

Role model

When leading sessions, you are representing the sport or activity in which participants are taking part and you must set an example. For example, in order to be an effective role model you should dress appropriately in every session you coach and lead.

Appropriate behaviour and language must be used at all times. Sports leaders should accept responsibility for the conduct of the sports performers whom they coach and encourage positive and non-discriminatory behaviour.

As a sports leader you are selling the sport or physical activity session to the sports performers. The more enthusiastic you are, the more likely the performers are to become enthusiastic too and to want to continue to participate.

Assessment activity 13.1

(P1) (M1) (D1) ·BTEC

You have been asked to support the tutor of a Year 10 PE group who is trying to encourage everyone to complete a Junior Sports Leader Qualification.

The tutor would like you to give the group a presentation about the importance and relevance of leadership in sport, and the qualities, characteristics and roles required to be an effective sports leader.

1. In your presentation you must describe four qualities, four characteristics and four roles common to effective sports leaders. **P1**

2. Explain four qualities, four characteristics and four roles common to effective sports leaders. **M1**

3. Analyse four qualities, four characteristics and four roles common to effective sports leaders. **D1**

Grading tips

- In order to attain **P1**:
  - select four qualities, characteristics and roles and define the meaning of each one
  - say what a sports leader has to do to fulfil each quality, characteristic and role.

- In order to attain **M1** provide examples of actual sports leaders who have fulfilled each quality, characteristic and role saying how they have met each one and how it has developed their ability to plan and lead sports and physical activity sessions

- In order to attain **D1** analyse each quality, characteristic and role by using examples of successful and unsuccessful sports leaders and provide recommendations of what a sports leader has to do to ensure each one is met in full and appropriately to support sports performers.

PLTS

By analysing each quality, and providing recommendations, you will develop your skills as a **reflective learner**.

Functional skills

When researching the attributes of a successful leader, you will develop your **ICT** skills in finding and selecting information

2. Know the importance of psychological factors in leading sports activities

2.1 Psychological factors

One of the roles of a sports leader is that of psychologist. He or she will need to develop their understanding of the variety of psychological factors which may affect the delivery of their coaching sessions and the performers who participate. (For more information about psychological factors see Unit 17 Psychology for sports performance in Student Book 1.)

Cohesion

When sports performers develop into groups they can be affected by each other. When a group forms, it is important that the sports leader manages and observes it to ensure that the formulation is successful and that there is a strong bond. A leader must ensure that the group or team has shared goals and objectives, is aware of each other's role within the team and that the team has strong **cohesion**.

Key term

Cohesion – the tendency for a group to stick together and remain united in the pursuit of its goals and objectives.

There are two major forms of cohesion – task cohesion and social cohesion.

- **Task cohesion** is the extent to which group or team members work together to achieve common goals and objectives. Although both types of cohesion influence performance to a certain degree, task cohesion is more closely related to successful sporting performance.

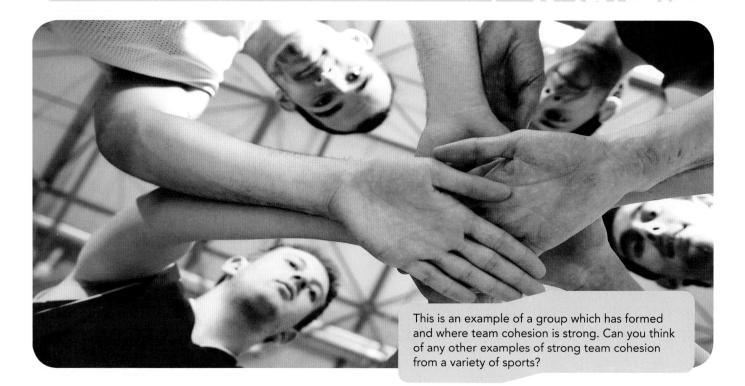

This is an example of a group which has formed and where team cohesion is strong. Can you think of any other examples of strong team cohesion from a variety of sports?

- **Social cohesion** is how much the team members enjoy each other's company. In recreational sport, all the players may get on well with one another and enjoy playing the game regardless of whether they win or lose.

To develop cohesion after a team or group has formed, the leader must ensure that everyone works together successfully and effectively. To achieve this, he or she should set appropriate goals and targets. The leader should always observe the group and ensure that no one is isolated or unaware of shared goals. The majority of successful sports teams need time to develop and so it is important to ensure that every opportunity is given for groups to formulate and bond.

Carron (1982) discovered that there are four major factors which can affect team cohesion:

1 environmental factors
2 personal factors
3 team factors
4 leadership factors

For a more detailed look into Carron's conceptual model of cohesion, refer to Unit 17 Psychology for sports performance in Student Book 1.

Group formation

For a group of people to become a team, they must go through four developmental stages (Tuckman, 1965). These are:

- forming
- storming
- norming
- performing.

For more detailed coverage, refer to Unit 17 Psychology for sports performance in Student Book 1. All groups go through these stages, but the time they spend at each stage and the order in which they go through the stages may vary. You need to understand the four stages.

Stage 1: Forming

The group members get to know each other and try to decide if they belong in that group. They then start to assess the strengths and weaknesses of other members, and test their relationships with each other. Individuals will get to know their roles and make decisions about whether or not they feel they can fulfil (or want to fulfil) their role within the group. The sport leader should be directive during the forming stage.

Stage 2: Storming

Conflict begins to develop between individuals in the group. It is common for individuals or cliques to start to question the position and authority of the leader and they will start to resist the control of the group. Often conflicts develop because demands are placed on the group members and because some individuals begin to try to acquire more status. The leader should take on more of a guidance role with decision-making and help the team to move towards what is expected.

Stage 3: Norming

The instability, hostility and conflict that occurred in the storming stage is replaced by cooperation and solidarity. Members of the group start to work towards common goals rather than focusing on individual agendas, and group cohesion begins to develop. As this happens, group satisfaction increases and the level of respect for others in the group increases. In the norming stage, the sports leader should expect the group members to become more involved in the decision-making process, and to take more responsibility for their own behaviour.

Stage 4: Performing

The team functions effectively as a unit. It works without conflict towards achieving shared goals, and there is little need for external supervision from the sports leader as the group is more motivated. The group is now more knowledgeable, able to make decisions and take responsibility for them.

Social loafing

Social loafing refers to a situation where group members do not put in 100 per cent effort in a group- or team-based situation due to a lack of motivation. This is most evident when the individual contributions of group members are not identified or are dispensable. Research demonstrates that social loafing affects performance. Ringelmann (1913) observed that groups of two, three and eight people pulling a rope did not pull as much as their individual efforts of pulling the rope suggested they would. **The Ringelmann effect** can occur when people are not as accountable for their own performance – as the group gets larger, athletes can 'hide' behind other athletes and not get noticed.

> **Key term**
>
> **The Ringelmann Effect** – the tendency for individuals to lessen their effort when working as part of a group.

A sports leader continually strives to motivate and set appropriate goals for each member of the team. By doing this you may be able to reduce the chances of social loafing happening. Cohesion in a sports team or group also reduces the likelihood of this.

Personality

Sports leaders should know the personalities of their athletes as they determine how an individual behaves, their motivation and the types of people within a group or team with whom they form relationships.

Personality is defined as the sum of those characteristics which make a person unique. There are several theories of personality; although we are all different and have different characteristics, these theories enable you to classify certain traits into personality groups. One of the most common methods for categorising personality is classifying whether an individual is an extrovert or introvert.

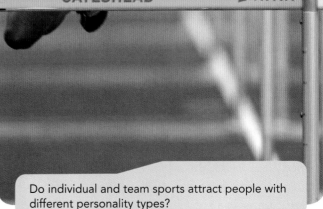

Do individual and team sports attract people with different personality types?

Activity: Introverts and extroverts from the world of sport

Make a list of the characteristics which you think make up introverts and extroverts.

In the table below, complete a list of sports performers from a variety of team and individual

sports and identify whether they are introverts or extroverts – discuss with your groups the reasons for each selection.

Sports performer	Sport	Team/individual	Personality type
Rio Ferdinand	Football	Team	Extrovert

- **Introverts** are individuals who don't actively seek excitement and would rather be in calm environments. Introverts are generally reserved and quiet; they are more likely to take part in individual sports.

- **Extroverts** tend to become bored quickly, are poor at tasks that require a lot of concentration and constantly seek change and excitement. Extroverts are very outgoing and good in social situations; they are more likely to take part in team sports.

For a more in depth analysis of each of these theories, refer to Unit 17 Psychology for sports performance in Student Book 1.

Motivation

Motivation refers to a sports performer's drive to take part and to persist in a sport or physical activity session. For more information about motivation, refer to pages 286–290 in Unit 17 Psychology for sports performance in Student Book 1.

There are two main types of motivation: **intrinsic** and **extrinsic**.

- **Intrinsic motivation**
  This is when someone participates in an activity without an external reward and/or without the primary motivation being the achievement of external reward. In its simplest form, this is when a sports performer participates in a sport for enjoyment.

- **Extrinsic motivation**
  This is when a sports performer behaves in a certain way because of an external reward. The most common forms of extrinsic motivation for a sports performer are in the shape of tangible and intangible rewards. Tangible rewards are physical things that can be given, like money, medals and trophies; intangible rewards are non-physical, such as praise or encouragement. Rewards must be used sparingly for extrinsic motivation to be successful in sports activity sessions. If the reward is given too frequently, it will be of little value as the sports performer will become accustomed to it and expect it.

Key terms

Motivation – the direction and intensity of your effort is critical to sporting success.

Extrinsic motivation – external rewards such as trophies, external praise and money.

Intrinsic motivation – internal rewards such as love of the game and health benefits.

Stress, anxiety and arousal

A sports leader must recognise the signs and symptoms of stress, anxiety and arousal. A good leader should be aware of the most effective state of mind in which an athlete performs. For example, the

Activity: Motivation

Ask a group of sports performers who participate in a local college, school or club team why they participate in sport. Complete the table below for each sports performer and identify what motivates them to play sport.

Performer	Why they play	Main type of motivation
James Arramayo	• love of the game • to keep fit • socialisation	• intrinsic

After you have completed the task for the whole team, complete a summary for the team's coach of the methods they could use during sessions to ensure their sports performers are motivated.

performance of some athletes is improved by higher levels of anxiety and arousal, whereas it can lead to a poor performance for others. It is the role of the sports leader to manage this.

Stress is defined by Lazarus and Folkman (1984) as 'a pattern of negative physiological states and psychological responses occurring in situations where people perceive threats to their well-being, which they may be unable to meet'. There are two forms of stress – eustress and distress:

- **Eustress** is a good form of stress that can give you a feeling of fulfilment. Some athletes actively seek out stressful situations as they like the challenge of pushing themselves to the limit. This can help them increase their skill levels and focus their attention on aspects of their sport. The benefit is that increases in intrinsic motivation follow.

- **Distress** is a bad form of stress and is what you normally associate with the term. It is an extreme form of anxiety, nervousness, apprehension or worry as a result of a perceived inability to meet demands.

Anxiety is a negative emotional state that is either characterised by, or associated with, feelings of nervousness, apprehension or worry. Anxiety can adversely affect sports performance. It is seen as a negative mental state that is the negative aspect of stress. These negative effects of stress can lead to lower levels of performance, and as performance levels decrease, this can lead to a corresponding decrease in the self-confidence of the athlete. Some symptoms of anxiety can be beneficial for sports performance, like increased blood flow, breathing rate and respiratory rate.

Arousal is referred to as a physiological state of alertness and anticipation that prepares the body for action. Arousal doesn't necessarily have a negative effect on the sports performance of a sports performer; it can be positive depending on the perception of the athlete. If the performer interprets the changes due to arousal as positive, this can have a positive effect on performance or prepare them for their event (psyching up the performer). However, if the changes are viewed as negative, this can negatively affect performance or preparation for performance (psyching out the performer). For more information on anxiety, and arousal, refer to Student Book 1 in Unit 17 Psychology for sports performance, pages 290–297.

Assessment activity 13.2 P2 M2 BTEC

A local sports leader is having some problems delivering sports sessions to one particular group of sports performers. He has tried using a variety of activities but the performers' motivation levels are low and their application and effort levels within sessions are very limited.

1. Produce a written report for this experienced sports leader that will develop his knowledge about the importance of psychological factors in leading sports activities. In your report you must describe four psychological factors that are important in the leading of sports activities. **P2**

2. In your report you must explain four psychological factors that are important in the leading of sports activities. **M2**

Grading tips

- In order to attain **P2**:
  - ensure you select four psychological factors that are important in the leading of sports activities and define each one
  - say what a sports leader has to do to support the development of another sports leader
  - discuss the impact each psychological factor can have on sports performance on individuals or teams.
- In order to attain **M2**:
  - provide examples of how psychological factors have supported the success of sports performers and examples of when sports performance has suffered because of psychological factors.

PLTS

Undertaking research for your report will provide evidence of your **independent enquirer** skills.

Functional skills

Describing four psychological factors that are important in the leading of sports activities will help you develop your **English** writing skills.

3. Be able to plan a sports activity

3.1 Planning

A sports leader has to plan thoroughly all aspects of a sports or physical activity session and take into account a number of factors.

Participants

When planning sport and physical activity sessions you must consider the participants. They will determine the types of activities that you use and the method of delivery and instruction used to support the learners.

Numbers

Prior to planning the session you need to know the number of participants to ensure that the resources and facilities are appropriate. You will have to adapt the session according to the numbers. Consider the session plan and specific activities for participants of different:

- ages
- ability
- gender
- specific needs.

Medical consent

Prior to delivering sessions you need to gather as much information as possible about the participants. Some of this information is a pre-requisite. To obtain medical information about the sports performers you could ask them to complete a health screening questionnaire and PAR-Q and, on completion of these, request that they obtain appropriate consent to participate within the session. (For more information and evidence of health screening procedures, see Unit 7 Fitness testing for sport and exercise in Student Book 1.)

Resources

You should highlight on a session plan the resources required within each component and how these will be used. There are several different types of resources which will be used in sport or physical activity sessions:

- **Human** – other people who may be involved with the delivery of a session including other coaches, assistant coaches, parents and spectators. When there are a large number of participants you need an appropriate ratio of coaches to participants. When there is more than one sports leader involved in the delivery of a session you should identify the roles and responsibility of each leader on the session plan.

- **Physical** – the facility and equipment required to deliver the session.
- **Fiscal** – the financial costs of running the sport sessions. This may include facility and/or equipment hire and could include depreciation costs or loss or damage costs to the equipment or facility.
- **Time** – allocate a time for each activity and ensure that the timings are appropriate for the duration of the session.
- **Environment** – ensure that you have chosen the appropriate environment for the session. In some instances you may need to adapt your session because of external forces. For example, if you are delivering a session outdoors and the weather becomes very severe, you will need to have alternative plans.
- **Transport** – in some instances you may need to provide transport. As the leader of the session it is your responsibility to coordinate the timings of the transport to and from the venue.
- **Targets** – these should be highlighted on a session plan. Targets should be set around the sports performer's strengths and areas for improvement. Within each session a sports leader should target particular sports performers and set realistic targets that can be achieved.

Expected outcomes

When planning a session, clearly set out what you would like each participant to achieve by the end of it. You should record these outcomes on the session plan. These outcomes are often called **aims** and **objectives**.

Key terms

Aim – something you want to achieve – a goal.
Objective – how you are going to achieve your aim.

The aims of a sports leadership session should be clearly stated on the session plan. (For an example of a session plan, see Student Book 1 Unit 5 Sports coaching, pages 138–139.) This should be agreed before the start of the session. An aim is something that you want to achieve or that is an overall goal for the session, for example, by the end of the session everyone will be able to execute a serve in tennis. In order to achieve your aim you need objectives. These will have to be clearly written on your session plan and should express how you will meet each of your aims (if you have three aims you will need to have three objectives). For example, 'In order for everyone in the group to execute a tennis serve effectively I must introduce, demonstrate and develop the required technique for the serve in tennis.'

Other considerations

When preparing to lead a sport activity you must consider a number of other factors including the legal requirements for delivering a session. Prior to delivering a session you should ensure that you have appropriate insurance. For some sports the legal requirements are much more complex than others. For example, the insurance required to run outdoor adventurous activities is much more difficult to obtain than that for leading a table tennis session. Getting insurance to run sports activity sessions may depend upon the qualifications held by the sports leader. The more qualifications and experience the leader has, the easier it will be to buy insurance.

A sports leader should be aware of all the other legislation which affects the delivery of sessions to different groups. For example, when working with children you must be aware of child protection legislation and the correct practices of delivering sessions to children and how to support children appropriately.

Activity: Failing to plan is planning to fail

Imagine you are taking a group of 15 12-year-old children in a minibus to a local park to participate in a multi-sports session. You have to plan a sports activity session for these 15 children. Draw up a list of all the considerations you will need to complete prior to the session taking place, taking into account the group for whom you are planning the session.

Assessment activity 13.3 (P4) BTEC

You have been asked to deliver a sports leadership session to a group of Year 10 students to demonstrate how their skills will develop as they become more experienced and confident as sports leaders. Produce a plan for leading a selected sports activity. (P4)

Grading tips

In order to attain (P4):

- select an appropriate activity, general sports coaching session, modified session or fitness session as your choice subject of delivery

- ensure your plan identifies the participants who will be involved in the session, the numbers, their age, ability, gender and any specific needs

- clearly state the expected outcomes of the session's aims and objectives

- complete a medical referral form for the learners to fill in prior to the session and gain consent for their participation

- ensure the session plan highlights the resources and organisation required for each activity

- indicate the time required for each component of the session

- identify the staff required to deliver the session (if more than one)

- identify the role of each member of staff leading the session (if more than one)

- ensure other considerations are catered for including insurance, and any other legal obligations, for example, CRB checks are carried out.

PLTS

When designing activities suitable for delivery in leadership sessions you will develop your **creative thinker** skills.

Functional skills

When producing a document template for leadership session delivery you will develop your **ICT** skills in the use of ICT systems.

3.2 Risk assessment

When planning sessions, it is a sports leader's priority to manage the health and safety of the participants before, during and after a session. When working with children and young adults under the age of 18 this responsibility becomes a legal obligation of duty of care. All sports carry an element of risk of injury; it is a requirement of the sports leader to:

- assess risk

- protect sports performers from injury and reduce the likelihood of risks occurring

- deal with injuries and accidents when they occur.

Risk assessment is an examination of what could cause harm and a consideration of how to reduce the risk of harm or injury to those involved in the session. The process of risk assessment requires you to identify hazards; to do this you must examine all equipment and the facility/playing surface where the activity is taking place. Once the hazard has been identified you must eliminate it. If the hazard cannot be eliminated then you must classify the degree of risk. Risks are usually classified as:

- low – no or minimal risk of injury

- medium – some risk of injury

- high – high risk of injury.

If the hazard is higher than low risk, you need to take action to eliminate it or reduce it to an acceptable level by reviewing and adding precautions as far as possible. If as sports leader you encounter hazards, you must consult a more senior coach or member of staff and discuss whether or not the session should proceed. (See Figure 13.4 for an example of a risk assessment form.)

Take it further

Risk assessment

In small groups, plan a circuit session for a group of 17-year-olds. Once you have planned the session complete a risk assessment (like the one in Figure 13.4). Then go into the sports hall and carry out the session. Individually, and as the session takes place, look for any other health and safety considerations which you have missed and add these to your risk assessment. Discuss your findings with the rest of your group.

Risk assessment form

Location: ....

Date: ....

Assessor: ....

Possible hazard	Risk	Likelihood of risk occurring (low/medium/high)	How to eliminate or minimise risk

Figure 13.4: An example of a risk assessment form. How might you need to adapt this form for different types of activities?

Assessment activity 13.4

P3   **BTEC**

Complete a risk assessment for the session plan that you completed in Assessment activity 13.3. This should demonstrate appropriate planning and preparation for the session to be delivered to the Year 10 students. The risk assessment will also be viewed by the sports leaders at the school to demonstrate how to monitor health and safety. **P3**

Grading tips

In order to attain **P3** ensure you:
- identify every risk or hazard that may cause injury or harm to the sports performers who participate in your session
- consider the type of activity, the learners participating, the location and how any of these could cause risk or injury to the participants and sports leader
- identify on the risk assessment who may be injured or harmed by the risk/hazards identified
- identify the likelihood of occurrence of injury by the identified risk/hazard
- identify the severity of the risk
- identify appropriate measures to minimise each risk/hazard.

Functional skills

When producing a risk assessment you will develop your **ICT** skills by bringing together information to suit content and purpose.

3.3 Activities

A sports leader does not just stand in front of a group and observe it participating in a session. He or she must consider appropriate activities within a session to ensure that the participants' needs are met. Sport and physical activity sessions come in many different forms and these are discussed below.

Figure 13.5: What types of sports activity have you recently participated in?

Basic sports coaching sessions

These sessions concentrate on one specific sport and are based around one or a number of the required skills, techniques or tactics for this sport.

Modified activities for special populations

A modified activity session will often require the sports leader to consider the ability of the participants. This may include physical differences or different levels of performance. A sports leader must ensure that everyone can participate and achieve the aims and objectives set within the session. For example, when working with sports performers with physical disabilities, activities and rules may need to be amended to ensure that all performers can participate. When working with beginners, the activity may need to be amended to make the session achievable and to develop the participants' skills.

Fitness sessions

Not all activity sessions need to be sport-related. Some client groups want to develop their fitness and this is when a sports leader needs the knowledge and ability to plan and deliver fitness sessions. There are many different forms of fitness sessions and because of their nature a sports leader will need appropriate qualifications to deliver them and gain insurance. (For more information on the types of training for different components of fitness see Unit 4 Fitness training and programming on pages 93–99 of Student Book 1.)

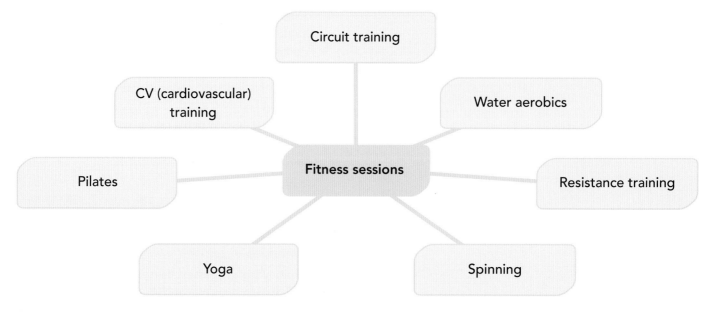

Figure 13.6: Can you think of any other types of fitness session?

Case study: Older sports performers

A local leisure centre has asked for your support to develop some of the physical activity sessions which they currently offer to a group of adults aged over 60. The sports performers have said that they are bored with the badminton sessions which have been run for the last six months. The group would like to participate in a wider range of activities and be introduced to some new sports and types of sessions as appropriate.

1. **Which other activities could this group be introduced to?**
2. **What health and safety implications might there be for these sessions?**
3. **What are the wider benefits of ensuring that sports sessions are available for everyone in a community?**

4.   Be able to lead a sports activity

4.1 Leading

A sports leader must deliver a session in an effective way and this can be measured by a number of factors explored below.

The safety and security of the coaching environment

You should ensure that the facilities and equipment are safe to use. You also need to provide a good level of instruction on how to use the equipment and facilities safely and effectively. You should constantly monitor the health and safety of all those involved and, in the instances where you identify health and safety issues, take appropriate action taken to prevent injury.

Communication

An effective session requires clear communication between the sports leader and the participants. He or she must give the group clear and concise instructions and when appropriate provide individuals with support and guidance on how to develop. This information can be given in three ways:

- Verbal communication – giving technical instructions to sports performers.
- Non-verbal communication – facial expressions and body gestures.
- Listening – after asking a sports performer a question and requesting a response.

Skills and techniques

A sports leader must help all performers to participate and enjoy themselves. One of way of measuring the success of a session is by looking at the participants' faces. If you think that they are not enjoying themselves then you should adapt the session. You do not always have to deliver a session directly from a session plan.

4.2 Review

The review stage of the delivery process is an important opportunity to assess the effectiveness of each session. This stage should influence the future planning of sessions. To complete an effective review of any session which you have delivered, you should examine a number of factors including these explored below.

Participants' performance

As a sports leader you should examine the strengths and weaknesses of participants when delivering sessions. For example, if you have delivered a session with the aim of improving the technique of a forward roll, you can review the session by asking yourself or an observer if the performers' technique has improved between the start and end of the session.

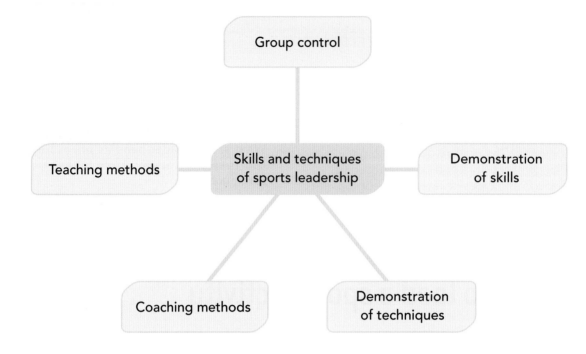

Figure 13.7: How will you be assessed? These are areas of performance as a sports leader that you will be assessed on in this unit.

Own performance

You should assess your performance and to do this you need feedback from observers. You could ask a mentor, supervisor or a friend with similar or more experience of leading sport activity sessions to observe you. In order to develop, you need feedback from more experienced sports leaders who can provide you with guidance and support your development.

Seeking feedback from the participants in a session can be done in several ways including asking them to complete questionnaires, surveys or short and fun evaluations. You should be able to use the results of the performers' feedback to find out if they enjoyed the session and the activities. (For more examples of methods of feedback see Unit 5 Sports coaching in Student Book 1 on pages 142–144.)

You can gain **formative** and **summative assessment** from participants, supervisors and observers.

Strengths

Using feedback, you should be able to identify the strengths of a session. This information should be drawn from the positive feedback and feelings that you obtained from the performers, summative feedback and listening to the responses and feedback from the observer/s of the session.

Key terms

Formative assessment – takes place informally and should support the development of a sports coach.

Summative assessment – takes place formally to assess the performance of a sports coach. This form of assessment is often used to assess a coach's ability (for example, when trying to gain a coaching qualification).

Areas for improvement

From the feedback, you should also be able to identify which components and elements of your performance require improvement. These factors will support your development and help you set your targets to improve your performance. Every sports leader should seek to improve at every stage of their career.

Development

After you have planned, delivered and obtained feedback from a session, you need to reflect on your performance and produce a development plan for improvement. This will include targets which you have set for yourself and which address the areas identified for improvement. This will increase your ability to deliver effective sports leadership sessions.

When setting targets for personal development a sports leader should use the SMART model for setting targets (see Unit 10 Outdoor and adventurous activities, page 21).

Opportunities

Within the development plan, specific goals should be identified. These might include:

- completing specific coaching/leadership qualifications
- working with specific sports leaders in the community
- observing effective sports leaders in action and when working with specific groups.

The development plan should clearly identify the methods which the sport coach plans to use to improve their performance with a justification of how and why.

Further qualifications

National governing bodies (NGBs) of sport have developed coaching and leadership awards which will support a developing coach. Almost all NGBs now have a coach education structure which produces qualifications from the assistant coach level (level 1) up to the elite sports coach level (levels 4 and 5). It is important that a sports leader aims to gain the appropriate qualifications required to coach and lead the performers with whom they are working. This ensures that the performers receive the support and experience recommended by the NGB.

Potential barriers

When producing a development plan it is important that a sports leader is aware of the barriers which could stop them meeting some of their targets. A sports leader, unlike a sports performer, will be left to their own devices to overcome potential barriers. These might include:

- geographical location
- cost
- time
- gender
- cultural background.

Despite such barriers, Sport England and NGBs are working with community groups to try to increase the number of coaches. Initiatives such as the McDonalds Coaching Scheme, run in conjunction with the Football Association, aim to increase the number of qualified coaches. The scheme offers football coaches an opportunity to gain a coaching qualification free of charge and is run through the regional FAs to support those coaches who, in the past, may have not been able to access such qualifications.

Assessment activity 13.5

P5 P6 P7 M3 M4 D2 · BTEC

You are going to deliver the session you planned in Assessment activities 13.3 and 13.4 to the Year 10 students. On completion of the session, you will ask the learners to give you feedback. You will also get feedback on from your supervisor/tutor and the teacher of the session. Using this feedback, you must review your performance and consider methods of further development.

1. Lead a selected sports activity with tutor support **P5** or lead it independently. **M3**

2. Review the performance of the participants within the activity identifying strengths and areas for improvement. **P6**

3. Review your performance in the planning and leading of the sports activity, identifying strengths and areas for improvement. **P7**

4. Explain the strengths and areas for improvement. **M4**

5. Justify the suggestions you have made relating to the development of participants. **D2**

Grading tips

- To attain **P5** ensure that the participants are safe and secure at all times, that you communicate effectively and demonstrate the correct leadership skills and techniques.

- To attain **M3** lead your session with no external support.

- To attain **P6** record the session and use it to analyse the strengths and areas for development of the performers.

- To attain **P7** watch the recording again and review your own performance identifying strengths and areas for improvement.

- To attain **M4** justify each strength and weakness of your performance by saying why it was a strength or why it was a weakness.

- To attain **D2** produce a development plan that identifies specific activities to support your future performance as a sports leader.

PLTS

When reviewing the performance of participants within an activity and identifying strengths and areas for improvement you will develop your **independent enquirer** skills.

When leading a selected sports activity you will develop your skills as a **team worker**.

Functional skills

When reviewing your own performance in the planning and leading of the sports activity you will develop your **English** writing skills.

Zach Armstrong

Volunteer

Zach is currently studying for a Sports Science degree at university after completing a BTEC National Diploma in Sport at his local college. During his BTEC studies, Zach enjoyed participating in leadership events and completed a number of leadership and coaching qualifications.

Now Zach is at university he has volunteered to support the Student Union in delivering a multi-sports activity event for a local primary school. The experience is completely voluntary but Zach sees the experience as valuable, not least because he wants to go on to gain a Post Graduate Certificate in Education and become a teacher.

The committee have met and discussed the organisation and planning required for the event. Zach has been given the role of Child Protection Officer and part of his role requires him to work with all the leaders who will be delivering the sessions. He must ensure that they meet the appropriate standards and that all the required paperwork is completed prior to the event.

The chairman of the event has also asked Zach to draw up several codes of conduct for the performers, sports leaders and spectators. These codes must be distributed in advance of the session. Zach must ensure that everyone agrees with the requirements of the codes and is aware of the consequences if they are broken.

Think about it!

- What legal obligations will Zach have to adhere to if he is the Child Protection Officer?
- What courses are available to support Zach in this role?
- What is a code of conduct and why are they important?

Just checking

1. Identify five successful sports leaders.
2. Identify four roles of a successful sport leader.
3. What is intrinsic motivation and what is extrinsic motivation?
4. List the characteristics of an introvert and an extrovert.
5. What is task cohesion and what is social cohesion?
6. List the four stages of Tuckman's stages of group development.
7. How can stress enhance and decrease sports performance?
8. What is a risk?
9. Provide some examples of the measures that can be taken to prevent injuries occurring during a five-a-side football session.
10. Provide a list of qualifications that could be completed to support your development as a sports leader.

edexcel ⠿

Assignment tips

- Remember that this unit will develop your skills as a leader.

- Ensure the activities within your sessions are appropriate for the target audience.

- When practising a leadership session remember that every performer has different strengths and so will develop at different speeds.

- Support your peers and they will support you. Work together giving each other tips and encouragement.

- Learn from other successful and experienced sports leaders. Watch them carefully. They will all be experienced and have plenty to teach you. Talk to them and gather information from them to assist with your assignments.

- Complete a sports leadership qualification to support you with the knowledge and ideas required to complete this unit.

- Ensure that you read the assignment briefs properly. Take your time and ensure you are happy with the task set for you. If not ask your tutor for additional assistance.

- Make sure you attempt all parts of the assignment briefs. If you only attempt the pass criteria this is all you will achieve – have a go at everything.

14 Exercise, health and lifestyle

This unit is particularly relevant to anyone aiming to work in health promotion or the fitness industry. It aims to develop your understanding of a range of different aspects which help maintain health and wellbeing. Good health helps you to achieve your maximum potential. Those who take part in regular physical activity, eat a healthy diet, do not smoke, drink alcohol in moderation and manage their level of stress, are likely to live longer and cope better with the demands of daily life.

You will gain the knowledge and skills to assess an individual's lifestyle, provide advice on lifestyle improvement and plan a health-related physical activity programme. You will explore the physical, social and psychological benefits of regular exercise, as well as barriers to participation, the importance of a balanced diet, not smoking and avoiding stress; and become informed about exercise and lifestyle programming for individuals. You will gain an understanding of behaviour change and models of change that can be adopted in the promotion of improved health behaviour.

Learning outcomes

After completing this unit you should:

1. know the importance of lifestyle factors in the maintenance of health and wellbeing
2. be able to assess the lifestyle of a selected individual
3. be able to provide advice on lifestyle improvement
4. be able to plan a health-related physical activity programme for a selected individual.

Assessment and grading criteria

This table shows you what you must do in order to achieve a pass, merit or distinction grade, and where you can find activities in this book to help you.

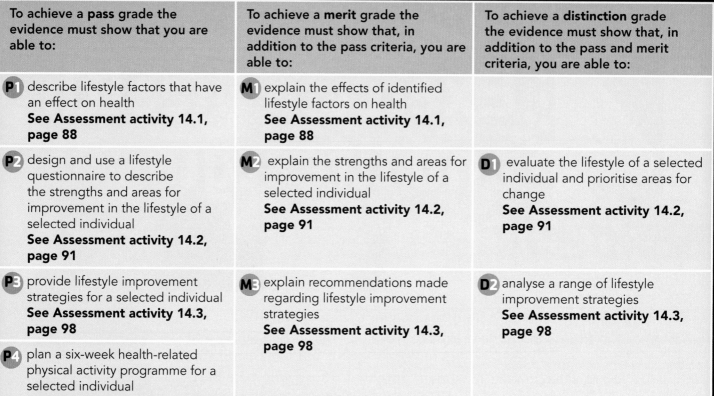

To achieve a **pass** grade the evidence must show that you are able to:	To achieve a **merit** grade the evidence must show that, in addition to the pass criteria, you are able to:	To achieve a **distinction** grade the evidence must show that, in addition to the pass and merit criteria, you are able to:
P1 describe lifestyle factors that have an effect on health **See Assessment activity 14.1, page 88**	**M1** explain the effects of identified lifestyle factors on health **See Assessment activity 14.1, page 88**	
P2 design and use a lifestyle questionnaire to describe the strengths and areas for improvement in the lifestyle of a selected individual **See Assessment activity 14.2, page 91**	**M2** explain the strengths and areas for improvement in the lifestyle of a selected individual **See Assessment activity 14.2, page 91**	**D1** evaluate the lifestyle of a selected individual and prioritise areas for change **See Assessment activity 14.2, page 91**
P3 provide lifestyle improvement strategies for a selected individual **See Assessment activity 14.3, page 98**	**M3** explain recommendations made regarding lifestyle improvement strategies **See Assessment activity 14.3, page 98**	**D2** analyse a range of lifestyle improvement strategies **See Assessment activity 14.3, page 98**
P4 plan a six-week health-related physical activity programme for a selected individual **See Assessment activity 14.4, page 104**		

How you will be assessed

This unit will be internally assessed by a range of assignments that will be designed and graded by your tutor. Your assignment tasks will allow you to demonstrate your understanding of the unit learning outcomes and relate to what you should be able to do after completing this unit. Your assignments could be in the form of:

- presentations
- practical tasks
- written assignments
- case studies.

Simon, 18-year-old gym user

I am a keen fitness enthusiast. I am a member of my local health and fitness club and attend three or four times a week. This unit gave me the knowledge and skills required to work as a health and fitness instructor. I particularly enjoyed learning about health and fitness screening and the consultation process. I have adopted the principles of training in my own exercise regimes and have begun to notice the benefits.

The practical tasks and activities made this unit more exciting for me. The bit I enjoyed most was interviewing my client for the assessment activities for the unit. I chose my uncle who has been sedentary and a smoker for much of his adult life. Helping him to explore ways of giving up smoking and embarking on a programme of physical activity has been extremely rewarding.

Over to you!

1. What aspects of this unit might you find challenging?
2. What preparation could you do to overcome these potential challenges?
3. What aspect of the unit are you most looking forward to?

1. Know the importance of lifestyle factors in the maintenance of health and wellbeing

Factors influencing your health and fitness

Take five minutes to think about all the factors that might influence your health and fitness. Awareness of these factors and their effect on health and wellbeing will help you to formulate realistic and achievable lifestyle goals and programmes when meeting some of the assessment requirements of this unit.

1.1 Lifestyle factors

Evidence suggests that leading a healthy lifestyle by following a sensible diet, participating in regular physical activity, maintaining a healthy body weight and avoiding smoking, excessive alcohol consumption and stress, is important to **health** and longevity.

Key term

Health – as defined by the World Health Organization, is a state of complete physical, mental and social wellbeing and not merely the absence of disease and infirmity.

Lifestyle refers to the way a person lives and reflects an individual's attitudes, values and behaviours. There are five lifestyle factors that are significant in maintaining health and wellbeing:

- physical activity
- a healthy diet
- not smoking
- avoiding excessive alcohol intake
- avoiding excessive stress.

Physical activity recommendations and guidelines

To gain health benefits the Department of Health recommends you do at least 30 minutes of moderate exercise on at least five days of the week. This recommendation should be viewed as the minimum required to achieve health benefits. The good news is it does not have to be achieved in a single bout. Several short bursts of activity can count towards your total. This approach may make it easier for some individuals to meet their daily physical activity target. Greater benefits will be gained from increasing the amount to 40–60 minutes each day, especially for those at risk of weight gain and associated diseases. The same recommendations apply to older people dependent on ability, but children are encouraged to achieve at least one hour of moderate intensity activity every day.

What is moderate activity and what type of activity should you undertake? Moderate means you must get a little warmer and slightly out of breath – the more vigorous the activity the greater the gains in cardiovascular health. In terms of type, it can be anything that raises your energy expenditure above resting level, enough to expend about 200 calories, and includes brisk walking, swimming, cycling and jogging, dancing, heavy housework and gardening.

Benefits of physical activity

There is overwhelming scientific evidence to prove that individuals leading active lives are less likely to die early or suffer from chronic disease such as coronary heart disease and diabetes, and are better able to cope with stress.

Remember

Physical activity is any activity that increases energy expenditure above resting level. Exercise is physical activity that is structured and undertaken usually for fitness gains. Physical activity undertaken for health benefits would be targeted at avoiding disease and delaying death. Exercise undertaken for fitness benefits would be targeted at improving one or more components of health-related fitness.

Activity: The benefits of exercise

Before you read on, take a few minutes to consider all the benefits a regular programme of physical activity or exercise can bring.

Are you able to group the benefits you have identified into the following categories:

- physical
- social
- psychological
- economic and environmental?

Many studies have demonstrated the numerous health benefits of physical activity and exercise.

Social	Economic
• Encourages connectedness. • Improves social skills. • Reduces isolation. • Enhances self-esteem and confidence.	• Reduces health costs. • Creates employment. • Supports local business. • Reduces absenteeism. • Enhances productivity.

Table 14.1: The wider benefits of physical activity and exercise.

As you can see from Table 14.1, when considering the health and wellbeing of the nation, there are wider social and economic benefits to an active lifestyle. At an individual level you can examine the short- and long-term benefits of physical activity in maintaining health and wellbeing:

- It's an opportunity for fun and enjoyment.
- The body is relaxed and revitalised, reducing muscular and mental tension.
- Exercise boosts self-esteem and confidence.
- It clears the head and improves concentration.
- It lowers the risk of heart disease and stroke.

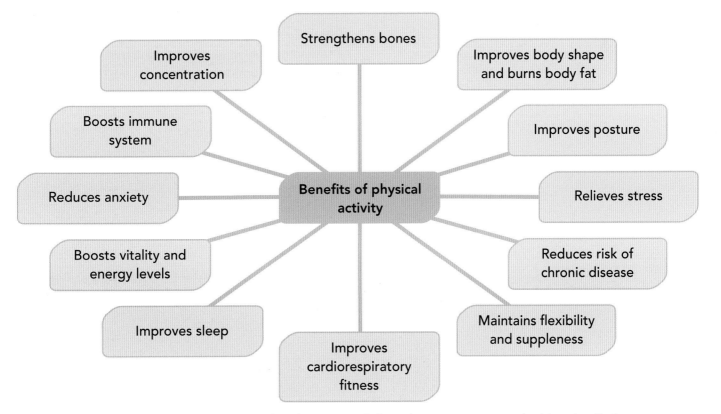

Figure 14.1: Consider the impact of these benefits of exercise and physical activity on your own health and wellbeing.

- It lowers body weight and body fat assisting in the maintenance of optimal body weight and composition.
- The risk of type 2 diabetes is lowered and the uptake of glucose in those who are sufferers is increased.
- It lowers the risk of certain types of cancer.
- It lowers the risk of osteoporosis.
- It alleviates the symptoms of arthritic pain.
- It combats ageing by maintaining the effectiveness of body systems, such as the respiratory, circulatory and musculoskeletal systems.
- Digestion is improved as exercise and activity support the proper functioning of the gut.

In addition, the **psychological** benefits of exercise should not be overlooked. Studies have shown that exercise brings about short- and long-term psychological benefits to health and wellbeing. Regular physical activity can improve mood, self-confidence and body image. Researchers have also found that regular physical activity reduces depression and anxiety and makes you better able to manage stress and tension.

Remember

Physical activity enhances mood, reduces anxiety and raises self-esteem and confidence. Surveys suggest that physically active individuals feel happier with life; even single bouts of activity can improve mood and energy. But for physical activity or exercise to have optimal benefits it is required to be current and continued.

Take it further

Research the benefits

While low levels of physical activity give some health benefits, moderate to high levels deliver major benefits to health and wellbeing. Undertake your own research of scientific journals and key authoritative sources on physical activity participation, such as the American College of Sport Medicine (ACSM) and British Association for Sport and Exercise Sciences (BASES), to investigate the scientific basis for this statement.

Alcohol

Alcohol is a drug that affects every organ in your body. It is a central nervous system depressant that is readily absorbed from your stomach and small intestine into your bloodstream. Binge drinking (excessive alcohol consumption) is a major public health concern.

Moderate alcohol consumption is thought to be beneficial in reducing the risks of heart disease. However, excessive intake causes health problems such as malnutrition, cirrhosis of the liver, certain forms of cancer and psychological health problems. Current safe limits recommended for alcohol consumption are up to three to four units per day for men, and for women up to two to three units per day. It is advised to spread alcohol intake throughout the week to avoid binges and include two or three alcohol free days each week. One unit is the equivalent to 8 grams of alcohol, typically a small glass of wine, or a half pint of beer, lager or cider and a single pub measure of spirits.

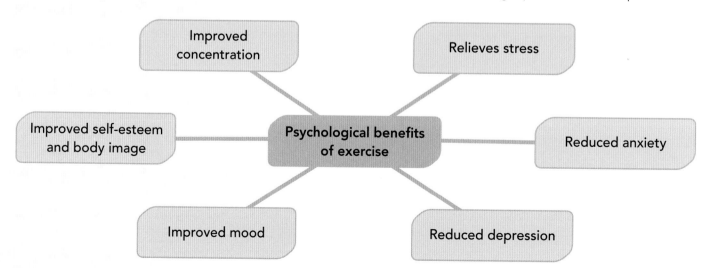

Figure 14.2: Consider the psychological benefits of regular physical activity on health and wellbeing.

Excessive consumption can have a detrimental impact on social and psychological health with the following associated risks.

- **Stroke** – this occurs when brain tissue dies as a result of a sudden and severe disruption of blood flow to the brain. Heavy alcohol use is associated with increased risk of stroke.
- **Cirrhosis** – chronic abuse of alcohol over a prolonged period can lead to cirrhosis of the liver, which may result in liver failure and death.
- **Hypertension** – the relationship between alcohol use and blood pressure is important as hypertension is a key factor in the risk of coronary heart disease and stroke. Hypertension is defined as a systolic blood pressure above 140 mm Hg and a diastolic pressure above 90 mm Hg.
- **Depression** – excessive alcohol consumption plays a part in causing depression. Alcohol dependence and depression may occur together. Depression is commonly reported in those being treated for alcohol dependence.

Smoking

Tobacco smoke contains nicotine and tar which are both damaging to health. Nicotine is a very powerful drug that causes addiction. It stimulates the central nervous system and increases heart rate and blood pressure. Tar is a complex mixture of chemicals, many of which cause cancer. It is largely deposited in the respiratory tract and gradually absorbed.

The risk of disease increases with the volume of smoking and number of years smoked, but also how deeply the smoke is inhaled. Some of the health risks associated with smoking include:

- **Coronary heart disease (CHD)** – a generic term to describe conditions caused by an interrupted or reduced flow of blood through the coronary arteries to the heart muscle. Smokers appear to have a higher risk of developing atherosclerosis (the build up of fatty deposits in the arteries) which is a primary contributor to CHD. Smoking presents an increased risk alone but when coupled with other risk factors such as high blood pressure, high cholesterol and physical inactivity it increases the likelihood of the blood to clot resulting in a heart attack.

- **Cancer** – worldwide, lung cancer is the most common form of cancer and the type most commonly associated with smoking. In terms of the risk of developing lung cancer the age at which smoking commences appears to be significant. Results of a study of ex-smokers showed that those who started smoking before the age of 15 had twice as many cell mutations (an instrumental factor in the development and initiation of cancer) than those who started after the age of 20. The impact of smoking on cancer risk is not limited to its effect on the lungs. Smoking is also implicated in cancers of the mouth, oesophagus, bladder, breast, cervix, colon, liver and kidneys.
- **Lung infections** – smokers are likely to suffer more respiratory tract infections than non-smokers. They are more prone to suffer from colds and flu, and take longer to recover. Pneumonia is a serious lung infection and is more common amongst smokers and more likely to be fatal. Bronchitis is a condition that inflames the lining of the bronchial tubes; it can be an acute or chronic condition. The most common symptom of bronchitis is a cough. Acute bronchitis is most often caused by a viral or bacterial infection, while chronic bronchitis is most often seen in smokers. Smoking causes damage to the cilia that line the airways; over time they become less efficient at clearing debris and irritants making the lungs more susceptible to infection.

Overall smokers have a higher risk of heart attack than non-smokers (a two- to three-fold increase in risk) while smokers under the age of 40 are five times more likely to suffer a heart attack than non-smokers. Exposure to other people's smoke (passive smoking) increases the risk of CHD in non-smokers. Passive smoking is becoming an increasing public health concern and has resulted in a ban on smoking in public places in the UK.

Stress

Stress can be defined as a physiological and mental response to triggers in our environment. Factors that produce stress are known as 'stressors' and they take different forms. Potential stressors include major life events, such as marriage, divorce and moving house, injury or trauma, and environmental situations such as a demanding work environment, but whatever the stressor the physical and mental responses usually include the feelings of anxiety and tension.

Chronic stress exposes your body to persistently elevated levels of stress hormones such as adrenaline and cortisol. The effects of chronic stress may manifest themselves in different ways, such as lowered resistance to disease, increase risk of heart disease, hormonal imbalances, back or joint pain and emotional and eating disorders. Other health risks associated with excess stress levels include:

- **Hypertension** – scientists remain unsure about the possible links between stress and hypertension. It is thought that long-term stress can contribute to hypertension through repeated blood pressure elevation. In the case of short lived stress we know that stress causes blood pressure to rise for a while, but once the stress is relieved blood pressure returns to normal.

- **Angina** – a pain or constricting feeling in the centre of the chest that can radiate down one or both arms, but most usually the left. This pain or tightness results from ischemia, or lack of oxygenated blood reaching the heart. It is an indicator of coronary heart disease caused by the build up of fatty deposits (atheroma) in the coronary arteries that supply blood to the heart muscle, which results in their narrowing. When stress causes an increase in blood flow to the heart, angina can occur.

- **Stroke** – stress can cause blood pressure to rise. Evidence suggests that those whose blood pressure rises with exposure to stress have a greater risk of stroke.

- **Heart attack** – stress is thought to increase the risk of coronary heart disease (CHD), although the direct links are unclear. It appears likely that stress may contribute to the development of other risk factors for CHD, such as smoking, inactivity, obesity and high blood pressure.

- **Ulcers** – the majority of ulcers (75 per cent) are caused by bacterial infection. There is support for the theory that stress is another cause. Stress may act by stimulating gastric acid production or by promoting behaviour that causes a risk to health.

Diet

The term 'diet' refers to your typical pattern of food consumption, while the term 'balanced diet' describes a diet that provides the correct amount of nutrients required by your body without excess or deficiency. A healthy diet should fulfil two primary objectives; it should:

- provide adequate energy and nutrients to maintain your normal physiological functioning, allowing for growth and replacement of your body tissues
- offer you protection against disease.

Scientific research provides evidence of direct links between good eating habits and disease prevention. The benefits of a healthy diet include increased energy and vitality, improved immune system function, maintenance of healthy body weight and reduced risk of chronic disease.

Deficiencies, excesses and imbalances in dietary intakes all produce potentially negative impacts on health which can lead to a range of dietary related disorders. Disorders of deficiency include scurvy (lack of vitamin C), osteoporosis (lack of calcium) and anaemia (lack of iron), while disorders of excess include obesity (excess calories) and coronary heart disease (excess fat). Imbalances of dietary intake may occur during periods of high nutritional demand such as growth or pregnancy, or when physical or psychological difficulties impact on meeting adequate nutritional intake such as during old age.

Targets for dietary intakes of the UK population were first established in the 1980s. These were reviewed in the 1990s in the COMA (Committee on Medical Aspects of Food Policy) report on Dietary Reference Values for UK Subjects. Healthy eating principles aim to assist the population in meeting these dietary targets. The current dietary targets for the UK population are listed in Table 14.2.

Table 14.2: How do you think your eating meets these dietary targets for the UK population? What activities could you undertake to assess if you meet them?

Nutrient	Recommendation
Total fat	Less than 35% of total energy
Saturated fat	No more than 11% of total energy
Protein	Less than 15% of total energy
Carbohydrate	50% of total energy
Fibre (non-starch polysaccharide)	18 g per day
Salt	6 g per day

A simple guide to healthy eating

- Eat the correct amount to maintain a healthy body weight.
- Reduce your fat intake, particularly from saturated sources.
- Eat plenty of foods with a high starch and fibre content.
- Don't eat sugary foods too often.
- Use salt sparingly and reduce your reliance on convenience foods.
- Ensure adequate intakes of vitamins and minerals by eating a wide variety of foods.
- If you drink alcohol keep within sensible limits.
- Enjoy your food and don't become obsessed with your diet or dieting.

The **eatwell plate** is the UK's national food guide. The model identifies the types and proportions of food groups you require to achieve a healthy, balanced diet. As you can see, the model shows a plate with divisions of varying sizes representing each of the five main food groups. Those that have a larger slice of the plate should feature in larger proportions in your diet, while those with the smallest slice should be consumed in smaller proportions or used only as occasional foods especially in the case of those with a high fat and/or sugar content.

Figure 14.3: Think about the foods you ate yesterday. How does your intake compare to the eatwell plate?

Figure 14.4: Do you practise these simple guidelines of healthy eating and lifestyle on a daily basis?

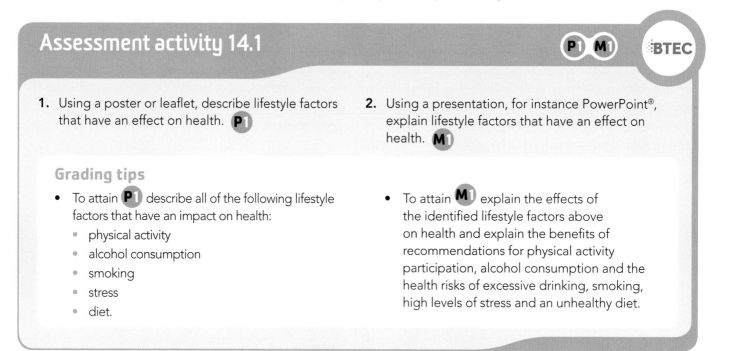

Assessment activity 14.1 **P1** **M1** BTEC

1. Using a poster or leaflet, describe lifestyle factors that have an effect on health. **P1**

2. Using a presentation, for instance PowerPoint®, explain lifestyle factors that have an effect on health. **M1**

Grading tips
- To attain **P1** describe all of the following lifestyle factors that have an impact on health:
  - physical activity
  - alcohol consumption
  - smoking
  - stress
  - diet.

- To attain **M1** explain the effects of the identified lifestyle factors above on health and explain the benefits of recommendations for physical activity participation, alcohol consumption and the health risks of excessive drinking, smoking, high levels of stress and an unhealthy diet.

Functional skills

By using the Internet to research the lifestyle factors that have an effect on health, and by writing a poster or leaflet, or designing a presentation, you are providing evidence towards skills in **ICT** and **English**.

2. Be able to assess the lifestyle of a selected individual

To provide advice on lifestyle improvement and plan a health-related physical activity programme you must be able to assess the lifestyle of an individual. One way to achieve this is via a questionnaire that assesses the five lifestyle behaviours already identified as important in adopting a healthy lifestyle.

2.1 Lifestyle questionnaire

You should assess health status prior to planning a health-related physical activity programme. An objective evaluation of current exercise, health and lifestyle provides information on the individual's strengths and areas for improvement. This provides the basis for the establishment of realistic goals and the avoidance of injury. Testing initial fitness levels is a useful benchmark against which progress can be measured, with periodic testing providing motivating feedback as the physical activity or exercise programme progresses.

Levels of physical activity

Fitness assessment may form part of the overall screening process. It is essential that health and lifestyle screening takes place prior to this assessment and to exercise prescription, preferably by a medical or fitness practitioner. This is particularly important for anyone who is contemplating starting a physical activity or exercise programme, particularly if they are unaccustomed to exercise. Pre-exercise health screening can take different forms and can range from a self-administered physical activity readiness questionnaire to a complete medical examination carried out by a medical practitioner. The choice of method will depend on a number of factors such as age and health status, previous training history and resources. Comprehensive lifestyle and pre-exercise screening helps to identify medical conditions that may prevent the participant from exercising safely. It will highlight the participant's objectives and ensure that the exercise and lifestyle prescription fulfils their needs.

An example of a Physical Activity Readiness Questionnaire is available from the **Canadian Society for Exercise Physiology** at **www.csep.ca.** This questionnaire is designed for use by individuals between the ages of 15–69 and aims to identify the small number of individuals for whom physical activity might be inappropriate, or those who would require medical advice before embarking on a programme or supervision during physical activity or exercise participation.

The key features of a good lifestyle screening protocol are that it:

- takes account of the participant's past and current medical history
- takes account of family medical history

Remember

When in doubt about an individual's suitability or readiness to exercise ensure they consult their doctor. Any information obtained from health and lifestyle screening should be stored in a secure place to maintain confidentiality. This information should only be accessed by authorised personnel.

- measures body composition
- measures current fitness status and exercise history
- records diet and alcohol history
- records smoking history
- investigates stress and sleep patterns.

Alcohol consumption

Questionnaires aimed at assessing alcohol consumption should address volume (units) and frequency (days) of consumption.

Smoking

Questionnaires aimed at assessing smoking habits should consider the type of smoking (cigarettes, cigars, pipe), the duration of smoking (the number of years) and volume (amount per day).

Stress levels

Questionnaires aimed at assessing stress levels may consider major life events and recent changes in personal situation such as marriage, divorce, bereavement, loss of job, but also issues related to recent health status, eating habits and sleep patterns.

Diet

There are five basic methods for assessing dietary intake. Two of these methods use records of food consumption made at the time of actual eating, one with the actual weight recorded, the other using estimates of weights of food consumed using standard household measures. The other three methods attempt to assess diet and food consumption in the recent past by asking about food intake during the previous day (24 hour recall), over the past few weeks (diet history), or in the recent or distant past (food frequency questionnaire).

2.2 Consultation

One-to-one consultation

You are likely to gather information to assess the lifestyle of an individual through a one-to-one consultation. Key factors in a successful consultation include effective communication skills and client confidentiality.

The activity on the next page should help you highlight which aspects of your lifestyle require changes to improve your health. If you have many aspects to change, prioritise these and begin with the easy things.

Communication: questioning, listening skills and non-verbal communication

Effective communication is crucial in the consultation process. Communication is about giving and receiving information. Your questioning, listening and non-verbal communication skills are important in ensuring you set the correct tone for the consultation. Whether the subject feels at ease and whether your information is received in the way you intend it to be will depend on the effectiveness of your communication skills. Remember, non-verbal communication such as facial expressions, hand gestures and general body language sends out messages without you even speaking.

Key factors to ensure effective communication in the consultation process include:

- maintaining eye contact with your subject
- making them feel at ease by welcoming them, introducing yourself and explaining the consultation process
- maintaining a professional approach and avoiding being over familiar
- seeking permission if you intend to keep notes of your consultation
- maintaining an open and friendly posture at all times.

Client confidentiality

Information about a client belongs to the client. The principle of client confidentiality ensures that you should not release information about your clients to a third party without their consent.

Activity: Lifestyle assessment questionnaire

Complete the following lifestyle assessment questionnaire. The purpose of this questionnaire is to raise your awareness of the healthy and unhealthy lifestyle choices you make before you move on to working with a selected individual. Please answer **True** or **False** to the following questions:

Diet

1. I usually try to eat three balanced meals each day.	True/False
2. I usually eat at least five servings of fruit/vegetables each day.	True/False
3. I eat the right amount to be a healthy body weight.	True/False
4. I only consume alcohol within the recommended guidelines.	True/False

Physical activity and exercise

5. I undertake at least 30 minutes of moderate intensity physical activity at least 5 times per week.	True/False

Stress

6. I get plenty of rest.	True/False
7. I seldom feel tense or anxious.	True/False

Sleep

8. I usually get at least 8 hours of sleep each night.	True/False

Smoking

9. I never smoke.	True/False

Drugs

10. I never take drugs.	True/False

To calculate your score, give yourself one point for each question you answered True.

- 9–10 = very healthy lifestyle
- 7–8 = generally healthy lifestyle
- 5–6 = average lifestyle
- Below 5 = unhealthy lifestyle with many improvements needed

Why is the consultation process an important part of assessing the lifestyle of a particular individual?

Assessment activity 14.2

P2 M2 D1 BTEC

Your college has invested in a new health and fitness suite with the primary emphasis on improving the health and wellbeing of staff and students. Your class has been asked to design a lifestyle screening questionnaire for use in this facility.

1. Design a lifestyle questionnaire to describe the strengths and areas for improvement in the lifestyle of a selected individual. **P2**

2. To assess the usability of the questionnaire, use it on a client and explain the strengths and areas for improvement in their lifestyle. **M2**

3. Evaluate the lifestyle of a selected individual and prioritise areas for change. **D1**

4. Write up your findings in a report format.

Grading tips

- To attain **P2** you need to collect information on the lifestyle of an individual using a self-designed questionnaire and one-to-one consultation.

- To attain **M2** you must explain the strengths and areas for improvement of a selected individual's lifestyle and explain your recommended lifestyle improvement strategies.

- To attain **D1** you need to evaluate the lifestyle of a selected individual and prioritise areas for change. In doing this you may need to make some value judgements about the strengths and areas for improvement.

PLTS

Using your questionnaire, seeking feedback on it and refining it will help you develop your skills as an **independent enquirer**, **creative thinker** and **reflective learner**.

Functional skills

By researching and designing your lifestyle questionnaire you are providing evidence towards skills in **ICT** and **English**.

3. Be able to provide advice on lifestyle improvement

Poor health is a drain on national resources. It increases the amount spent on healthcare by the government. As individuals we may encounter difficulties in attaining **wellness**. Our age, ethnicity and socio-economic status may present challenges to achieving wellness.

3.1 Strategies to improve lifestyle

Take it further

The health of the nation

Use the Internet or your local health promotion office to investigate the range of local and national initiatives aimed at improving the nation's health. Awareness of these initiatives will assist you in meeting assessment requirements for the unit.

Ways to increase physical activity levels

Despite the strong case for keeping active, many find it difficult to take up exercise. The mere notion of physical activity or exercise conjures up unpleasant thoughts, images of boring exercise classes, or rough competitive sports where the risk of injury is a deterrent. Those who have never exercised before, or who are in poor shape, should not expect immediate results. Achieving physical fitness requires time and consistency. Ways of getting fit are explored below.

- **Walking** – scientific evidence supports the benefits of regular walking for health and wellbeing. It is an easy and economical way to become and stay active. All ages can participate and it is a social activity.

  To achieve the health benefits associated with walking, a target of 10 000 steps a day (about 5 miles) is required. The average sedentary individual achieves around 2000–3000 steps per day. A **pedometer** can be used as a motivational tool to measure progress towards achieving this target. A sensible approach to reaching the

10 000 a day target is to aim to increase average daily steps by 500 each week until the 10 000 target is reached.

Key terms

Wellness – can be viewed as our approach to personal health that emphasises individual responsibility for wellbeing through the practice of health promoting lifestyle behaviours.

Pedometer – a portable electronic device usually worn all day on the belt which counts each step taken.

- **Stair climbing** – encouraging the use of stairs in the workplace and other settings may have significant health benefits. Evidence suggests that moderate intensity lifestyle activities like taking the stairs (instead of the lift or escalator) may be more successfully promoted than vigorous exercise programmes. Stair climbing can be accumulated throughout the day and with an energy cost of approximately 8–10 kcals per minute, it can help with weight control. It also has benefits in terms of leg power and bone strength and cardiovascular fitness.

- **Cycling** – this can be an effective and enjoyable aerobic exercise. Daily cycling has been shown to be sufficient to lead to significant health benefits. People of most fitness levels can participate in cycling, although anyone with heart disease or other pre-existing conditions should consult their doctor before they start a cycling programme. Cycling offers a healthy leisure activity and with around 70 per cent of all car trips reported to be less than 5 miles, it is an alternative mode of transport.

Remember

The risks associated with participation in a regular programme of physical activity or exercise are commonly less than the risks associated with that of living a sedentary lifestyle. However, the potential benefits of exercise must outweigh the potential risks to the participant.

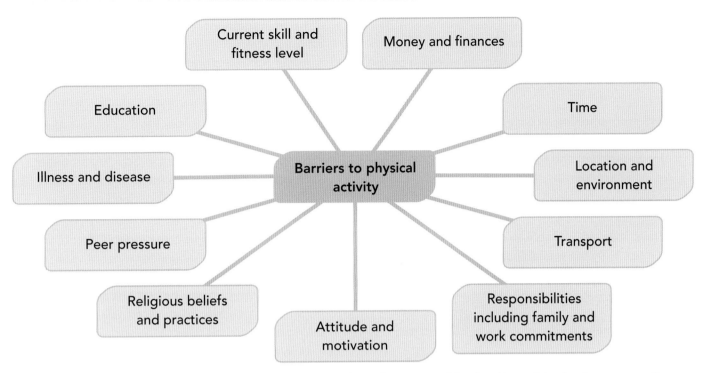

Figure 14.5: Consider the impact of these potential barriers to physical activity participation. How might they be overcome?

Alcohol

When alcohol consumption becomes so excessive and frequent that it has a severe and negative impact on health it is termed alcoholism. Alcoholics exhibit intense cravings for alcohol and become physically dependent on it.

Problem drinking and alcoholism is serious, but recovery is possible if the alcohol user is strongly motivated to stop drinking. Treatments might include counselling and therapy, self-help groups, either face-to-face or online, or alternative treatments and therapies.

Individual or group counselling is provided by specially trained therapists; often this might involve other family members. Exploring and developing awareness of triggers for alcohol consumption and the breaking of habitual behaviours are areas of focus for counselling and therapy. Relapse is often high for alcohol abusers and preventing relapse is a key feature of the counselling and therapy process.

Treatment for alcohol abuse often begins with detoxification and withdrawal from alcohol. This is necessary when alcohol consumption has continued for long periods of time. It can be an uncomfortable process with unpleasant withdrawal symptoms.

In extreme cases it can be fatal (which is why detoxification is usually undertaken under supervision within an alcohol treatment facility).

Successful treatment of alcoholism depends on recognition of the problem by the sufferer. Self-help groups such as Alcoholics Anonymous (AA) have helped many sufferers through a step-by-step programme of recovery. Some alcohol users may seek alternative treatments and therapies such as acupuncture and hypnosis which are thought to lessen the symptoms of withdrawal. However, there are mixed views about their value within the medical fraternity.

Smoking

Smoking increases the risk of lung and heart disease. As with most behaviour modification goals, in order to quit smoking the smoker must want to stop. Once this is realised there are a number of approaches than can be taken to help them.

- **Acupuncture** – a traditional Chinese therapy which may help someone to stop smoking by increasing the body's production of mood enhancing endorphins that reduce or alleviate withdrawal symptoms.

- **NHS smoking helpline** – this was launched in 2000 as part of a government initiative to encourage 1.5 million people in the UK to give up smoking by the year 2010. The helpline offers information, advice and support.

- **NHS stop-smoking services** – the range of services promoted include group and one-to-one counselling and information on nicotine replacement therapy.

- **Nicotine replacement therapy** – this refers to a range of products (gums, patches, lozenges and sprays) that are available to help the smoker to give up. They are available on prescription and are suitable for most smokers, although those that are pregnant or taking regular medication should consult their doctor first. Unlike cigarettes they do not contain the harmful cancer-causing toxic chemicals.

Stress management techniques

To control stress there are two general approaches that can be taken:

- Try to reduce the amount of overall stress.

- Develop coping or stress management techniques.

To reduce overall stress, the factors that promote stress, usually known as stressors, should be identified and, if possible, eliminated or reduced. Careful time management and prioritisation of workload and commitments may help an individual to manage their stress better.

It is not possible to eliminate all the stresses faced in daily life. Therefore, having techniques or participating in activities that reduce levels of stress will have a positive impact on health and wellbeing. Exercise can be viewed as a positive stress for the body. Other ways to manage stress are outlined below.

- **Assertiveness** – the ability to express your feelings and rights while respecting those of others. While assertiveness may come naturally to some, it is a skill that can be learned. Once mastered, it can help you deal with conflict situations that may be a cause of stress in daily life.

- **Goal setting** – properly set goals can be motivating and rewarding – achieving these goals can build self-confidence and reduce stress.

- **Time management** – this is a critical element of effective stress management. Time management is about achieving our tasks in good time by using techniques such as goal setting, task planning and minimising time spent on unproductive activities.

- **Physical activity** – this can have a positive effect on anxiety, depression, self-esteem and mood. It can be a stress reliever by producing an outlet for frustration, releasing endorphins, the 'feel good' hormones that lift mood, and providing a distraction from the stressor.

- **Positive self-talk** – this is the inner dialogue you have with yourself. It influences most of your emotional life and reflects how you respond to your thoughts, feelings and actions and it can be negative or positive. Positive self-talk involves taking an optimistic view of life and your situation. In daily life you face constant challenges, difficulties and deadlines – being able to take a positive view of these and have constructive ways of dealing with them helps to reduce and manage stress.

- **Relaxation and breathing exercises** – focusing on breathing exercises is a simple way of trying to control or reduce stress. It involves controlled inhalation and exhalation, best undertaken when you are quiet and comfortable.

Diet

To meet the learning outcomes of this unit it is necessary for you to be able to critically evaluate your own eating habits and what influences them.

The timing of meals is a key component of food habits. Food habits develop over time and are resistant to change. They are subconscious as they are acquired at a young age. In areas of the world where food is readily available 24 hours a day, intake can occur at any time. However, most of us do not eat continually but stick to reasonably defined mealtimes with snacks between. In western culture this has lead to a 'three meals per day' approach supplemented by snacking. As lifestyles become more busy and flexible, more snacking may occur, but overall nutritional density of the diet remains important.

Activity: You are what you eat

Keep a record of all food and fluid intake for at least a **3 day period** which should include **1 weekend day**. For a more detailed evaluation you can record your intake for a full week.

Write down **everything** you eat and drink. Be as accurate and honest as possible and don't modify your diet at this stage, otherwise you will not be evaluating your typical diet. Carry your record around with you at all times. This will allow you to record food and drink as it is consumed to avoid forgetting anything.

Record as much information as possible to include:

- the type of food and drink consumed and how much, either as an estimation of portion size using household measures such as slices of bread, pints

of fluid, tablespoons of vegetables, etc. or as an actual weight, either weighed or recorded from the packaging

- the time that the food and drink was consumed and where you were when consumed (these points are often useful to consider when assessing external factors that affect your dietary intake)

- the cooking method and type of food preparation.

Once you have completed your record, compare it to the eatwell plate guidelines and write a short account of your evaluation on the strengths and areas for improvement in your diet.

The government has set targets or dietary intake goals aimed at improving the nation's health and reducing the risk of chronic disease. Your diet should be balanced across the five main food groups to ensure adequate energy and nutrients without excesses or deficiencies. As a population we are advised to eat more wholegrain starchy carbohydrate food and fruits and vegetables and to eat less fatty and sugary foods. This is expressed in the percentage contribution of food groups within the **eatwell plate** model.

Most foods require some form of preparation before consumption. Food preparation depends on cooking skills and facilities and the time available to prepare it. Awareness of these factors is important when suggesting strategies for improving dietary intake to ensure realistic and achievable goals are set. Food handling and safety are also important aspects of food preparation in ensuring health and wellbeing.

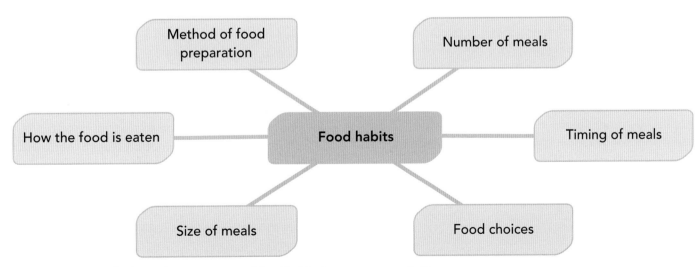

Figure 14.6: How do the main components of food habits impact on your diet?

Activity: What, when, where and why you eat

Your food record should allow you to further examine your normal eating patterns. As well as the types and amounts of food consumed, it should give you an idea about how your lifestyle dictates what, when, where and why you eat. Take another look at your record and consider the following questions:

- In relation to healthy eating principles, is your diet better than you first thought or is there room for improvement? What healthy eating goals might you not be achieving and why?

- Are your mealtimes structured and regular? Do you eat any differently at weekends? Does where and what time you eat dictate your food choice and selection?

- Do you rely heavily on convenience foods and takeaways? If yes, what influences this?

- What constraints do you foresee that may prevent you from making any changes you have identified as a result of your evaluation? Do you think you will be able to overcome them?

Suggest realistic strategies for improvement where necessary. Try to implement these changes over the coming weeks while studying this unit.

To monitor the effectiveness of your dietary changes, repeat this exercise in a month's time to see if you have successfully managed to implement the changes you identified to eat a healthier diet.

Take it further

Information and leaflets

Visit your GP surgery or local health promotion unit to collect information and leaflets on the treatment and management of lifestyle issues such as smoking, physical activity, diet, drug and alcohol use. You may find this exercise useful in assisting you with providing lifestyle improvement strategies for a selected individual.

Behaviour change

Behaviour modification has its basis in psychological principles of learning theory and is used to change or modify a person's behaviour. Behaviour modification techniques can be used to eliminate unhealthy lifestyle behaviours. One of the most common approaches applied by practitioners in promoting lifestyle behaviour modification is the Stages of Change Model (Prochaska, Diclemente and Norcross, 1992).

This model recognises that change occurs through a process of stages identified as:

- pre-contemplation
- contemplation
- preparation
- action
- maintenance
- termination.

In the **pre-contemplation** stage you are not considering changing behaviour in the near future. In fact, most people in this stage will fail to notice or have any concerns about a particular behaviour (for example, overeating or a lack of physical activity). When you become aware that a change may be desirable you are considered to be in the **contemplation** stage (for example, you've decided you can't fit into your clothes and need to lose weight by eating less and exercising). In the **preparation** stage, you will begin to set yourself targets and goals to improve behaviour. During the **action** stage you start to implement your plan of behaviour change – obstacles should be expected and strategies for overcoming them may need to be considered. In the **maintenance** stage you should be able to acknowledge that setbacks will come along from time to time, but you remind yourself of your goals and the positive benefits of the change so that you are able to cope with relapses. The **termination** stage is achieved when you are able to overcome all temptation towards your previous behaviour.

Simple steps to behaviour modification include:

1. Identify the problem (or problems) and understand the need to change.

2. Understand the influences on the problem.

3. Establish short-, medium- and long-term goals for tackling the problem and record them.

4. Develop a strategy to facilitate change and understand the resources or skills required for success.

5. Implement the strategy and record and monitor progress.

6. Evaluate progress and consider strategies to maintain change in behaviour if successfully achieved.

Different **barriers** may present themselves in tackling the five health behaviours identified in this unit. However, some common barriers may apply across all including:

- lack of knowledge about the benefits of the behaviour change
- lack of self-efficacy (or confidence) in making the behaviour change
- setting unrealistic goals for behaviour change
- lack of commitment or motivation to make the change
- lack of control over your environment to make the change
- lack of support from others to make the change
- falling at the first hurdle (relapse).

Cognitive and behavioural strategies are approaches to behaviour change based on concepts and principles derived from psychological models of human behaviour. They include a broad range of approaches along a continuum from structured individual psychotherapy at one end to self-help at the other. In cognitive behavioural therapy (CBT), a 'skills based' approach, the client and therapist work together to identify and attempt to understand the client's problem behaviour. A key element of this approach is to help the client to understand the relationship between thoughts, feelings and behaviour. The client and therapist then attempt to establish a shared understanding of the problem. This leads to some personalised goals and strategies for tackling the problem that are monitored and evaluated over time. During this process the client learns to develop psychological or practical skills for problem solving or management. The overall aim of cognitive and behavioural approaches is for the client to attribute improvements in their behaviour to their own efforts and not those of the therapist.

Case study: Beat the bulge

Carl is a 43-year-old male maintenance worker who was screened at his company's occupational health centre and found to have a high percentage of body fat. The occupational health nurse has told him he needs to lose some weight and begin a programme of physical activity. He smoked 40-a-day up until three years ago when he quit on his 40th birthday, but since giving up smoking he has gained weight.

He admits to a sedentary lifestyle away from work, preferring to watch sport, rather than participate in it, from the comfort of his armchair. He was a competitive athlete in his early youth, winning medals for distance running, but can't seem to get motivated to do any exercise at present. He has thought about joining his local health club but is sensitive about his current size and poor level of fitness.

1. **What benefits would a regular programme of physical activity or exercise bring for Carl and how long might it take before he would notice these benefits?**

2. **What do you think would be the most appropriate types of exercise to include in a regular programme of physical activity or exercise at this stage?**

3. **What strategies could you use to overcome Carl's current barriers to participation in a regular programme of physical activity or exercise and get him motivated to start?**

How would Carl benefit from lifestyle improvement strategies?

Possible approaches for helping people change unhealthy lifestyle behaviours include:

- individual advice and leaflets
- individual counselling and support
- group counselling and support
- campaigns and displays
- community-based activities.

Assessment activity 14.3   (P3)(M3)(D2)   BTEC

Select an individual who would benefit from lifestyle improvement. This could be a friend or relative who wishes to lose weight, follow a more healthy diet, give up smoking, reduce their alcohol intake or increase their physical activity.

1. Provide the individual with appropriate lifestyle improvement strategies. **P3**

2. Explain the recommendations you have made regarding lifestyle improvement strategies. **M3**

3. Analyse the range of lifestyle improvement strategies that are appropriate for your selected individual and how you can monitor and evaluate their effectiveness. **D2**

Grading tips

- To attain **P3** include advice where appropriate on stress management, smoking cessation, alcohol reduction and diet. You could achieve this though the production of a written report or a video recording of your consultation.

- To attain **M3** explain the lifestyle improvement strategies in terms of their suitability for the selected individual.

- To attain **D2** investigate the strengths and weaknesses of different strategies and how you can monitor and evaluate their effectiveness with your selected individual.

PLTS

By providing lifestyle improvement strategies for an individual, you are developing your skills as an **effective participator** and as a **creative thinker**.

Functional skills

By providing lifestyle improvement strategies for an individual you are demonstrating your skills in **English**.

4. Be able to plan a health-related physical activity programme for a selected individual

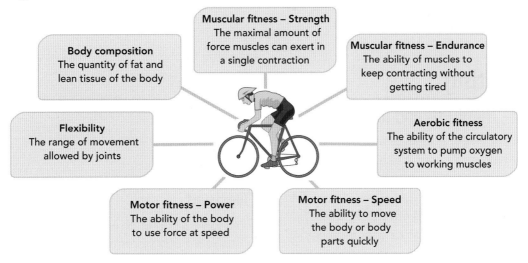

Figure 14.7: Evaluate each component of fitness in relation to your own health and fitness.

Health-related fitness has several components and you require a minimum level of fitness in each of these individual components to cope with everyday living with ease.

4.1 Collect information

Before you plan a health-related physical activity programme for a selected individual it is necessary to collect relevant information. This will help you to produce a plan which meets their personal goals and takes account of their relevant lifestyle, medical and physical activity history. There should also be some consideration of their attitude towards physical activity and exercise, and their motivation to adhere to your plan.

In order to maintain interest and motivation, you should carry out regular evaluations of the individual's fitness. Monitoring fitness goals and outcomes can provide useful information in the design and progression of physical activity and exercise programmes.

Personal goals

An individual's motivation to embark on a physical activity or exercise programme is influenced by a wide range of personal goals ranging from improving all or specific elements of health-related fitness, to weight loss and maintenance, to getting fit for a particular occasion or challenge. Knowing what these are will allow you to tailor your programme and provide a focus for boosting motivation if it dips.

Lifestyle

The key features of lifestyle screening have been covered on pages 88–90, but the most important elements in a lifestyle history should relate to:

*   type of occupation and family commitments
*   smoking and alcohol use
*   perception of stress
*   perceived challenges or barriers to success in achieving personal goals.

Medical history

The most important elements of a medical history should relate to:

*   any current existing medical condition(s)
*   any previous medical history
*   any family history of chronic disease
*   previous medical examination results if available
*   medications or drug use.

Physical activity history

The most important elements of a physical activity history should relate to:

*   exercise and activity history (frequency, intensity, time, type)
*   exercise and activity preferences.

Attitude and motivation

It is vital that progress is monitored in order to sustain motivation and to develop a lifetime commitment to staying fit. Progress can be monitored by keeping training logs or diaries which record the distance walked or run, or the amount of weight lifted.

4.2 Goal setting

Goals (short-, medium- and long-term)

The first step in undertaking a physical activity or exercise programme is to commit to it. It is important to set short-, medium- and long-term goals to keep you on track. Setting goals, providing they are realistic, will give you a target and an incentive to continue, especially if the going gets tough or your motivation starts to wane – attaining your goals will improve self-esteem and motivation.

Short-term goals should be achievable within the first six to eight weeks of a programme, while long-term goals might look ahead to 12 months; medium-term goals aim at the first three, six and nine months. Long-term goals can be modified to meet changes in need or circumstances, or if progress is faster than expected and the goals are achieved.

Remember

Achieving short-term health-related fitness goals provides great motivation to continue with the programme.

SMART targets

By setting SMART targets or goals you are much more likely to be successful. Remember that 'SMART' stands for specific, measurable, achievable, realistic and timed (refer to Unit 10 Outdoor and adventurous activities, page 21 for more details).

4.3 Principles of training

Being physically fit is about having enough energy, strength and skill to cope with the everyday demands of your environment. Individual fitness levels vary greatly from the low levels required to cope with daily activities to optimal levels required by some performers who are at the top of their sport.

The preparation and construction of an effective exercise or physical activity programme must be based on the way the body adapts to different training regimes. Programmes can be constructed to emphasise one or many aspects of fitness, for example, strength, aerobic endurance and flexibility, but the following factors should be given careful consideration:

- individuality
- specificity
- reversibility
- overload
- progression.

Overload

To achieve a higher level of fitness it is necessary to stress your body systems and place them in a state of overload. This is a point above and beyond that which is usually achieved. If this greater level is not achieved, adaptation will not occur. To avoid the problems associated with injury, illness and motivation, it is important that the training load is progressively increased. Rest and recuperation are also important too. Remember that when working with the general population to develop health-related fitness, the overload required may be very small and could take some time to achieve.

Consider the novice gym user who at the start of their training programme can only perform six repetitions of a press-up. After training two or three times a week for two to three weeks, they should be able to increase the number of repetitions achieved beyond this. They can then think about including sets of repetitions.

Specificity

Adaptations to training are specific to the type of activity undertaken and the intensity at which it is performed. Specificity relates to the muscle groups involved and the energy sources used. Training for one sort of activity does not lead to fitness for all activities. For example, a squash player can sprint around the court returning every shot, and keeps going long after their opponent looks exhausted and concedes defeat. Enter the same squash player in a long distance road race and they may manage to get round the course, but they are unlikely to win the event and may even get out of breath and have to stop along the way. Similarly there is little transfer of training from strength training to cardiovascular efficiency. For example, a marathon runner would not spend a great deal of time lifting heavy weights or doing short sprint intervals. The power lifter would not overemphasise distance running or low intensity resistance training, while prolonged long distance running is unlikely to improve endurance swimming time.

Progression

When exercise is performed over a period of weeks or months, your body adapts. The physiological changes that occur with repeated exposure to exercise improve your body's exercise capacity and efficiency. With aerobic training, such as running and cycling, the heart and lungs become more efficient and endurance capacity increases, while the muscles become stronger with resistance modes of training such as weight training. Adaptations derived from training are highly specific to the type of exercise or activity undertaken.

Individual differences

Genetics plays a large part in determining how quickly and to what degree you will adapt to a specific exercise regime. Two individuals are unlikely to show the same rate and magnitude of adaptation in response to the same training programme. As a result the principle of individual differences must be taken into account when designing health-related physical activity and exercise programmes.

Variation

Variation in a physical activity or exercise programme is important to progression of fitness goals, but also motivation to continue with the programme. Variation can be achieved by manipulation of the training variables:

- frequency (how often you undertake the activity)
- duration or time (for how long)
- intensity (how hard)
- the type of activity.

Reversibility

Training effects are reversible. This means that if the benefits of adaptation to an exercise programme are to be maintained and improved, then regular activity must be adhered to. It is possible to 'lose it by not using it'. All components of fitness can be affected by non-activity. However, once a level of fitness has been achieved, this level can be maintained with a

lower degree of effort than was initially required for its development.

FITT principles of exercise prescription

- **Frequency** of exercise refers to the number of times the exercise is undertaken, usually expressed in times per week.
- **Intensity** of exercise refers to how hard, or the amount of stress or overload that is to be applied.
- **Time** (duration) of exercise refers to how long the activity is to be carried out.
- **Type** of exercise refers to the mode of exercise performed.

S	M	T	W	T	F	S
	✔		✔	✔		✔

Frequency 3–4 times a week

Intensity 60–80% maximum heart rate

Time 20–30 minutes (minimum)

Type 'Aerobic' exercise

Figure 14.8: How could the principles of exercise programming be applied to the case study of Carl on page 97?

Take it further

Exercise prescription

Undertake your own research to investigate the American College of Sports Medicine's guidance on exercise prescription.

4.4 Appropriate activities

Different types of exercise provide different health benefits. Once fitness goals have been set, the exercise prescribed must lead to the desired benefits, such as weight control, stress management, prevention of disease, muscle definition or the maintenance of flexibility. Important factors to be taken in to consideration are convenience, cost, motivation and enjoyment.

Walking

Do not underestimate walking as a form of exercise – it is possibly the perfect aid to weight loss and improving general fitness.

Cycling

A study carried out by the Department of Transport found that even a small amount of cycling can lead to significant gains in fitness. One study found that aerobic fitness was boosted by 11 per cent after just six weeks of cycling short distances four times per week.

Hiking

Hiking trails range from the easy to challenging. Beginners are advised to start on the flat while those with more experience and fitness may take on the challenge of a mountain trail. Hiking is generally free and usually involves covering longer distances over more varied and rugged terrain than walking, but this is not always the case. It also requires more specialised equipment to ensure personal safety, such as a good pair of boots, windproof and waterproof clothing, a backpack to carry food and fluid, and a map and compass.

Hiking conditions the cardiovascular system and also the major muscles of the legs, while carrying a backpack will increase energy expenditure and burn more calories to assist with weight loss.

Swimming

Swimming is a great aerobic activity to improve cardiovascular fitness. Nearly all major muscle groups are recruited when you swim, offering a total body workout to improve muscle tone and strength. However, as swimming is non-weight bearing it does not offer the same benefits as other forms of aerobic activities in terms of bone strength. It is appropriate for all fitness levels, particularly those who are unaccustomed to exercise, overweight, pregnant or who suffer from joint problems or injury.

Investigate the walking and hiking groups in your local area.

4.5 Exercise intensity

Exercise intensity is usually set at a percentage of maximal capacity, communicated as a percentage of maximal heart rate and provides a measure of how hard you are working (see page 212).

Rating of perceived exertion (RPE)

The best way to monitor intensity during exercise is to use a combination of heart rate measures and ratings of perceived exertion or RPE. Heart rates can be taken manually or by wearing a heart rate monitor. RPE is a ten point scale that focuses on tuning in the body to physical cues for recognising intensity of effort, such as a quickened breathing rate, breathlessness or flat out effort. The RPE scale provides a way of quantifying subjective exercise intensity, but has been shown to correlate well with heart rate and oxygen uptake.

Table 14.3: Modified rate of perceived exertion (RPE) chart.

Rating of perceived effort (RPE)	Intensity of effort
0	Nothing at all
1	Very weak
2	Weak
3	Moderate
4	Somewhat hard
5	Hard
6	Moderately hard
7	Very hard
8	Very, very hard
9	Near maximal
10	Extremely strong or maximal

The original scale was from 6 to 20, with 6 representing complete rest and 20 exhaustion. The reason for this numbering was reflected in the subjects that were used in the original exertion studies. They were all fit individuals who had heart rates that corresponded to around 60 beats per minute (bpm) at rest and a maximum heart rate of around 200 bpm.

Maximum heart rate

Heart rates are dependent on age (children have relatively higher rates than adults). When the body is in action, cardiac output can increase five to seven times in order to accelerate the delivery of blood to exercising muscles, and meet their demand for increased oxygen.

During participation in sport and exercise, cardiac output will be increased as a result of increases in either heart rate, stroke volume or both. Stroke volume does not increase significantly beyond the light work rates of low intensity exercise, therefore the increases in cardiac output required for moderate to high intensity work rates are achieved by increases in heart rate. Maximal attainable cardiac output decreases with increasing age, largely as a result of a decrease in maximum heart rate. Maximum heart rate can be calculated using this formula:

maximum heart rate = 220 – age (in years)

Exercise heart rates are used to assess the strenuousness of the exercise. This information is then used in the formulation of training intensities in the exercise programme.

Maximum heart rate reserve

Maximum heart rate reserve (or the Karvonen method as it is also known after the Finnish physiologist who introduced the concept) provides somewhat higher values for exercise intensity compared to heart rates calculated simply as a percentage of maximum heart rate. The Karvonen formula calculates training heart rate threshold as:

heart rate threshold = heart rate at rest + 0.60 (heart rate maximum – heart rate at rest)

For example, the heart rate training threshold for a sedentary adult female with a heart rate at rest of 85 beats per minute and a maximum heart rate of 185 beats per minute would be calculated as:

$$
\begin{aligned}
\text{heart rate threshold} &= 85 + 0.60(185 - 85) \\
&= 85 + 0.60(100) \\
&= 85 + 60 \\
&= 145 \text{ beats per minute}
\end{aligned}
$$

Talk test

The best way to monitor intensity during exercise is to use a combination of heart rate measures and ratings of perceived exertion – but when neither is available the talk test method can be applied. It is a simple method that sets a marker to avoid overexertion; if you are able to comfortably talk during exercise you are likely to be exercising at an appropriate intensity.

Take it further

Your own plan

Now that you have been introduced to a variety of training methods for different components of fitness, plan a six week training programme suitable for yourself. Before you start you will need to give consideration to the fitness components that you wish to develop.

Assessment activity 14.4

(P4) **BTEC**

Using the same individual you worked with in Assessment activity 14.3, devise a six week health-related physical activity programme taking into account current recommendations for physical activity. (P4)

Grading tips

- To attain (P4) ensure you give consideration to the principles of training when you design of your programme.

PLTS

By drawing up an activity programme, you are demonstrating your **creative thinker** skills.

Functional skills

When you produce your activity programme, you have the opportunity to use your **ICT** skills.

Jay Stevens
Health and fitness instructor

I work in an independent health club as part of a team of ten fitness instructors and studio teachers who deliver health and fitness services to a wide range of clients. Everyone in our team is a qualified fitness instructor and a member of the Register of Exercise Professionals (REPs). My work responsibilities include:

- client health and fitness assessments
- exercise prescription and programming
- individual and group exercise instruction
- maintenance of health and safety
- mentoring junior colleagues.

A typical day for me involves making sure all health and safety checks of the equipment and gym environment have been undertaken. I also spend time in individual consultations carrying out lifestyle and fitness assessments. I may spend one or two hours each day on the development and review of health-related exercise programmes for clients, instructing them on new programmes or new equipment. If I have time I'll try to fit in a training session of my own.

The best thing about my job is that I enjoy meeting people and helping them set realistic and achievable goals for improving their health. Most people join the gym to lose weight but once they see all the other benefits of a regular programme of physical activity and exercise, they find it easier to maintain their programme, even if weight loss doesn't happen. It gives me a sense of satisfaction knowing that I have helped clients to achieve their personal fitness goals.

Think about it!

- What knowledge and skills have you covered in this unit that would provide you with an understanding of the role of the health and fitness instructor?
- How would you rate your current level of competency at using the knowledge and skills you have developed in this unit? What further knowledge and skills might you need to develop to pursue a career in the fitness industry?
- Investigate the requirements for joining the Register of Exercise Professionals (REPs). You can do this at www.exerciseregister.org.

Just checking

1. Identify five major benefits of regular physical activity and exercise participation.
2. Explain why it is important to undertake a thorough health, fitness and lifestyle assessment prior to formulating a health-related physical activity programme for an individual.
3. What key components would you include in the design of a lifestyle assessment questionnaire?
4. Define stress and consider why the control of stress is important to maintain health and wellbeing.
5. Describe the components of a healthy balanced diet.
6. Describe and evaluate three strategies to support the cessation of smoking.
7. What dietary modification techniques could be implemented to assist with weight loss?
8. Describe behaviour modification and the steps that might be involved in changing unhealthy behaviours.
9. In relation to physical activity and exercise prescription, what is overload and why is it important?
10. How would you determine maximum heart rate?

edexcel

Assignment tips

- Take a look at the following websites for information on lifestyle factors that affect health and wellbeing:

American College of Sports Medicine	www.acsm.org
British Nutrition Foundation	www.nutrition.org.uk
Department of Health	www.dh.gov.uk
Food Standards Agency	www.eatwell.gov.uk
The World Health Organisation	www.who.int

- Visit a range of health and fitness environments to gather information on lifestyle improvement. You may choose to use some of this information in meeting the assessment requirements of this unit.

- Remember, prior to being able to plan a health-related physical activity programme for a selected individual, it is necessary to collect relevant information. This will help you in the planning process that will meet the personal goals of the individual and take account of their relevant lifestyle, medical and physical activity history, as well as consider their attitude towards physical activity and exercise and their motivation to adhere to your plan.

- Before you embark on your assessment activities, role play activities with your fellow students and gain feedback from your tutor on your consultation skills. This will help you to effectively carry out a successful consultation with your client and design an appropriate six week health-related physical activity programme. You could also practise your technique on friends and relatives. This will help you to gain confidence in your interview technique.

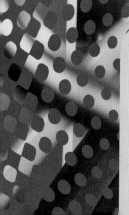

15 Instructing physical activity and exercise

Ensuring that clients have a detailed and suitable training programme is essential for their sporting success. It is vital that these programmes are devised and instructed in a clear, safe and professional manner. Improving people's health and personal fitness through physical activity instruction remains a primary goal throughout the ever-changing fitness industry. This unit will help to develop the knowledge, skills and understanding required to successfully plan, deliver and evaluate a range of exercise programmes.

You will explore the principles behind planning a safe and effective exercise session. This includes the use of pre-screening questionnaires and planning activity sessions to meet individual clients' needs. This unit introduces you to the theories and practices required to instruct physical activity and exercise.

Activities will help develop practical skills, including group teaching, enhancing communication skills, and being aware of different ability levels. Finally, you will investigate the importance of reviewing personal performance and identifying strengths and areas for improvement.

Learning outcomes

After completing this unit you should:

1. know the principles of safe and effective exercise sessions
2. be able to design an exercise programme
3. be able to plan and lead an exercise session
4. be able to review the design of an exercise programme and leading of an exercise session.

Assessment and grading criteria

This table shows you what you must do in order to achieve a pass, merit or distinction grade, and where you can find activities in this book to help you.

To achieve a **pass** grade the evidence must show that you are able to:	To achieve a **merit** grade the evidence must show that, in addition to the pass criteria, you are able to:	To achieve a **distinction** grade the evidence must show that, in addition to the pass and merit criteria, you are able to:
P1 describe the principles of fitness training **See Assessment activity 15.1, page 119**		
P2 describe the health and safety considerations associated with exercise programmes and sessions **See Assessment activity 15.1, page 119**	**M1** explain the health and safety considerations associated with exercise programmes and sessions **See Assessment activity 15.1, page 119**	
P3 describe the importance of warm-up and cool down in exercise programmes and sessions **See Assessment activity 15.2, page 120**		
P4 design a six-week exercise programme for two selected contrasting clients **See Assessment activity 15.3, page 128**	**M2** explain choice of activities for exercise programmes for selected clients **See Assessment activity 15.3, page 128**	**D1** justify choice of activities for exercise programmes for selected clients, suggesting alternative activities **See Assessment activity 15.3, page 128**
P5 plan a safe and effective exercise session **See Assessment activity 15.4, page 133**	**M3** explain choice of activities for the planned exercise session **See Assessment activity 15.4, page 133**	**D2** justify choice of activities for the planned exercise session and suggest alternative activities **See Assessment activity 15.4, page 133**
P6 deliver a safe and effective exercise session, with tutor support **See Assessment activity 15.4, page 133**	**M4** independently deliver a safe and effective exercise session **See Assessment activity 15.4, page 133**	
P7 review own performance in the designing of exercise programmes and the planning and delivery of the exercise session, identifying strengths and areas for improvement **See Assessment activity 15.5, page 136**		

How you will be assessed

You will be assessed using a variety of methods. These will include:

- presentations
- practical sessions
- reports
- posters
- programme design.

Liz, 16-year-old netball player

I am excited about my future and I am hoping to become a personal trainer. This unit helped me to attain the skills and knowledge that are needed to design and implement training programmes for different clients. I learned that everybody is different and that people will have different training goals and needs.

I also learned about the importance of having clear and realistic goals or targets that I could aim to achieve and how these must be reviewed at regular intervals to ensure that I was motivated. The unit taught me that a well planned training programme is vital in achieving personal training goals.

There were lots of practical aspects to this unit and I really enjoyed putting the theory I had learned into practice and watching progress being made as part of my training ideas. I enjoyed working with people and helping them to reach their personal goals.

Over to you!

1. **What areas of the unit might you find challenging?**
2. **What aspect of training are you most looking forward to?**
3. **How can you prepare yourself for assessment in this unit?**

1. Know the principles of safe and effective exercise sessions

Warm-up

What makes an exercise session safe and enjoyable?

A good understanding of anatomy and physiology is essential for designing safe and effective training programmes. You also need to be able to communicate ideas so that the sessions you design are safe and enjoyable. In groups, discuss what you think are the main components of a safe and enjoyable exercise session. You should consider the skills that you would need to lead a session, and how you can develop these.

1.1 Principles of fitness training

A personal trainer identifies areas for improvement as part of a training programme. Such a programme will have clear targets such as weight loss or a gain in muscle size. So if you are a personal trainer or instructor, both you and your athlete must understand the principles of training, and relate these to the client's personal targets.

Components of fitness

The five key components of fitness are:

- strength
- aerobic endurance
- muscular endurance
- flexibility
- body composition.

Strength is the ability of a muscle – or group of muscles – to exert a maximal force or overcome a maximal resistance in a single contraction. The amount of strength generated is in direct proportion to the size of the muscle or muscle group. Some sports require specific muscle training to improve muscle size and strength.

Aerobic endurance can be thought of as the ability of the heart, lungs, blood vessels (arteries and veins) and skeletal muscle to take in, transport and use oxygen efficiently, and over a prolonged period. Aerobic endurance is achieved as a result of continuous training. 'Aerobic' means that energy is produced with oxygen present, which allows long and steady physical activity. Activities such as swimming, cycling, jogging and exercising to music are all associated with aerobic endurance.

Muscular endurance is the ability of a muscle – or group of muscles – to make repeated contractions against light-to-moderate resistance over a prolonged period. Muscular endurance is different from aerobic endurance as it depends on the ability of muscles to perform without oxygen present (anaerobically) for a few minutes. The principal method of improving muscular endurance is to train at a medium intensity for a reasonable duration – more than ten repetitions. Muscular endurance can be improved using the same equipment as that used for strength training, to increase both muscular and cardiovascular endurance.

Flexibility is the ability to move a joint through a complete – and natural – range of motion without discomfort or pain. Many sports require great flexibility, not least to prevent injury. Sports such as gymnastics require the performer to have a wide range of movement. Factors affecting flexibility include the condition of muscles, **connective tissue**, ligaments and tendons, the bones that form the **synovial joint**, and the amount of excessive body fat around the joint.

Boxing is an example of a sport where muscular endurance is important. How can a boxer improve his or her muscular endurance?

Key terms

Connective tissue – (tendon) is used to attach muscles to bones, and is used for structure and support of the skeleton.

Synovial joints – freely movable joints that allow movement. A synovial capsule between the bones prevents bones rubbing together and lubricates the joint cavity.

Body composition is the body's physical make-up in terms of fat and non-fat (or 'lean') body tissue. It is measured as a percentage. Body composition – particularly the fat percentage – can be measured in several ways:

- The most common method is to use a set of skinfold callipers to measure the thickness of fat in various places on the body. These include the abdominal area, the sub-scapular (shoulder blade) region, arms, buttocks and thighs. These measurements are then used to estimate total body fat and can be compared to 'norms' data.

- Another method is bioelectrical impedance analysis, which uses the resistance of electrical flow through the body to estimate the amount of body fat.

A person's weight is not a key consideration within the context of his or her body composition. It is possible for a person to be considered heavy according to standard guides, but to have only a moderate percentage of body fat. This is because lean muscle tissue weighs more than an equal volume of fat tissue.

Activity: Key components of fitness

In small groups, discuss the following sports and identify the key components of fitness: rugby, sprinting, tennis and gymnastics. Why do the components of fitness differ for each of the sporting activities? How might these differences affect a training programme?

Adaptations to training

The human body undergoes changes both during and after exercise. These changes can be described as:

- short-term – there is an immediate change, such as an increase in heart rate or breathing rate
- long-term – such as improved aerobic endurance or an increase in muscle size.

An understanding of why these changes happen will allow you to explain to a client their physiological responses to your prescribed training programme.

Hypertrophy – this is the term used to describe an increase in the size of individual muscle fibres (myofibrils). Skeletal muscle is composed of many individual fibres. These fibres are responsible for muscle contractions. Generally, the bigger the individual muscle fibres, the bigger the muscle and the greater the muscular strength. For hypertrophy to occur, the muscle has to be actively stimulated. The easiest method of doing this is as part of a weight-training programme. This is most effectively done by undertaking resistance training.

Increased muscle tone – some people use the term 'muscle tone' to refer to how 'in shape' a person is. Health clubs, for example, might tell you they are 'improving muscle tone' when they are actually aiming to reduce the amount of fat in your body mass. Technically, what they are referring to is muscular strength, or a lower fat-to-muscle ratio. 'Toned' in this sense means 'fit' or 'trim'. The fat-to-lean body mass ratio can be improved by exercising both aerobically and anaerobically. By training using resistance at a moderate level while using more frequent repetitions, a client might improve muscle definition. Dietary considerations should be taken into account. The person needs to decrease his or her body fat percentage while increasing the lean body mass (body mass excluding fat).

Decreased resting heart rate (RHR) – one of the principal long-term adaptations to aerobic exercise is a decrease in a person's resting heart rate. The heart pumps blood around the body to deliver oxygen to working muscles and remove waste products such as carbon dioxide and water. The demand for oxygen increases during exercise, so the heart must work harder. After training aerobically over a period of time, the body will make physiological changes in order to improve its ability to transport and use oxygen:

- The heart muscles become larger and stronger (through hypertrophy), allowing it to pump greater amounts of oxygenated blood. Blood circulation to the muscles thus improves to meet the demand for oxygen.
- Haemoglobin – which is needed to transport oxygen in the blood – is produced in greater amounts.
- The skeletal muscles increase their ability to produce energy using oxygen and are therefore more efficient.

Increased stroke volume – because the person's heart is now bigger and stronger, it has an increased **stroke volume**. This describes the amount of blood that can be pumped from the heart's ventricles in one contraction. Therefore, at rest the heart is able to pump more blood in one beat than in a person who is less aerobically fit.

Cardiac output is the amount of blood that is pushed out of the heart in one minute. It is defined as:

$$cardiac\ output\ (CO) = stroke\ volume\ (SV) \times heart\ rate\ (HR)$$

Stroke volume is defined as the volume of blood ejected from a ventricle with each beat of the heart. Long-term aerobic exercise increases the size and efficiency of the heart and the stroke volume, which in turn results in a slower heart rate.

Key terms

Stroke volume – the amount of blood pushed out of the heart in one contraction.

Cardiac output – the amount of blood pushed out of the heart in one minute. This is the equivalent of stroke volume × heart rate.

FITT – frequency (how often), intensity (how hard), time (how long) and type (how appropriate).

FITT principles

When designing any training programme, it is important that you consider the main factors that will make it safe and effective. These are known as the principles of training, and you should follow them when devising any fitness or training programme. **FITT** refers to:

- frequency
- intensity
- time
- type.

Table 15.1: Intensity of exercise. Are there any sports that could vary in intensity?

Light	Moderate	Vigorous
Golf	Swimming	Squash
Fishing	Football	Football (if out of breath)
Darts	Tennis	Running
Bowls	Brisk walking	Swimming (if out of breath)
Slow walking	Cycling	Tennis (if out of breath)
Table tennis	Aerobics	Cycling (if out of breath)
Gardening		

Table 15.2: Exercise recommendations for fitness and for general health. Consider your own levels of physical activity. Which category do you fit into?

Variable	Fitness-related	Health-related
Frequency	3–5 days per week	Most days, preferably every day
Intensity	60–90% of maximum heart rate (MHR)	At least moderate intensity
Time (duration)	20–60 minutes continuously	At least 30 minutes
Type	Any aerobic activity	Not specified

Frequency refers to how often a person will train, for example twice a week. Time available will be limited by a person's lifestyle and commitments. If an exercise plan is undertaken over a long period, then it is more likely to be included in a person's hectic lifestyle.

Intensity refers to the level of effort required to perform an exercise session – in other words, how hard the exercises are. Exercise intensity can be measured in a number of ways for a variety of exercises. Simple equipment such as a heart-rate monitor can provide valuable information in measuring exercise intensity. Intensity is sometimes referred to as 'overload'. This means that for any improvements to be made, you must work the body beyond what it is normally used to. If overload is not achieved then the best a person can expect is to maintain his or her current level of fitness or health.

Time refers to how long each session will last. Generally speaking, higher-intensity exercises can be performed for a short period, while lower or moderate levels of intensity can be maintained for longer. Either way, any form of exercise can have a beneficial effect on everyday health. However, for significant benefits to occur, a training session should be longer than 30 minutes.

Tables 15.1 and 15.2 show categories of intensity as well as exercise recommendations for health and fitness, according to one survey.

Type refers to the category of training performed. This could be aerobic or resistance training. Your proposed training programme for a client should have the correct exercises to achieve the client's specific goals. You should consider strength, flexibility, muscular endurance, aerobic endurance and body composition.

1.2 Health and safety

There are many reasons why a training programme might be unsafe. You must be especially aware of all of these factors:

- poor technique
- incorrect clothing or footwear
- poor or broken equipment
- individual medical conditions
- pre-existing injury.

You must ensure that both you and your client are properly prepared before any training session commences. This will involve several things.

PAR-Q

One of the easiest ways to determine a client's background in terms of activity and fitness level is to use a Physical Activity Readiness Questionnaire (PAR-Q). Completion of a PAR-Q is a sensible first step to take if a client is planning to increase the amount of physical activity in his or her life. For most people, extra physical activity should not pose a problem or hazard.

The PAR-Q has been designed to identify those people for whom physical activity might be inappropriate, and those who should seek medical advice concerning the type of activity most suitable for them.

A PAR-Q will include questions on health such as high blood pressure (hypertension), experiences of chest pains, dizziness, recent injuries or operations or back and joint mobility problems.

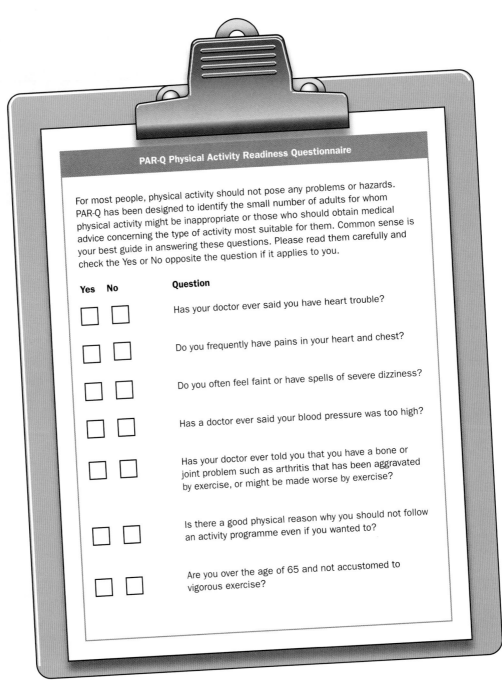

PAR-Q Physical Activity Readiness Questionnaire

For most people, physical activity should not pose any problems or hazards. PAR-Q has been designed to identify the small number of adults for whom physical activity might be inappropriate or those who should obtain medical advice concerning the type of activity most suitable for them. Common sense is your best guide in answering these questions. Please read them carefully and check the Yes or No opposite the question if it applies to you.

Yes	No	Question
☐	☐	Has your doctor ever said you have heart trouble?
☐	☐	Do you frequently have pains in your heart and chest?
☐	☐	Do you often feel faint or have spells of severe dizziness?
☐	☐	Has a doctor ever said your blood pressure was too high?
☐	☐	Has your doctor ever told you that you have a bone or joint problem such as arthritis that has been aggravated by exercise, or might be made worse by exercise?
☐	☐	Is there a good physical reason why you should not follow an activity programme even if you wanted to?
☐	☐	Are you over the age of 65 and not accustomed to vigorous exercise?

Figure 15.1: An example of a PAR-Q. Why is such information important to both the instructor and the client?

Contraindications

> ## Key term
>
> **Contraindication** – a physical or mental condition or factor that increases the risk involved when engaging in a particular activity. Contra means 'against'.

You must be aware of a client's **contraindications** before he or she starts any exercise programme. This can be done by completing a short questionnaire or conducting a short, informal interview. This will ensure you are aware of any conditions that are likely to affect a person's ability to train safely.

Some examples of contraindications include:

- asthma
- pregnancy
- a history of heart disease
- an injury
- operations
- diabetes.

Remember that all exercises may have a risk. If you have one of the above contraindications it does not mean that you cannot exercise at all. For example, Paula Radcliffe has asthma but by taking medication and advice she is still able to compete at the highest levels. If you are unsure then always seek professional medical advice.

Risk assessment

A risk assessment is performed to ensure that all facilities and equipment are safe for use. You should carry out a review of these before each training session. The risk assessment will identify the possibility of harmful effects to individuals from certain human activities or facilities. (For a full exploration of risk assessment, refer to Unit 3 Assessing risk in Student Book 1.)

> ## Take it further
>
> ### Exercise and risk
>
> Poor behaviour can be a risk factor, and this must be taken into consideration when performing a risk assessment. In small groups discuss the behaviour that could be dangerous and why this may occur in an exercise environment.

Table 15.3: Why is a knowledge of contraindications so important?

Contraindication	Activity	Restriction
Asthma	Running	Running should be at a level that will not aggravate the condition. Medicine such as inhalers should be used as required.
Pregnancy	Swimming	Exercise should be encouraged during pregnancy as it improves flexibility, increases heart rate and blood flow and can relieve stress. Exercises should be low impact.
Heart disease	Walking	Light exercise such as walking is permissible although a doctor should be consulted first.
Diabetes	Football	People with diabetes are encouraged to exercise as it will improve blood flow around the body and gives better blood sugar control. However precautions must be taken to ensure that exercise is at the correct intensity and that you have a suitable diet that contains extra carbohydrates.
Operation	Cycling	If you are returning to sport after an injury or operation it is advisable to start slowly and use low impact exercises. This will ensure that you don't do any further damage to key areas.
Injury	Swimming	Always return slowly and at a lower level than before you were injured. It is wise to build up and not take unnecessary risks as this may cause you to injure yourself again. Remember rehabilitation from injury takes time.

Risk assessment checklist

☐ Complete a consent form ensuring the client understands the risk involved in exercise training.

☐ Check equipment is working properly.

☐ Ensure trainer is qualified and insured for personal injury.

☐ Perform induction to show how each piece of equipment should be used safely.

☐ Check client before every session for injuries or illness.

☐ Conduct a full warm-up and cool down each session.

1.3 Warm-up

The purpose of a warm-up is to prepare the athlete for activity both physically and mentally. The warm-up generally consists of a gradual increase in intensity of physical activity. For example, before running or playing an intense sport, you might slowly jog to warm the muscles and increase the heart rate.

It is important that the warm-up should be specific to the activity that will follow. This means that warm-up exercises should prepare the muscles that are to be used and activate the energy systems required for that particular activity.

Functions of a warm-up

The main functions are to:

- increase heart rate
- raise body temperature
- prepare the major joints of the body
- mentally prepare the participant for the exercise ahead

The warm-up should increase the heart rate in order to pump more blood around the body to the working muscles, in preparation for exercise. This, in turn, will allow more energy to be produced using oxygen, and increase the body and muscle temperature. Increasing muscle temperature will, in turn, improve the elasticity of the working muscles so that they are less likely to become injured. In addition, a warm-up should involve a wide range of movements that are specific to the exercise or sport to be undertaken. For a warm-up to be most effective, it should be tailored to the individual client.

Components

The warm-up can comprise a variety of exercises. These can be categorised as either pulse-raisers or stretches.

Raising of the pulse – as the name suggests, a pulse-raiser is a simple cardiovascular exercise that will raise a person's heart rate (pulse) in readiness for further exercises. The pulse-raiser should gradually increase in intensity as time goes on, and normally lasts 5–10 minutes. At the end of a pulse-raising warm-up, the heart rate should be near to the level that will be expected during the main activity. Types of pulse-raiser commonly used as part of a warm-up include:

- walking and/or jogging
- swimming
- cycling
- rowing.

Stretches – these are used as part of a warm-up to improve joint mobility. Stretching will induce the body to produce more fluid in synovial joints, in readiness for more exercise. The joints will become warmer and allow a full range of motion to be achieved. Stretching should start with small movements and then progress to larger, full ranges of motion. The main joints that should be mobilised by stretches are the shoulders, elbows, spine, hips, knees and ankles.

Dynamic stretching – this involves moving muscles through their full range of motion in a controlled manner. Dynamic stretching keeps the heart rate raised and gets the muscles ready for further exercise. Dynamic stretching promotes a form of flexibility that is beneficial in sports using momentum from an effort to propel the muscle into an extended range of motion (not exceeding the static/passive stretching ability).

Which joints are being mobilised here?

Duration

The warm-up should be customised to the physical capabilities of the client and the intensity of the activity. A brief warm-up of 10 minutes' jogging and stretching will adequately prepare a 'weekend' client for a run. In contrast, an athlete's preparation for a run might include 10–15 minutes' jogging, 5–10 minutes' stretching, 5–10 minutes' running with gradual increase to race pace, and finally 5–10 minutes' jogging.

A specific warm-up should be included in the programme for each activity that will follow.

Types of warm-up

A range of techniques can be used to raise heart rate and body temperature and prepare the body for further exercise.

Specific (aerobic routines) – aerobic (cardiovascular) exercise is a good way of raising heart rate and body temperature, and increasing joint mobility.

- The first phase of the warm-up should raise the heart rate, leading to an increase in the speed of delivery of oxygen to the muscles and the temperature of the body. Performing a cardiovascular exercise such as jogging can easily increase the heart rate.

- The second stage should include mobility or stretching exercises. Press-ups, lunges and squat thrusts are good for this.

- The final stage of a warm-up should involve a sport-specific or skill-related component. This should work the neuromuscular mechanisms related to the activity. For example, if you were warming up to play soccer you might practise kicking a ball to a team-mate.

General (low repetitions on resistance machines) – a general warm-up will still aim to raise heart rate, increase body temperature and improve joint mobility. Resistance machines can be used with low weight resistance and low repetitions to help. A general warm-up will start at low to medium intensity, with the intensity increasing after stretching.

1.4 Cool down

The purpose of a cool down is to return the body to its pre-exercise state.

Functions

The three main objectives of a cool down are to:

- return the heart rate to normal
- remove any waste products that may have built up during exercise
- return the muscles to their original state (or length if stretched).

A cool down will also keep the metabolic rate high and capillaries dilated to enable oxygen to flush through the muscle tissue, which helps remove lactic acid waste created by the exercise. This should stop the blood from staying in the veins, which can cause dizziness if the exercise is stopped too quickly. A cool down can also reduce the effect of **delayed-onset muscle soreness (DOMS)**, which often follows strenuous exercise that the body is not used to. It was once thought to be caused by lactic acid build-up, but a more recent theory is that it is caused by tiny tears in the muscle fibres caused by eccentric contraction such as downhill running, or unaccustomed training levels.

The final part of the cool down should include stretching that is designed to facilitate and improve flexibility, as the muscles will be very warm at this stage.

Key term

Delayed-onset muscle soreness (DOMS) – the pain or discomfort often felt 24–72 hours after exercising. It subsides generally within 2–3 days.

Take it further

Cool downs

Clients may not feel like doing a cool down after a strenuous workout, but they must understand that because of the possible benefits, it is worth doing. By getting into the habit from an early age, clients will be more disciplined about performing a cool down. Consider why a cool down is important and what the consequences are of not performing a full cool down.

Components

Lowering of the pulse – you should select cardiovascular exercises that involve all the major muscle groups. Start at a high intensity and slowly lower so that a drop in heart rate can be achieved. This normally lasts for approximately five minutes, and it is common to use an exercise bike as the client can sit down after strenuous exercise.

Stretches – stretching as part of a cool down will allow the muscles to return to their normal working length. It will also aid the removal of waste products that may have built up in the muscles. Stretching can be either maintenance or developmental:

- Maintenance stretching allows the muscles to return to their normal length.
- Developmental stretching is used on muscles that may have become tight and shortened during exercise.

Developmental stretches involve stretching and holding the working muscle for about ten seconds until it relaxes. Following this, the muscle should be stretched again but at an increased level, and again held for ten seconds. This process should be repeated three times.

Proprioceptive neuromuscular facilitation (PNF) is a combination of passive stretching and isometrics, in which a muscle is first stretched passively and then contracted. The technique targets nerve receptors in the muscles to extend muscle length.

PNF stretching was developed as a form of rehabilitation. It can also be used to target specific muscle groups. As well as increasing flexibility and range of movement, it can also improve muscular strength.

- First the relaxed muscle is stretched by an external force, such as an exercise partner, or by the person's own body weight against the floor, wall or similarly resistant object. Where a partner is available, the athlete and a partner assume the position for the stretch, then the partner extends the body limb until the muscle is stretched and tension is felt.
- The athlete then contracts the stretched muscle for 5–6 seconds, and the partner must inhibit all movement. The force of the contraction should be appropriate to the condition of the muscle. For example, if the muscle has been injured, do not apply a maximum contraction.

- The muscle group is now relaxed, then immediately and cautiously pushed past its normal range of movement for about 30 seconds.

- Allow 30 seconds' recovery before repeating the procedure two to four times.

Figure 15.2: A PNF cool down exercise. How can PNF be used to improve flexibility and why is this important in sport and exercise?

Assessment activity 15.1   P1 P2 M1   BTEC

1. You have been asked by the local leisure facility where you work to prepare a presentation for a local athletics club describing the principles of fitness training. The presentation should include essential information on the components of fitness and the short- and long-term adaptations to exercise. **P1**

2. Following your presentation, you need to prepare a document that describes the health and safety requirements an instructor must consider when planning and delivering an exercise programme or session. The document should clearly describe the importance of health and safety in exercise, and the ways in which an instructor can limit the risk of injury or illness. **P2**

3. You must further explain the health and safety considerations associated with exercise programmes and sessions. **M1**

Grading tips

- To attain **P1**:
  - make the presentation interesting by using a wide variety of sports or exercises to highlight the key components of fitness and the adaptations to a training programme
  - consider how your body changes immediately during exercise, and explain why this happens. Also consider how your body would change during longer, sustained periods of exercise.

- To attain **P2**:
  - prepare a PAR-Q form that can be used to identify health- and injury-related problems that may affect safe exercise
  - outline and explain common contraindications and highlight why these must be considered.

- To attain **M1** prepare and conduct a risk assessment on a sports facility at your school or college – explain the purpose of a risk assessment and outline what you would do if a potential risk was identified.

PLTS

By considering the changes that occur during exercise you could gain evidence as a **reflective learner**. By considering the health and safety requirements you could produce evidence to show your skill as an **independent enquirer**.

Functional skills

By preparing your presentation and your document you could provide evidence of your skills in **English** and **ICT**.

Assessment activity 15.2

P3 **BTEC**

Design a suitable warm-up and cool down for a sport of your choice. Remember that your warm-up should be specific to the exercise you are about to undertake, and contain a variety of stretches and pulse-raising exercises. Having designed the warm-up and cool down, demonstrate them to a small group, describing the need for each chosen exercise. **P3**

Grading tip
- To attain **P3** consider how your body changes immediately during exercise, and during longer, sustained periods of exercise. You must consider the sport you are warming up to perform and should identify the specific muscles that will be used during performance.

PLTS
Designing a warm-up and cool down will help you show your skills as a **creative thinker**.

Functional skills
By developing a warm-up and cool down you could provide evidence of your skills in **English**.

2. Be able to design an exercise programme

2.1 Structure

In your role as a professional trainer, you must be able to plan and deliver safe and suitable training programmes. This section will give you an understanding of the key considerations you must follow in order to do that. It also outlines some of the common mistakes people make, and the reasons why training programmes are not always successful.

Introduction to a session

Remember
At the start, it is always necessary to be aware of any medical issues you might need to take into consideration. This is especially important when a new client – or one who has not undertaken an activity programme recently – is involved. A simple medical screening questionnaire can be used in consultation with the client and a medical professional. This might result in ensuring that adequate facilities are available during training sessions (for example, an asthma inhaler).

The first step in designing a programme is to gather as much information about your client as possible. This will allow you to build up a picture of their lifestyle and goals. At your first meeting, a short interview and completion of a pre-exercise questionnaire (or PAR-Q) will give you the information you need to plan an individual training programme. You must take into account that not all clients will be the same as you in terms of their level of fitness or their exercise goals. You must identify relevant lifestyle factors before an accurate plan can be devised including:

- current activity level
- occupation
- leisure activities
- diet
- smoking
- alcohol intake
- stress levels
- time available to train or exercise
- current and previous training history.

Some common reasons given for wanting to exercise include:

- cardiovascular fitness
- weight (fat) loss
- to overcome injury (rehabilitation)
- improve flexibility
- muscular strength
- improved health
- muscle size
- power
- muscle tone
- muscular endurance.

Remember

A word of caution – if you ask a client what he or she wants to achieve, the answer will often be simply 'to get fit'. Make sure that you identify specific targets or goals.

The warm-up

Your proposed exercise programme must incorporate a range of suitable warm-up activities that involve both the cardiovascular system and stretching, to prepare the client for exercise. Warm-ups should be tailored to meet a client's specific needs

Duration of sessions

The duration of a session refers to how long each session will last. This will be progressive and should get longer over a period of time. Different training methods will last different lengths of time.

Activities

A variety of training methods and activities can be adapted to suit the individual client. They include:

- continuous training
- interval training
- Fartlek training
- resistance training.

Continuous training describes training in a steady, aerobic way. Continuous training involves comparatively easy work performed for a relatively long period – for example, cycling at a slow speed for 30 minutes or more. This helps to develop aerobic fitness and muscular endurance. Top athletes such as Paula Radcliffe use continuous training. It is one of the best ways to build a solid aerobic base on which to add more specific types of fitness. It is also one of the easiest types of training when it comes to monitoring your heart rate. Essentially, it involves running, cycling, swimming, etc. at a set pace, usually for 30–45 minutes.

Table 15.4: A continuous training programme for a rugby player. How could it be changed in order to progress?

Element	Duration (minutes)	Intensity (% of MHR)
Warm-up	10	50–60
Workout	20–45	70–80
Cool down	10	50–60

Interval training is broadly defined as repetitions of work at high speed or intensity followed by periods of low activity or rest. For example, a runner will improve his or her workload by combining high-intensity bursts of fast running with recovery periods of slower jogging. Interval training can be any cardiovascular workout (stationary biking, running, rowing, etc.) that involves brief bouts at near-maximum exertion interspersed with periods of lower-intensity activity.

Fartlek training is a form of interval training. Developed by Swedish coach Gösta Holmér, it is a form of conditioning that puts stress mainly on the aerobic energy system due to the continuous nature of the exercise. The difference between this type of training and continuous training is that the intensity or speed of the exercise varies, meaning that aerobic and anaerobic systems can be put under stress. Most Fartlek sessions last a minimum of 45 minutes and can vary from aerobic walking to anaerobic sprinting. Fartlek training is generally associated with running, but it can include almost any kind of exercise including cycling, rowing or swimming.

Fartlek training can benefit participants in sports such as soccer, field hockey and rugby, as it develops aerobic and anaerobic capacities that are both used in these sports.

Fartlek training

☐ Warm-up – light/easy running for 10–15 minutes

☐ Steady, hard speed for 0.75 to 1.5 miles – like a long repetition

☐ Rapid walking for about five minutes – recovery

☐ Easy running interspersed with sprints of about 50–60 metres, repeated until a little tired – start of speed work

☐ Easy running with three or four 'quick steps' now and then – simulating suddenly speeding up to avoid being overtaken by another runner

☐ Full speed uphill for 175–200 metres

☐ Immediately, fast pace for one minute

☐ Repeat the whole routine until the total training period has elapsed

---

Resistance training is often referred to as strength training, because it is used to develop the strength and size of skeletal muscles. It involves using resistance or weights during a muscular contraction. Resistance training may also be used to improve muscular endurance.

Resistance training can use the body's own weight to produce the resistance, or it can use fixed or free weights. Using such weights involves a number of repetitions and sets, with the following training principle applied:

muscular strength = high resistance and low repetitions

muscular endurance = lower resistance and high repetitions

Activity: Training for tennis

Research how the four types of training discussed here – continuous, interval, Fartlek and resistance training – might be used by a tennis player. Decide which would be the most beneficial, and discuss your results. Remember to consider what the key fitness components of tennis are.

Exercise intensity

This refers to how hard you are exercising. It is often measured as a percentage of your maximum heart rate (MHR), with common applications being rated low, medium or high intensity.

- low intensity – training at up to 70 per cent of MHR, used to improve general fitness
- medium intensity – up to 80 per cent of MHR, used to improve aerobic threshold or endurance
- high intensity – up to 90 per cent of MHR, used by athletes to improve their strength or anaerobic threshold

Training zones

These are used to determine the level of intensity at which you are working. This is particularly important for cardiovascular training or exercise.

Heart rate training zones are calculated by taking into consideration your maximum heart rate (MHR) and your resting heart rate (RHR). To work out your MHR you should subtract your age in years from 220:

$MHR = 220 - age$

Your RHR can be measured by taking your pulse at rest, preferably before any form of movement or exercise. Because it is difficult to exercise and measure your heart rate manually, it is useful to use a heart rate monitor.

The Karvonen formula

Knowing how fast your heart is beating is no help unless you know how fast it should be beating. The Karvonen formula is a method used to specify training intensities in relation to the heart rate training zones explained in Table 15.5.

The Karvonen formula will allow you to determine how fast your heart should be beating when you are in one of the heart-rate training zones:

desired heart rate (HR) = RHR + [(MHR − RHR) × % intensity]

Consider an example of a client with an MHR of 180 beats per minute (bpm) and an RHR of 70 bpm. So:

for 60% intensity: 70 + [(180 − 70) × 0.60] = 136 bpm

for 85% intensity: 70 + [(180 − 70) × 0.85] = 163 bpm

Using a heart rate monitor, the client will be able to exercise using cardiovascular training at the correct level, not allowing his or her heart rate to exceed the required level or zone.

Rating of Perceived Exertion (RPE)

Another method of describing exercise intensity levels uses the so-called Borg rating of perceived exertion (see Table 15.6). Perceived exertion is how hard you feel your body is working. It is based on physical sensations during activity, including increased heart rate, increased respiration or breathing rate, increased sweating and muscle fatigue.

A heart rate monitor is an essential tool for measuring heart rate during and after exercise. How can you use a heart rate monitor to determine training zones and how will this benefit the user?

The four main training zones are described in Table 15.5.

Table 15.5: The four main training zones. Why must a personal trainer understand training zones?

Zone	Percentage of MHR	Training
Fitness	60–70	Develops basic endurance and aerobic capacity – all easy recovery running should be completed at a maximum of 70% MHR.
Aerobic	70–80	Develops your cardiovascular system – the body's ability to transport oxygen to, and carbon dioxide away from, the working muscles is developed and improved; as fitness improves it will be possible to run at up to 75% MHR and get the benefits of fat-burning and improved aerobic capacity.
Anaerobic	80–90	High-intensity – your body cannot use oxygen quickly enough to produce energy so relies on energy that can be used without oxygen, namely glycogen stored in the muscles. This can be used for only a short period – a build-up of lactic acid will rapidly cause fatigue.
Red line	90–100	Maximum level of exercise – training possible only for short periods, effectively trains fast-twitch muscle fibres and helps develop speed. This zone is reserved for interval running – only for the very fit.

Through experience of monitoring how your body feels, it becomes easier to know when to adjust your exercise intensity. For example, a walker who wants to engage in moderately intensive activity would aim for a Borg scale level of 'somewhat hard' (12–14). If she described her muscle fatigue and breathing as 'very light' (9 on the Borg scale) she would want to increase the intensity. On the other hand, if she felt her exertion was 'extremely hard' (19 on the Borg scale), she would need to slow down her movements to achieve the moderate intensity range.

Cool down

A cool down should be included in all training programmes and must be designed to lower heart rate, decrease body temperature and return the muscles to their original state. It also helps to remove waste products that have built up during exercise. A combination of reduced-intensity cardiovascular exercise and stretching will help a client recover. A minimum of ten minutes should be allocated at the end of a session for an effective cool down, although this time can be increased if necessary.

Table 15.6: The Borg rating of perceived exertion. Consider how you feel when you exercise. Can you think of some examples to place along the scale?

6	No exertion at all
7	Extremely light
8	
9	Very light – easy walking slowly at a comfortable pace
10	
11	Light
12	
13	Somewhat hard – quite an effort, you feel tired but can continue
14	
15	Hard (heavy)
16	
17	Very hard – very strenuous, you are very fatigued
18	
19	Extremely hard – you cannot continue for long at this pace
20	Maximal exertion

This marathon runner has been through all of the levels of perceived exertion. How can this experience help the athlete in future training and competition?

2.2 Factors to consider when designing an exercise programme

Screening

Each client should complete a screening session with you. This may involve a short, informal interview and the completion of a pre-exercise questionnaire (such as the PAR-Q, see page 114). The questionnaire should include questions about the client's medical history and exercise history. This should give you a clear picture of the exercise that it will be safe to undertake.

> **Remember**
>
> Never take chances. If, at any point, you are unhappy with the responses the client has made, then you should get the approval of a qualified doctor first.

Motives

Clients are motivated to exercise for a variety of reasons. They include losing weight, health benefits, preparation for a competitive sport, or recommendation by a doctor. It is important that you understand why a particular client wants to exercise, or why he or she may need an individual fitness programme. Understanding their motives will allow you to get a picture of your client's short- and long-term aims or goals.

Barriers

Why people don't exercise, or why they drop out of exercise programmes, is an area that all instructors need to understand. Having knowledge of common barriers to participation will allow you to address these and overcome them.

One of the most common reasons for not exercising is lack of time. People have busy lives with work, education and family commitments, and fitting in exercise can often be difficult. Therefore you must consider how and when a client can exercise, and adapt the proposed programme to their life.

Current physical activity level

The pre-exercise questionnaire and interview will allow you to determine the client's current level of activity. This is important, so that you do not prescribe exercises that are too easy, so that little progress is likely to be achieved. And you must never prescribe exercise that is too hard for the client, as this can be dangerous and cause discomfort or injury. Each client must be comfortable with his or her exercise programme.

Goals (short- and long-term)

A client should identify specific goals, with your help. What goals are to be achieved in the long-term, and how will they be approached in the short term?

Goal setting can follow the SMARTER principle. Goals should be:

- **S**pecific
- **M**easurable
- **A**djustable
- **R**ealistic
- **T**imed
- **E**xciting and challenging
- **R**ecorded.

Short-term goals are used as 'stepping stones' to achieve the final goal. An example is a client who wishes to lose 5 kilos in weight. His long-term goal would be to lose this total weight, while his short-term goal might be to lose 0.5 kilos per week over a ten-week period.

2.3 Clients

There are many different types of client for whom you might have to write exercise programmes – individuals, groups, adults or children.

Various abilities

Some clients may be highly experienced athletes, while others will be undertaking exercise for the first time. You must be aware of the different levels in ability and adapt training programmes accordingly. You must ensure that each client is safe when exercising, and your recommended programme must be suited to his or her ability, fitness level and enjoyment.

Individuals and groups

Training programmes can be set in the form of individual or group exercise. Group training can prove challenging, as there is likely to be a wide range of abilities within the group. Exercises must be adapted so that individuals are able to exercise at their specific level.

Group exercise can be a good motivator, as other people encourage the individual who may be struggling within the session. Group activities are also a good way of meeting people, and are commonly used as a social experience.

Specific groups

Groups that may wish to exercise together can include the elderly, children or those who are obese. Again, it is important that any programmes are adapted to meet the needs of the group and the individuals, so that training is safe.

- **Older people** will generally undertake programmes that are low in intensity, with little resistance and several repetitions. This is aimed at achieving a good level of general fitness.

- **Children** should not undertake *any* weight training exercise as it can cause permanent damage, especially to the skeletal system that is still growing. Children should undertake exercise that is low in resistance and high in repetitions (such as aerobic exercise). This can be used to improve general health and fitness as well as improve aerobic capacity.

- **The obese** – a simple way of tackling obesity is to exercise aerobically. Activities should be based predominantly on low-resistance that will improve the client's ability to exercise over a period of time. Gentle walking or slow jogging can be recommended – although it is important that the client is given a full health check prior to any exercise, especially if he or she has not exercised for some time.

For any exercise programme to be effective, lifestyle and dietary advice may also be given so that any goals outlined are realistically achievable.

For more information on specific groups, refer to Unit 16 Exercise for specific groups.

Code of ethical practice

A code of ethical practice is a set of guidelines that exercise professionals should follow to ensure they are working at the highest standards. The Register of Exercise Professionals describes such a code as 'good practice for professionals in the fitness industry by reflecting on the core values of rights, relationships and responsibilities'.

Older people will tend to exercise at low intensities. What are the benefits of exercise to older participants?

People who work in the exercise profession must accept their responsibility for those who participate in exercise, for other fitness professionals and colleagues, for their respective fitness associations, professional bodies and institutes, for their employer, and for society. They should follow the four main principles of ethical practice:

- rights
- relationships
- personal responsibilities
- professional standards.

Rights – an exercise professional will promote the rights of every individual, and recognise that every person should be treated as an individual. Professionals must treat all clients equally regardless of race, gender, age, disability, religion, ethnic background or sexual orientation, and should keep all client information confidential.

Relationships – exercise professionals should develop a rapport with their clients based on openness, trust, honesty and respect. They must always promote the welfare and best interests of their clients, and encourage them to accept responsibility for their own behaviour and actions during training sessions.

Personal responsibilities – exercise professionals should agree to demonstrate proper behaviour at all times. They should be fair, honest and considerate to all clients and others working in the fitness industry, and display control, respect, dignity and professionalism. They should also ensure that they do not over-train clients or undertake any practices that are likely to result in injury.

Professional standards – the exercise professional will ensure that he or she is suitably qualified and undertake regular, up to date retraining. The professional will accept responsibility for his or her actions and continuously evaluate personal performance with the aim of improving.

Activity: Pre-exercise questionnaire

Design a pre-exercise screening questionnaire that would be suitable to use in the sport of your choice. Ensure the questions are relevant and cover areas such as illness, disease and injury. Ask your fellow students to fill in the form, then check if you have managed to gather all the information you need. What questions could you add?

2.4 Activity selection

Understanding the needs of a client means that you must take into account a variety of factors, such as his or her likes or dislikes, accessibility, culture, commitments, personal goals and time. This will allow you to devise a programme that is suitable for the individual, and allow the individual to maintain a high level of commitment.

Likes and dislikes

These influence what activities the client will be prepared to undertake. However, there may be some exercises that the client needs to do in order to achieve specific goals. You must ensure that he or she recognises the importance of exercising using a variety of methods.

Accessibility

Provision varies from place to place, so activity sessions may be limited by a lack of facilities and the difficulty of reaching them. A client who has to travel a long distance to a session may drop out because of the inconvenience – the time commitment and possibly the cost of transport. This should be discussed with the client at the beginning and exercises that can be adapted may be considered. Price is also a consideration – low-income groups may only have access to the cheaper sessions or facilities.

Culture

Some cultures experience barriers due to social or religious taboos or traditions, different attitudes to sport, little experience of structured sport, or a lack of role models. An exercise professional must consider how to overcome these barriers and adapt programmes accordingly.

Commitments

A client's other commitments tend to come in the form of either work or family, and generally these will take precedence over formal exercise. Sessions must be fitted around these commitments, so the ideal exercise programme may have to be adapted.

Goals

All goals must be realistic and achievable, and clearly time-defined. This will help the client to decide whether the goals are truly realistic over a given period. The programme should ideally outline short-, medium- and long-term goals.

Time

Probably the most quoted reason for not exercising – or dropping out – is lack of time. Time can be swallowed up by work, family duties and social preferences.

You can encourage clients to incorporate exercise into a busy lifestyle by walking rather than using the car, or getting off the bus one stop earlier than usual. Using the stairs instead of lifts or escalators can also contribute to improving health.

Take it further

Useful web links

Visit the following websites for further research:

- www.publichealth.nice.org.uk – the National Institute for Health and Clinical Excellence (NICE) is responsible for providing national guidance on promoting good health and preventing and treating ill health.
- www.sportengland.org – Sport England (supported by the National Lottery) advises, invests in and promotes community sport, and aims to get two million people more active in sport by 2012.

Assessment activity 15.3   P4 M2 D1   BTEC

The athletics club has been impressed by your knowledge of instructing physical activity. They are now keen to appoint a fitness instructor on a part-time basis who can work with the emerging young athletes.

1. As part of the application process for this post, you are required to design a six-week exercise programme for the following two athletes:
   - 100-metre sprinter
   - 1500-metre runner.

   Consider the key requirements of fitness for each athlete and design your programme accordingly. **P4**

2. Explain why you have chosen each of the different exercises outlined in your six-week training plan for each athlete. **M2**

3. Justify why you have chosen each of the exercises for the two athletes. **D1**

Grading tips

- To attain **P4**:
  - think about how the body will adapt to the exercise you recommend over the six-week period
  - make sure your programme is varied and progressive
  - ensure you consider warm-up and cool down exercise to reduce the chance of injury
  - remember to consider any health and safety factors.
- To attain **M2** you should explain the key differences between the exercises you have chosen.
- To attain **D1** you should explain the purpose of each exercise, highlighting the component/s of fitness it is designed to train. You should then give examples of other exercises the athletes may wish to undertake so that the sessions are varied and enjoyable.

PLTS

By designing a training programme you are able to gain evidence as a **reflective learner**, a **self-manager** and a **creative thinker**.

Functional skills

By using maths to work out a suitable training programme with weekly development you could provide evidence of your skills in **mathematics**.

3. Be able to plan and lead an exercise session

A number of factors must be considered when planning and delivering an effective exercise session. Apart from health and safety, an exercise professional must also consider the venue, equipment and his or her communication skills. You must understand the importance of each of these if you are to be successful.

📱 3.1 Plan an exercise session

Screening

Health screening must take place before any exercise or testing is performed by the client, and must be administered by the sports practitioner. Screening usually takes the form of a questionnaire and interview, and its aim is to identify any medical condition that would prevent the client from exercising safely.

Screening and testing are normally carried out before induction, or during the induction process. At this stage, the practitioner will complete the relevant paperwork, taking down personal details.

A high-quality health screening programme should involve a number of health checks, which may include the following components:

- taking the client's past medical history
- taking the family medical history
- recording blood pressure
- measuring lung function
- checking cholesterol level
- measuring body composition.

Risk assessment

The fitness and health club sector has grown in recent years. It has seen the development and enhancement of facilities and services, and one of the key areas of improvement is the necessity to deliver safe, well-structured practice.

Before you start any exercise programme, it is essential that a full risk assessment has been fully considered. Before the session starts, you must check the equipment that is to be used, and the facility. The following points that must be considered:

- Is the equipment suitable and in full working order?
- Is there enough equipment?
- Is the area to be used free from cables or wires?
- Does the area have good ventilation?
- Is the temperature suitable for physical activity?

The lifestyle questionnaire should include questions about:

- diet
- alcohol and tobacco use.

Aims

The success of a session has to be judged against a set of aims. These are the principal targets. The aims must be achievable, but they must not be too easy so that the participants are not challenged at all. If that happens, the individuals or team will fail to improve.

There should also be a time constraint attached to the aims. For example, a marathon runner might set an aim of being able to run 10 km at four months prior to the event – to allow for progression to be made to complete the full distance of just over 42 km (26.2 miles).

Objectives

Objectives will accompany the session's aims – these refer to how the aims will be achieved. The objectives will outline very specific goals, which may be short- or medium-term goals. For example, an objective of a marathon runner may be to identify suitable training methods to improve muscular and cardiovascular endurance.

Structure of sessions

Structure is very important if the client is to enjoy the exercise and avoid injury. In general terms, a session will follow the order: warm-up, main activity and cool down.

The warm-up – this generally consists of a gradual increase in intensity in physical activity. For example, before running or playing an intense sport you might slowly jog to warm muscles and increase heart rate. It is important that warm-ups should be specific to the exercise that will follow, which means that exercises should prepare the muscles to be used and to activate the energy systems that are required for that particular activity. Stretching the active muscles is also recommended after doing a warm-up.

The main activity – it is important that a number of rules are followed.

📱 *Rule 1: exercise major muscles in pairs*

When using resistance training, it is important that corresponding muscles are trained equally. Muscles help stabilise a joint, so if one is stronger than another this may cause joint instability and injury. It can also cause long-term problems with posture and may affect sporting performance. The main pairs of muscles are:

- pectorals and trapezius
- biceps and triceps
- latissimus dorsi and deltoid
- abdominals and erector spinae
- quadriceps and hamstrings.

Rule 2: do the difficult exercises first

A simple exercise will involve only one joint (for example, a bicep curl), whereas a more difficult exercise will involve two or more joints (for example, a chest press). The more difficult exercises will need more focus, so they should be done early on before the onset of fatigue.

Rule 3: train the large muscles first

The large muscles of the body are:

- trapezius
- latissimus dorsi
- pectorals
- quadriceps
- hamstrings
- gluteus maximus.

The main reason for exercising these muscles first is that they will require the most effort, so they should be exercised before they start to tire. The smaller muscles of the body help the larger muscles to work, so should remain relatively fresh when exercising.

📱 *Rule 4: exercise the abdominal muscles last*

The abdominal and muscles of the lower back are used to provide support to the main core of the body. These should remain free from fatigue so that injury to the back can be avoided and correct posture can be maintained.

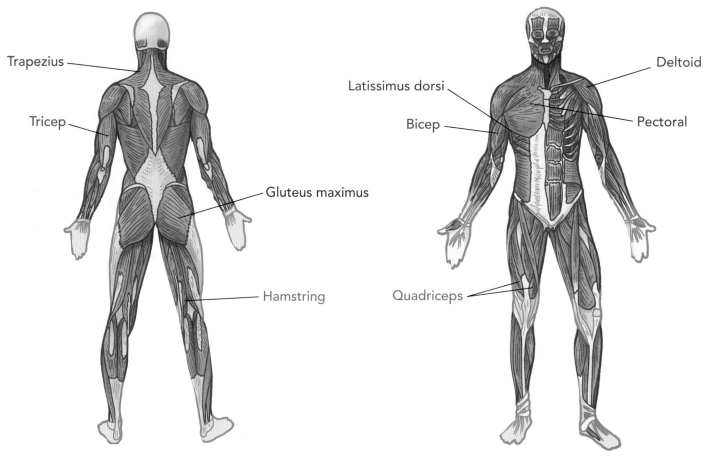

Figure 15.3: The main pairs of muscles. How would you exercise each pair?

The cool down – the purpose of this is to return the body to its normal level. This will involve light exercise to lower the heart rate and body temperature, while stretching is used to prevent muscle soreness.

Activity: Skeletal muscles

In pairs or small groups, identify the major skeletal muscles that are being used for each phase of the following simple exercises:

- press-up
- tricep dip
- step up
- chest press.

Venue

Being able to lead an effective session will depend on the venue used. Is it the correct size for the number of people, and is it suitable for exercises? You should also consider whether the venue will provide the necessary equipment. If clients have to provide their own, this will have a financial implication and may prevent some people from taking part.

The venue must be safe. A full health and safety check should be conducted prior to all sessions.

Marketing

Marketing can be broadly defined as the need to identify, anticipate and satisfy customers' needs. It is particularly important if you are to run a successful business. It will be vital to promote your service in a way that attracts clients, makes them want to return in the future, and recommend it to their friends and family.

The way in which you perform during sessions will also help. You must be professional and competent at all times, and be clearly willing to help people achieve their fitness goals.

Setting-up

To present a professional image, all sessions should be planned in advance. You must identify the venue, the time of the session and the equipment needed. In advance of the session, you should set up the equipment to be used so that it is ready when the clients arrive. The equipment should be checked for damage, and not used if you are unsure.

Checking and maintaining equipment

Equipment should be checked for damage before and after a session. Any damaged equipment should be either repaired or replaced before the next session.

3.2 Deliver an exercise session

Your introduction to the session

All participants should be aware of:

- what is expected of them
- how the exercises should be completed
- health and safety issues
- variations of activities for male and female participants
- ability levels or factors that may affect existing/past injuries.

In order to communicate these messages, time should be taken to determine how people learn best, and how they will be able to replicate movements that in some cases are new to them and complex in nature. To demonstrate a session effectively, the acronym IDEA presents a natural progression suitable for exercise classes, gym inductions, coaching sessions or on a one-to-one personal training basis. IDEA stands for:

Introduction – of the exercise, its purpose, its benefits and basic technique. ☐

Demonstration – this should be non-verbal, allowing participants to observe the movements without a spoken message that might distract from their observation. ☐

Explanation – of the basics of the exercise: mention perhaps two or three technique-related points, but avoid information overload. ☐

Application – give participants an opportunity to practise the movements and gauge whether there are any potential problems or areas for improvement – it is essential to ensure correct technique, so this is a key phase in the introduction to a session. ☐

Instruction delivery

When clients begin to exercise, they will need ongoing support to ensure correct technique and avoid injury. This support should come from you in a number of forms.

- **Communication** – an essential tool for developing relationships and interacting. The key to good communication is to provide the amount of information the receiver can use effectively, rather than the amount you would like to give. Your message should be transmitted in a clear voice and be free from jargon. The use of jargon and slang terms is commonplace but can cause confusion.

- **Technique correction** – this must be addressed early. Leaving small errors to develop will result in serious problems later, which will take valuable time to correct. Poor technique will often fail to deliver the preferred results. People engaging in weight-training programmes are a prime example of this, because they tend to fail to target the desired muscle regions and see little or no improvement. Poor technique may also lead to injury.

- **Correct body alignment** – the development of 'core stability' is a fairly new phenomenon in the fitness world. It basically seeks to develop an equilibrium or balance throughout the skeletal and muscular systems. Body alignment will target areas of posture and balance as fundamental factors to ensure the body remains functional and efficient. Core stability achieves this by highlighting the core (abdominal and lower back regions) as the framework to generate a solid platform to work from.

  Body alignment also deals with creating a balance between muscle groupings. For example, the quadriceps are capable of producing substantial power output but should not be too powerful for the opposite muscles – the hamstrings – to deal with, otherwise one of the hamstrings is likely to sustain damage.

- **Modification of exercises** – not everyone is built the same way. Some people will find an exercise easily achievable, while others might have difficulty with it. As an exercise professional you should always have contingency plans available to ensure everyone has an opportunity to attempt the activity. The art of modifying exercises is an essential tool.

- **Observation** – when leading an exercise session, you will be able to gauge levels of experience and

potential from simply watching. With experience, technique correction can be completed by studying running styles, arm positioning, foot strike on the floor or head position – to name but a few – during a phase of movement.

- **Motivation** – a common reason why people leave exercise and training programmes is a drop in motivation. This may be caused by previous poor experience, lack of enjoyment, or failure to achieve aims and objectives. You must motivate your client, especially when the going gets tough.

  Imparting motivation will involve verbal encouragement as well as considering your own body language. You must be positive at all times to make sure that you are pushing the client into working as hard as is reasonable to achieve his or her goals safely.

- **Rapport with clients** – having a friendly and open rapport with clients will help you to produce effective training programmes. Being honest and respectful will keep up the clients' motivation. Clients should feel that they are able to discuss their programmes with you, and feel comfortable in trying to achieve their targets.

Remember

It is important to be friendly and patient, especially when the client is struggling. Ensure that you are positive and motivate the client.

Activity: Non-verbal communication

In small groups, explore the importance of non-verbal communication (body language). Try and communicate a common phrase or expression without using any gestures. For example, you may wish to describe a recent sporting performance that you have witnessed.

Your group should list examples of body language that you used, highlight any positive and negative examples, and compare them.

- List examples of positive/negative body language.
- What are the problems of displaying negative body language?
- Why must a leader be enthusiastic and confident?

Ending a session

Once the session has been completed (including the cool down), you have the opportunity to ask clients how they feel it went. This time is important, as it gives you valuable feedback as part of your own personal evaluation. Through discussion with your clients, you can amend their programme as well as improve areas of your delivery.

This time should also be spent giving the clients feedback. Explain how you thought they did.

Finally, check all equipment for damage, and arrange for repair or replacement as necessary. Store it in a manner that is likely to prevent accidents or damage. The setting down of equipment should be performed efficiently and safely. In particular, heavy items should be carried correctly.

Assessment activity 15.4

P5 M3 D2 P6 M4   BTEC

Having designed a successful six-week training programme for the two contrasting athletes, you have been shortlisted for an interview at the athletics club. The club manager has decided that the best way of recruiting a suitable exercise instructor is to see them perform a practical exercise session.

1. You are required to plan a one-hour, safe and effective exercise session for a group of young athletes. **P5**

2. Within your plan, explain the exercises you have chosen for the proposed session. **M3**

3. Justify why you have chosen the exercises outlined in your proposed session plan. **D2**

4. Having prepared a suitable one-hour session as part of your job interview, you are now required to deliver the session. The session must be safe and effective, and you may seek support if you need to. **P6**

5. Alternatively, you could deliver the session without support. **M4**

Grading tips

- To attain **P5** the session plan should include the following information:
  - aim and objective of the session
  - health and safety considerations
  - risk assessment
  - equipment required
  - warm-up and cool down
  - structure of the session.

- To attain **M3** it is worth considering what each chosen exercise actually trains – what component of fitness is being addressed?

- To attain **D2** think about why these exercises are beneficial to the athletes, and what alternative activities you could choose if you needed to.

- To attain **P6** ensure you have:
  - checked for any injuries and illnesses.
  - checked if there are any reasons why anybody should not participate
  - checked the facilities and equipment prior to the session
  - outlined the aims of session at the beginning of the session.

- To attain **M4** be confident enough to deliver the session without support. Don't forget your verbal and non-verbal language (body language) – be enthusiastic. Remember to encourage and motivate all the participants during the session. Be confident!

PLTS

By designing a training programme you are able to gain evidence to show that you are a **reflective learner**, **independent enquirer**, **self-manager** and **effective participator**.

Functional skills

By using maths to work out a suitable training programme with weekly development you could provide evidence of your skill in **mathematics**. By delivering a programme you are working towards your speaking and listening in **English**.

4. Be able to review the design of an exercise programme and leading of an exercise session

4.1 Review performance

Methods

After any exercise programme, it is important that you review your own performance as well as that of your clients. There are many different ways of doing this, including peer evaluation, questionnaires and self-evaluation. Each method should be understood and used if you are to improve your sessions in the future.

- **Peer evaluation** – you can gain information from your peers about your performance. This evaluation can be in the form of interviews or questionnaires. Peer observations are useful because they highlight strengths and weaknesses of performance and give valuable information on how to improve.

- **Questionnaires** – these can be given to clients after sessions have been completed. Again, valuable information can be gained about what they enjoyed or disliked. This information can then be applied in future sessions.

  Here are some examples of questions that can be asked:

- Did the session meet your original objectives?
- Did you enjoy the session, and if not, why not?
- Did you feel safe throughout the session?
- In what ways would you like to see future sessions developed?
- **Self-evaluation** – you should always ask yourself questions after each session, and you must answer these honestly, even if the answers are likely to identify weaknesses in your performance. Self-evaluation is an important tool as it means future sessions will be safe and effective, and clients will remain motivated and make targeted progression. Self-evaluation will also help you to identify any future training needs you have to update your skills.

Remember

Evaluate your performance immediately after you have finished. This will ensure that any ideas are fresh in your mind.

Fit for purpose

By reviewing performance, you can identify whether your selected activities are fit for their purpose. This means making sure the exercises are actually addressing the short- and long-term goals of the client.

- **Track progression** – have clear targets that are measurable, so that any improvements can be tracked. If a specific aspect of the programme is not effective, then changes can be made and the session adapted.

- **Adaptation session** – perform regular session reviews. If the client's goals are not being met, then it is important that the session is amended. Such adaptations should take into account the client's needs, and may address whether a client has become demotivated. Adaptations will also allow variety, which can further enhance enjoyment.

- **Modify activities** – activities may be modified to take into account factors such as injury, illness, unexpected changes to the length of sessions, and client demotivation. Modifications should be discussed fully with clients so that they are aware of what to expect in the future.

- **Improve own performance** – conduct a full personal performance review to identify areas of strength and weakness. This may include whether you can improve your clients' motivation, and the way in which you instruct them. Remember that you may have to adapt your approach and instructor skills for each individual – what works for one client may not work for another.

- **Codes of practice** – a code of practice should be a clear set of rules that identifies how you and your clients should behave before, during and after each session. Exercise and fitness professionals should follow the four main principles of ethical practice: rights, relationships, personal responsibilities and professional standards. A code of practice will also clearly define safe behaviour, which will help reduce the risk of injury to clients and others.

- **Continued professional development** – it is important that an instructor identifies his or her areas of weakness and addresses them through continued professional development. Attending up to date courses will ensure that the instructor is imparting the correct techniques and up to date information to the client. In addition, clients will have confidence in the training programmes you provide.

Modifying

When modifying a programme, it is important to be specific in the changes you make and to outline why they are being made. There are a number of reasons why changes are made. They may include FITT progression, increased motivation and the achievement of goals.

- **FITT progression** – this refers to frequency, intensity, time and type of exercise within a training programme. You should be able to modify these specific aspects in order to achieve a client's outlined goals. For example, the intensity may be too high, so that a client struggles to complete a session. Training at too high an intensity can also result in injury, so should be addressed immediately.

  Here are some questions to ask yourself and each of your clients:

  o Is the frequency of each session too high or too low? In other words, can the clients commit to each session?

  o Is the intensity or level of work too easy or too hard for the clients?

o Is the time allocated for each session too long or too short? In particular, do the clients struggle to complete the sessions fully?

o Are the types of exercise used appropriate and effective?

o Do the clients enjoy the range of exercises used?

- **Changes to maintain interest and motivation** – each training session should involve a variety of exercises. Too much repetition can cause boredom and may demotivate the client. Talk to the client and find out what he or she is enjoying, and what is boring or disliked. Regular modifications can help enhance commitment by the client.

- **Achievable goals** – any targets that you set should follow the SMARTER principle (specific, measurable, adjustable, realistic, timed, exciting/challenging and recorded). By following this principle, you and your clients can conduct continuous reviews of performance and ensure that identified goals are achievable. This will also allow you to make any modifications as necessary.

Development needs

All people working in the exercise industry must ensure that their knowledge and skills are up to date and that they are giving out the correct information. It is vital that instructors attend regular update training and continued professional development. These courses will maintain the high standards that clients will expect from a trainer.

SMART targets

All exercise programmes must be reviewed on a regular basis to ensure that they are valid and meeting their specific targets. To do this an instructor should use the SMART principle. By following this system an instructor will ensure that long-term goals are achievable.

Assessment activity 15.5

P7 | **BTEC**

Having successfully completed your session, it is essential that you evaluate how it went. Review your own performance in designing, planning and delivering the exercise session. Remember – you must be honest in your evaluation, and you should be able to identify both your strengths and weaknesses, so that further areas for improvement can be identified. **P7**

Grading tip

To attain **P7** prepare an evaluation sheet for participants to complete at the end of the session. Be honest in your personal performance evaluation. List the strengths of the session – what went well? List the weaknesses of the session – what would you change next time?

PLTS

By reviewing your performance you are able to demonstrate your skills as a **reflective learner**.

Rebecca Pett
Personal trainer

Rebecca is a personal trainer in a health club. She has done this job since she left college although she still attends many courses to ensure that her knowledge and skills are up to date. Rebecca works in a variety of situations with a wide range of people and her working day can vary enormously. For example, she may work on a one-to-one basis with a client who is wishing to lose weight or she may find herself training with an elite athlete. Either way, she must ensure that any programme she devises is specific to the client's needs and that she reviews it on a regular basis.

Sometimes Rebecca will find herself working with large groups of people, for example, when she teaches aerobics. This will present her with different challenges and she must be well prepared for all her sessions.

'A typical day starts at 7 a.m. where I will check that I have all the equipment ready for the day's sessions. I will have already planned a session for each of my clients and I make sure that I arrive at the venue in good time. When I get there I check all the facilities are safe and that they are suitable. When my client arrives I ensure that they are wearing the correct clothing, have water for hydration and that they are free from injury or illness. Following a warm-up I then perform the individual session including posture, core stability, aerobic workout and resistance training. Each session will end with flexibility training.

On a normal day I will see clients either early in the morning or in the evening when they return from work. What I enjoy most about my job is helping people to achieve their goals. In terms of skills, enthusiasm, empathy and good communication are essential. I work with a wide variety of people, each of whom will have specific requirements.'

Think about it!

- Rebecca often works long hours starting early in the morning and finishing late at night. Why are sessions at these times?
- What forms of communication might Rebecca use for a training session? Why are motivation and enthusiasm important in her role as a personal trainer?
- Why must Rebecca regularly review her own performance as well as the success of her clients?

Just checking

1. What are the principles of training?
2. When planning an exercise or training programme, outline and explain the main health and safety considerations.
3. Warm-ups and cool downs are an important part of any exercise programme. Describe why these must be used, and their purpose.
4. Using your knowledge of exercise programmes, design a six-week training programme for a client of your choice. Then select a different client and design an individual programme for them.
5. Having previously designed a six-week programme, explain why you selected your outlined activities and suggest alternative exercises that may be used.
6. What factors must you consider when delivering a safe and effective session?
7. What is the purpose of a performance review?
8. How can a performance review be conducted?
9. What is a risk assessment and why should it be performed?
10. What is screening, and what information should be collected?

edexcel

Assignment tips

- Remember that leading exercise sessions are meant to be fun. Enjoy the experience and you are far more likely to see improvements in your skills and techniques as well as those that you are leading.
- When practising a practical activity, work at your own pace. Everyone has different strengths and so will develop at different speeds. Do not be too hard on yourself if you do not achieve what you want first time.
- Support your peers and they will support you. Work together giving each other tips and encouragement.
- Learn from your teachers and instructors. They will all be experienced and have plenty to teach you. Talk to them and gather information from them to assist with your assignments. Evaluate their performances.
- Use websites to help you gather research material. They contain plenty of useful information.
- Ensure that you read the assignment briefs properly. Take your time and ensure you are happy with the task set for you. If not ask your tutor for more help.
- Make sure you attempt all parts of the assignment briefs. If you only attempt the pass criteria this is all you will achieve. Talk to your tutor if you're not sure.

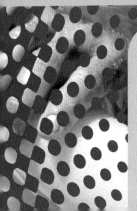

16 Exercise for specific groups

The government's drive for increasing the health of the nation means that the general population are aware of the benefits of exercise. In this unit you will learn about the professional organisations which are responsible for delivering exercise programmes for specific groups, each with their individual needs.

These groups are children and young people, elderly, pregnant women and new mothers, disabled people and referred clients. Exercise has many benefits, but the type of exercise you might take up can differ very greatly from someone else. You will discover how exercise for specific groups is provided in your local area and will examine the exercise referral process.

In this unit you will also learn about the physiological and psychological benefits that exercise has for each group, the importance of adapting activities to suit the needs of individuals and exercise prescription guidelines. You will learn how to plan, deliver and review an exercise session for a chosen group.

Learning outcomes

After completing this unit you should:

1. know about the provision of exercise for specific groups
2. know the benefits of exercise for different specific groups
3. be able to prescribe exercise for specific groups
4. be able to plan, deliver and review an exercise session for a specific group.

Assessment and grading criteria

This table shows you what you must do in order to achieve a pass, merit or distinction grade, and where you can find activities in this book to help you.

To achieve a **pass** grade the evidence must show that you are able to:	To achieve a **merit** grade the evidence must show that, in addition to the pass criteria, you are able to:	To achieve a **distinction** grade the evidence must show that, in addition to the pass and merit criteria, you are able to:
P1 describe the provision of exercise for three different specific groups **See Assessment activity 16.1, page 148**	**M1** compare and contrast the provision of exercise for three different specific groups, identifying strengths and areas for improvement **See Assessment activity 16.1, page 148**	**D1** analyse the provision of exercise for three different specific groups providing recommendations relating to identified areas for improvement, and the benefits to specific groups **See Assessment activity 16.1, page 148**
P2 describe the exercise referral process **See Assessment activity 16.1, page 148**		
P3 describe four benefits of exercise to each of three different specific groups **See Assessment activity 16.2, page 155**	**M2** explain four different benefits of exercise to each of three different specific groups **See Assessment activity 16.2, page 155**	
P4 produce safe and effective exercise prescriptions for three different specific groups **See Assessment activity 16.3, page 159**		
P5 plan and deliver an exercise session for a selected specific group, with tutor support **See Assessment activity 16.4, page 166**	**M3** independently plan and deliver an exercise session for a selected specific group, explaining chosen components **See Assessment activity 16.4, page 166**	**D2** independently plan and deliver an exercise session for a selected specific group, justifying chosen components **See Assessment activity 16.4, page 166**
P6 review the planning and delivery of an exercise session for a specific group, describing strengths and areas for improvement **See Assessment activity 16.4, page 166**		

How you will be assessed

This unit will be assessed by an internal assignment that will be designed and marked by the tutor at your centre. Your assessment could be in the form of

- presentations
- written assignments
- case studies
- planning sessions
- delivering sessions.

Archie, 17 years old, trains regularly at the local athletics club

This unit has helped me plan and deliver an exercise programme for a group of clients with specific needs. It was interesting to gain knowledge of the provision of exercise for such a wide variety of people. This knowledge enabled me to analyse the provision of exercise for specific groups in my home town. After visiting a health centre, my local GP and health clubs, and talking to different practitioners, I understood the exercise referral process and the real benefits of exercise for specific groups. I needed to understand the needs of specific groups.

Observing practitioners working with specific groups and individuals on referral programmes helped me to design and deliver my exercise session. I enjoyed teaching my group from a residential care home and was very pleased with the feedback I got from my tutor and other people doing the unit.

Over to you!

1. Which part of the unit do you think will be difficult to research?
2. Will you enjoy visiting, questioning and even working alongside professionals in their workplace?
3. Can you organise some observation sessions of specific groups to enhance your learning?

1. Know about the provision of exercise for specific groups

Warm-up

What kinds of specific groups are there?
Make a list of specific groups and then in pairs write down the five most important benefits of exercise for one of the named groups. Get into larger groups and agree on the main benefit.

1.1 Specific groups

Groups can be divided into different categories depending on the age, condition and physical ability of the people within the group.

Specific groups are those which have something unique to that group, for example, an antenatal group is one in which all the women are pregnant.

People with disabilities

A person may have an impairment that means they require a wheelchair but they may still be able to exercise independently. You have probably heard of the following terms:

- wheelchair bound
- visually impaired
- hearing impaired
- physically impaired
- learning impaired.

People with disabilities have a wide variety of exercise needs depending on the individual.

Antenatal

This group is pregnant women. The **antenatal** period is from conception to birth. Exercise during pregnancy helps women to stay healthy and keep their weight gain within a safe range. However, there are certain restrictions on what kind of exercise they should do to keep them and their baby safe. A pregnancy can be divided into first, second and third trimesters. This will be important when you are organising and planning exercise sessions for this group later in the unit.

Post-natal

This group of women have just had their babies. Some women have trouble bringing their abdomen back to its original size after having a baby and certain exercises can help them tone this area. However, you would not expect a woman who has recently had a caesarean to exercise at the same level as someone who has given birth without undergoing surgery. **Post-natal** exercise can start after the six week check-up with permission from the health practitioner.

Key terms

Antenatal – relating to pregnancy, this is the period from conception to birth.

Post-natal – this relates to the period after childbirth.

Post-natal classes encourage mums to swim with their babies. Why?

Talk with a partner about the importance of play for children.

Older adults

Older people used to be defined as those who had reached retirement age or older. Now, older adults are defined as people aged 50 or over. Individuals do not grow old in the same way and so this group can have a wide variety of exercise needs. The main providers of exercise for this specific group are classes run by the local authority at leisure centres, within private health clubs, voluntary groups and partnerships. The range of activities is vast but so too is the range of possible medical conditions, ability levels and interests of the clients.

Children and young people

This group is defined as 4 to 14-year-olds. There are lots of points to consider about this group. Girls and boys have different body shapes. Boys are larger than girls and usually have less body fat. Boys who mature early tend to be strong and more naturally physically able than those with average or delayed maturity, whereas girls who mature early are generally less naturally physically able than those who are delayed in maturity, who tend to have leaner physiques. So boys and girls show physical ability at different stages of development and the onset of puberty can create changes.

Referred clients

This group of people includes those who have been asked to join a fitness and exercise programme by their doctor or another healthcare professional. There can be many reasons why someone is referred by a doctor or health specialist to a referral programme.

1.2 Provision

Providers

Providers are organisations which offer exercise opportunities, usually under guidance, for specific groups. Providers may be found in the public, private and voluntary sector and partnerships will form within local organisations.

- **Public sector organisations** receive their funds from central and local government. Providers in this sector will be schools, local authority-run leisure centres, swimming pools, youth clubs and National Health Service (NHS) schemes.

- **The private sector** consists of commercially-run organisations that aim to make a profit. Private health clubs, private leisure centres, private physiotherapists, sports therapists, personal trainers, football clubs and rugby clubs come under this heading.

- **Voluntary providers** have charitable status and are run by volunteers, although some have paid employees. Voluntary organisations do not aim to make a profit and any profit is reinvested into the provider. An example of a voluntary provider is the YMCA. The YMCA offers many opportunities for young people with excellent facilities and coaches.

- **Partnerships** occur when two or more of the sectors above come together to provide opportunities for exercise. For example, football clubs in partnership with the FA have set up initiatives for young people and adults, and local authorities work in partnership with voluntary sector groups such as the British Heart Foundation to provide rehabilitation programmes for heart patients.

Types of provision for specific groups

Primary Care Trusts work closely with surgeries to provide a GP referral pathway for inactive patients with established forms of disease. The Primary Care Trusts provide funding for the scheme and work in partnership with local authorities to provide opportunities for people to become healthier by being more active. Providers of exercise include sports centres, leisure centres and clinics. GPs, practice nurses, hospital consultants, physiotherapists and dieticians may all refer a patient onto an exercise programme (but always through the patient's GP).

A tailored exercise programme is devised for the client who will take part in a health assessment at the beginning and end of a 12-week programme. Once the programme is completed, clients will be encouraged to continue with regular exercise through the Active Lifestyle for All (ALFA) programmes. These provide opportunities for everyone to get involved in exercise in a fun and friendly environment. The programmes provide walking, cycling and swimming groups and such schemes may be funded by councils and Primary Care Trusts. ALFA programmes can also offer dance and a variety of sports programmes, some free and others for a small fee, by private enterprises, for example, Burnley Community Enterprises Ltd. Facilities such as leisure centres, swimming pools, playing fields, parks, schools and clubs are provided for the use of specific groups.

The NHS provides facilities at hospitals, clinics and doctors' surgeries for exercise for antenatal and post-natal women. Schemes such as wellbeing classes,

water aerobics, low impact aerobics, stretching, toning and breathing exercise classes are provided at leisure centres, swimming pools and clinics.

Exercise on prescription classes are run for specific identified groups referred by their doctors to sports therapists/instructors who work at leisure centres or with other appropriate organisations. Fitness suites in leisure centres are equipped with machinery and personnel for exercise on referral schemes. Hospitals have specialist equipment for cardiac rehabilitation.

Children and young people may have classes provided through Community Youth Provision which is an initiative started in conjunction with Sport England. Additional equipment aimed at providing teachers and coaches with options around the inclusion of young people with disabilities is provided by Active England.

Private health schemes, for example BUPA, provide opportunities for a variety of specific groups. They provide initiatives such as walking groups, exercise on prescription, prenatal and post-natal classes, over 50s programmes, swimming, cycling and running.

Exercise provision includes the following range of activities:

- aqua mobility
- long-term condition circuit classes
- healthy walks
- mighty movers
- rowing.

Adult further education classes also provide a range of exercise opportunities for the over 50s including aerobics classes, walking and golf.

Activity: Public and private provision

Visit public and private sector organisations that provide exercise for specific groups. Describe the difference between a public sector and private sector organisation. Identify the specific groups who use the organisations for exercise programmes. Interview an instructor from each sector and find out if the instructor believes there is sufficient provision of exercise for specific groups in their sector, for example the public sector. Do any of these organisations offer referral programmes?

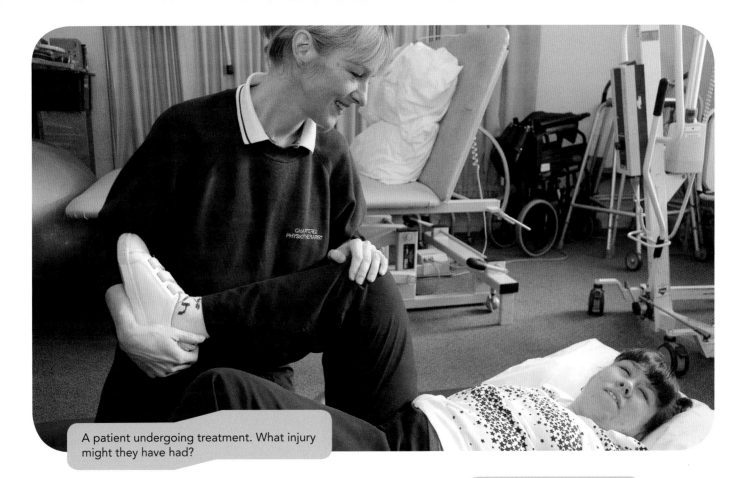

A patient undergoing treatment. What injury might they have had?

1.3 Exercise referral process

The referral process introduces the referred client to trained people and facilities where structured and individually tailored physical activity programmes can be designed and delivered. The process is initiated by a primary care practitioner who will refer an individual to a programme that encourages physical activity or exercise. It will involve an initial assessment and lead to a programme tailored to individual needs, as well as providing monitoring and supervision.

Initial screening procedures

Screening is a legal procedure. The purpose of initial screening of participants is to identify:

- those who have symptoms of a disease
- those who are at increased risk of disease.

There are three stages to the screening process:

1. Identify participants who need medical checks.
2. Completion of a consent form on which the participant and their doctor will provide information.
3. Completion of a questionnaire by the participant.

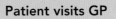

Patient visits GP

↓

GP recommends exercise on prescription

↓

Patient makes first visit to leisure centre

↓

A professional makes an assessment of the client

↓

Exercise begins under supervision of a qualified instructor

Figure 16.1: A patient goes through the exercise referral process.

Referral professionals

Referral professionals can be sports therapists, physiotherapists, GPs or consultants. Sports therapists train to work with people who have sport injuries. Physiotherapists play a big part in the healthcare system, particularly in rehabilitation programmes and intermediate care.

Although therapists and nurses may initiate exercise referral schemes, the GP is responsible for the overall management of the programme of exercise.

Referral conditions

Referral schemes aim to encourage and support people to engage in regular physical activity, often working in partnership with primary care and leisure services. The two most common reasons for referral, in addition to sedentary behaviour, are musculoskeletal conditions and cardiovascular risk factors. Reasons for referral are explored in more detail below.

- **Obesity** – Active for Health Schemes include referral schemes for clients with conditions that can improve through physical activity, including obesity. The scheme is designed to assist the client in beginning a healthy and active lifestyle. Kids Active 4 Health is a scheme which targets obesity at its early stages to prevent it continuing into adult life. This type of intervention is important for improving children's health and wellbeing. Slimming on referral is a scheme set up in partnership with local services and Slimming World.

- **Sedentary people** should start an exercise programme slowly and choose an activity that they enjoy, such as walking. Thirty minutes on five or six days a week is ideal. Eligible participants can be recruited during routine consultations and the suggested programmes take place in leisure centres, swimming pools or private gyms.

- **A cardiac rehabilitation** programme:
  - aids recovery
  - prevents the problem getting worse
  - reduces the risk of further heart problems.

  The levels of cardiac rehabilitation service provision within the UK vary. There are hospital-based supervised cardiac rehabilitation programmes providing early, low level and short-term exercise training programmes which can improve the cardiac and physical function status of patients. If there is no medical facility with a cardiac rehabilitation centre, then the exercise rehabilitation therapist can work closely with the client's local fitness facility.

- **Pulmonary disease** includes conditions like chronic bronchitis and emphysema. Chronic obstructive pulmonary disease is usually caused by smoking.

- **Metabolic disease** comprises a large class of metabolic disorders. In most of these, problems arise due to the accumulation of substances which are toxic and interfere with normal function. An example of a metabolic disease would be a person with a defect in their carbohydrate pathways. Exercise referral process would be through the GP.

- **Injury** – if you have suffered an injury, you will know that exercise is a vital part of the rehabilitation process. An athlete will receive a course of treatment from a physiotherapist but will also be set specific strengthening and flexibility exercises. Always ask your doctor before exercising after an injury.

- **Arthritis** is from the Greek words 'arthro' meaning joint and 'itis' meaning inflammation. Arthritis disease includes rheumatoid arthritis and psoriatic arthritis, which is septic arthritis caused by infection in the joints. Osteoarthritis mainly affects older people and is the degeneration of joint cartilage. Research has shown that moderate exercise can bring a wide range of benefits to people with arthritis. Exercise is seen as an essential part of pain management.

- **Osteoporosis** – our bones begin to thin after the age of 30. With this condition a person can break a bone following a simple knock or fall because their bones have become fragile. With osteoporosis the bones have become too porous. The wrist, hips, hands and spine are the sites where these fractures occur most commonly.

- **Mobility problems** – exercise referral schemes for people with mobility problems are usually water-based. Schemes offer 12 weeks of supervised water-based mobility exercises that are ideal for those with joint pains and mobility problems such as arthritis or recovering from injuries. Active Lifestyle Exercise referral schemes provide a variety of programmes to meet the needs of defined medical problems such as mobility, and these assist the individual to become more physically active.

- **Multiple sclerosis** is an autoimmune disease which attacks the central nervous system. Exercise referral schemes have been set up to provide exercise programmes for people with this disease. People with neurological conditions can be referred independently with written agreement from their GP to schemes at council-run leisure centres and gyms.

- **Mental illness** may impact on the way a person thinks, behaves and interacts with other people. Mental illness includes the following disorders: bipolar disorder, depression, anxiety disorders, eating disorders and panic.

Take it further

Visit a surgery

Visit your local surgery or clinic and research the procedures for referring a client onto an exercise referral scheme. Imagine that a patient has asked their GP if they can be referred on to an exercise programme. What is his role in the referral scheme? What exercise programmes are available to them in your area and who will take care of them while on the programme?

Exercise prescription

One of the roles of the National Health Service is to help people take more exercise, especially when they are at risk of illness or recovering from it. Exercise prescription schemes provide opportunities for fitness professionals to work in partnership with GPs and other health professionals on schemes that target people who do not normally take exercise. Primary Care Trusts incorporate exercise programmes into the rehabilitation programme of, for example, coronary heart disease, hypertension and falls, particularly among older people.

A person is prescribed an exercise programme by a healthcare professional that matches the frequency, intensity, duration and type of exercise to meet their fitness and health needs. There is a professional register for exercise and fitness professionals in the UK. This is supported by Sport England and operated by the Fitness Industry Association. The quality assurance framework set up in 2000 for exercise referral recommends registration as a prerequisite for exercise instructors working at this level.

Recommended guidelines

Below are the national guidelines set up by the National Assurance Quality Framework for Referral Schemes.

- Healthcare professionals are referral specialists who should keep a regularly updated file of local physical opportunities and support groups for their prospective clients.

- Referral specialists will select the most appropriate strategy to encourage exercise outside the programme. There should always be a follow-up briefing at the end of the programme.

- The exercise programme must be tailored to the participant's needs and the professional's skills.

- Records of progress have to be filed or a logbook kept by the participant.

- Records of all communication must be securely filed within the exercise setting.

- There should be a mid-point assessment (after five to six weeks).

Remember

Children should exercise for 60 minutes every day. This exercise should get their heart beating faster than usual. Why? Because children need to burn off calories to prevent them storing up excess fat in their body which can lead to heart disease, cancer and type 2 diabetes. Exercise will also keep their bones healthy, encourage muscle strength and flexibility.

Monitoring

The monitoring process consists of pre-assessment, the exercise programme, post-assessment and evaluation. If a client does not attend the pre-assessment, the exercise professional will follow this up with the client's GP. During the 12 week programme the instructor will guide the client through the individually designed exercises. If the client does not attend for two consecutive weeks then this too will be followed up by the exercise professional. All patients are provided with a programme review and a client satisfaction questionnaire. They will then be encouraged to join mainstream activity by joining activities through the Get Active schemes.

There is strong evidence to support the positive impact of physical activity on a variety of health problems. National standards for GP exercise referral schemes were published in 2001. This has improved the delivery of existing referral schemes and encouraged the development of effective high-quality projects nationwide.

Assessment activity 16.1   P1 M1 D1 P2   BTEC

Mrs Johnson (35) is five months pregnant and well. Mr Johnson (40) is diabetic but lives a healthy lifestyle. Their two children, Laura (10) and Daniel (8, and partially sighted), both enjoy sport. Granddad (74) is healthy while Gran's (76) activities are limited because she has osteoporosis. Choose three members of the family who you would like to help.

1. Having researched exercise provision, describe where three members of the family can go to find provision for their exercise needs. This can be written or verbal. **P1**

2. Compare and contrast the opportunities available for exercise provision for the three different groups. Identify strengths and areas for improvement. **M1**

3. Write a short report based on your findings. Detail the information discovered about three specific groups analysing the provision of exercise for them. Make recommendations based on your findings relating to the areas for improvement and the benefits to your selected groups. **D1**

4. Design a leaflet which describes all Mrs Johnson needs to know about the exercise referral process before she visits her GP. **P2**

Grading tips

- To attain **P1** you need to give a clear and full description and include all the relevant points.

- To attain **M1** explore if there is a group that has less opportunity for exercise. Are there groups that can find provision easily? Don't forget to support your opinions with examples.

- To attain **D1** consider your selected groups carefully by examining your research and discuss the exercise opportunities in your area for them. Think about how each group benefits from exercise. How could these benefits be enhanced? What might be done to increase provision?

- To attain **P2** gather information about exercise referral schemes from your local GP, health centre, leisure centre or other private health clubs in the area.

PLTS

When you research the provision of exercise for different specific groups and the exercise referral process you can develop your skills as an **independent enquirer**.

Functional skills

When you research the provision of exercise for three different specific groups and the referral process you could provide evidence of your **ICT** and **English** skills.

2.   Know about the benefits of exercise for different specific groups

2.1 Physiological benefits

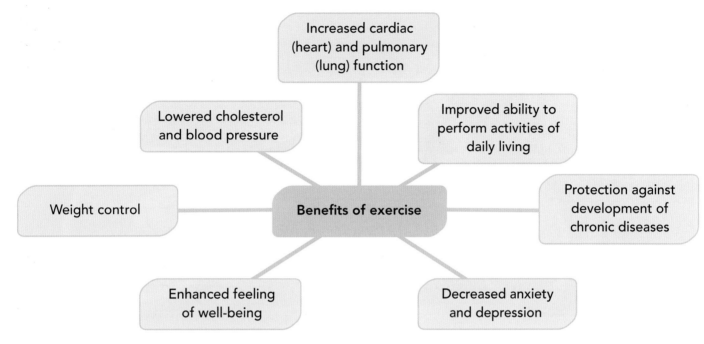

Figure 16.2: Discuss the physiological benefits of exercise.

Antenatal

Recent studies have identified several benefits of exercise during pregnancy, including:

- less backache
- increased wellbeing of the mother-to-be
- increased wellbeing of the foetus
- improved sleep patterns
- improved muscle tone in the upper body and abdominal area.

The better the cardiovascular system, the more stamina a woman will have for birth. Exercise helps circulatory problems such as fatigue and varicose veins. Good circulation supplies the baby with more oxygen and nutrients because the woman and the baby are linked by the placenta. Exercise reduces the problem of haemorrhoids, cramps and constipation.

During pregnancy there are increased fluid volumes and retention and reduced blood flow back to the heart. Exercise in water helps improve venous blood flow reducing swelling in the lower limbs. As a woman's body grows during pregnancy, her centre of gravity changes and this affects her posture and balance. Better muscle strength and coordination help her to adjust to her changing shape.

Post-natal

Benefits of post-natal exercise include:

- speedier healing and recovery from the birthing process
- a faster return to the woman's pre-pregnancy shape
- an increase in energy levels to cope with the demands of motherhood
- reduced likelihood of stress and depression.

Post-natal exercises help to regain shape but ligaments and joints will still be soft for at least three months following birth, so vigorous stretching and high impact activities should be avoided. During pregnancy

The weekly pram push. Why is walking good exercise for new mothers?

the weight of the baby will have altered the woman's centre of gravity. This, combined with the softening effects of the hormone relaxin on her ligaments, may have led to bad posture. Through exercise she can strengthen her abdominal and back muscles. This improves posture and reduces her chances of backache while carrying the newborn baby.

A strengthened cardiovascular system will give the mother more endurance and stronger muscles allowing her to accomplish tasks with less effort. The new mother will have more energy to get through the day.

A woman who has exercised during pregnancy will not have to lose a significant amount of weight. Post-natal exercise helps the mother to lose weight and regain her shape (although she should not expect too much too soon). Through regular exercise the mother will feel good about herself.

Children and young people

The benefits of exercise to children will vary according to the activity. Children learn by doing, being motivated, achieving, through encouragement and by copying others. Children learn and develop skills by:

- understanding the task
- performing and practising the task
- receiving feedback from performance which reinforces learning

Exercise is fun! What do children learn from team sports?

- practising the skill until it becomes automatic
- evaluating their performance and completing the self-assessment process.

Sport may help children to work together and develop positive attitudes and fair play. Children need to play sport in a positive atmosphere where participation and effort is as good as winning. As they become older they learn to cooperate with others, enjoy teamwork and there is a greater awareness of their own and others' skills.

Motor skills can be divided into fine motor skills and gross motor skills. Fine motor skills allow children to develop the ability to write, draw and manipulate. Gross motor skills require balance and coordination. Exercise increases motor skills. Examples of gross motor skills include running, jumping, catching and throwing.

Referred clients

Referred clients are more likely to belong to specific groups like cardiac rehabilitation, mobility, exercises on prescription or accident.

Referred clients increase fitness by exercising. The three main types of exercise which increase fitness are flexibility (stretching) exercises, strengthening (resistance) exercises and cardiovascular (aerobic exercise) like walking, dancing, swimming or cycling.

Rehabilitation programmes used to be suggested for the young who needed to return to work after an illness or surgery. Today, with improved programmes and close monitoring, rehabilitation programmes are an option for people of all ages and with any form of disease or injury.

Studies show that older adults who exercise three or more times a week have a significantly lower risk of developing dementia than adults who exercised less (*Annals of Internal Medicine, 2006*). Aerobic exercise, done for a period of three months, can improve elasticity in the arteries of older adults who suffer from type 2 diabetes. This reduces the risk associated with cardiovascular diseases. Other studies have investigated exercise reducing invasive cancers.

Some specific groups need to work with qualified referral specialists such as sports therapists, physiotherapists or on an appropriate scheme recommended by their doctor. Exercise can enable these groups to manage and sometimes improve their condition.

2.2 Psychological benefits

The psychological benefits of exercise include improved self-esteem, mental alertness and an increased perception of acceptance by others. Exercise sharpens your brain and improves focus and concentration.

Benefits also include a reduction in depression and when feeling stressed people exercise to relieve their anxieties. In the early 1980s a neuropeptide (a brain chemical) was discovered which showed remarkable morphine-like qualities. Small amounts of beta-endorphin promoted feelings of exhilaration and reduced feelings of depression and anxiety. Exercise is now a major part of stress reduction programmes and self-care for depression.

People who exercise regularly suffer less from anxiety. They are able to concentrate more and sleep deeply at night. Regular exercise decreases the level of stress hormones released during stressful responses such as anger and fear.

Case study: Exercise brings rewards

Sheila Barker, aged 68, has always been healthy and active but lately she has been feeling tired and lacking in energy. Winter is approaching and she is dreading the long, dark nights. Her friend Margaret is a member of her local gym and attends regularly twice a week. She follows one of these sessions with a swim at the local pool. Margaret invites Sheila to accompany her and, after much persuasion, Sheila agrees. The following spring Sheila looks back over the winter months and wonders where the time has gone. She is now an active member of her local gym,

attends a weekly coffee morning and has found a new group of friends. She devotes one day a week to working in a charity shop. Sheila has even found time to start her spring cleaning.

1. **Describe four benefits which Sheila has gained through exercising at the gym.**

2. **Could Sheila have gained the same benefits from joining a 'book club'? Explain the benefits gained and give details to support your answer.**

When you are in control of your body size and weight through exercise your self-confidence and self-esteem are increased. The strength and endurance gained from regular exercise makes you more confident about your daily tasks such as shopping, gardening and meeting other people.

2.3 Specific groups

Older adults

There are physiological benefits for older adults:

- Exercise can reduce pain and stiffness.
- It can build strong muscles around the joints.
- Exercise can build stronger bones.
- There will be more flexibility and endurance.
- The person will feel better because they will have more energy.
- Exercise aids sleep because the person is more active during the day.
- Exercise controls weight.

Take it further

Healthy bones

Have you ever noticed an older person who is very round shouldered or stooped and begins to look smaller? Can you explain why they stoop and how exercise can be beneficial to them? Research how many hip operations are performed in the UK per year on older people. What could you do now to build and maintain healthy bones?

People with disabilities

In order to participate in and benefit from exercise, a person must be able to physically perform the required skill.

There are different ways and levels of performing the same task. The physiological and psychological benefits can be similar to those covered in the section for children or older adults, as many people with disabilities are included in mainstream exercise with adaptations.

Wheelchair-bound people can physically perform many tasks. Wheelchair-bound games are very popular. Discuss the many skills which can be performed while in a wheelchair.

Antenatal and post-natal exercise

Moderate exercise that makes pregnant women feel slightly out of breath is good especially if the body is used to exercise. Being fit is excellent preparation for the physical effort required during labour. Many obstetricians recommend that both aerobic and resistance exercise is reduced in the third trimester. However, others say a reduction in exercise after the first two trimesters results in the mother gaining unnecessary weight and foetal fat mass.

Pilates is an excellent exercise programme and can be started by mothers in varying post-natal stages to assist recovery.

Children and young people

Children learn by taking part and doing exercises. All children should be set activities where they can achieve and be successful. This means that they remain motivated and on task. You should always encourage children, allow them to experiment, copy others and make mistakes. The motivation for doing exercise comes from enjoyment.

Referred clients

Many referred clients are suffering stress as a result of pain. How does exercise help them to manage their pain? Some of the key issues are explored below.

- **Obesity** – being overweight forces the heart to work harder. Exercise will improve heart efficiency, lower blood pressure and lower blood cholesterol levels. It will also reduce weight, maintain weight loss and fight obesity. Men tend to lose abdominal fat which lowers their risk of heart disease faster than reducing body fat. Women who undergo aerobic exercise and strength training lose fat in their arms and legs. Obesity is a risk factor for heart disease. Obese adults should always consult their doctor before starting an exercise programme.

Activity: School meals

Did your school meals help you to keep a healthy body weight? Explain why.

Why is diet so important to children and young adults? Research the differences Jamie Oliver has brought to school meals.

- **Sedentary living** increases the risk of chronic health conditions. The physical benefits of exercise will indirectly influence sedentary people's psychological wellbeing, as exercise eliminates nervous energy and aids relaxation. The number of overweight children and adolescents has accelerated over the last ten years and children now show risk factors for chronic health conditions related to their sedentary lifestyle.

- **Cardiac** – exercise strengthens the cardiovascular and respiratory systems and increases fitness. The circulation of the blood goes through the heart and blood vessels. A build up of plaque in your arteries is caused by cholesterol and other products in the bloodstream. This can interrupt the blood flow and cause life-threatening damage to the cardiovascular system.

- **Pulmonary or metabolic disease** – clinical research has shown that pulmonary or metabolic disease like asthma, emphysema and bronchitis can be improved by exercise. Studies have shown that regular exercise helps people with serious lung disease reduce anxiety and depression and improves endurance and some intellectual functions. A person with a metabolic disease has difficulty exercising. They become easily tired. For this group, prolonged moderate exercise may not be beneficial and may be painful. Professional therapists should work with the individual to satisfy their exercise needs.

- **Injuries** – a study found that exercise had benefits for individuals with traumatic brain injuries. Those who exercised were found to be less depressed and their general state of health was better. It was found that exercise improved mood and general health but did not affect aspects of disability and handicap. People who suffer from back pain have found that exercise and physical therapy aids recovery. Active exercise, as well as creating the physiological conditions for the injured area to heal, relieves emotional distress and also aids recovery.

- **Arthritis** – arthritis sufferers benefit from flexibility exercises that involve basic stretching movements to improve their range of motion. After feeling comfortable with these, endurance exercise such as weight training and cardiovascular (aerobic) exercise can begin. If there is a great amount of pain, exercise programmes in water are better because the body's buoyancy reduces stress on the hips, knees and spine. A qualified instructor will assess their specific exercise and joint protection needs.

accidents. Muscles can be strengthened and bone density maintained. This decreases the risk of fractures should an older adult fall. Muscle strengthening increases synovial fluid, which increases flexibility and reduces the risk of falling.

Mental health – evidence shows that supervised programme of exercise on prescription can be as effective as antidepressants in treating mild depression and exercise has far fewer side effects. Exercise releases endorphins that make us feel good physically and mentally. Being active is one of the best things you can do to protect yourself against depression and anxiety.

Janice really enjoys her referral programme for osteoporosis. Can you suggest why?

> **Remember**
>
> A referral professional will help the client to get started on the programme which could improve their quality of life.

> **Activity: How good is your balance?**
>
> Stand on one leg and stay as still as possible for as long as possible. Are you completely balanced? Is your body still? Could you explain why some people can remain balanced and others would find it very difficult? Practise balancing activities. How good are you at balancing?

- **Osteoporosis** – three types of exercise will bring benefit to osteoporosis sufferers:
  - strength-training exercises
  - weight-bearing aerobic activities
  - flexibility exercises.
- **Mobility problems** – strength training can work directly on bones to slow mineral loss. Weight-bearing exercises could be walking, dancing or gardening. These exercises work on the bones in your legs, hips and lower spine to reduce mineral loss. Flexibility exercises increase joint mobility. If joints are stiff, then abdominal and chest muscles tighten and this pulls the body forward giving the stooped position. Chest and shoulder stretches benefit posture.

Balance exercises improve agility and flexibility. Older adults should safeguard and improve their balance. Lack of balance is the cause of many

Assessment activity 16.2

P3 **M2** **BTEC**

On your recommendation, the Johnson family begins classes. Laura joins a gymnastics class and the swimming club, while Daniel becomes a member of a football team and a running club. Mr Johnson joins a gym and plays badminton and Mrs Johnson is referred to a prenatal exercise group and also enjoys taking the children swimming. Granddad is now playing golf and walking. Finally, Grandma has joined a rambling group and also an exercise on prescription class at the local gym. The family is very interested in the benefits they will gain from exercise.

1. Create a wall chart that identifies the same three specific groups chosen in Assessment activity 16.1 through photographs, images or drawings. Next to the images, describe four different benefits of exercises for each group. **P3**

2. Add another section to the report you compiled for Assessment activity 16.1 in which you discuss the benefits of exercise for the chosen groups, and provide further evidence as to why these groups should have many opportunities locally for exercise. **M2**

Grading tips

- To attain **P3** you can select the same three members of the family as you selected for Assessment activity 16.1. Can you describe how each one of them has benefited from exercise? Remember to describe four different benefits for each.

- To attain **M2** you have to explain that exercise does bring benefits to your chosen groups. Having identified and described the benefits, you need to give a fuller explanation of each one to convince the family to look for opportunities to exercise for their specific needs.

PLTS

When you research four benefits of exercise for each of the three specific groups independently, and create a wall chart, you can develop your skills as an **independent enquirer**, **team worker** and **creative thinker**.

Functional skills

When you research four benefits of exercise for each of the three specific groups independently you could provide evidence of your skills in **ICT** and **English**.

3. Be able to prescribe exercise for specific groups

3.1 Exercise prescription

This is an exercise programme designed specifically for an individual. An exercise prescription should be FITT – it should include:

Frequency – how often the client exercises.

Intensity – how hard the client exercises.

Time – how long the client exercises.

Type – the type of exercise the client is doing, for example, walking or running.

When the client exercises at sufficient intensity, time and frequency, their body will improve and they will see a change in their weight, body fat percentage, cardiovascular endurance and strength.

3.2 Contraindications

A contraindication is when a treatment should not be used because it may be harmful to the client/patient. Exercise prescription may have dangerous effects on certain individuals within specific groups. A doctor must be consulted regarding exercise for all medical conditions. More information on contraindications can be found in Unit 15 Instructing physical activity and exercise, page 115.

Absolute contraindications

Certain exercises would be absolutely contraindicated for the following specific groups.

- **High blood pressure** is a serious condition that can lead to coronary disease, heart failure, stroke and other health related problems.
- **Tachycardia** is a rapid heart beat. This is usually defined as greater than 100 beats per minute.
- **Uncontrolled medical conditions** – exercise programmes would only be prescribed when the doctor knew that the patient had the illness under control. These include:
  - **asthma** – a condition which affects the airways (the small tubes which carry air in and out of the lungs)
  - **diabetes** – a disease in which the body does not properly produce or use insulin (the hormone needed to convert sugar, starches and other nutrients into energy)
  - **acute heart failure** – common symptoms include anxiety, tachycardia and dyspnoea. Dyspnoea is difficulty in breathing often associated with lung or heart disease. Pallor and hypotension are present in severe cases. These cases may be related to extensive myocardial infarction (another term for heart attack), sustained cardiac arrhythmias, when the heartbeat is too slow, too rapid or irregular, or mechanical problems like acute papillary muscle rupture (papillary muscles are small muscles that anchor the heart valves in the heart)
  - **unstable angina** – a chest pain produced when the heart muscle is not getting enough blood flow. Unstable angina is often caused by a partial blockage of the artery.

Specific to certain groups

- **High impact exercise** – examples include running and jumping. High impact exercising is one of the things you can do to help build and maintain healthy bones. Activities for bone health are generally described as weight-bearing. Weight-bearing exercises put stress on the skeletal structure and your bones react by supporting the stress. Walking and weightlifting fall into this category, but current studies are showing that some higher impact activity can make a more significant contribution to bone health. It makes sense if you think about it – when you lift weights your muscles react by becoming

stronger and toned. If you jump up and down, your bones react similarly. Performing high impact activity can also have other benefits. Some high impact exercises can also improve coordination, agility, balance, and endurance. The jarring and intensity of higher impact activities means you need to closely evaluate if it is appropriate for you to start an exercise routine that involves high impact movement. If you are currently diagnosed as having osteoporosis, the risk factors (such as fractures) may outweigh the benefits. Activities that are lower in impact could be more appropriate in this case and a discussion with your GP about an exercise plan is vital. If you have a cardiac condition, an autoimmune disorder, any joint problems, or other medical conditions, consulting your GP before starting a high impact exercise routine should also be considered the first step. Obese clients should avoid high impact aerobic activity and take part in non weight-bearing exercise, for example, water aerobics and swimming.

- **High intensity exercise** – this is not recommended for beginners and can contribute to injuries in individuals who are not prepared for a strenuous workout. If you are just starting an exercise programme, a slow and steady progression of longer and less intense exercise is a better option. Children training for teams could be involved in high intensity exercise. Low workouts of short duration and frequent intervals would be more beneficial to patients with pulmonary disease than longer duration and few intervals.
- **Heavy weights** – cardiac patients are usually asked to refrain from lifting heavy weights but moderate strength training is safe and beneficial for people at low risk. Clients with back pain would only increase the weights to their tolerance level and under guidance.
- **Abdominal exercise** – specific static abdominal and pelvic floor exercises are beneficial in pregnancy but only if you exercise frequently. It is not advisable to begin a new activity during pregnancy apart from Aqua Natal (water based exercises) or gentle walking. If you wish to begin exercising outside of these activities, seek medical advice. Lower abdominal exercise is very effective for back pain. Obesity and a sedentary lifestyle have increased the number of people suffering with back pain. If you lack strength and stability in your core muscles then you risk muscle strain or weakness, ligament damage and disc problems.

Take it further

Specific exercise for specific groups

What group of clients would be prescribed high intensity exercise? Can you suggest a safe high intensity exercise for this group?

A sports therapist prescribed exercises using weights for his client. What specific group do you think this client belonged to and can you suggest an exercise which would have been suitable for their problem?

Abdominal exercises were prescribed by a GP for his patient. Why might this patient need this form of exercise? Produce a safe and effective prescription for this patient.

3.3 Specific groups

Older adults

For older adults there are four types of exercise that are key to staying healthy and independent. These are strength, balance, stretching and endurance exercises.

People with disabilities

For those who have disabilities, t'ai chi and yoga can both be performed from a chair or bed and many other forms of exercise can be adapted for them.

Antenatal and post-natal exercise

Antenatal and post-natal exercise can be prescribed in the form of yoga which improves breathing, strength and stamina. Many antenatal and post-natal exercise plans include Kegel exercises, specific exercises to strengthen the pelvic floor muscles. There are also schemes which provide aerobic classes for pregnant women and most health clubs run these. Swimming is encouraged as this keeps the body toned without putting weight and stress on the joints. Walks are organised for new mothers called 'pram pushes', which help them to regain their shape and meet other new mums.

Children and young people

Children and young people need to do at least 60 minutes of physical activity that increases their heart rate every day. This keeps their bones healthy and encourages muscle development. Activities like jumping, skipping, dancing and running will exercise them and protect against brittle bone disease. Swimming is another way of using every muscle group and is good for cardiovascular fitness.

Swimming keeps children fit. What other type of exercise would you encourage for this age group?

Referred clients

- **Obesity** – people with mobility problems are more likely than others to be obese or grossly overweight. Swimming and walking are recommended for those who are overweight. **Sedentary** – walking, gardening, cycling, swimming, football and golf are types of activities in which sedentary people could be involved.

- **Cardiac** – an exercise programme for referred cardiac patients can be divided into three sections:

  Programme 1 – in hospital: the client begins with non-strenuous activities including:
  - sitting up in bed
  - self-care
  - walking
  - limited stair climbing
  - being involved in activities they will face at home.

  Programme 2 – early recovery: exercises introduced will be those that the client can do safely at home (for example, walking).

  Programme 3 – late recovery: the client's exercise regime and lifestyle must become a long-term programme.

- **Pulmonary or metabolic disease** – recent research has shown that intensive work for several months after a stroke, including work on the treadmill, increases aerobic capacity and motor function. Strength exercises have also been found to have beneficial effects in patients with stroke history. Before undergoing an exercise programme, a stroke patient would undergo an electrocardiogram (ECG) as part of a monitoring programme before beginning exercise. The Diabetes Wellness scheme consists of circuit-based exercises adapted to differing levels of fitness and ability.

- **Injury** – if you have a back injury you become aware that back muscles are used in almost any activity – even sitting or standing. Walking and swimming are low impact activities that can be started before back pain has totally resolved, as recommended by your doctor. Others include:
  - gentle stretching
  - strengthening exercises
  - warm water exercises.

Breaks are common injuries. How can you help recovery from a broken leg?

- **Arthritis** – exercises which are beneficial to clients with arthritis include:
  - gentle stretching exercises which can be done every day
  - strengthening exercises (resistance exercise) to make muscles stronger.

Arthritis sufferers need to include aerobic exercise in their programmes. It may begin with 5 minutes three times a week, increasing to 30 minutes. The client would work within their target heart rate. Water exercises are beneficial for people with arthritis.

- **Osteoporosis** – exercises for the neck, hips, back, arms and legs are appropriate for those with osteoporosis and exercises to increase balance to prevent falls and fractures. Weight-bearing and weight training exercises benefit beyond osteoporosis treatment, for example, reduced risk of heart disease, weight management and the prevention of high blood pressure. Calcium, the major component of bones, is not well absorbed unless a demand for it is created through exercise. Walking is a weight-bearing exercise that puts full weight on a person's bones and so reduces the risk of osteoporosis. Exercise will increase muscle strength, improve balance and reduce the risk of falls.

- **Mobility problems** – the following are examples of exercise for the elderly which would help with mobility problems:
  - side stepping – to increase leg and hip strength and balance
  - sitting and getting up and down

  - shoulder shrugs – to strengthen back, stretch chest muscles, and improve posture
  - toe, heel and leg rises – to improve ankle strength for balance
  - eyes closed balance exercises – to improve posture, balance and range of motion.

- **Multiple sclerosis (MS)** – if a client has multiple sclerosis they should check with their doctor before beginning any exercise programme. Water aerobics, swimming, t'ai chi and yoga are examples of exercises that work well for this specific group. People with MS are sensitive to heat, and symptoms become worse when body heat rises therefore swimming keeps them cool.

- **Mental health** – studies have shown that self-esteem improved along with fitness in a four week jogging programme. Other studies showed reductions in trait anxiety and depression when walking and swimming. People with alcohol problems coped better with life stresses after aerobic exercise.

Assessment activity 16.3

P4 · BTEC

Working in groups of three, each person in the group should research a case study which focuses on one specific group. Each person should then share their research with the group and produce safe and effective prescriptions for each specific group. Each prescription could be presented in the form of a teaching manual as examples of individually assessed prescriptions. **P4**

Grading tip

To attain **P4** you must consider three different specific groups and ensure that the exercise prescriptions for these groups are safe and beneficial.

PLTS

By producing safe and effective exercise prescriptions for three different specific groups you can develop your skills as a **creative thinker**, **self-manager**, **effective participator** and **team worker**.

Functional skills

By producing exercise prescriptions for three different specific groups you could provide evidence of your skills in **ICT** and **English**.

4. Be able to plan, deliver and review an exercise session for a specific group

4.1 Planning a session

Aims

These are the goals you are setting for the individuals in your group that they will be able to achieve by the end of the session.

Outcomes

These are the learning outcomes. What will you want your group to have learned at the end of the activity session?

Resources

These can be divided up into three areas: human, facilities and equipment. Human means 'you' because you are leading the session and also anyone else who is there to help you. You must know where your session is taking place, for example on a field, in a sports hall, a fitness room or a church hall. Equipment will depend on your chosen group and topic. You must check equipment for safety, and make sure it is the right equipment for the group. Your resources may include any questionnaires, checklists, and self evaluation sheets for individuals.

Screening and medical history

A simple questionnaire could provide you with details that help you to identify the healthy participants and those who might be at risk and require clearance from their doctor. A PAR-Q is an example of an appropriate questionnaire. Refer to Unit 15 Instructing physical activity and exercise, page 114, for more information on PAR-Qs.

Informed consent

The participant will receive consent from their GP, health professional or other qualified instructor regarding their ability for exercise. The participant will then sign an informed consent form for exercise participation along with the doctor or health professional. Refer to Unit 15 Instructing physical activity and exercise for more information.

Other considerations

There are considerations to take into account before delivering a session.

- **Health and safety** – it must be safe and appropriate. Ask yourself:
  - Have I carried out a risk assessment?
  - Do I know where the nearest telephone is?
  - Do I know where the first aid box is kept?
  - Have I planned an appropriate warm-up? (See pages 116–117.)
  - Is there water available for the participants?
  - Have I checked the condition of the equipment?
  - What are the participants wearing? Are they suitably dressed?
  - Who are the participants? Have all the appropriate checks been made, for example the screening and medical history? (See Unit 15 Instructing physical activity and exercise, page 129.)
  - Do I know the correct procedure for reporting an accident?
- **Contraindications** – some exercise programmes may be dangerous for certain groups, for example, people with high blood pressure. Therefore all information about your session participants must be thoroughly checked.
- **Timing and sequencing of activities** – you must deliver your session in a structured and logical way. If you don't, the participants will not understand or learn. Planning an exercise session helps you to time each section so that you don't spend too much time on one area.
- **Ability level** – no two people have the same abilities. Everyone in your group should have equal opportunity to participate. You may have to adapt exercises and activities to meet individual needs.
- **Marketing** – this is the promotion of your ideas, the possible pricing and the exchange that satisfies the customer.

Take it further

Promoting exercise for older people

Design a poster advertising a specific exercise session for older people. Write a newspaper article analysing the benefits of the exercise programme. Use this to advertise your exercise session for a specific older group. Are you targeting a particular activity?

4.2 Deliver your session

Safe and effective

When planning a safe and effective exercise session you should consider:

- the level of fitness of your participants
- the range of movement of the participants
- their body types
- what kind of exercise they enjoy doing.

You will also consider clothing and footwear, equipment and how it is used, and during the exercise session you should be aware of participants who may over-stretch themselves.

Warm-up

The purpose of a warm-up is to prepare the body for exercise, to improve performance and to protect against injury. The aim of a warm-up is to promote circulation and generate heat. This will take longer with older adults. The warm-up should build up gradually. Warm-ups include pulse raising exercises for older people (circling arms, leg extensions or bending arms at elbows alternately). A pulse raiser for children could be a tag game as a warm-up for a rugby session.

Stretching should be selected according to the type of activity which is to follow. Stretches as part of a warm-up may involve stretching the front of the upper leg, the chest, and the muscles across your back or down the side of your upper body. Joints should not be overworked and support given where necessary, for example a chair or partner.

Session components

In order to deliver your session you will need a plan. Table 16.1 shows the kind of detail it should include.

Table 16.1: Discuss the checklist headings.

Detail	Information
Specific group Number of people Related problems	
Detail of activity	
Venue Time Date	
Number of helpers	
Space and equipment	
Aims and objectives of session	
Details of session (+ times for each section): • introduction • warm-up • main content • cool down • evaluation	

- **Cardiovascular training** will include activities which increase stamina and aerobic fitness. This will increase the efficiency of the cardiovascular system to deliver oxygen to working muscles and carry carbon dioxide and other waste products away.

- **Resistance training** can include flexibility exercises; participants will be more able to use muscles and joints throughout the full range of natural movement. Participants will also become more agile, have better coordination, reaction time, power and speed.

- **Games and skills** – if you plan to play a game, ensure the participants have the appropriate skills. The skills you teach will relate to the game or activity which follows. Skills can be introduced in a similar way with chair-based games for older people. The games you select will depend on the participants – you may choose to play games such as tag rugby, high five netball, short tennis, mini soccer or Kwik cricket with young children.

Take it further

Games and skills

Select a skill that you could teach to a specific group for use in a games activity. What adaptations will you have to make to the teaching of the skill and the skill itself for your selected group? Why would this skill be physically beneficial to this group of people? How could you add progression to challenge the participants? What social benefits would your group gain from this activity?

Cool down

The cool down is a calming down activity that lowers the pulse. It decreases the intensity of movement developed in the main content of the session. The emphasis during stretches should be on relaxation. All major muscles should be stretched and related to everyday activities. When cooling down, an older adult should not be asked to get up and down from the floor frequently. Cool downs gradually decrease the intensity of the exercise.

Delivery

One of your aims is to ensure that all participants have an enjoyable and safe exercise session. Through detailed planning, your session will give everyone the opportunity to participate fully and have fun. You and the group should enjoy being together. This will happen if you build a rapport with your participants. If you fail to motivate participants in your exercise session, they will not have fun, nor will they achieve. To deliver an interesting and enjoyable exercise session, you can motivate participants by:

- planning the session carefully
- showing enjoyment and enthusiasm
- being confident and energetic
- learning with your group
- acting responsibly.

When delivering your session, you must:

- communicate clearly using verbal and non-verbal skills
- always position yourself where you can see all of the group
- listen to what others are saying
- check that others have understood what you have communicated
- remember that body language is important.

Verbal communication is powerful. It involves you with individuals and allows them to give you feedback. Non-verbal communication or body language is also important because you need to be able to read the participants' body language and they need to be able to read yours. How you stand gives messages. Do you stand confidently? Facial expression is vital. Do you look nervous and anxious, or do you look happy and pleased to meet everyone?

When delivering your session you must correct techniques according to the participants' ability. This is important, especially if a participant could be injured by performing the wrong technique. Some participants, especially older adults, may find the correct technique difficult so adapt the skill to suit them. Many exercises can be adapted to suit the specific needs of individuals. Exercise can also be adapted for chair-based activities or for those who need the support of a chair.

Why is it important to speak clearly? Why is good communication so important?

Games and exercises can be modified. You can modify a game in the following ways by changing the:

- playing area
- equipment
- team structure
- individual roles and positions
- rules
- scoring.

Participants can give feedback at any time during the session. Through questioning you can check knowledge and understanding. You may even give the participants a questionnaire. Questions should be a mixture of open and closed questions. Closed questions can be answered with 'yes', 'no' or a short phrase. Open questions require thoughtful and reflective answers and give opinions or feelings.

Remember

When delivering an exercise session for older adults:

- encourage good posture, a good starting position and ensure effective and safe techniques
- keep balance to a minimum and give support if it is needed
- do not spend long periods with the knees bent
- emphasise that participants should work at their own level
- ensure that the older participant does work
- give clear instructions as someone may have a hearing problem
- deliver the warm-up where you can be seen by everyone
- encourage chatting and laughter
- encourage partner work for social interaction
- allow time for the heart rate to return to pre-exercise rate.

4.3 Reviewing your session

Reviewing is the process of looking back over the planning and delivery of a session and evaluating what was successful and what could be improved. Your participants and peers can give you feedback. Your tutor can help by discussing the strengths and weaknesses.

Methods

Methods of evaluation such as the use of questionnaires to provide feedback from participants and peers, feedback observation sheets, charts, checklists and self evaluation methods can assist you in identifying areas of strength and areas for improvement. You can receive feedback from questioning during and at the end of your exercise session, as well as using observation skills. Questionnaires can be used to gain feedback from participants, peers, teachers and for self-assessment. Questions can be open or closed.

Feedback from your peers should be given in a way that helps you to self evaluate. Your peers can give you information which would be difficult for you to gain while delivering your session. The observer will collect data for you to analyse. A feedback observation sheet which could be completed by your peers would consider the factors shown in Table 16.2.

Table 16.2: Ask your peers to use this observation checklist to give you feedback.

Warm-up	Did I explain the activity clearly?	
	Did the activity relate to the sport/game?	
	Was everyone involved?	
	Were the participants aware of safety issues?	
	Were my aims achieved?	
Skills practice	Did I follow a progressive structure?	
	Did the methods of adaptation work?	
	Was the practice session enjoyable?	
	Did I achieve my aims?	
The game/activity	Were the instructions clear?	
	Did everyone participate?	
	Did everyone enjoy themselves?	
Cool down	Was it explained clearly to the participants?	
	Was everyone involved?	
	Did the activity achieve its aims?	
General	What could have been improved? Be specific.	
	Did I communicate well?	
	What worked really well?	

Direct observation assessment techniques can assess the process of your delivery session as well as the overall session. By using a checklist like Table 16.2 your peers or tutor can assess whether you performed all aspects of the session successfully.

At the end of your session reflect on how well or badly it went. Consider highlights and lowlights. Checklists, rating scales and questionnaires will help you to evaluate your session. Headings used in a checklist can be turned into a questionnaire, or rate yourself using a scale (for example, 1 = poor, 4 = excellent).

Strengths

Strengths can be determined by completing a SWOT analysis:

Strengths

Weaknesses

Opportunities

Threats

The information you have collected from questionnaires, observation sheets, teachers and self-evaluation will help you complete the analysis. Under strengths, you might consider the following:

- What did you do well?
- Which part of the session was the most enjoyable?
- What do you feel confident doing?
- What did your participants achieve?
- How did you encourage your participants?

Areas for improvement

Under areas for improvement consider your weaknesses, threats and opportunities. Ask yourself:

- What else do I need to learn to improve?
- What barriers do I need to overcome?
- How can I overcome my weaknesses?

Development plan

After considering your strengths and areas for improvement, make a development plan. This is a specific plan which sets out in writing/diagrams what you want to achieve. List targets to guide your development. The plan should contain short- and long-term goals. When designing your development plan think of the word SMART. This means that any targets you set yourself should be:

Specific: identify your targets.

Measurable: how will you measure progress towards the targets?

Achievable: how will you achieve your targets?

Realistic: check that your targets can be achieved.

Timed: what time will you give yourself before re-assessing the target?

Assessment activity 16.4

P5 P6 M3 D2 · BTEC

1. Plan and deliver an exercise session for a group of your choice. Your session plan should use the following headings: aims, outcomes, equipment, venue, time, forms of adaptation to be used, warm-up, main content, cool down and debrief. The session should include the warm-up, skills practice, exercises or a game, adapted game or fun game, the cool down and a session debrief. You may have the support of your tutor. **P5**

2. If you choose to complete the plan and delivery of an exercise session for a selected group *without support*, explain why you have chosen the specific exercise and activities for this group. Give reasons for selecting the warm-up, main content and cool down. **M3**

3. Having completed the session plan and delivery of an exercise session independently for a selected group, justify why you selected the exercise and activities with the warm-up, main content and cool down sections. Support your reasons for selecting the chosen exercises and activities by providing evidence that the selections achieved the aims of the chosen components. **D2**

4. Review the planning and delivery of your exercise session for a specific group describing strengths and areas for improvement. **P6**

Grading tips

- To attain **P5** you can have tutor support when planning and delivering an exercise session for your selected specific group. Select a group that you are familiar with and have researched well.

- To attain **M3** you must independently plan and deliver an exercise session for your selected specific group. You must also explain the contents of your lesson.

- To attain **D2** go further and explain how and why the contents of your lesson were suitable and beneficial for your selected group.

- To attain **P6** ask your participants to complete a questionnaire and listen to feedback from your peers and tutor. Reflect carefully on both the planning and delivery of your exercise session for your selected specific group and describe everything you believed was strong in your planning and delivery and what you could have improved.

PLTS

If you plan and deliver an exercise session for a selected specific group then you can develop your skills as an **independent enquirer**, **team worker**, **creative thinker** and **self-manager**. If you review the planning of an exercise session for a specific group, describing strengths and areas for improvement, then you can develop your skills as a **reflective learner**.

Functional skills

If you plan and deliver an exercise session for a selected specific group and review the planning of this session, describing strengths and areas for improvement, you could provide evidence towards your **ICT** and **English** skills.

Martine Done
Sports therapist

Martine is a sports therapist based at a health and fitness club which is very interested in the exercise on prescription scheme. She has been on several courses and manages the scheme for the club. Lucy has been referred to her through the scheme by her GP in consultation with a clinical psychologist.

Lucy is 38 and has been diagnosed with clinical depression. She is married with an 11-year-old son. She often refers to her weight as a major contributory factor to her depressive feelings; she blames her medication as the cause for her excess weight gain in recent years. Lucy wants to reduce her body fat and become more active, both physically and mentally. Lucy's participation in exercise in the past has been limited and, while she was physically active as a child, she has not been able to maintain regular exercise in recent years. Now Lucy's son has become older she wants to become more actively involved in his life by improving her physical fitness and health so that she can 'keep up with him'.

Before starting an exercise programme, Martine meets Lucy at the gym, shows her the facilities and discusses the exercise plan which covers a 12-week period. Her programme consists of 60 minute sessions using indoor and outdoor facilities. Martine then goes through the initial screening process and completes the appropriate forms.

During the 12-week programme, Martine introduces Lucy to exercise opportunities outside the scheme, for example, at the local leisure centre where she has joined a walking group. She also ensures that Lucy is aware of the many opportunities that exist to promote exercise for people with depression in her area.

During the exercise on prescription programme, Lucy is set small targets each week. She might walk 20 minutes each day one week and another week aim to swim at least twice. These targets, along with her exercise programme, have increased her confidence because she feels better and can exercise with her son.

Think about it!

- Can you prescribe an interesting exercise session which would help Lucy reduce her body fat?
- What sort of exercise opportunities are there in your area that would be suitable and available to Lucy?
- Can you describe Lucy now, at the end of the programme? Think about her appearance, mental and physical fitness, confidence, self-esteem and her relationship with the rest of her family. How would you feel if you were able to help someone in this way?

Just checking

1. Identify three different specific groups and give a short description of each one.

2. Choose three specific groups and explain the physiological benefits and the psychological benefits of exercise for these groups.

3. Why is maintaining bone density important? What benefits are there in exercise for someone with:
   - osteoporosis
   - diabetes
   - multiple sclerosis?

4. What do you mean by a rehabilitation programme? Describe a rehabilitation programme for a specific group.

5. What do you mean by the exercise referral process?

6. When planning a session, why would you consider factors such as aims, outcomes, resources, health and safety?

7. What do you mean by participants of an exercise programme?

8. Why is communication so important when delivering an exercise session to people with a disability, or older adults?

9. Why is it important to include a warm-up when delivering an exercise session?

10. When would you adapt a game when planning and delivering an exercise session?

edexcel

Assignment tips

- Access the Internet. There is a great deal of information about specific groups and exercise on prescription.

- Read and research books, magazines and leaflets about the specific needs of your selected groups.

- Visit health centres, health and fitness clubs, schools, care homes, special needs schools and your GP. These are examples of where you will find professionals to help you. Examine the referral process in real situations.

- Speak to your tutors and ask them to help you arrange visits to observe professionals working in your areas of interest. How do the professionals adapt activities to suit client needs?

- Discuss ideas and exercises with other learners and tutors.

- Practise delivering your session to your peers. Ask for feedback and use this to improve and strengthen your planning and delivery of the exercise session.

- Remember practice does make perfect!

18 Sports injuries

Sports injuries can be a major cause of physical pain, frustration, heartache and financial loss for players of all sporting disciplines and at a variety of performance levels. However, technological advances in the diagnosis and treatment of injuries are being developed all the time. This is due partly to a dramatic increase in the number of individuals studying a wide variety of sport and exercise disciplines as an academic subject. The huge amount of money involved in sport at the highest level has also contributed to major developments in the sports sciences on a worldwide scale.

In this unit you will investigate the identification of risks and the prevention of injuries. You will also examine the types, causes and symptoms of a range of injuries and the treatments available, identifying which methods are applicable. Putting into practice the knowledge that you will develop, you will produce an initial treatment plan, along with a long-term rehabilitation programme, for two commonly occurring sports injuries.

Learning outcomes

After completing this unit you should:

1. know how common sports injuries can be prevented by the correct identification of risk factors
2. know about a range of sports injuries and their symptoms
3. know how to apply methods of treating sports injuries
4. be able to plan and construct treatment and rehabilitation programmes for two common sports injuries.

Assessment and grading criteria

This table shows you what you must do in order to achieve a pass, merit or distinction grade, and where you can find activities in this book to help you.

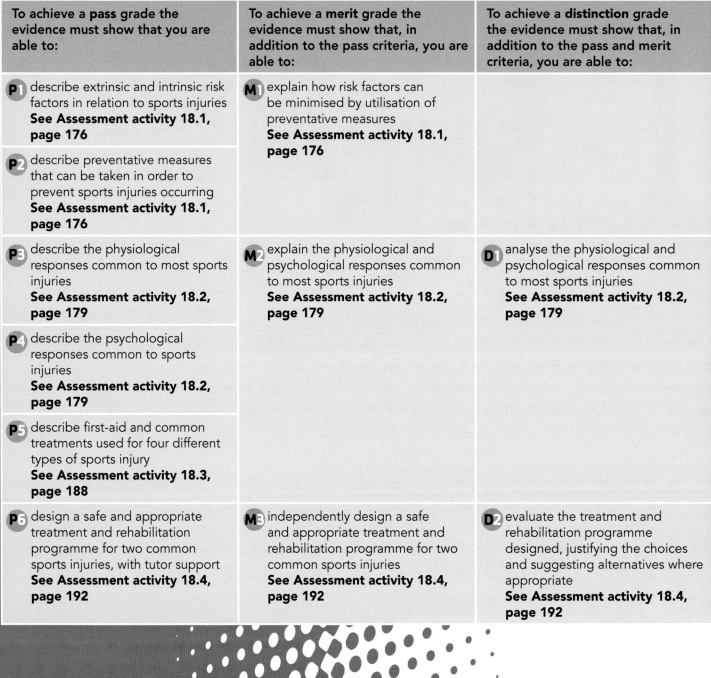

To achieve a **pass** grade the evidence must show that you are able to:	To achieve a **merit** grade the evidence must show that, in addition to the pass criteria, you are able to:	To achieve a **distinction** grade the evidence must show that, in addition to the pass and merit criteria, you are able to:
P1 describe extrinsic and intrinsic risk factors in relation to sports injuries **See Assessment activity 18.1, page 176**	**M1** explain how risk factors can be minimised by utilisation of preventative measures **See Assessment activity 18.1, page 176**	
P2 describe preventative measures that can be taken in order to prevent sports injuries occurring **See Assessment activity 18.1, page 176**		
P3 describe the physiological responses common to most sports injuries **See Assessment activity 18.2, page 179**	**M2** explain the physiological and psychological responses common to most sports injuries **See Assessment activity 18.2, page 179**	**D1** analyse the physiological and psychological responses common to most sports injuries **See Assessment activity 18.2, page 179**
P4 describe the psychological responses common to sports injuries **See Assessment activity 18.2, page 179**		
P5 describe first-aid and common treatments used for four different types of sports injury **See Assessment activity 18.3, page 188**		
P6 design a safe and appropriate treatment and rehabilitation programme for two common sports injuries, with tutor support **See Assessment activity 18.4, page 192**	**M3** independently design a safe and appropriate treatment and rehabilitation programme for two common sports injuries **See Assessment activity 18.4, page 192**	**D2** evaluate the treatment and rehabilitation programme designed, justifying the choices and suggesting alternatives where appropriate **See Assessment activity 18.4, page 192**

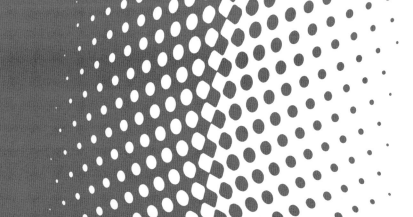

How you will be assessed

Your assessment could be in the form of:

- presentations
- case studies
- practical tasks
- written assignments.

Don, 18-year-old rugby player

While competing in the national trials I suffered from a sprained shoulder joint. This left me very disappointed as I did not fulfil my full potential and make the squad, and I could not train or compete for a while. Rehabilitation from my injury seemed to be taking a long time and I started to feel frustrated and disillusioned with my physical progress.

Through this unit I have developed a great deal of insight into the different stages of the rehabilitation process. This knowledge has made me realise the need for specific goals during rehabilitation and that my injury had, in reality, improved tremendously. My experiences throughout the unit also developed my appreciation that sports injuries produce both psychological and physical impacts on athletes.

Over to you!

1. Have you ever suffered from an injury and wondered what physiological responses were taking place within your body?

2. After suffering an injury have you ever considered the various treatment and rehabilitation methods available?

3. What aspect of this unit are you particularly interested in?

1. Know how common sports injuries can be prevented by the correct identification of risk factors

Warm-up

How can injuries be prevented or minimised?

The type and severity of injuries vary greatly between different sports, with contact sports often having higher rates of traumatic injury. Various individuals, as well as athletes, can help to reduce the likelihood of accidents. The most important issue surrounding sports injuries is how to prevent them, or minimise the severity if they occur. Can you think of ways in which to achieve this?

Sports injuries can be caused by a variety of different factors which fall into two categories – **extrinsic** and **intrinsic**. Identifying the risk factors can dramatically reduce the chances of someone developing the different types of injury.

Key terms

Extrinsic – a risk or force from outside the body. These are external forces, such as from objects or other individuals making contact with someone

Intrinsic – a risk or force from within the body. These are internal forces, which are stresses from within the body.

📱 1.1 Extrinsic risk factors

Coaching

If a coach demonstrates poor communication and leadership methods and suggests incorrect techniques and exercise, this can pose risks for sports players. The rules of sports are designed by the governing bodies, in part, to protect the players. Non-adherence to these will involve risks for both the player breaking the rules and other players participating.

Incorrect technique

Using inappropriate or incorrect techniques is an injury risk. As well as poor sports techniques, incorrect methods of setting up and lifting and handling equipment will cause risks to those involved.

Environmental factors

Weather can have a huge impact on playing conditions in sport. Poor playing conditions potentially increase the risk of injury. For example:

- slips and falls from slippery surfaces
- falling on uneven ground
- cold conditions which make playing surfaces harder and potentially dangerous
- poor conditions may mean the style of play may change, and create further risks to players via the movements that they carry out.

Clothing and footwear

Not wearing the correct equipment for your sport will create major extrinsic risk factors. Examples of incorrect equipment include wearing:

- the wrong footwear for the activity or playing surface
- damaged, or too much or too little, protective equipment
- the wrong protective equipment for the sport.

Safety hazards

It is important for coaches, support staff and players to be aware of hazards and risks associated with the activities being undertaken. Various health and safety considerations must be applied to all activities both before and during participation.

- **Environment** – a safety check of the sporting environment should be carried out before a game or training. It is vital to remove any dangerous objects, or any slippery or uneven areas of a playing surface, along with a general consideration of potential risks.

- **Sports equipment** – the equipment we use as training aids, for protection, and to enhance performance can also act as a potential extrinsic risk factor, and it is essential that equipment is checked by players and coaches before use. A referee should also check equipment before the players enter the playing area (for example, checking studs before a rugby or football match).

- **Misuse of equipment** – the misuse and abuse of equipment will cause risks to sports players – equipment is specifically designed to do a particular job. Tampering with or modifying equipment will make it less useful and often dangerous.

- **First-aid provision** – a lack of preparation for any potential accidents on the sports field may cause undue risks to sports players. Experienced first-aiders and/or medical professionals and, crucially, a fully equipped first-aid kit should be available at all sports sessions.

- **Safety checklist** – this is a useful tool to make sure all activities and equipment are safe.

The process of risk assessment is covered in detail in Student Book 1, Unit 3 Assessing risk in sport.

1.2 Intrinsic risk factors

Training effects

Due to anatomical differences and abnormalities (such as muscle imbalance), undue stresses can be placed on different parts of the body, potentially causing injuries.

Inadequate or poor preparation for sports training and competition places risks on athletes. It is essential to prepare for sport both mentally and physically before participating. The warm-up is an essential aspect of preparation for sport (Unit 15 Instructing physical activity and exercise, pages 116–117). Appropriate flexibility is an important component of fitness, and a lack of flexibility will place physical stress and risk on an athlete. Inappropriate general fitness levels will also yield intrinsic risks. Particularly when combined with other intrinsic risks, overuse injuries are also potential risk factors athletes must be aware of.

Individual variables

Having the correct fitness levels to play your chosen sport minimises the risks of injury. Playing at an appropriate level is also critical, as playing sport with individuals of either superior or inferior fitness levels and/or age and physical development will involve risk to yourself and others.

Your anatomy can predispose you to certain injuries and a history of certain injuries can make you more susceptible to anatomical abnormalities. A history of injury increases the intrinsic risk of that injury recurring during future sports participation. Differences or problems associated with your anatomy are classed as an intrinsic risk factor.

Insufficient sleep before training and competition is another risk. Being alert and refreshed for sport is a key ingredient for focus and success in training and competition. A crucial method of preparing for physical activity is sufficient nutrition (including hydration). Not eating or drinking enough before an activity will cause serious risks to the body (see Student Book 1, Unit 11 Sports nutrition).

Postural defects

Abnormal curvature of the spine is a potential risk that can become degenerative and inhibit sporting potential. Examples of such malalignment of the vertebrae include:

scoliosis – a lateral imbalance or sideways bending of the spine

kyphosis – an excessive arching of the upper part of the spine

lordosis – an excessive inward curve at the lower part of the spine.

These problems can occur independently or sometimes together to a certain degree.

Overuse and insufficient recovery following exercise and excessive strain on a body part can also exacerbate injuries and worsen existing postural defects.

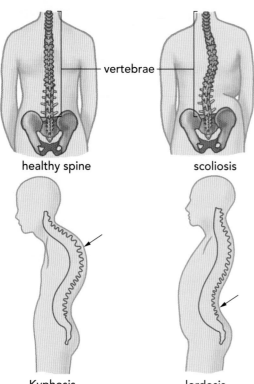

Figure 18.1: What measures can be used to minimise the risks and severity of vertebral malalignment?

(Labels in figure: vertebrae, healthy spine, scoliosis, Kyphosis, lordosis)

1.3 Preventative measures

The role of the coach

The coach will play a major role, particularly for younger athletes, in preventing mishaps on the playing field. As a physical trainer, sports leader or sports coach, you must:

- have up to date knowledge of all your players' abilities, including strengths and weaknesses in their physicality and skills

- have up to date and relevant knowledge and qualifications in the sport that you are coaching

- be able to adapt your coaching style based on ability, age, fitness, gender and motivation of the athletes being coached

- stress the importance of health and safety in well planned training sessions and match situations – communication skills are vital for all coaches

- check that all equipment is safe to use, that it is being used correctly, and that the environment is safe for the activity being undertaken

Activity: Intrinsic or extrinsic?

Complete the table below to check your understanding of the categorisation of risk factors.

Table 18.1: Categorisation of risk factors.

Risk factor	Intrinsic (I) or extrinsic (E)?
Lack of organisation for an event	
Inadequate preparation for a game	
Muscular imbalance	
Postural defects	
Poor technique	
Poor coaching and/or leadership	
Playing surfaces	
Age	
Inadequate fitness levels	
Overuse	
Growth and development	
Environment (weather)	
Insufficient flexibility	
A history of previous injury	
Nutrition	
Sleep disturbances	

- ensure that players are aware of all governing body guidelines and adhere to the rules and regulations that have been set out
- ensure sufficient first-aid provision is available for all training and competition scenarios – this is critically important
- make a detailed assessment of the risks of all activities.

Activity: Risk fact sheet

In small groups, produce a fact sheet explaining the different types of risks associated with sporting activity. Include a section indicating the roles of different individuals in minimising extrinsic and intrinsic risk factors.

Equipment and environment

As previously highlighted, a thorough risk assessment of the training and competition environment must be carried out. It is also important to go through this procedure for the equipment that is used (for example, protective equipment). In many sports, the protective equipment available has changed dramatically over the years. Technological advances in the materials available and biomechanical analysis techniques (research and analysis of movement) have allowed dramatic improvements in the quality of protective equipment available. Advances have been in both specific protection of body parts, and limiting the negative impact of the protection on playing performance (such as excess weight and decreased range of movement).

Sports players need to ensure that specialist protective equipment is used correctly. If it is used incorrectly, this can be a hazard, putting yourself and other players at risk. When using different types of protective equipment, you should:

- ensure that the equipment is thoroughly checked prior to use
- use the equipment only for the sport for which it is designed
- use only the correct size
- not share your personal equipment (for example, boots, pads, etc.) with other people
- not use damaged equipment
- not make modifications to equipment

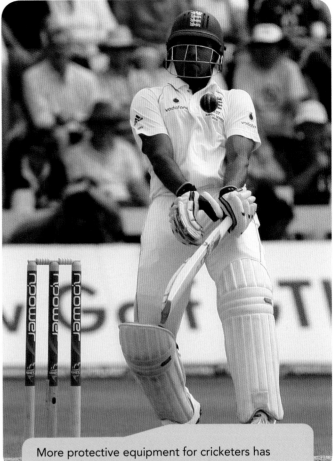

More protective equipment for cricketers has become available in recent decades. Can you trace some technological developments that have occurred over the last 50 years?

- be aware that protective equipment does not make you invincible
- use the equipment for both practice and competition
- be aware that some equipment can protect both you and other players.

Take it further

Research protective equipment

The protective equipment for many sports has changed dramatically over the years. Choose three sports and highlight the developments in equipment.

Remember

Many individuals can play a role in preventing injuries – including players, coaches, support staff and parents, among others.

Assessment activity 18.1

P1 P2 M1

BTEC

You are a trainee working with the coach of a local youth sports team (choose a sport that is relevant to your background). Considering all the various risk factors associated with sports injuries, you are going to describe the range of measures you could put in place to prevent injuries to players in your team.

1. Describe extrinsic and intrinsic risk factors in relation to sports injuries. **P1**

2. Write a detailed explanation of how risk factors can be minimised with the use of preventative measures. **M1**

3. Describe preventative measures that can be taken in order to prevent sports injuries occurring. **P2**

Grading tips

- To attain **P1** break down your answers into a table of extrinsic and intrinsic risk factors and how they can lead to sports injuries.

- To attain **M1** write a detailed explanation of the relationship between specific preventative measures and the risk factors they relate to.

- To attain **P2** highlight the different individuals involved, and explain their role in injury prevention. Explain the different tasks that should be done before a sporting activity (for example, equipment and playing area checks).

PLTS

If you describe sports injury risk factors and preventative methods you can develop your skills as an **independent enquirer**, **creative thinker** and **self-manager**.

Functional skills

If you describe the range of measures you could put in place to prevent injuries to players in your team you could provide evidence of your **ICT** and **English** skills.

2. Know about a range of sports injuries and their symptoms

Knowledge of the signs and symptoms of different sports injuries is vital to ensure the correct treatment is applied from the onset of the problem. You should try and gain as much knowledge as possible about the injury, as early as possible, so the best care can be implemented at each stage of treatment.

2.1 Physiological responses

Key term

Physiological response – the body's physical mechanisms that respond when an injury takes place. These are initiated to repair and protect the damaged tissue.

Damaged tissue

As soon as an injury takes place, the body responds in a number of ways. Damage to body tissue initiates the primary damage response mechanism. The two main signs and symptoms are pain and inflammation. Causes such as external trauma, overload (this is excessive use of one or more of the FITT principles, see page 112), repeated load, pressure and friction can cause inflammation, which is associated with the majority of sports injuries. Inflammation is caused by a number of factors, which trigger other signs and symptoms:

- accumulation of fluid surrounding the injury
- redness due to an increase in blood flow

- tender to the touch
- impaired functioning and range of motion (ROM).

When you bleed because of an injury, the blood clots to initiate the healing process. Platelets, which are cells within the blood, are activated by chemical reactions when trauma causes blood loss. These platelets make the blood sticky, and quickly cause a clot as they stick to the surface of the blood vessels. The clotting mechanism is important as this process acts as a preliminary phase of the healing process.

Bleeding is a major physiological response to all injuries. When an acute injury occurs to the body, the damaged tissue will bleed into the surrounding tissues. The amount of bleeding that takes place will be specific to the type and severity of injury. There are two types of haematoma:

- intermuscular haematoma – bleeding occurs within the compartment of the muscle, but does not seep into the surrounding tissue
- intramuscular haematoma – blood escapes into the surrounding tissue (for example, different muscle compartments).

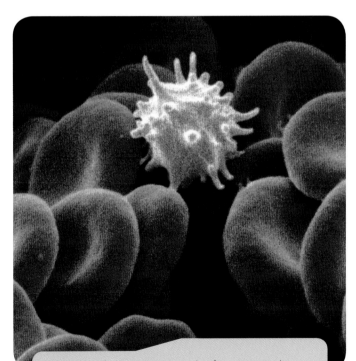

Scanning electron micrograph of an activated blood platelet among red blood cells (unactivated platelets are smooth and oval-shaped) – platelets clump together to prevent bleeding and assist in clot formation (magnification: × 10,2000). What other substances are present in blood and what are their roles?

The different types of haematoma are described in more detail on page 181.

Importance of scar tissue in the remodelling process

The remodelling process (the development of scar tissue) restores the tissue at the site of an injury as close as possible to its original state. From the time when an injury takes place, scar tissue starts to form. It is crucial that the correct treatments are applied to regain the original functioning of the body part. The more severe an injury, the more difficult it will be to restore damaged tissue to its original state.

A more detailed explanation of the remodelling process is given on page 189.

Specific to injury

The signs and symptoms of various injuries may differ and this must be considered during initial diagnosis. For example, first, second and third degree sprains and strains will be different, and the physiological responses will be more pronounced.

2.2 Psychological responses

Response to injury

As well as the physiological responses of the body to injury, **psychological responses** can cause stress to an athlete. The way a person deals with an injury varies between individuals and some potential negative psychological responses are listed below.

> **Key term**
>
> **Psychological response** – the mental aspect of how an athlete copes and comes to terms with their injury and treatment.

- Fear – this can take many forms, including the fear of recurrence of an injury, and fear of not returning to full fitness.
- Stress and anxiety – this can be felt by an athlete during competition. If the athlete then suffers an injury, these feelings will be increased. As an injury progresses, concerns regarding the athlete's long- and short-term sporting prospects can become a psychological issue.

- Motivational issues – some injuries can take a long time to heal. As the duration of an injury increases, an athlete's motivation towards their sport may decrease.

- Depression – some athletes may demonstrate symptoms of clinical depression, such as decreased energy levels, constant sadness, withdrawal from social contact, etc.

- Anger – this can be towards oneself, the injury, and also other people (particularly if the injury is the fault of someone else).

- Decreased confidence – this is very common for athletes who are returning to training and competition. An athlete may suffer from a lack of confidence in their own skill levels, and decreased confidence in their fitness and ability to push their body physically.

- Denial – sometimes an athlete may try to deny the severity of an injury, and try to return to their sport too quickly. It is important that those supporting sports players (for example, coaches and family) are aware of the nature of the injury and take guidance from medical professionals.

- Frustration – this is a common issue for many athletes, particularly for long-term injury. The majority of sports players will crave to return to competition, and become frustrated by a lack of physical exercise and/or their specialist sport.

- Isolation from team mates – many team sports players' frustration can be exacerbated by the fact that they will not be involved in competition and training. This can lead to players becoming mentally withdrawn from their team.

Response to treatment and rehabilitation

As well as the athlete's physiological response to the injury, psychological responses also take place during rehabilitation and these can either hinder or assist the healing and rehabilitation processes. They include:

- anxiety – this can occur during many phases of an injury often due to uncertainty regarding the treatment and rehabilitation methods used

- frustration – when an athlete cannot see immediate improvements, or if there is a plateau in progress, frustration will often set in

- need for motivation – athletes will need to remain motivated during the often long road to recovery from injury. Those involved in rehabilitation can often support with such motivational issues

- use of goal setting – to ensure that athletes stay motivated, goal setting strategies are useful to keep track of progress and to see the improvements that have been made.

The psychological responses to a sports injury vary dramatically between individuals. Some may suffer no or few negative responses, whereas others may experience a number of psychological issues.

Remember

Often, when we consider sports injuries, we think of the traumatic injuries that occur due to a mishap on a specific occasion, in a game or in training. But many injuries are caused by an accumulation of stress over a period of time, or to overuse of a body part.

Chronic injuries are long-term injuries that have developed slowly.

Acute or traumatic injuries occur suddenly through instant trauma to the individual.

Examples could be:

- chronic – a runner develops a stress fracture due to repetitive overloading

- acute – an individual suffers a sprained ankle when cockling over while playing badminton.

Note: the severity of the injury is not determined by any of these categorisations.

Assessment activity 18.2

P3 P4 M2 D1 BTEC

You are a first-aider working for a large local voluntary sports club. Produce a poster to raise awareness of how the body responds to a sports injury. Specifically you must cover the following:

1. Describe the physiological responses common to most sports injuries. **P3**
2. Describe the psychological responses common to sports injuries. **P4**
3. Explain the physiological and psychological effects common to most sports injuries. **M2**
4. Analyse the physiological and psychological responses common to most sports injuries. **D1**

Grading tips

- To attain **P3** you could include some specific examples of sports injuries you are familiar with.
- To attain **P4** think about the types of feeling that you may experience at the time of an injury taking

place and also as time progresses when you cannot train or compete. Brainstorm some ideas and provide a description of how some psychological reactions might affect a sportsperson.

- To attain **M2** you should explain *why* the physiological responses are taking place and their role in the healing process following an injury. You should also explain why any psychological issues occur, and the short- and long-term effects they may have on the athlete.

- To attain **D1** think about how the psychological and physiological factors interact when a sports player suffers an injury. Which individual characteristics may contribute to psychological effects of sports injuries in the long- and short-term? How can the body's physiological and psychological responses change during the different stages of the healing process?

PLTS

By producing a poster raising awareness of the physiological and psychological responses to sports injuries, you can develop your skills as an **independent enquirer**, **creative thinker** and **self-manager**.

Functional skills

By producing your poster you could provide evidence of your skills in **ICT** and **English**.

3. Know how to apply methods of treating sports injuries

Some common trends have emerged regarding the types of sporting injury. Collisions with other performers or objects, and twists or turns beyond the body's capabilities, are common causes of acute injury. Continued excessive force on a specific body part (for example, the knee) is associated with chronic injuries. This section details the anatomy and physiology of some common sports injuries. It is important that you are aware of the types of sport that may cause the different injuries outlined, and the specific preventative measures that can be taken.

Hard tissue injuries are to bones, joints and cartilage, whereas **soft tissue injuries** are to muscles, tendons, ligaments, internal organs and the skin. A combination of both hard and soft tissue injuries can occur, and this must be taken into consideration during the treatment and rehabilitation processes.

Key terms

Hard tissue injury – injury to bones, joints and cartilage.

Soft tissue injury – injury to muscles, tendons, ligaments, internal organs and skin.

3.1 Types of sports injury: hard tissue damage

Hard tissue injuries are particularly prevalent in contact sports such as football, and in individual sports such as skiing, gymnastics and riding. Hard tissue injuries include fractures, dislocations and cartilage injuries. Although sport can cause skeletal injuries, as with other parts of the anatomy, exercise can result in strengthening and thickening of bone, making injury less likely.

Fractures

A **fracture** is a partial or complete break in a bone – a common form of hard tissue injury. The way an injury takes place causes bones to break differently. Most are due to direct impact, but the site of the injury and how it occurs will result in different types of fracture. The treatments for different fractures are slightly different and so the correct category of injury has to be diagnosed. Fractures can be categorised into many different types.

- **Open and closed fractures** – a closed fracture is one where relatively little displacement of bone has occurred, which therefore does not cause much damage to the soft tissue surrounding the injury. An open fracture is one in which the fractured ends of the bone/s break through the skin. Open fractures have a high risk of infection, so it is vital that they are dealt with immediately after injury occurs. All fractures are relatively serious injuries, and specialist professional attention should be sought in all cases.

- **Complete and incomplete fractures** – some fractures do not crack the full length of the bone. This is an incomplete fracture. Fractures where a complete break in the bone occurs (when more than one fragment exists) are called complete fractures.

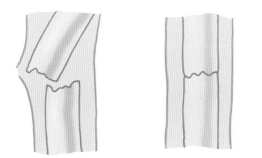

Figure 18.2: An open fracture (left) and a closed fracture (right). How will the treatment differ for each category?

- **Greenstick fracture** – the bone bends and splits without causing a full break in the bone (resembling a bending tree twig). This type of fracture is common among children, because children's bones are not fully developed and not as hard as fully matured bone.

- **Transverse fracture** – a crack that is perpendicular (at right angles) to the length of the bone.

- **Oblique fracture** – similar to a transverse fracture, but the break occurs diagonally across the bone, resulting in sharp ends where the break occurred.

- **Spiral fracture** – very similar to an oblique fracture, but the break is in a spiralling motion along the bone. This often occurs due to a twisting motion accompanied by a high amount of stress to the bone.

- **Comminuted fracture** – produces multiple fragments of bone. With these types of injury, it is often necessary to use screws and wires to assist with healing of the bone, and long rehabilitation is often required.

- **Impacted fracture** – both ends of the bone are forced together in a compression motion. Again, this type of fracture can be complicated, and rehabilitation is needed to restore normal functioning.

- **Avulsion fracture** – a fragment of bone becomes detached at the attachment point (either ligament, tendon or muscle).

Dislocation

A **dislocation** occurs when the correct alignment of bones becomes disrupted, moving them out of their normal position. Such injuries are often caused by impact with another player or object, or by a fall. Typical sites of dislocation due to sports are shoulders, hips, knees, ankles, elbows, fingers and toes. If you suspect that a dislocation has occurred, it is important to seek medical attention to ensure the bones are replaced in correct alignment without damaging the joint. Very often, a dislocated joint will result in ligament damage. The joints in the body are held together by ligaments – when a dislocation occurs they can become stretched, sometimes permanently. If this happens, you become more susceptible to a recurrence of the same injury, particularly in joints such as the shoulder or kneecap.

A subluxation is an incomplete or partial dislocation.

Fracture – a partial or complete break in a bone.

Dislocation – a displacement of the position of bones, often caused by a sudden impact.

Stress fracture

This is different from the other forms of **fracture** as it is not caused by a traumatic injury, but develops due to overuse or fatigue. A stress fracture can also be called a fatigue or insufficiency fracture, and generally occurs in weight-bearing bones.

Stress fractures can be particularly difficult to spot using traditional X-ray equipment, particularly at the early stages of development.

Take it further

Types of fracture

Of the different types of fracture, which are more likely to produce an open fracture, and why?

Shin splints

These are another hard tissue injury to the front of the tibia (shin bone). This is often caused by inflammation to the periostium (sheath around the bone's surface) and is common in runners.

3.2 Types of sports injury: soft tissue damage

Haematoma

A **haematoma** is a pocket of congealed blood caused by bleeding to a specific area of the body. Haematomas may be small bruises, or can be more serious when they occur to different organs (such as the brain), or cause large amounts of blood flow disruption. The majority of haematomas caused by sports injuries occur to the muscles, and are caused by impact or rupture. Muscular haematomas fall into two main types: intermuscular and intramuscular. The size and shape of skeletal muscles vary dramatically, but the general structure remains similar. Muscle fibres (cells) are bundled together in groups and surrounded by a membrane. These are grouped in further bundles, again surrounded by a membrane. These groups of muscle fibres mean that the structure of a muscle is broken down into a number of compartments. For a more detailed overview of the muscular system, see Student Book 1, Unit 1 Principles of anatomy and physiology in sport. Whether a muscular haematoma is inter- or intramuscular depends on where the bleeding takes place.

An intermuscular haematoma is when damage to the muscle causes blood flow within the muscle belly. In this case, the bleeding does not seep into the surrounding tissues, but is restricted to specific compartments within the muscle. An intramuscular haematoma, in contrast, results in blood escaping to the surrounding tissue. With these types of injury, the resultant bruise can spread to areas where the injuries did not occur. Both intra- and intermuscular haematomas can be either superficial or deep (superficial being towards the surface and deep being further inside the muscle).

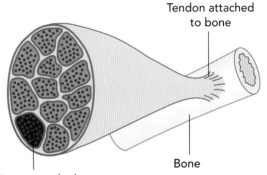

Intermuscular haematoma: bleeding is confined to one bundle of muscle fibres

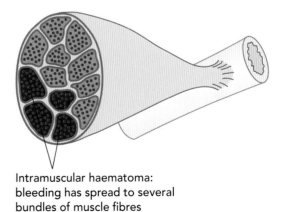

Intramuscular haematoma: bleeding has spread to several bundles of muscle fibres

Figure 18.3: Intermuscular (left) and intramuscular (right) haematomas. How does the recovery differ for the different types of haematoma?

Abrasion

An abrasion is superficial damage to the skin. In the majority of cases, abrasions (often friction burns) are relatively minor and cover a small area of skin. Many abrasions are caused by contact with a playing surface (for example, falling and slipping), or clothing rubbing on the body.

Sprains and strains

Many people find it difficult to differentiate between a sprain and a strain. It is quite simple, as long as you have a reasonable understanding of basic anatomy:

- a **sprain** is damage to ligaments (stretch or tear)
- a **strain** is damage to muscle or tendon.

Sprain – the causes of a sprain are generally a sudden twist, impact or fall that makes the joint move outside its normal range of movement. Sprains commonly occur to the ankle, wrist, thumb or knee, generally the parts of the body that are at risk when involved in specific sporting activities. The severity of sprains depends on different factors. More than one ligament can be damaged at the same time, and the more ligaments affected, the more severe the injury. Also, whether the ligament is stretched or torn (either partially or fully) determines how severe the injury is. Sprains can be categorised as either first-, second- or third degree, depending on severity:

- first-degree sprain – stretching of ligament (no tear)
- second-degree sprain – partial tear of ligament
- third-degree sprain – complete tear of ligament, or detachment of ligament from the bone.

Strain – a strain is damage to a muscle or tendon caused by overstretching that particular area. Similar to a sprain, a strain can result in a simple overstretching of the muscle or, in more serious examples, partial or even complete rupture. Strains can be common in sports involving dynamic lunging, particularly when combined with sprinting activities, and in contact sports (for example, tackling in football). The

severity of a strain is determined by a three-grade categorisation system:

- Grade 1 – relatively minor damage to the muscle fibres (cells) – less than 5 per cent.
- Grade 2 – the muscle is not completely ruptured, but more extensive damage to the fibres has occurred.
- Grade 3 – a complete rupture of the muscle has occurred – in most cases this will require surgery and rehabilitation.

Concussion

Concussion is caused by the brain shaking inside the skull. This causes a temporary loss of consciousness or functioning. Other signs and symptoms include:

- partial or complete loss of consciousness, usually of short duration
- shallow breathing
- nausea and vomiting can occur when the person starts to regain consciousness
- the injured person will often describe 'seeing stars'
- loss of memory of what has happened just before and immediately after the incident
- headache may occur.

Tendonitis

The repetitive and high-impact nature of sporting activity involves continued muscle actions, pulling on tendons, resulting in movement of the skeleton. Tendons will normally glide smoothly with the contraction of the muscles, allowing efficient movements. The varied and dynamic movements involved in sports can, from time to time, place friction on the tendons causing irritation and inflammation.

This inflammation is called tendonitis, and is generally caused by overuse, particularly with increased or different training demands. The symptoms normally subside within a few days, but without care the problem can last weeks or even months. Typical locations of tendonitis could be the achilles tendon and within the complex structures of the shoulder joint.

Tendon rupture

A tendon attaches muscle to bone. A tendon rupture (tear) can be particularly serious depending on the location of the injury and may need surgery.

Blister

Blisters are caused as a defence mechanism to help repair damage to the skin. They are a response to a burn or friction, and are fluid that develops under the upper layers of the skin. Avoid popping a blister, as this will make it more susceptible to infection.

Cramp

Cramp is an involuntary contraction of muscles. Muscles that are particularly susceptible are the gastrocnemius (calf), the quadriceps (thigh), the hamstrings, the abdomen and the feet and hands, depending on the type of activity. Cramp is caused by a lack of oxygen to the muscles, or a lack of water or salt. Deep breathing can alleviate cramp if poor oxygen supply is the cause. In the case of a lack of water and salt, stretching, taking on more fluids and gentle massage can reduce the problem.

Tennis elbow

Symptoms of tennis elbow include pain and tenderness on the outside of your elbow and this may spread to the forearm. Inflammation or a tear to the tendon that joins the forearm muscles to the humerus bone is the cause of tennis elbow.

Back pain

Back pain is a common problem for many people – not just sports players. The back is central to the posture and movements in the majority of sports skills, so pain can cause major disruptions to performance. Four out of five adults have at least one bout of back pain sometime during their lives. In fact, back pain is one of the most common reasons for health care visits and missed work.

Activity: Sports and their injuries

Working in groups, discuss the nature of the following sporting activities and suggest (with appropriate reasons) the types of injury that might be prevalent:

- field hockey
- football
- boxing
- netball
- cricket
- equestrianism.

Based on the injuries you have highlighted, suggest strategies to decrease the risk/likelihood of such injuries taking place. Consider the following:

- protective equipment
- specific rules and regulations
- possible future schemes that could be implemented.

Make a table of your suggestions like the one below.

Table 18.2: Strategies to reduce the risk of sports injuries.

Sport	Common injuries	Protective equipment	Governing body guidelines	Future schemes
Field hockey				
Football				
Boxing				
Netball				
Cricket				
Equestrianism				

Treatment may involve anti-inflammatory drugs, physiotherapy, massage and many other approaches, depending on the specific cause of the pain. Sometimes the actual cause of pain can be very difficult to pinpoint, increasing the difficulty of treatment.

Cartilage injuries

Cartilage comes in different forms, serving various purposes in the body. Cartilage acts as ossification (bone growth) sites, acts as the skeleton for a foetus, keeps tubes of the body open (such as the epiglottis), supports areas of the body requiring tensile strength (such as between the ribs), and lines adjoining bones. Cartilage minimises the impact of internal skeletal forces during sports and general activities. During intense exercise such as running, the forces on the knee, for example, can be huge. Cartilage absorbs the impact of bones while reducing the friction. Damage to cartilage is often due to wear and tear from long-term overuse. Alternatively degenerative conditions (such as osteoarthritis) would also result in chronic cartilage problems. Acute trauma can also cause damage to cartilage, which can occur alongside other injuries (such as a dislocation).

Friction burns

Friction burns are a form of abrasion. In sport these are often caused by falling on playing surfaces or skin rubbing on kit.

3.3 First-aid

First-aid is the immediate treatment given to an injured person. The severity of sporting injuries can vary, from minor cuts and bruises to life-threatening problems. Some knowledge of first-aid can potentially save a person's life, and can also help with minor problems to speed the recovery process and limit potential complications.

Completion of this unit does not qualify you as a first-aider. If you do witness a serious accident, the most qualified and experienced individual should be the one who carries out the first-aid procedures. Do not crowd the injured person, and assist in any way that the first-aider asks.

Remember

Completion of first-aid qualifications can be a great benefit to your sports team. Also, formal first-aid qualifications improve your general employment potential through an enhanced CV.

Emergency/immediate treatment

The priority of first-aid is to preserve life and reduce the risk of further complications from an injury. With potentially serious accidents, a specific primary survey should be carried out.

Primary survey

This is to ensure that a patient is breathing, so it is of paramount importance that it is carried out first.

- **Danger** – check the area for potential danger to yourself. Another casualty will worsen the problem. Also remove any potentially hazardous objects from around the casualty.

- **Response** – check if there is any response from the injured person. If not, call for help immediately. Do not leave the injured person.

- **Airway** – be aware of potential neck injuries. Gently tip the head backwards and check if there are any foreign objects in the person's mouth, blocking the airway.

- **Breathing** – check to see if the person is breathing (up to 10 seconds). If not, send someone for an ambulance (dial 999).

- **Circulation** – check for signs of circulation. If not, cardiopulmonary resuscitation (CPR, see below) should commence.

Secondary survey

A secondary survey should be carried out if an unconscious person is breathing. This is done to check all areas of the body for damage. The process should be carried out quickly and in a systematic way.

- **Bleeding** – check the area, and check the patient head-to-toe for blood.

- **Head and neck** – check for bruising and/or deformity. Gently feel the back of the neck for damage.

- **Shoulders and chest** – compare the shoulders; feel for fractures in the collarbones and ribs.

- **Abdomen and pelvis** – feel around the abdomen for abnormalities and to see if the person feels any pain.
- **Legs and arms** – check legs, then arms, for fracture and any other clues.
- **Pockets** – check the pockets of the person to make sure that when you roll them into the recovery position, items do not injure them. Be very cautious of sharp objects (for example, needles). If possible, have a witness if you remove anything from their pockets.
- **Recovery** – making sure that you don't cause further damage to the person, place them in the recovery position (see below). If a neck injury is suspected, this should be done with the assistance of other people supporting the casualty's whole body.

Be aware of jewellery to make sure it is not worsening the problem – remove it in such cases. Also look for medic alerts (such as diabetes bracelets/necklaces).

Make a mental and/or written note of anything you have observed during the primary and secondary surveys. This information should be passed on to the emergency services to help with treating the patient.

The recovery position is a way of positioning an unconscious casualty, minimising the risk of their airway becoming compromised. Two potential dangers that are avoided are:

- the tongue relaxing and blocking the airway
- the patient vomiting and the vomit blocking the airway.

Figure 18.4: The recovery position – turn the casualty onto their side; lift their chin forward in the open airway position and adjust their hand under their cheek as necessary; check the casualty cannot roll forwards or backwards.

Cardiopulmonary resuscitation (CPR)

CPR is performed when a person is not breathing and does not show any signs of circulation. This process is carried out to keep the vital organs alive until help arrives. An oxygen supply to the brain is needed to sustain life, and this is done via inhaled air and the movement of blood in the body. If a person is not breathing and their heart is not beating, this will need to be done for them. CPR involves breathing for the casualty and performing chest compressions. This is represented in Figure 18.5.

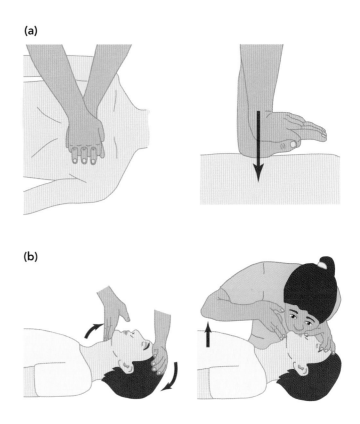

Figure 18.5: The CPR process: (a) chest compressions, (b) rescue breaths. What is the ratio of chest compressions to rescue breaths?

Shock

Shock is caused by a drop in blood pressure or blood volume. Shock can be a secondary reaction to many serious injuries (for example, with major blood loss). There are three classifications:

- cardiogenic shock – the most common type, caused by the heart not pumping effectively
- hypovolaemic shock – caused by a loss in bodily fluids resulting in low blood volume (can be common for traumatic injuries such as major sports injuries)
- anaphylactic shock – caused by a severe allergic reaction.

The signs and symptoms of shock include:

- increased pulse rate (can become weaker as the condition worsens)
- pale and clammy skin, sweating as shock worsens (lips can become blue)
- fast, shallow breathing
- nausea or vomiting
- dizziness
- feelings of weakness
- with severe shock, deep breathing can develop, with confusion, anxiety and possibly aggression
- casualties can become unconscious.

To treat shock:

- the cause of shock must be addressed (for example, a fracture must be immobilised)
- lay the person down and, if possible, raise the legs (keeping the flow of blood to the vital organs)
- keep the person warm
- loosen any tight clothing.

With all cases of shock, the emergency services should be contacted immediately. The casualty should be monitored continuously (breathing, pulse and response).

Bleeding

Loss of blood is common in many sports. Causes of blood loss can vary from minor scratches to serious lacerations and puncture wounds. With all cases of blood loss you should prevent infection in both the casualty and the person treating the wound. Disposable gloves should be worn when dealing with blood. The main priorities of blood-loss treatment are to stop the bleeding, prevent the person from going into shock, and reduce the risk of infection to a wound.

To treat bleeding, direct pressure should be applied to the site of bleeding using an appropriate bandage or gauze. Do not remove any large, impaled objects from a person. If an object is imbedded in a person, pressure can be applied at either side of the object. An absorbent, sterile dressing large enough to cover the wound completely should be applied firmly without restricting blood flow to the rest of the body. Fortunately, the majority of sports injuries are not serious enough to require CPR or treatment for shock. However, appropriate treatment is required for all injuries – if in any doubt, a professional opinion is

required. The correct treatment of injuries is critical to ensure that the healing process can occur without complications.

Further considerations

Special attention needs to be paid in certain situations following an injury.

- For an unconscious casualty you must be aware of the potential of both head injuries and the chance of concealed injuries. These can be identified through the primary and secondary surveys already discussed.
- If fractures are a possibility it is essential to minimise the movement of the injury.
- Where the risk of infection is high it is important to minimise this risk, often through appropriate covering of the injury.
- With any of these injuries, it is important to summon qualified assistance and the emergency services.
- Whether an accident takes place in the workplace or during sporting competition, it is essential to complete an accident report form if treatment of injury is required. This process is a legal requirement for insurance purposes.

3.4 Common treatments
SALTAPS

In assessing sporting injuries, you are likely to have seen the accident take place, and you will already have a reasonable understanding of the specific body part that may be damaged. In this context, some aspects of the primary and secondary survey can become obsolete, and a more specific sports-related assessment is more relevant. One such technique is performed by using the acronym **SALTAPS**.

To ensure the best efforts are made to carry out an accurate assessment of the signs and symptoms, and hopefully diagnose the injury itself, the following specific guidelines are used to assess injured people at the point of occurrence.

Stop – observe the injury.

Ask – ask questions about the injury, where it hurts, type of pain, etc.

Look – for specific signs, for example, redness, swelling, foreign objects.

Touch – palpate the injured part to identify painful areas and swelling.

Active movement – ask the injured person if they can move the injured part of the body without help.

Passive movement – if the person can move the injured part, gently move it through a full range of movement (ROM).

Strength testing – can the player stand or put pressure on the injury? Can they resume playing? If so, make sure you continue to observe them.

Note: with increasingly serious injuries, it is important to stop the SALTAPS process at an appropriate stage.

In the treatment of all sports-related injuries, the most appropriate individuals to give treatment are the most experienced. The aim of the SALTAPS process is to make an accurate assessment of the type, severity and location of an injury. This can be difficult for some sports injuries – even the most experienced practitioners can find an initial on-site diagnosis difficult.

Activity: SALTAPS

You are a first-aider on work experience alongside the sports therapist for a youth football team. During a match, two players collide in a tackle. After the incident, one of the players clutches their leg and is clearly in substantial pain. Following the SALTAPS procedure, highlight some typical responses that you may encounter, and the possible injuries. For the injuries you identify (for example, strains, sprains, fractures, bruises), highlight the point at which you should stop the SALTAPS procedure.

PRICED

For acute but less severe traumatic injuries, the initial treatment should involve the **PRICED** procedure. When soft tissues are injured they become inflamed, and the purpose of treatment is to reduce swelling, prevent further damage and ease pain.

Protect – the person and injured part of the body to minimise the risk of further injury.

Rest – allows healing and prevent any further damage.

Ice – stops the injured area from swelling.

Compression – acts as support and also prevents swelling.

Elevation – reduces blood flow to the area, reducing swelling with the aid of gravity.

Diagnosis – needs to be done by a professional.

Key terms

SALTAPS – procedure for the assessment of an injured person – stop, ask, look, touch, active movement, passive movement, strength testing.

PRICED – procedure for the treatment of acute injuries – protect, rest, ice, compression, elevation, diagnosis.

More common treatments

Common treatments that can be used when dealing with an injury are often used to minimise movement of the injured area and therefore limit further damage. Such methods could include:

- taping
- bandaging
- tubigrips
- splints
- limb supports.

Other common treatments that can be used could include:

- cryotherapy – this is the local or general use of **low** temperature that reduces swelling, prevents bleeding and provides pain relief
- thermotherapy – this is the use of **heat** treatment used to assist the healing process
- anaesthetic spray
- electrotherapy.

Medical referrals for specialist help as appropriate

Depending on the nature of the injury it may be necessary to refer an individual to a specialist. Such individuals could include:

- GP
- physiotherapist
- specialist consultant
- surgeon
- strength and conditioning coach
- nutritionist.

Assessment activity 18.3

P5 BTEC

Working in a coaching, teaching or performance environment will expose you, or other participants, to sports injuries from time to time. In your role as first-aider on work experience alongside a sports therapist, describe the steps you would take when you witness the following injuries taking place:

- a suspected fractured femur
- a head injury resulting in an unconscious casualty
- a potential hamstring tear
- a suspected anterior cruciate ligament tear. **P5**

Grading tips

To attain **P5** choose four contrasting types of sports injury to demonstrate your knowledge of a range of treatment methods. Try to include injuries at different severity levels to show your understanding of a range of treatment methods. Describe how you would approach the injury, and what you would expect to see using the SALTAPS procedure. Indicate at what point you would stop the SALTAPS procedure. Consider the first-aid methods that are most appropriate for each specific injury.

4. Be able to plan and construct treatment and rehabilitation programmes for two common sports injuries

4.1 Treatment

Based on accurate diagnosis

Rehabilitation is concerned with restoring a sportsperson's functionality to a normal state, or as near as physically possible. Progress during rehabilitation is dependent upon accurate diagnosis to enable effective healing processes of damaged tissue. The immediate first-aid and initial diagnosis and treatment of the injury can be critical to the long-term healing of the injury. If rehabilitation is not done effectively, and/or the person returns to activity too quickly, the injured body part is far more susceptible to a recurrence of the injury.

As previously highlighted, GPs, physiotherapists, medical specialists, consultant surgeons, strength and conditioning coaches and nutritionists provide specialist help and advice and this advice can be for the long-term success of a rehabilitation programme. This is particularly important for serious injuries where rehabilitation can be a long, time-consuming, and often painful and frustrating process.

Key term

Rehabilitation – the process of restoring a person's physical functionality to a normal state, or as near as physically possible.

4.2 Rehabilitation

Identification of the stages of rehabilitation

There are five stages of rehabilitation:
1 acute stage
2 re-establishing functional activity
3 strengthening exercises
4 ongoing treatments
5 gradual increase in activity.

These five stages are designed to ensure the functions of rehabilitation are systematically undertaken to ensure the athlete has the best potential to return to normal functional activity. A combination of strengthening exercises, ongoing medical treatments and gradual increases in activity are central components of a programme design. Some important functions of a programme are to:

- ensure correct immediate first-aid is provided
- reduce pain and swelling
- minimise pain in subsequent hours, days and weeks
- re-establish neuromuscular control of the injured area of the body
- restore ROM of the affected joints
- restore lost muscular strength, power and endurance
- develop core stability, posture and balance
- maintain cardiovascular fitness to an attainable level.

The healing process

Many of the physiological responses to injury follow a clear sequence and timescale. The signs and symptoms of an injury can be a clear indicator of the progression of the healing process.

- Inflammatory response phase (see page 176) occurs as soon as an injury takes place, and is the start of the healing process. Inflammation ensures that healing properties in the blood can access the injured part of the body while simultaneously disposing of injury by-products.
- Repair phase – occurs after a few hours of injury, and can last as long as six weeks. Some of the signs and symptoms are similar to the inflammatory response phase. Involves rebuilding the damaged structure and healing the damaged areas. Scar tissue will develop during this phase.
- Remodelling phase – scar tissue development will imitate the original structures prior to the injury. If appropriate care is given to the injury, long-term scarring will decrease, and strength and ROM will improve at the site of the injury.

Remember

Each phase of the healing process can be prolonged by inappropriate management techniques. It is important to encourage movement exercises, as developing scar tissue can shrink over time and can limit ROM.

4.3 Programme

Methods to improve lost range of motion

Restoring flexibility is vital to limit the chances of an injury recurring. With the majority of injuries, inflammation and general damage will have dramatically reduced the movement possible at the joints near or at the site of injury. Potentially, ROM at other joints of the body will also have decreased, because exercise levels will have dropped. Stretching of muscles is an important ingredient of any warm-up and cool down and will minimise the risk of injury (see Unit 15, Instructing physical activity and exercise, pages 116–118). Stretching should be incorporated into a rehabilitation programme to regain ROM.

Advice on the best stretching methods has changed over the years, with some methods being replaced (some can cause damage to different parts of the body, for example, bouncing while touching your toes puts stress on your lower back). Distinctly different methods of stretching are used in ROM exercises:

- dynamic stretching – controlled movements towards the limits of ROM (for example, swinging arms and legs)
- static stretching – holding a stretch at the furthest ROM
- passive stretching – similar to static stretching, but involves stretching using either a piece of apparatus or another person
- active stretching – similar to static stretching, but involves holding a position with only the assistance of the surrounding muscle groups
- proprioceptive neuromuscular facilitation (PNF) stretching – combines stretching with muscular contraction.

PNF is fast-developing and is used in a number of sports (for example, gymnastics and dance) as well as for rehabilitation. A stretch is performed by moving the limb or joint toward the limits of ROM, then force is applied by the person stretching against a resistance (either a partner or apparatus) (see Unit 15 Instructing physical activity and exercise, page 118).

Strengthening and coordination exercises

Strengthening exercises are important throughout rehabilitation, as this aspect of fitness will have deteriorated as a result of an injury. Developing muscular strength, endurance and power is an essential element of rehabilitation. Muscle atrophy is a decrease in muscle size that will take place due to injury and reduced physical training. Static and dynamic strength training methods can be used to address the problem, with increased resistance and impact later in a programme. Resistance machines, free weights and some endurance machines (for example, an exercise bike) can be used for this aspect of rehabilitation. Exercises should be specific to the injured area, but the whole body should be considered to prevent muscular imbalances. Coordination losses will often occur following an injury. A range of coordination training exercises, specific to the injured area of the body, should be incorporated into a rehabilitation programme to complement other treatment procedures. An example is wobble board exercises.

Remember

A rehabilitation programme must be designed specifically to take into account an individual's abilities and characteristics. Depending on the speed of recovery, and any problems that arise, modifications may be needed on a regular basis.

Psychological considerations during rehabilitation

The psychological aspect of how well an athlete deals with rehabilitation and the often slow return to competition is often neglected. Athletes, and any individual who suffers an injury, can experience a very wide range of emotions. Individual differences dictate that athletes will vary dramatically both in the physical aspects of the programme (including pain threshold and speed of recovery) and also in how well they deal with the mental aspects of an injury. Motivation and anxiety are common issues that must be considered during each phase of rehabilitation.

Activity: Treatment techniques

Research the following treatment techniques and identify the stage of the healing and rehabilitation process at which it would be best to use the different methods for different injuries. Working in groups, make a table like the one below.

Table 18.3: At which stage should each method be used?

Method	Inflammatory response	Repair	Remodelling phase
Flexibility stretching			
Taping			
Cryotherapy			
Strengthening exercises			
Coordination exercises			
Electrotherapy			
Massage			
Thermotherapy			
Acupuncture			

Many of the psychological techniques used to enhance performance and other coping strategies can be useful in dealing with the problems associated with sporting injuries. These techniques are covered in Student Book 1, Unit 17 Psychology for sports performance. Such psychological intervention techniques can be implemented alongside a rehabilitation programme to complement the processes.

Remember

Psychological issues can also influence physical recovery following an injury.

One of the most important aspects of a rehabilitation programme for an athlete is that they can see improvements in the injury and that they are progressing towards competition fitness. It important to set appropriate goals for the athlete to strive towards during rehabilitation. Goal-setting can incorporate both long- and short-term goals. These should be designed in a progressive manner – a number of very specific short-term goals (week by week) are assembled to construct a more generalised set of long-term goals. Goal-setting can be a vital tool enabling a progressive rehabilitation programme, and well planned goals can act as a powerful psychological tool, helping the athlete to see significant progression and to remain focused on returning to fitness.

The need for a careful, structured approach to rehabilitation

The physical and mental strain that can be placed on an athlete during their rehabilitation from injury can elicit motivational issues and also anxiety. Such factors must be acknowledged when designing and modifying programmes to suit individual needs.

Recording documentation and tracking of treatment

When developing a rehabilitation programme you should be proficient in both the practical aspects and the accurate recording of the entire process. The records kept should detail accurately all the factors of the rehabilitation, from the initial injury evaluation to the end of the programme. Things to consider when documenting a rehabilitation programme include:

- background information about the client (for example, medical issues, injury history, specific requirements of rehabilitation)
- the activities undertaken
- the levels and development of the client
- problems or issues arising from the session
- complications (for example, allergies or illness) that affect the quality of the client's progress during the session
- important legal documents and forms such as parental consent for younger sports players
- dates for review/functional testing (aims, objectives, etc.)
- accurate and up to date information that may change during the duration of the treatment
- specific objectives including appropriate and measurable timescales and review dates.

Take it further

Potential complications

Research into the potential complications that could arise during the rehabilitation of injury for the following scenarios:

- a 9-year-old football player experiencing a hairline fracture to the fibula and an ankle sprain
- a 55-year-old, physically healthy man who has developed knee cartilage problems
- a 17-year-old student representative hockey player who has developed lower back muscular spasms
- a formerly inactive 32-year-old individual who has developed achilles tendonitis two weeks after starting at a gym with the intention of losing weight.

Assessment activity 18.4

P6 M3 D2 BTEC

1. In your role as a first-aider on work experience alongside the sports therapist, design a rehabilitation programme for two selected athletes who have suffered different, common sports injuries. You can do this with support from your tutor. **P6**

2. Alternatively, you can perform this task without tutor support. **M3**

3. Finally, you should evaluate your rehabilitation programme and justify your choice of methods and, where appropriate, suggest alternative methods. **D2**

Grading tips

- To attain **P6** you must demonstrate your research skills and knowledge of a range of rehabilitation protocols. Ensure you provide appropriate timescales for a rehabilitation programme for the two different injuries.

- To attain **M3** you must ensure you do all of the above but independently.

- To attain **D2** explain how unforeseen circumstances may require changes and modifications to a rehabilitation programme. Consideration is needed of how the rehabilitation process will change in response to each specific phase of the healing process. Link the type of activity to the injury and the duration/phase of healing process.

PLTS

By designing your rehabilitation programme, you can develop your skills as an **independent enquirer**, **creative thinker** and **self-manager**.

Functional skills

By producing your rehabilitation programme you could provide evidence of your skills in **English**.

Ian Harris

Physiotherapist

Ian is a registered physiotherapist and leads a small team in a sports injuries clinic. He is responsible for the evaluation and rehabilitation of clients who have suffered a wide variety of sports injuries. The roles and responsibilities that Ian fulfils are very diverse including:

- dealing with professional athletes who have suffered injuries of various severities
- supporting elderly people with a variety of health-related problems and injuries
- treating and rehabilitating young people who have been injured while participating in youth sport
- rehabilitating individuals with long-term chronic injuries requiring technical modifications to their physical movements.

'A common scenario that I sometimes encounter involves elite athletes feeling concerned that they will not be able to compete at the level they did previously and that their injury might be career threatening. In a situation like this I often prioritise both the physiological and psychological demands on the athletes. Furthermore, in cases like this, a team of individuals may be used to support the athlete including me (the physiotherapist), a sport psychologist, coaches, family and team mates.

Based on the physical and mental demands on an athlete it is essential to provide realistic but challenging goals that they can work towards. When an athlete becomes disillusioned with their progress I often find it particularly useful to sit down with them and explain how far they have developed since the injury by reviewing their previous short-term goals.'

A physiotherapist is continually dealing with people and Ian has not only the scientific know-how and academic qualifications but also the interpersonal and counselling skills that are often demanded in his job.

Think about it!

- What steps would you take when dealing with an athlete who has become frustrated with their rehabilitation progress and is considering retiring from their sport?
- What are the skills most often applied by professional physiotherapists? Write a list of the main personal attributes needed to become a physiotherapist and discuss these with your peers.
- Research the qualifications required to become a physiotherapist.

Just checking

1. What is the difference between intrinsic and extrinsic injury risk factors?
2. What steps can you take to reduce your risk of injury before training or competition?
3. What can coaches do to protect their team from injury risk?
4. Provide three examples of the primary damage responses that are likely to occur as a result of a sports injury.
5. Define the following:
   lordosis
   kyphosis
   scoliosis
6. What are the different categorisations of fractures?
7. What is the difference between hard and soft tissue damage?
8. What do the following acronyms stand for?
   PRICED
   SALTAPS
9. Which psychological problems may occur as a result of suffering from a sports injury?
10. Provide three examples of typical procedures that are common during injury rehabilitation.

edexcel

Assignment tips

- Choose to investigate injuries from that are common within sports that you have an interest in.
- Remember that extrinsic and intrinsic sports injury risk can be minimised using a variety of control measures.
- Ensure that you match the appropriate preventative measures to the specific sport.
- Utilise a range of sources of information to help write your treatment programme.
- Keep a record of the different injury classification methods.
- Remember that sport injuries manifest both psychological and physiological responses.

19 Analysis of sports performance

Coaches and athletes need to know how movement and physiology affect performance. There is also increasing awareness of sports psychology, and how the mind can affect performance – factors such as stress and motivation can make the difference between winning and losing. Performance may also depend on a technical or tactical aspect. This unit introduces the need to analyse sporting performance.

During his or her career, every high-level or world-class athlete will suffer from a loss of form or a significant setback. By analysing their performance, athletes can address the issues that are affecting them and make the changes necessary to gain success. If no evaluation takes place after a poor or unsuccessful performance, athletes may continue to perform badly and miss out on medals or other measures of success. Coaches should understand the importance of this area, and how they can influence and support the athlete, both in training and in competition.

Learning outcomes

After completing this unit you should:

1. know the performance profile of a sporting activity
2. be able to analyse sporting performance
3. be able to provide feedback to athletes regarding performance
4. understand the purpose and resources required for analysing different levels of sporting performance.

Assessment and grading criteria

This table shows you what you must do in order to achieve a pass, merit or distinction grade, and where you can find activities in this book to help you.

To achieve a **pass** grade the evidence must show that you are able to:	To achieve a **merit** grade the evidence must show that, in addition to the pass criteria, you are able to:	To achieve a **distinction** grade the evidence must show that, in addition to the pass and merit criteria, you are able to:
P1 describe the performance profile of a selected sporting activity **See Assessment activity 19.1, page 209**	**M1** explain the performance profile of a selected sporting activity **See Assessment activity 19.1, page 209**	**D1** analyse the performance profile of a selected sporting activity **See Assessment activity 19.1, page 209**
P2 describe five factors that may influence the performance of an athlete **See Assessment activity 19.2, page 213**		
P3 perform an assessment of a selected athlete undertaking sporting activity using three components of their performance profile, with tutor support **See Assessment activity 19.2, page 213**	**M2** independently perform an assessment of a selected athlete undertaking sporting activity using three components of their performance profile **See Assessment activity 19.2, page 213**	**D2** analyse the performance of a selected athlete using three components of their performance profile **See Assessment activity 19.2, page 213**
P4 provide feedback to the athlete based on the assessment of their performance, with tutor support **See Assessment activity 19.3, page 216**	**M3** independently provide feedback to the athlete based on the assessment of their performance **See Assessment activity 19.3, page 216**	
P5 explain the purpose of, and the resources required for, analysis at two different levels of sports performance **See Assessment activity 19.4, page 220**		

How you will be assessed

Your assessments could be in the form of:

- written reports
- case studies
- presentations
- interviews
- role play
- video analysis.

Helen, 17-year-old gymnast

This unit helped me to understand how I can improve as a gymnast. It made me think of the factors that affect my performance and how I can measure them. I particularly enjoyed using video analysis to film and watch my performances over a period of time as part of a performance profile assessment. I also liked the fitness testing aspects of the unit as I enjoy practical sport and the results helped me to set specific targets for the future and see how specific components of fitness changed with the aid of a training programme.

The unit also helped me compare my performances with other gymnasts and it helped me understand the specific techniques and requirements that I need to perform to the best of my ability. I enjoyed working with both coaches and my peers and their feedback was invaluable in giving me the information that would help me to improve.

Over to you!

1. What aspects of this unit are you looking forward to studying?
2. What parts of your sport can you analyse?
3. How will video analysis help you to improve as a sports performer?
4. How will target setting help you to improve your performance?

1. Know the performance profile of a sporting activity

How can analysis improve performance?

A good understanding of **performance analysis** is vital in measuring team and individual performance and making recommendations for future improvements. Being able to analyse will enable you to set clear targets in order to achieve personal and sporting success.

In groups, discuss what areas of performance can be analysed and how you can do this. You should consider the skills you would need and how each identified area can affect performance and success.

Key term

Performance analysis – the provision of objective feedback to performers trying to achieve a positive change in performance.

Performance profiling is a way of giving the athlete information about what *actually* happened in their sport – rather than what they *think* happened. It involves both analysing the athlete's performance through observation, and also understanding the athlete's state of mind. There may be occasions when the athlete has underperformed due to nerves or lack of concentration. Therefore the purpose of performance profiling is to:

- assist the athlete with both their physical and their psychological needs
- assess scope for technical and tactical improvement
- improve the athlete's motivation and performance.

The coach should assess the athlete before and after the event, discussing physical, technical and tactical issues, and the following important psychological factors:

- confidence
- concentration
- commitment
- control
- refocusing of effort.

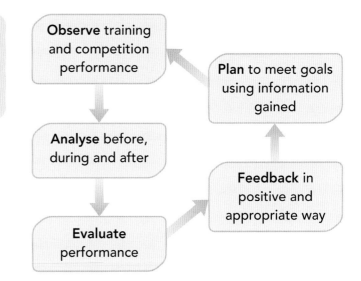

Figure 19.1: A performance analysis will follow a clear process. What are the advantages of using such a model of analysis?

Understanding each of these will allow you to prepare a strategy to address the issues highlighted by the profiling.

1.1 Sporting activity

Different sports have very different requirements, and the athlete and coach should be aware of the specific physical and psychological demands needed in order to achieve success. For example, a midfield player in football will need different physical and mental skills from a goalkeeper.

What factors may affect an archer's concentration?

Performance profiling should take into account the individual and specific demands of both the sport, and the position within that sport. Performance profiling and analysis can be used to document, assess and predict the ability of a goalkeeper to meet the demands of performance, covering various aspects of physical capacity, psychological factors, technical skill and tactical awareness. These may include:

- physical tests of speed, strength, power and flexibility, core stability and endurance
- psychological assessment of personality, anxiety and confidence
- biomechanical analysis of movement technique
- notational analysis of performance.

While some of these factors may be relevant to other positions within the team, any profiling or analysis must identify requirements specific to goalkeeping.

Take it further

Four key areas of performance

The four key areas of performance are physical, psychological, technical and tactical. Consider each of these areas and highlight how they affect performance in a chosen sport. You may wish to consider the role of the coach as well as the performer in this analysis.

Individual based

Examples of individual based sports are archery or shooting. These are unusual sports because the opposing player has no effect on the player in action. Archers are required to concentrate for long periods, and the skills they use are described as 'closed'. A closed skill is one that takes place in a stable, predictable environment – the performer knows exactly what to do, and when. However, skills can be affected by the environment, for example, the weather. Movements follow set patterns and have a clear beginning and end. The skills tend to be self-paced. An archer may have to wait for long periods before performing.

Specific position

Different sports make different demands on athletes – and different positions within the same sport also make very different demands. An example is a goalkeeper (in any sport), who will need to concentrate for long periods without being directly or physically involved in the action.

Once the individual physical, psychological, technical (biomechanical) and tactical strengths and weaknesses have been identified in relation to the unique demands of goalkeeping, the next step is to use this information to set short- and long-term goals for training. Setting goals gives purpose and direction to the training programme, and promotes the intrinsic motivation, self-confidence and sense of responsibility that will strengthen the goalkeeper's adherence to the training programme. The profiling process should be repeated at regular intervals to monitor the effectiveness of the specific training programme, and highlight any areas of good or poor progress.

Research shows that, on average, a soccer goalkeeper spends 86 per cent of a match walking or standing still, and the remaining 14 per cent performing activities at moderate to high intensity. This equates to approximately 12 minutes' pressure on the goalkeeper throughout the duration of the match.

The goalkeeper must also be prepared mentally throughout the match. From a psychological perspective, the goalkeeper must be constantly alive to potential dangers, remaining focused and concentrating on the build-up of play, which will be linked to his or her physiological ability to recover quickly after each exertion in preparation for the next attack.

Specific action

Many sports require the analysis of a specific action. Complex actions, such as a tennis serve, should be broken down into smaller stages so that a clear analysis can be made.

Using a whole–part–whole method of analysis, it is possible for the coach and player to investigate key parts of a technique. This means that the whole skill can be analysed and practised, while more detailed or complex elements are learned and practised specifically and separately, in order to make up the whole skill. For example, the initial throw may be too far in front of the tennis player, so that he or she keeps serving into the net.

1.2 Performance profile

The purpose of analysing a sporting performance is to provide detailed feedback to the athlete or team in order for them to improve their game. When analysing the performance of an individual or team, you should consider a variety of questions, which might include:

- How well are specific skills executed?
- How focused and motivated are the athletes?
- Are the athletes using the correct techniques?
- Are the correct tactics adopted at the right time?

This example of a performance profile can be adapted to suit any sport. It compares where the athlete views their level of performance for each category against the perfect model of performance. Any differences can then be identified and discussed.

Technical and tactical

Sport involves many complex skills and techniques. As we learn and practise these skills, they become more 'natural' and we are able to refine and perfect them. For example, a cricketer will practise specific shots as part of his or her training programme, to the standard needed to execute them as part of a competitive match. All sports require athletes to have good techniques in order to achieve success. Therefore it is essential that the athlete and coach focus on how individual skills are performed. This may involve observational analysis and feedback, and examining complex skills broken down into simpler parts. Skills can be divided into three categories:

- Discrete skills which have a very clear beginning and end, for example, a serve in tennis.
- Continuous skills which have no obvious beginning or end but tend to merge and flow into one another as the skill or sport progresses, for example, cycling or swimming.
- Serial skills which are composed of both discrete and continuous skills, for example, a tennis player playing a shot on the run.

All sports require tactics or strategies in order to achieve success. Sport contains many examples of tactics that a coach, athlete or team may adopt in order to win. These may include playing the offside trap in football, batting defensively in cricket, or using zone marking in basketball. When devising and using

Table 19.1: A completed performance profile.

Characteristics identified by the athlete	Athlete's perceived level of importance (API)	Athlete's self-assessment (ASA)	Discrepancy (10 – ASA) × API
Confidence	8	8	16
Concentration	10	6	40
Control	6	7	18
Commitment	8	8	16
Refocusing after errors	6	5	30
Enjoyment	10	8	20

tactics, it is important that all the players understand the tactic and when to employ it. Failing to do this may lead to confusion and disrupt performance.

- Shooting – sports such as football, netball, basketball and hockey all require players to hit a target in order to achieve points or goals. Therefore an important performance analysis is measuring how many shots either an individual player or team make, how many of these are on or off target, and how many are successful. Using notational analysis and evaluation of this data will allow the coach to recognise whether specific training and coaching is needed, or to devise specific tactics.

- Crossing – further analysis will allow the coach and athletes to determine the number of crosses that were successful in reaching a team mate, or in a shot on or off target. For example, if a player makes ten crosses in a game but only three of them reach a team mate, then further coaching is likely to be needed.

- Catching – many sports, such as rugby, cricket and basketball, require players to catch a ball either to defeat an opponent or to continue a pattern of play. Again, analysis will determine the number of catches that were successfully caught or dropped – if an area of weakness is discovered, further analysis can be carried out and training focused on this area.

- Passing – a key component of most team sports is passing a ball between players in order to reach a goal. Analysis could include the number of successful passes made, the number of passes that fail to reach their target, and whether short or long passes were more successful. It is important that both coach and players are clear about what is being observed, and clear definitions are made of 'success', and 'short' and 'long' passes. Tactics often use either long or short passes depending on previous analysis of individuals or opponents.

- Tackling – gaining possession through tackling is an important tactic. The coach and players should conduct an analysis that counts the number of successful tackles made, or the number of fouls committed (resulting in free or penalty kicks) through poor tackling.

- Heading – football requires players to head the ball. Heading may be necessary to pass the ball between players or to shoot at the goal. Notational analysis will count the number of successful headers, while a qualitative analysis will allow more detailed and descriptive feedback to be given, correcting poor technique.

- Dribbling – the skill of dribbling can be analysed both quantitatively and qualitatively. The time and distance an individual player dribbles with the ball can be observed and analysed, or the coach may prefer to observe dribbling technique, ensuring that the correct skills are used.

- Striking – similar to shooting, the way a soccer player strikes a ball will have a direct effect on where it goes (either successfully or unsuccessfully). Players such as Didier Drogba will use video analysis to observe their striking technique, and practise to perfect this skill. This quantitative analysis allows the player to observe a perfect model.

- Positional play – modern technology allows coaches, players and even spectators to observe the movements of players throughout a match. Television pundits use this information to offer their expert opinion on why a team is either successful or unsuccessful. Being able to observe the position of individual players can help a coach identify why, for example, a goal was scored or conceded. The information can be used to develop patterns of play and tactics such as attacking or defensive play. This is particularly important in sports such as basketball, where a coach may prefer to use man-marking in preference to zone-marking.

- Style of play – performance profiling will allow a coach to devise tactics suited to both his or her team, and the opposition's style of play. A team may prefer to focus on attacking rather than defensive play, and their tactics may be to play long balls forward. Or a team may play defensively and try and score goals on the counter-attack. Various formations have been developed by coaches that will suit their players, tactics and strategies.

Case study: The English Institute for Sport

The English Institute of Sport provides elite athletes with the opportunity to undertake performance analysis in order to prepare for competition. The Institute describes performance analysis as the provision of objective feedback to performers trying to achieve a positive change in performance. In simple terms, this means providing the athlete with information on what they actually did, as opposed to what they think they did.

1. **For a sport of your choice, visit the English Institute of Sport's website (www.eis2win. co.uk) to investigate how your sporting performance can be enhanced through performance analysis.**

Physical (health- and sports-related fitness)

Sport requires participants to have a high level of fitness in order to perform. It is also important to be physically fit simply for health reasons. There are five main components of fitness:

- Strength – the ability of a muscle or group of muscles to exert a maximal force, or overcome a maximal resistance, in a single contraction.

- Aerobic endurance – the ability of the heart, lungs, blood vessels and skeletal muscle to take in, transport and utilise oxygen efficiently and over a prolonged period.

- Muscular endurance – the ability of a muscle or group of muscles to make repeated contractions against light to moderate resistance and over a prolonged period.

- Flexibility – a measure of ability to move a joint through a complete and natural range of motion without discomfort or pain.

- Body composition – the body's physical make-up in terms of fat and lean or non-fat body tissue, measured as a percentage.

Being able to measure these will help the coach and athlete develop a training plan that will meet the specific requirements of the sport and the chosen area of fitness. Fitness tests can be conducted to measure each area, and the results analysed in order to develop a training programme.

Physiological

- **Heart rate** – this can be measured during exercise with a heart rate monitor. Athletes can train within target zones of their maximum heart rate, at a controlled intensity.

Activity: Heart rate

The measurement of heart rate is a good indicator of cardiovascular fitness. Using a simple test, you can measure your resting heart rate (RHR) by taking your pulse, with lower readings indicating a healthy cardiovascular system. An RHR between 60 and 70 beats per minute (bpm) is considered normal. Maximum heart rate (MHR) can be calculated as 220 – age.

- What is your RHR?

- What is your MHR?

- How can you use knowledge of heart rate as part of your training? Calculate your maximum heart rate, and the workout training zones of 60, 70 and 80 per cent of your maximum heart rate.

- **Warm-up** – to perform at the highest level, physical preparation before training and competition is paramount. A warm-up generally consists of a gradual increase in intensity in physical activity. For example, before running or playing an intense sport, you might jog slowly to warm your muscles and increase your heart rate. It is important that a warm-up should be specific to the exercise that will follow, preparing the muscles to be used and activating the energy systems that are required for that particular activity. Stretching the active muscles is also recommended after doing a warm-up.

The three main functions of a warm-up are to:

○ increase heart rate

○ raise body temperature

○ prepare the major joints of the body.

The warm-up should increase the heart rate in order to pump more blood around the body to the working muscle, in preparation for exercise. This in turn allows more energy to be produced using oxygen, and increases the body and muscle temperature. Increasing muscle temperature will improve the elasticity of the working muscles, making them less likely to become injured. The warm-up should involve a wide range of movements specific to the exercise or sport to be undertaken.

For a warm-up to be most effective, it should be tailored to the individual client.

- **Cool down** – the purpose of a cool down is to return the body back to its pre-exercise state. The three main objectives of a cool down are to:
  - return the heart rate back to normal
  - remove any waste products that may have built up during exercise
  - return the muscles to their original state (or length, if stretched).

A cool down will keep the metabolic rate high and the capillaries dilated to enable oxygen to flush through the muscle tissue, which helps to remove lactic acid waste created by the exercise. This should stop the blood from staying in the veins, which can cause dizziness if exercise is stopped too quickly. A cool down can also reduce the effect of delayed-onset muscle soreness (DOMS), which often follows strenuous exercise that the body is not used to. The final part of the cool down should include stretching designed to facilitate and improve flexibility, as the muscles will be very warm at this stage.

- **Lung function** – being able to analyse lung function allows athletes to determine not only the size of their lungs, and therefore how much air they can inhale, but also the strength and efficiency of their lungs. Being able to inspire oxygen and deliver it to working muscle is essential to athletes of all abilities. Likewise, being able to expire waste products such as carbon dioxide is also vital to sporting performance.

Recently there has been much scientific research into lung function and aerobic sports such as cycling, long-distance running and rowing. Results indicate that the larger and stronger the lungs, the more able they are to deliver oxygen to the working muscle, especially during intense exercise. For example, an elite rower may be able to deliver up to 240 litres of air per minute in and out of the lungs. To put this in perspective, a typical value for an untrained male would be between 100 and 150 litres per minute during maximal exercise.

A spirometer is used to measure lung function. The athlete takes the deepest breath he or she can, then exhales into the spirometer as hard as possible, for as long as possible. The spirometer is then able to determine the following measurements:

- Forced vital capacity (FVC) – the total amount of air that you can forcibly blow out after full inspiration, measured in litres.
- Forced expired volume 1 (FEV 1) – the amount of air that you can forcibly blow out in 1 second, measured in litres per second (along with forced vital capacity, considered one of the primary indicators of lung function).
- Peak expiratory flow (PEF) – the speed of the air moving out of your lungs at the beginning of the expiration, also measured in litres per second.

Psychological

- **Motivation** – understanding what motivates athletes to train and compete will help the coach devise varied and enjoyable training sessions. Motivation is the desire or need to perform a certain task; it is why we choose to do something. Motivation has been defined as 'the direction and intensity of effort' – meaning what we choose to do, and the amount of effort we put in. There are many theories on motivation but in general it can be regarded as **intrinsic** (internal) or **extrinsic** (external).

- **Anxiety** – a certain level of stress is needed for optimum performance. If you are under too little stress, then you will find it difficult to motivate yourself to give a good performance. Too little stress expresses itself in feelings of boredom and not being stretched.

But too much stress and anxiety can seriously affect your ability to focus on your skills and performance. Both coach and athlete should recognise the symptoms of stress and anxiety to ensure performance is not affected.

Excessive levels of stress damage performance and damage your enjoyment of your sport, and may occur:

- when you think what is being asked of you is beyond your perceived abilities
- when too much is asked of you in too short a time
- when unnecessary obstacles are put in the way of achieving goals.

An optimum level of stress will give the benefits of alertness and activation that improve performance.

Anxiety is different from stress. Anxiety comes from concern about a lack of control over circumstances. In some cases, being anxious and worrying over a problem may generate a solution. But normally it will just result in negative thinking, and have a detrimental effect on performance. An example would be an athlete worrying about what the spectators think about their performance and fearing making a mistake.

- **Arousal** – this is how interested we are in performing a specific sport or action. Every sport will develop a sense of excitement, but if this becomes too great then the athlete may feel anxious, with a negative effect on performance. It is important that the levels of arousal are suitable to the skills that are being performed.

- **Attention** – a sportsperson will be presented with a wide variety of information when they are training and competing. Some of this information will be important and relevant, such as instructions from the coach and other players, while some will be of no use, such as negative comments from the crowd. It is essential that the athlete is able to focus on the relevant information that will lead to a successful performance. By selectively attending to only the important information, we are able to ignore negative factors that could affect performance. The demand for concentration varies with the sport:
  - sustained concentration – distance running, cycling, tennis, squash
  - short bursts of concentration – cricket, golf, athletic field events
  - intense concentration – sprinting events, skiing.

  Common distractions include anxiety, mistakes, fatigue, weather, public announcements, coach, manager, opponent, negative thoughts, etc.

- **Confidence** – confidence describes the feeling that you are going to succeed in a given situation: you will have self-confidence if you believe that you can achieve your goal. The more confident you are, the more likely you are to achieve your goals, which in turn is likely to result in sporting success. A confident athlete is likely to persevere even when things are not going to plan, show enthusiasm, be positive in their approach, and take their share of the responsibility for both success and failure.

Why is aggression important in rugby? Is aggression acceptable in *all* sports?

- **Aggression** – sports such as rugby require the players to show aggression, and in this context can be considered a good thing. A player may make a hard tackle and win possession of the ball. But in most sports, and beyond a certain level, aggression is seen as bad. A player throwing a punch is seen negatively, and is normally punished by the laws of the game.

  It is important that athletes are able to control their emotions and only use aggression in a controlled and appropriate way. Becoming frustrated by their own or others' performance may lead to feelings of anger, resulting in a lack of concentration on the task, deteriorating performance and a loss of confidence in their ability, which fuels the anger – a slippery slope to failure.

  A coach must teach players that while aggression can be positive in trying to win, winning should only be achieved by playing within the rules of the game.

- **Relaxation** – relaxation is a technique that can be used to reduce anxiety and therefore enhance performance. There are many ways in which the coach can help athletes to relax, including mental imagery, progressive muscular relaxation and meditation.

  Mental imagery is a technique used by athletes to imagine themselves in a variety of situations – perhaps performing a certain skill at a specific place, or in a relaxing situation such as lying on a beach. Research indicates that the more detailed the imagery, the more likely the athlete is to feel prepared for a specific situation. Imagery is useful in:

o developing self-confidence

o developing strategies to teach athletes to cope with new situations before they encounter them

o helping athletes focus their attention on a particular skill they are trying to learn or develop.

Progressive muscular relaxation involves the purposeful contracting and relaxing of specific muscles. Each muscle is contracted for between 4–6 seconds and then consciously relaxed, with the athlete making a mental note of how they feel. This process allows the muscles to return to a more relaxed state.

Meditation is used to reduce stress before an event, and with experience athletes can learn to relax different muscle groups and appreciate subtle differences in muscle tension. By making a note of their breathing and muscle tension, the athlete is able to relax and focus on the competition ahead.

- **Concentration** – the ability to focus and concentrate will aid performance and success. Concentration can be described as the ability to focus on a specific task. Due to the nature of sport, many factors may cause an athlete or team to become distracted – the crowd, the weather or negative thoughts. Therefore an athlete should learn how to concentrate, especially under pressure.

Remember

You must always concentrate on your sporting performance. Do not get put off by other players or spectators as this will have a negative effect on your performance.

Biomechanical (quantitative and qualitative)

Biomechanics is the science that examines forces acting on the human body in sport, and explains how performance can be affected by these forces. At the highest levels of sport, in which techniques play a major role, biomechanics provides an opportunity to investigate and analyse specific movements in order for improvements to be made.

Activity: Biomechanics in action

Forces play a significant part in many sports. However some sports people actually use these forces to aid their performance. One example of this is a cricket bowler. A bowler will keep one side of a cricket ball shiny and the other rough. This enables the ball to swing through the air as it is bowled because of the drag created by the rough side.

Consider your sport. How do forces affect performance? Are there examples of spin being used? How do playing surfaces affect performance? How can an understanding of biomechanics enhance a sportsperson's performance?

Quantitative analysis involves a detailed, scientific approach to observation analysis. It uses direct measurement of a technique or performance, and is often very time-consuming due to the need for detailed data collection. One method of collecting information is to watch a game and write down the action as it occurs – this is known as real-time analysis. However, sport is fast-moving and it is often necessary to video record a performance – this is known as lapsed-time analysis. For example, in a basketball match it would be very difficult to collect statistical data such as successful shots as the action occurred.

As technology has advanced, suitable equipment such as video cameras and laptop computers has become affordable. This means that a coach will be able to collect data at training and competition and analyse it afterwards. Examples of quantitative analysis may include:

- recording patterns of play
- recording successful passes in basketball
- examining the techniques used by a bowler in cricket
- the number of successful tackles in football
- the number of turnovers in a basketball match.

Key term

Quantitative analysis – uses numerical data or statistics to describe sporting performance.

Qualitative analysis is much simpler than quantitative analysis, as it simply requires general observation of a performance to be carried out. This can be done by a coach, spectators or even other players. Because this method is largely subjective (or open to interpretation), the information gathered may be biased. Therefore the more experience and knowledge an observer has, the more accurate the analysis is likely to be.

> **Key term**
>
> **Qualitative analysis** – uses descriptions and words to describe sporting performance.

An example of biomechanics being used as part of a performance analysis is the study of linear displacement. This describes how far and how quickly a person or object moves in a straight line. The information can then be used to determine the velocity and the acceleration of the object. Such information (quantitative data) may be useful for a 100-metre sprinter, for example. A coach will be able to determine if the runner is slow out of the blocks, or if they get slower (or decelerate) during the race.

Sports such as the javelin or shot-put involve the athlete throwing the object the furthest distance. By using both qualitative and quantitative analyses, the performer and coach can determine technique and velocity of release. Qualitative analysis can aid the athlete by observing and analysing the technique during the throw. A coach can then highlight key aspects of the technique and give descriptive feedback, with demonstrations if necessary. Collecting numerical data through video observation (quantitative analysis), the coach can work out if the velocity of release is too low. This would result in the javelin or shot put being thrown shorter distances. Biomechanics and analysis will also allow the coach to investigate the optimum angle of release so that maximum distances can be reached.

1.3 Factors influencing performance

Many factors can affect an athlete's performance in competition and training. It is important that the athlete and coach recognise and understand each of these, and adapt their training and competition accordingly. These factors can be divided into two broad categories: intrinsic and extrinsic.

Intrinsic factors

- **Age** – this constantly affects a person's level of fitness. For all forms of competitive sport there are age divisions, usually junior, youth and senior. Your body changes as you get older. The stages are shown in Figure 19.2.

Some activities are regarded as young people's sports and some as older people's sports. If an activity requires a great deal of physical exertion, it is more difficult to compete at a high level as we get older and our fitness levels begin to deteriorate. For example, an athlete's flexibility will decrease over time and will affect performance, especially in sports such as judo or gymnastics. It is important that the athlete and coach realise how the following key components can affect sporting performance:

- practising and learning – very young people can't cope with too much information and are unlikely to be able to learn complex skills
- strength – a young person will not achieve their maximum strength until they reach full adulthood

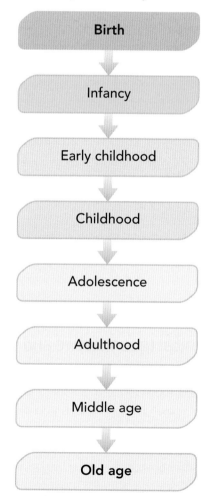

Figure 19.2: Life stages.

- skill – this can improve due to growth (high jumpers may appear more skilful as they get taller)
- flexibility – this decreases with age, with a negative effect on sports that require a wide range of movement, such as gymnastics
- diet – the body's metabolism slows down as we get older, so weight is likely to be gained
- reaction time – this decreases with age and, as many sports require quick reactions, can have a negative effect on performance
- injury and disease – older people are more likely to suffer from injury and disease, and take longer to recover.

It is also worth remembering that experience comes with age – and will generally have a positive effect on sporting performance and success.

- **Health** – recently there has been a massive growth in the number of health clubs offering both exercise classes, and complementary and relaxation therapies. For an athlete to perform at an optimum level of performance, they must be in excellent health and free from injury or illness.

However, recent studies suggest that some athletes may be exposing themselves to a range of health problems associated with inadequate dietary intake. Such behaviour is thought to stem from an obsessive desire to win, coupled with pressure from coaches and society's overwhelming obsession with body image.

- **Diet** – a suitable and balanced diet is the key to both health and the foundation of high sporting performance. An athlete's diet should contain food for energy, food for growth and repair, and food for general physical and mental health.

As athletes are more likely to need higher levels of energy than an average person, it is important that they eat suitable amounts of carbohydrates. Research indicates that the following nutrient intakes are optimum for most sports:

- 60–70 per cent of calories in the diet from carbohydrates
- 12 per cent from protein
- 18–28 per cent from fat.

What an athlete eats on a day-to-day basis is extremely important for training. Diet affects how fast and how well they progress, and how soon they reach their personal goals.

A common question that is often asked is 'When is the best time to eat?'. Many athletes will feel nervous before a competition and may not have an appetite. However, not eating should be avoided as the body's glycogen stores are likely to be low and will be needed when activity starts. The athlete should ideally have a high-complex-carbohydrate meal at least three hours before activity. This will allow the body to digest and absorb the food and to 'top up' the glycogen stores. It is also important that the athlete considers rehydration both during and after performance.

Activity: Food diary

Think about the types and amount of food that you eat. Keep a diary of the food that you eat in one day and using the packaging work out how much fat, protein and carbohydrates you have consumed.

How does this compare to recommended daily allowances?

- **Previous training** – when analysing sporting performance, it is useful for the coach to have a picture of what the athlete has achieved previously. This may be through observation and working on a regular basis with an athlete or team, or it may be through asking questions, either in person or via questionnaires. Likewise, a coach can examine previous training sessions and determine what was successful and what was less successful. Using this knowledge, future sessions can be designed to meet the specific needs of the athlete or team.

- **Motivation** – this can be defined as 'direction and intensity of effort' and it is important for any athlete who wishes to succeed in training or competition. Motivation can be viewed as either intrinsic or extrinsic.

- **Self-confidence** – the belief that they can succeed in their sport – is important to athletes. When an athlete has self-confidence they will tend to:
  - persevere even when things are not going to plan, both in training and competition
  - show enthusiasm and a desire to win
  - be positive in their approach to their sport and to others involved in the sport, such as coaches

○ take their share of the responsibility for both success and failure.

Self-confidence will also allow the athlete to remain calm under pressure, be assertive when required, and set challenging and realistic personal or team goals. A confident athlete will take risks in their sport because they are playing to win, and will never give up even if defeat seems likely.

To improve their self-confidence, athletes can use a variety of techniques. Naturally, success will tend to lead to an increase in self-confidence, and praise and recognition of achievements can improve confidence.

It is important to recognise that a lack of confidence may lead to poor performance. An athlete suffering from a lack of confidence is likely to suffer from stress under pressure from outside factors, such as spectators or mistakes, avoid taking risks and making mistakes, and lose concentration because they are worrying about failing.

Equally, overconfidence or false confidence can be dangerous because it can lead to inadequate preparation, low motivation and low arousal.

- **Ability level** – one of the main factors affecting performance is the ability level of the performer. Much research has been conducted to determine whether a person has a fixed level of ability, or whether anyone can be coached into a world-class athlete. What is certain is that clear and professional coaching will allow an individual to maximise their natural ability in their chosen sport.

Remember

Remember the phrase TCUP. This means Think Correctly Under Pressure and ensure that you focus only on the important aspects of your performance and not on outside factors that may hinder you such as the opposition or spectators.

Extrinsic factors

- **Group dynamics** – the success of a sports team will be affected by the dynamics within the team or group. It is important that athletes and coaches understand the importance of group dynamics and how this can affect performance and success. A group should have a collective identity and a sense of shared purpose. Successful groups will have:

○ opportunities for members to socialise
○ members who share goals and ambitions
○ members who are able to communicate effectively
○ strong cohesion
○ members who value relationships within the group
○ a successful coach or leader who ensures that all members' contributions to the group are valued.

The development of a group normally goes through the following stages:

○ forming – the group gets together; a level of formality is common
○ storming – heightened tension associated with competition for status and influence
○ norming – rules and standards of behaviour are agreed
○ performing – the group matures to a point where it is able to work together as a team.

- **Group cohesion** – this describes the desire of a group of players to focus on a common goal and strive towards achieving that goal together. Group cohesion also describes the identity of a team. Social cohesion, where team members socialise with one another, is important for successful team cohesion. Research indicates that groups that get on with one another are likely to exhibit high levels of cohesion and ultimately team success. It is important to understand the factors that can affect team cohesion which include:

○ stability – cohesion develops the longer a group is together with the same members, so a coach should attempt to keep the same players playing together
○ similarity – cohesion develops where group members are similar in terms of age, skills, goals and attitudes
○ size – cohesion develops more quickly in small groups
○ support – cohesive teams tend to have managers and coaches who provide support to members and encourage them to support one another openly; this may include players sharing their thoughts and concerns in an open and honest forum
○ satisfaction – cohesion is associated with the extent to which team members are pleased with each other's performance, behaviour and conformity to the norms and values of the team.

Take it further

Successful teams

A successful team will be more than a sum of its parts. Think about a successful team and explain how they show group cohesion. How can a coach ensure that a team works together?

- **Temperature** – this can affect the athlete in terms of both physical and psychological performance.

  The effects of extreme cold in sport are quite common. Through being cold, and a lack of appropriate warm-up, an athlete may suffer from torn muscles or tendons. Hypothermia (low body temperature) can also occur in extreme cases where the athlete is unable to maintain a suitable body temperature and loses heat. This can be very dangerous and can even result in death. However, it is more common for heat loss to simply affect sporting performance. To avoid hypothermia you should:
  - try and stay dry, as moisture increases the speed at which body temperature drops

  - wear suitable clothing for the conditions and the environment
  - avoid direct wind exposure if possible.

  High temperatures can cause the athlete to overheat, and fluid loss can cause performance to drop. Athletes must take on sufficient fluid before, during and after training or competition.

- **The time of day** when an athlete trains or competes may also affect performance. If an athlete performs at the end of the day, after work or education, they may be tired and unable to concentrate. Training very early in the day may also have a negative effect on performance, as the athlete will have a slower metabolism, making it harder to produce energy.

  Some major sports events are now restricted by media coverage, and television companies may dictate at what time the match should take place. This has resulted in evening fixtures as well as fixtures at midday, where the sun will be at its strongest in terms of heat.

Assessment activity 19.1

A local tennis coach has asked you (as a sports science student) how her junior players could improve through detailed analysis. Using your underpinning knowledge, help provide the coach with example player profiles for a sport of your choice.

1. Describe the performance profiles of the junior tennis players. Consider specific techniques within this sport, as there may be different requirements. **P1**

2. Having described what is required in order to perform, discuss these factors with the performers for your chosen sport, making sure you explain them fully. To help you and the performers, prepare a short report that fully explains the profile you have outlined. **M1**

3. The performers are keen to understand how the profile you have outlined will help them improve in their sport. Analyse each aspect of the profile fully, and as part of your report explain the effect this may have on successful performance. **D1**

Grading tips

- To attain **P1** don't forget to describe the physical, mental, tactical and biomechanical factors as part of the performance profile.

- To attain **M1** you should fully explain why each aspect of the performance profile is important and how being able to measure each component will allow a training programme to be developed.

- To attain **D1** you should fully examine each aspect of the profile and begin to reflect on developing a suitable training programme for a selected athlete.

PLTS

Reflecting on your findings will allow you to address your skills as a **reflective learner**.

Functional skills

By completing the report you are able to achieve skills in **English** and **ICT**.

2. Be able to analyse sporting performance

Being able to analyse sporting performance clearly is vital if weaknesses are to be identified and remedied. An athlete should always evaluate his or her performance both during and after training or competition. They should also seek the advice of others, such as a coach or tutor. It is important that when performance is analysed, an honest, clear approach is adopted. This will enable the athlete to make decisions affecting future performance. It is also important to recognise the many factors that can affect performance. These may be unavoidable (such as age or the weather) or may include factors that can be controlled by the athlete (such as diet and training).

Science has proved an important asset in improving and enhancing performance. Scientific principles are often applied to help record sporting performance, and the use of data can be analysed by the athlete, the coach or a sports scientist, with the aim of improving future performances.

A modern coach will no longer simply try to improve an athlete or team by instructing them to 'try harder'. To be an effective coach, you should be able to analyse and correct specific techniques as part of a training programme. Being able to break down complex movements into simple tasks allows the athlete to identify and correct specific aspects of his or her technique. A coach may identify movements that are ineffective or unnecessary, and these can be altered or removed from a performance.

2.1 Performance profile assessment

Technical and tactical assessment

When profiling sporting performance, good technical skills are required for success. These skills are often compared with a 'perfect model', and training and analysis should focus on developing skills that are technically correct to perform a range of motions or shots

The use of tactics and strategy is a key aspect of all sports. Tactics can be described as a specific, predetermined plan that can be implemented during a sporting performance. For tactics to be effective, it is important that all players understand what is required and are able to execute it effectively.

When studying sport it is possible to analyse performance through observation. This may be done either 'live', actually at the sports event, or by video after the event.

Notational analysis studies movement patterns in team sports, and is primarily concerned with strategy and tactics. Patterns of play that led and did not lead to scoring against specific opponents can be identified, and this information is then used as a tactic or strategy in subsequent matches to outperform opponents.

Being able to analyse past performances and the performances of upcoming opponents is an essential tool used by modern football managers, and it is now common to see a laptop on the training ground, or a television and video recorder in the changing room. Most managers now have their team's matches filmed, so they can be reviewed afterwards to highlight the strengths and weaknesses of players as well as patterns of play. This enables the manager to give players feedback as part of the coaching process, highlighting specific areas to address.

Key term

Notational analysis – the collection of data either by using a computer or by hand. This process normally involves counting the frequency of an event, such as a shot on target.

Tally charts are a useful tool when observing sporting performance. The tally chart may include simply counting performance factors such as:

- shots on target in football
- number of fouls committed in basketball
- wide balls bowled in cricket
- number of double serves in badminton
- number of shots played to the forehand and backhand in tennis.

Activity: Tally analysis

In small groups watch a recording of a volleyball match and conduct a basic tally analysis. You should count:

- successful serves
- unsuccessful serves
- shots to the front of the court
- shots to the back of the court
- smashes completed
- unforced errors.

Using the information that you have collected, discuss your finding with your group and identify any areas for improvement.

Physical

- **Multi-stage fitness test** – you are probably familiar with the multi-stage fitness test (commonly referred to as the 'bleep test') to measure **VO$_2$ max**. This is a predictive test that can be used by individuals or teams to estimate their current VO$_2$ max. Undertaking the test is relatively straightforward. Two cones are placed as markers 20 metres apart, and the participants have to run to each cone in time with the predetermined bleeps. These get progressively quicker, decreasing the time it takes to reach each marker cone and increasing the intensity of the exercise. The results are then recorded according to the stage you have reached, and can be converted to a predictive VO$_2$ max level. The multi-stage fitness test is a cheap and valid alternative to individual laboratory testing, which is expensive and requires specialist training to analyse performance. For more information see Student Book 1, Unit 7 Fitness testing for sport and exercise.

  The results can be used by the athlete or the coach as the foundation of an aerobic training programme. The athlete and coach can re-test at set intervals to gauge whether aerobic fitness has improved or decreased.

  This test is very good for games players, as it is specific to the nature of the sport, but due to the short turns it is less suitable for rowers, runners or cyclists.

Key term

VO$_2$ max – the maximum capacity to transport and utilise oxygen during incremental exercise.

- **Repeated anaerobic sprint test** – a repeated sprint test allows the athlete and coach to analyse sprint performance. Using quantitative analysis the coach can determine the time it takes to complete a sprint, the speed or velocity of the sprinter, and areas of acceleration and deceleration. Using this information, areas that need further training can be identified and specific training programmes can be devised. By repeating the sprint test over a number of weeks or even sessions, the coach is able to see whether improvements have been made. The repeated sprint test is also a good way to train the anaerobic systems of the body.

Motor

Test such as the T-run or Illinois agility test analyse motor skills and the ability to move in different directions. Analysing an athlete's ability to complete these as part of a training programme will help a coach identify specific movements and the ability to change direction quickly. For more information see Student Book 1, Unit 7 Fitness testing for sport and exercise.

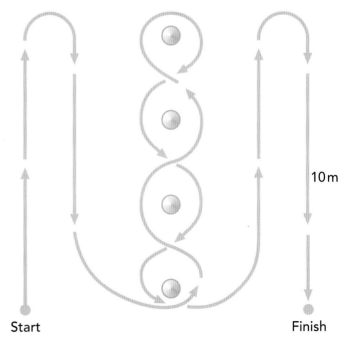

Start　　　　　　　　　　　　　　Finish

10 m

Figure 19.3: The Illinois agility test assesses an athlete's ability to change direction quickly. What sports require the athlete to use agility and how can this test improve this?

Physiological

A **heart rate monitor** is a convenient way of measuring heart rate before, during and after exercise. A strap attached round the athlete's chest sends an electrical impulse to a watch worn on the wrist. This allows the athlete to measure their heart rate and work within aerobic training zones (training zones are used to determine the level of intensity at which you are working; see below). Some heart rate monitors allow the recorded data to be downloaded to a computer, and the coach and athlete can analyse their training performance further. The use of such data gives valuable information so that training programmes can be devised or amended to suit the individual.

There are four main **training zones** (in percentage of maximum heart rate (MHR)):

- **fitness zone:** 60–70 per cent MHR
- **aerobic zone:** 70–80 per cent MHR
- **anaerobic zone:** 80–90 per cent MHR
- **red line zone:** 90–100 per cent MHR

Training zones are used to determine the level of intensity at which you are working. This is particularly important for cardiovascular training or exercise. Heart rate training zones are calculated by taking into consideration both your MHR and your RHR (resting heart rate). Because it is difficult to exercise and measure heart rate manually at the same time, it is useful to use a heart rate monitor.

There are a number of important factors that can affect heart rate, including:

- stress
- illness
- overtraining
- medication
- time of day
- food and drink (caffeine)
- altitude
- temperature
- hydration levels
- weather conditions.

Peak flow – strong, efficient lungs are essential to sporting performance. The ability to obtain and utilise oxygen will be affected if the lungs are unable to deliver oxygen (and remove carbon dioxide) in relation to exercise intensity.

Case study: Calculating heart rate

Using heart rate as a training tool is an easy and effective way of ensuring that you train at the correct intensity. Before any cardiovascular training, an athlete should determine their specific and individual training zones. To do this you should use the following method:

Calculating the heart rate for a training zone:

Helen wants to train for a period of time in the aerobic zone (75 per cent intensity). Her resting heart rate is 60 beats per minute and her maximum heart rate is 204.

$HR = RHR + [(MHR–RHR) \times \text{percentage intensity}]$

So in Helen's case:

$HR = 60 + [(204–65) \times 0.75]$

So the heart rate to aim for is 149 bpm.

1. **Now measure your own RHR and MHR and work out the target heart rate for 85 per cent intensity.**
2. **What are the benefits of training at the correct level?**
3. **Why should Helen review these targets on a regular basis?**

Peak flow is a measure of how fast you can blow air out of your lungs, using a spirometer. This measures how wide the airways in your lungs are. Factors that can cause the airways to become narrow include:

- swollen lining
- mucus in the airways
- tubes constricted by the special muscles surrounding the airways.

All these may happen if you have asthma. For people with asthma, this simple test shows how well their asthma is being controlled.

Psychological assessment

- **Interviews** – one of the easiest methods of analysing sporting performance is to interview the performer after training or competition. This gives valuable feedback on how they felt their performance went, and what areas they feel they need to improve. Using information on the athlete's personal strengths and weaknesses will allow the coach to develop a strategy for future performances. Interviews can also be used to discuss tactics they may wish to use against a particular team or individual.

- **Questionnaires** can be designed to gain valuable information about performers. This information can be used to develop tactics and strategies as part of training preparation. The information gained as part of the questionnaire may include strengths and weaknesses, likes and dislikes in training, and concerns about past and future performances. Key areas can then be addressed by the coach and players. Some questions to ask might include:
  - Why do you play sport?
  - On a scale of 1–5 how much do you enjoy training? (1 = not at all; 5 = completely)
  - What aspects of training do you find particularly enjoyable?
  - What do you dislike about training?
  - How do you feel before a competition?
  - How do you cope with the pressure of competition?
  - What are your strengths in terms of sporting performance?
  - What areas do you feel you need to address in order to improve?

- **Biomechanical** – being able to assess how the body moves during the execution of specific techniques will enable the coach to analyse if improvements or changes need to be made. For example, a tennis player may be struggling with their first serve so the coach will be able to watch or video this movement and make recommendations on changes in technique that are required.

Assessment activity 19.2  BTEC

An amateur cricketer has approached you and asked you to help them prepare for an upcoming match. They are particularly keen to understand how different factors can affect their performance.

1. Write a report describing at least five factors that can have an effect on performance. **P2**

2. Having outlined various factors that may affect performance, produce a performance profile for the cricketer to help them recognise what is required to improve. You should consider at least three components of their performance profile. **P3**

3. To gain the merit grading criterion, you should perform this profile without tutor support. **M2**

4. To assist the cricketer, prepare a report that fully analyses three of the factors outlined in their performance profile. This analysis is designed to help the athlete improve, and should give clear feedback as well as making recommendations on areas that need to be addressed. **D2**

Grading tips

- To attain **P2** you must fully describe both physical and psychological factors that can affect sporting performance.

- To attain **P3** you should also make specific recommendations for the cricketer and describe why you have suggested these proposals. Fully consider their performance profile and identify at least three components that can be addressed by the cricketer.

- To attain **M2** you should work independently and without additional support from your tutor.

- To attain **D2** you must further explain why you have made your profile suggestions and how these will improve specific aspects of performance. Ensure that you feed back your recommendations and explain why you have made these choices.

PLTS

By planning a specific performance profile you are able to achieve skills as a **reflective learner**.

Functional skills

By preparing a written report you are able to provide evidence of your skills in **English**.

3. Be able to provide feedback to athletes regarding performance

3.1 Feedback

Strengths

When providing feedback, it is important that the coach highlights the strengths of an athlete's performance and does not focus on what is being performed incorrectly or badly. Being able to understand what went well and to develop this area further will enhance future performances both within training and in competition and boost the performer's confidence.

Areas for improvement

Being able to identify areas for improvement will underpin all coaching. As such the coach must be able to identify these weaknesses and be able to develop these in order for future performances to improve. It is important that the coach can communicate these changes in an open and honest way so that the athlete can understand what is required and why.

SMART targets

Target-setting is a vital aspect of sporting performance and analysis. Being able to set clear, well defined targets is a valuable tool when giving feedback to the athlete. Target-setting is a powerful technique that appears to work by providing a direction for our efforts, focusing our attention, promoting persistence and increasing our confidence (provided we achieve the targets we set ourselves). When setting targets, there are a number of aspects to consider, generally defined as the SMART principle:

Specific

Measurable

Achievable

Realistic

Timed

- **Specific** – targets should be specific or definitive. For example, instead of saying that a player is a 'poor batsman' in cricket, a coach may identify specific aspects of batting that need to be improved, such as defensive play or a cover drive.

- **Measurable** – goals or targets should be capable of being measured. For example, if you are trying to improve your possession of the ball in football, you may wish to count successful passes, long passes, short passes or successful crosses. This can be done before, during and after a training programme, and any improvements can be recognised. It is important that, when measuring targets, clear criteria are used and that any data collected are analysed correctly.

- **Achievable** – it must be possible to achieve any target or goal that you set yourself in a fairly short period of time. It is pointless setting targets that are impossible, too difficult or too far off. It is also important that targets are not too easy, as this will have a demotivating effect on the athlete. An example of poor target-setting would be for a novice runner to complete a marathon in under two hours. Failure in meeting goals is useful in improving technique and long-term success, as long as you draw useful lessons from it and feed these back into your training programme. ('A' is sometimes taken to stand for 'adjustable' – meaning that the achievability must be monitored and the goal can be changed to suit the circumstances if necessary.)

- **Realistic** – if targets are too difficult or impossible, it is likely the athlete will become demotivated and may even give up training or competition. Targets should be challenging and realistic, pushing the athlete in their desire and ability.

- **Timed** – targets must have defined time limits so that a coach or athlete can review progress. Open-ended targets tend to be less successful than those that have a set period in which to achieve the target. For example, an athlete may be set a six-week training programme to improve their muscular strength. After (and even during) this six-week period, a review can be carried out to see whether the specific targets have been achieved. If not, the programme can be amended to take into account any personal changes.

Goals

When setting goals, it is important to understand that to achieve the 'dream' goal there should be a number of short- or medium-term targets to achieve on the way. The athlete who dreams of winning an Olympic gold medal will need to set short-term 'day to day' goals in order to focus their effort. Goals can be classified into short-, medium- and long-term.

- **Short-term or daily goals** are most important because they provide a focus for training in each session. Past research on Olympic athletes found that setting clear daily training goals was one factor that distinguished successful performers from their less successful counterparts.

- **Medium-term or intermediate goals** are markers of where you want to be at a specific time in your training programme. For example, if your long-term goal was to lower your 1500 metres personal best time by one second over ten months, a medium-term goal could be a half-second improvement after five months.

- **Long-term goals** are those that seem a long way off and difficult to achieve. In time terms, they may be anything from six months to several years away. These goals should comprise short- and medium-term goals.

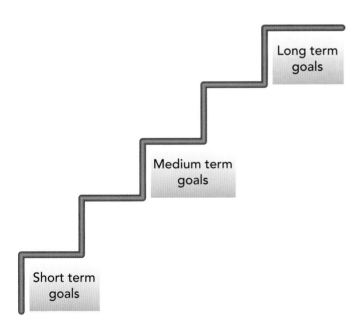

Figure 19.4: Small steps will allow you to achieve your medium- and long-term goals. Consider your own goals and using the diagram outline your own short-, medium- and long-term goals. How do your short-term goals affect medium- and long-term goals? Are these goals realistic?

Recommendations

The purpose of any performance analysis is to provide feedback to the athlete so that improvements can be made. Identifying specific areas of weakness is essential if changes are to be made.

- **Skills training** – feedback may provide information to address a specific skill that has been identified by observation. A coach may have identified that a golfer has poor balance when addressing a ball on the tee. The feedback would be very specific to the balance skill component. Using effective feedback will enable the coach to observe, demonstrate and correct the poor skill, and as part of the training a specific drill can be used to address this problem.

- **Training for specific components of fitness** – having observed and evaluated performance, the results may indicate that the athlete needs to address a specific component of fitness. The key components of fitness are:
  - strength
  - aerobic endurance
  - muscular endurance
  - flexibility
  - body composition.

  By identifying the specific area, the coach can design a new training programme or adapt existing ones so that improvements can be made.

- **Technique coaching specific to movement** – a typical training programme will contain an element that addresses an athlete's technique. Coaches will regularly observe, demonstrate and correct poor technique. This feedback can be through discussion, observation or watching a video of the performance so that the athlete can see their own actions. A training programme should give the athlete an opportunity to practise a specific technique so that the 'perfect' model can be achieved. For example, a coach may observe a cricketer's bowling action and decide that, by videoing the action, clearer feedback can be given. Through discussion, the bowler can address poor technique and correct it as part of their training or practice.

- **Psychological training** – as you will have discovered in Student Book 1, Unit 17 Psychology for sports performance, it is now recognised that an athlete's performance can be affected by their mind and it is important that the coach understands the psychological requirements. Therefore a coach may use interviews or questionnaires to find out how the athlete feels both during and after performance. This information can be used to design specific psychological training methods such as imagery or meditation.

Assessment activity 19.3 — P4 M3 BTEC

1. Having completed a performance assessment for the amateur cricketer, it is important that you give clear feedback. This may be in the form of a short presentation or interview, and should allow the player to ask questions. This may be done with the support of a tutor. **P4**

2. To gain the merit grade you should give your feedback independently, without the help of a tutor. **M3**

Grading tips

- To attain **P4** and **M3** you should fully prepare questions you would like to ask the athlete. You may want to practise these with a friend beforehand to ensure that they are relevant. Also spend some time considering the questions you are likely to be asked and the answers you may give in response.

PLTS

By providing feedback to an athlete, you can demonstrate your skills as an **effective participator**.

Functional skills

By delivering feedback to the athlete, you can provide evidence of your **ICT** and **English** skills.

---

4. Understand the purpose and resources required for analysing different levels of sporting performance

4.1 Levels of performance

There are many different levels of performance, depending on ability. This is best illustrated in what is commonly known as the sports development continuum.

Each level of the 'pyramid' represents the stage you are at in your chosen sport. The terms can be described as follows.

- Foundation – the early development of sporting skills (throwing, catching, hand–eye coordination), on which most subsequent sports development is based. These are normally the skills taught as part of PE lessons in schools. Without a sound foundation, young people are unlikely to become long-term sports participants.

- Participation – sport undertaken primarily for fun and enjoyment, often at basic levels of competence. This includes people who play sport on a regular basis, such as a Sunday league football player.

- Performance – a move from basic competence to a more structured form of competitive sport at club or county level. This includes performers who have been identified as having potential in their sport and may be selected to represent district or county teams.

- Elite – about reaching the top – this applies to performers at the highest national and international levels. Players such as Olympians or professionals are considered to be in the excellence category.

These four levels are explored in more detail below.

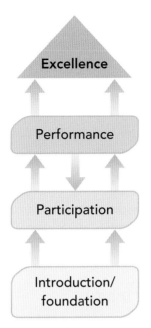

Figure 19.5: The sports development continuum. What level are you at on the continuum? How can you progress higher up the continuum?

Foundation

School is, very often, where children will have their first taste of organised and varied sport. This is part of the National Curriculum, which states that children must be taught at least two hours of high-quality PE and sport at school each week. In addition, the government aim is that by 2010, children will be offered two or more hours beyond the school day, delivered by a range of school, community and club providers. The government's overall objective is to enhance the take-up of sporting opportunities by 5–16-year-olds. The ambitious target is to increase the percentage of schoolchildren who spend a minimum of two hours a week on high-quality PE and school sport.

It is important that as many children as possible are actively involved in foundation sport. Not only does this provide fun, enjoyable and healthy activities, it will also mean that more children are likely to excel in sport and progress further in their sporting abilities.

Foundation level also includes sport for all beginners, regardless of age. Many organisations offer beginners lessons in their chosen sports, and these taster sessions often lead on to regular participation.

At this level, it is important that the fundamental skills are taught correctly and that participants are given an opportunity to practise these in an enjoyable environment.

Participation

Participation sports are undertaken mainly for fun and enjoyment. Other reasons may include health and fitness, and participants will also enjoy other aspects associated with physical activity, such as social aspects and a sense of purpose and achievement. An example may be a Saturday league player who enjoys being part of a team, and has progressed from foundation level. The player will have a range of basic skills that have been practised and developed so that they are competent in their sport. A coach will aim to analyse these skills through observation and discussion, and areas such as tactics can be introduced to improve performance and success. There are many highly skilled and talented players who choose to play at the participation level simply because they enjoy the sport, or for general health and fitness.

A key area that the government is keen to develop is the number of out-of-school sports clubs that offer a range of sports. Their purpose is to ensure children are able to take part in sport after their school day or at weekends. Strategies have been devised to link local schools together, as well as linking to local sports clubs. This is to ensure that if children wish to continue in sport, they have a local opportunity to do so. The government invested over £1.5 billion between 2003 and 2008.

Performance

When a player has consistently participated at a good standard, they may have their sporting talents recognised by local, regional or county organisations. These will provide the player with further opportunities to develop and enhance their skills using high-quality coaching and equipment. Players at this level will compete at county or even national standard.

Many local sports development units will have strategies in place to ensure talented athletes are offered opportunities for competition and training, and to support talented performers.

Through high-quality coaching and analysis, the performer may have an opportunity to further their sporting career and develop to the excellence level of the continuum.

Elite

An Olympic or world-class athlete will need a high level of analysis as part of their training and performance in order to maximise their potential. Using the latest analytical techniques, combined with advanced technology and coaching, the high-level athlete will be able to develop their skills and aim for the 'perfect' model. The use of sports science is now common, and an athlete is just as likely to find him- or herself in a laboratory as on a training field.

4.2 Purpose

Talent identification

Observation is used to identify talented athletes or produce a report on an opposing team. This is commonly referred to as scouting, and involves an experienced coach observing a performance and evaluating their findings. Reasons for doing this may include identifying new players, or preparing for a match where information about the opposition will allow you to devise a specific tactic.

Monitoring current fitness levels

Another purpose of analysis is to gain data about an individual's current fitness level. Using a variety of fitness tests, we are able to measure the various components of fitness, and this information can be used as a starting point of any training programme. Throughout training programmes, regular fitness tests can be conducted to ensure that the benefits are being gained. If results indicate that targets are not being met, training can be adjusted to take into account any changes.

Identification of strengths and areas for improvement

A key reason for undertaking a performance analysis is to identify areas of strength and weakness. This is of particular importance when investigating technique. Once you have identified areas that need to be improved, it is possible to develop a training programme to address these issues. For example, analysis may show that a goalkeeper is poor at gathering crosses. A training programme will incorporate specific training to improve this key area.

Performance assessment

By assessing a team or an individual in a competition situation, you are able to see whether players are affected by outside factors such as the crowd or the opposition. This type of analysis will allow you to develop specific tactics that can be used under game conditions. Using defined conditions during training will allow a team to develop both their techniques and their tactics. An example of this would be if a team struggles to defend using man-marking in basketball. A practice may include using specific drills to highlight marking, and every time this happens the coach can stop the practice and demonstrate if it has been effective or not.

Recovery after injury

If an athlete has been sidelined because of a short-term or long-term injury, it is useful to perform a number of assessments before they recommence training or performance. This ensures that the athlete has recovered sufficiently so that injury does not recur. Simple fitness tests can be conducted both on the injured area, and also generally to identify a base level from which to start training again. It is important that the athlete does not over-train, as this can result in continued injury and will prevent them from performing.

The coach may also wish to talk to the athlete about their injury in case there are problems or concerns about a recurrence. A player may have been hurt by a tackle, and may have developed a fear of tackling. Using this information, the coach will be able to support and encourage the athlete to overcome any psychological factors.

Assessment of health status

It is common to use fitness testing and health screening to analyse whether a person is able to participate in exercise programmes. This may be specific to an individual who has not taken part in sport for a long time, or to a high-level athlete recovering from illness or injury. Either way, assessment of health will provide the coach with information regarding whether or not they are able to perform specific exercises, or to gauge the level at which a training programme should be set.

Squad selection

Analysis can be used to monitor player performance both in training and in competition. Sports such as rugby and football now use large squads of players, and through performance analysis a coach will be able to select the players most likely to achieve success. If a player has been underperforming, this can be addressed and additional support given. A coach can analyse the opposition team in preparation for a match, so that tactics involving certain players can be developed and used.

Goal setting

By using detailed analysis and evaluation of performance, it is important that clear and well defined targets or goals are set by the coach and athlete. These goals can be seen as a target that the performer wishes to achieve, and may be either short- or long-term goals. Goals should be set using the SMART principle (see page 214) and should be discussed openly by the coach and the athlete. By including the athlete in the decision-making, it is likely that they will remain more motivated to train as they feel they are in control of their training.

4.3 Resources

Fiscal resources

Equipment for analysis costs money. As noted above, the ways in which performance can be analysed vary greatly. An effective evaluation can be performed by a coach simply watching a performance and feeding back their findings or thoughts to the athlete or team. Alternatively, technologically advanced equipment can be used to video techniques and computer software used to analyse specific movements. The benefit of this equipment is that it can slow techniques down to tiny movements, and measurements can be made, such as velocity of movements or joint angles. But this can be both expensive and time-consuming.

Equipment

The equipment a coach can use to perform an analysis varies greatly. A clipboard can be used to record observations during a match, and a simple stopwatch can be used to record times. But more elite performers will require highly detailed analysis with more advanced equipment, such as movement-analysis software, force platforms and respiratory analysers. Such performance equipment is commonly found in sports science laboratories that are designed specifically to record human performance.

(see page 214)

Activity: How sports equipment has changed

Tennis is a sport that has seen many changes to the equipment. Traditionally tennis was played with wooden racquets. However synthetic materials in the form of carbon fibre are now used. This has allowed players to hit the balls harder and faster and as a result tennis is more demanding on the players.

For the sports shown below, identify how the equipment has changed in recent years and how this has changed the sport:

- golf
- cricket
- football.

Time

Performance analysis can be a very time-consuming process. If a video analysis is conducted, the coach will have to review the performance, interpret the data that has been collected, fully evaluate it, and develop the results into training programmes or tactics. For an analysis to be effective, it is important that the coach and players allocate sufficient time to evaluate findings as part of the coaching process. If evaluation is hurried, errors are likely to occur and the findings may be inaccurate.

Facilities

It is common for high-level athletes to find themselves in a sports science laboratory as part of a performance assessment. Such laboratories will contain up to date scientific equipment which allows highly accurate and detailed physical performance information to be collected and analysed. Unfortunately, this equipment can be very expensive, and coaches may need specialist assistance in gathering information. But it is still possible to collect relevant information using common equipment such as stopwatches and simple notational analysis.

What are the benefits of using a sports science laboratory? What information could you obtain from having access to such research?

It is also important to remember that performance can be affected by *where* the athlete is performing. This must be taken into account when undertaking any form of assessment.

Human

The best asset in developing sporting performance is people who are enthusiastic about the goal. These may be coaches, players, family or spectators, and each plays a valuable role in improving an athlete's or a team's performance. Gaining feedback from people will aid training and performance, and using such advice should be part of the coaching process. Sharing the experiences of other players will also aid performance, and a young or inexperienced athlete should seek advice from others.

Scientific support and equipment

Having access to analysis equipment and qualified support will enable the athlete to focus on specific parts of their performance and training and be able to develop strategies to improve. However, such scientific support is usually only accessible to elite athletes because of the costs involved.

Assessment activity 19.4   P5   BTEC

Your voluntary work at a local sports college involves you working with a range of performers of different abilities. It is important that you are able to identify the different forms of analysis that can be used for the four different levels of sport. To help the athletes, prepare a presentation that outlines and describes the purpose of analysis for a sport at two different levels (for example, foundation and excellence) and the resources you require. **P5**

Grading tip

- To attain **P5** be realistic. If you are working at the foundation level you may not have the expensive, technological resources available to you. How can you overcome this? What types of analysis can you perform at this level that do not require advanced technology?

PLTS

By describing the resources required for the analysis of different levels of sport, you can demonstrate your skill as a **creative thinker**.

Functional skills

By preparing a presentation you can demonstrate your **ICT** skills.

Rizana Suhail
Performance analyst

Rizana works at a human performance centre where she carries out sporting performance analysis on individuals and teams. She uses the latest technology and equipment to perform a variety of analyses including:

- technical analysis that looks at individual sporting performances
- match analysis that will look at the tactical performance of a team.

An example of her job is noting a football match which may include the numbers of passes made, the numbers of corners conceded or the shots on or off target. Such data will be collected and analysed. Rizana is then able to set specific targets, tactics and training techniques to help improve performance.

'I start work at 8 a.m. and my first job is checking my schedule for the day. I can see if I am working with an individual or a team. I will then check the specific equipment that I might need such as a video camera, laptop and any notational checklists.

When the individual or team arrive I will have a brief meeting with them to explain the purpose of the analysis and how their performance is going to be measured. Any questions can be asked and I can highlight the specific aspects of performance that will be measured.

Having completed a session I will then analyse the measured data and prepare a report. This will outline my findings and I will have a meeting with the people involved to discuss and explain them. This will allow the individual or a coach to set specific targets or goals as part of their training programmes.

The best thing about my job is working with so many different athletes. Every day presents me with new challenges and I get lots of satisfaction from helping athletes reach their performance goals.

In terms of skills, I have to communicate with other members of the team and clients every day so this is at the top of the list. The practical skills I practised during my Sport BTEC, I now use every day to analyse performance and make specific recommendations. My knowledge of a wide variety of sports has also developed.'

Think about it!

- What are the benefits of using a performance analyst like Rizana?
- How can the use of video analysis help an athlete or team improve?
- What skills do you think you need to be successful in this job?

Just checking

1. Giving examples, explain what is meant by discrete skills, serial skills and continuous skills.
2. For a sport of your choice, explain the specific skills that are required to perform at excellence level.
3. Discuss how an understanding of sports psychology can aid performance.
4. Name two methods of psychological training that can be used to enhance performance, and discuss why these methods may work.
5. Outline the psychological factors that can affect a performance, and explain how a coach can address these as part of a training programme.
6. What is notational analysis and how is it used in sport?
7. What is meant by goal setting? Use examples from a chosen sport to explain this.
8. List and explain the four levels of sporting performance.
9. How may a coach use performance analysis for a group of beginners?
10. How can technology improve sporting performance?

edexcel :::

Assignment tips

- Remember that you will need to be able to communicate with a wide range of people. Enjoy the experience and you are far more likely to see improvements in your skills and techniques.
- Support your peers and they will support you. Work together giving each other tips and encouragement.
- Practise by watching performances in a wide variety of sports. Remember a successful sports analyst will need knowledge of many sports.
- Make sure that you are well prepared when performing an analysis. Remember sports action takes place very quickly so you need to know what to watch in advance.
- Use the national governing body websites to help you gather research material. They contain plenty of useful information.
- Ensure that you read the assignment briefs properly. Take your time and ensure you are happy with the task set for you. If not ask your tutor for additional assistance.
- Make sure you attempt all parts of the assignment briefs and not just the pass criteria.

20 Talent identification and development in sport

Do you remember when you started playing sport and possibly dreaming of being the next superstar? There will have been millions of people worldwide who have started with that same dream. This has posed a challenge for everybody involved in identifying and developing talented athletes. The key question for many people involved with sport is how to find, and then develop, the best athletes.

Professional sports clubs and organisations make huge financial investments in trying to produce the best athletes every year. Money is invested in the development of coaches and facilities and research into key factors associated with talent identification and development. There is a worldwide industry in identifying and developing young athletes. However, talent is not always apparent from an early age. You should not only think about who will be the next international superstar, but recognise that young people should be encouraged so they can enjoy and achieve at all levels of sport.

This unit will help you to learn about the factors associated with talent identification and development and to develop the necessary understanding to be able to design talent identification and development programmes for a chosen sport.

Learning outcomes

After completing this unit you should:

1. know the key predictors of talent for performers in sport
2. be able to design a talent identification programme for a chosen sport
3. know key factors in talent development in sport
4. be able to design a talent development programme for a chosen sport.

Assessment and grading criteria

This table shows you what you must do in order to achieve a pass, merit or distinction grade, and where you can find activities in this book to help you.

To achieve a **pass** grade the evidence must show that you are able to:	To achieve a **merit** grade the evidence must show that, in addition to the pass criteria, you are able to:	To achieve a **distinction** grade the evidence must show that, in addition to the pass and merit criteria, you are able to:
P1 describe the different types of talent **See Assessment activity 20.1, page 230**		
P2 describe five different predictors of talent for performers in sport **See Assessment activity 20.1, page 230**		
P3 describe one current talent identification programme in a selected sport **See Assessment activity 20.2, page 235**	**M1** evaluate one current talent identification programme in a selected sport **See Assessment activity 20.2, page 235**	
P4 using a standard structure, design a talent identification programme for a selected sport **See Assessment activity 20.2, page 235**	**M2** explain the chosen activities for a talent identification programme for a selected sport **See Assessment activity 20.2, page 235**	**D1** justify the choice of activities for a talent development programme for a selected sport **See Assessment activity 20.2, page 235**
P5 describe, using examples, five different key factors in talent development in sport **See Assessment activity 20.3, page 240**		
P6 describe one current talent development programme in a selected sport **See Assessment activity 20.4, page 246**	**M3** evaluate one current talent development programme in a selected sport **See Assessment activity 20.4, page 246**	
P7 using a standard structure, design a talent development programme for a selected sport **See Assessment activity 20.4, page 246**	**M4** explain the chosen activities for a talent development programme for a selected sport **See Assessment activity 20.4, page 246**	**D2** justify the choice of activities for a talent development programme for a selected sport **See Assessment activity 20.4, page 246**

How you will be assessed

This unit will be assessed by internal assignments that will be designed and marked by the tutors at your centre. Your assessments could be in the form of:

- written reports
- posters
- presentations
- information leaflets.

Thomas, 18-year-old sports coach

This unit has helped me get used to coaching different age groups in different sports. As I work in a range of sports, I really liked how this unit doesn't just look at one sport but helps you look at lots of different sports. It has been really useful for me to look at the different ways of identifying talented athletes so that I can pass any recommendations onto the local professional clubs.

I enjoyed learning about the Long Term Athlete Development plans for the different sports as they have given me lots of ideas about how I could structure my coaching sessions over the course of the season to meet the needs of my players. I have also been able to learn more about the role of other people and that has helped me to work with them more closely to benefit my athletes even more.

There were lots of opportunities for me to apply my learning to the different areas that I wanted to work in, so that really helped me to see the vocational relevance of this topic.

Over to you!

1. **Which areas of this unit are you looking forward to?**
2. **Which parts do you think you might find difficult?**
3. **What do you think you will need to do to get yourself ready for this unit?**

1. Know the key predictors of talent for performers in sport

1.1 Types of talent

Before you can understand the key predictors of **talent** in sport you need to first understand the definition of talent and the different types of talent. Howe, Davidson and Sloboda (1998) state that talent has five main properties:

1 Talent is at least partly innate.

2 Trained people will in advance be able to identify advanced indications of talent.

3 Early indications of talent provide a basis for predicting who is likely to excel.

4 Only a minority are talented.

5 Talents are relatively domain specific.

Sports coaches have identified four main types of talent known as unidimensional talent, multidimensional talent, unisport talent and multisport talent.

> **Key term**
>
> **Talent** – a natural ability to be good at something that can be developed through appropriate training.

When so many young people want to play sport, how can you find out who is the most talented?

Unidimensional talent

This is talent in one dimension only, which means that you have a very limited amount of transferable skills that can be used in other sports or events. An example of this would be a sprinter who can only sprint the 100 metres.

Multidimensional talent

Multidimensional talent means having a range of skills that are transferable to other sports, positions or events. Most team sports players require multidimensional talent as they will often have to make decisions quickly, change direction, react to the position of others and combine a range of skills.

Unisport talent

Unisport talent means that you are proficient to an elite level in one sport. Most world-class athletes have unisport talent, for example David Beckham is a world-class football player but is not world-class in any other sports.

Multisport talent

Multisport talent means that you are able to play a range of sports at the highest level. It is now almost unheard of for athletes to be able to play more than one sport at an elite level.

Case study:
C.B. Fry – the greatest English athlete ever?

C.B. Fry is seen as possibly the greatest English sportsman ever. He played cricket for Surrey as well as captaining England, scoring 94 first class centuries as well as six consecutive centuries. During his time as England captain, he never lost a test match and had a batting average of 50.

As well as playing cricket, Fry also took part in the first ever international athletics match between Yale and Oxford where he won both the 100 metres and the long jump. In 1893, he equalled the world record for the long jump (7.17 metres).

In addition to being world-class in both athletics and cricket, Fry also played rugby for Oxford University, Blackheath and Barbarians.

Finally, Fry also played professional football for Southampton (reaching the FA Cup final in 1901 and 1902) and was capped for the England football team.

1. **What type of talent did C.B. Fry possess?**
2. **Do you think it would be possible for any modern day athlete to emulate Fry's achievements? Justify your answer.**

1.2 Predictors of talent

There are a number of different predictors of talent and they can be categorised as:
- physical
- physiological
- sociological
- psychological
- skill-related.

Whereas some of these factors provide everybody with an equal chance, others (such as the physical characteristics of height, weight and muscle girth) can put some young athletes at a disadvantage if they are a late developer or at the latter end of their age group. This is known as the relative age effect.

Take it further

Relative age effect

Research the relative age effect in your favourite sport.

1. **Do you think that it is a positive or a negative aspect to talent development in your sport?**
2. **How do you think that you could minimise the relative age effect?**

Physical predictors of talent

The main physical predictors of talent in sport are height, weight, muscle girth and somatotype. When considering the physical predictors of talent, it is important to look at which are important or advantageous for your sport. For example, height can be advantageous for some positions in basketball, but can actually put some gymnasts at a disadvantage.

- **Height** be measured using a stadiometer or a tape measure. You measure it when you are standing barefoot, with your back to the wall and it is the distance from the floor to the top of your head.

- **Weight** is your body mass and it is measured in kilograms. In some sports, being heavier can be an advantage whereas in others it can be a disadvantage if your body mass is too great. Body mass can be measured using normal bathroom scales.

- **Muscle girth** is the size and mass of muscle that you possess. Generally, if you have greater muscle girth, you will be stronger (and potentially faster and more powerful) which will be an advantage in most sports. As well as the main factors highlighted above, speed, quickness, strength and power are also often considered as key physical predictors of talent.

- **Somatotype** is your body shape and it is separated into three categories: endomorph, mesomorph and ectomorph. Endomorphs tend to be rounded in shape, have low levels of muscle and are often considered to be the least 'athletic' of all

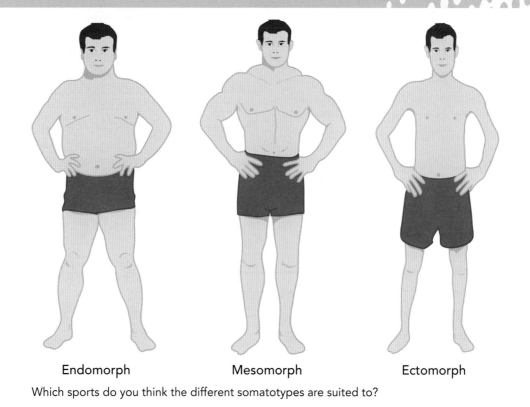

| Endomorph | Mesomorph | Ectomorph |

Which sports do you think the different somatotypes are suited to?

the somatotypes. Mesomorphs have an upright posture, have a higher level of muscle mass and are often considered to be the most 'athletic' of the somatotypes. Mesomorphs are often found in sports such as heavyweight boxing and rugby league. Ectomorphs have the slightest build and the lowest level of muscle. This somatotype is often found in sports such as marathon running.

Physiological predictors

There are two key physiological predictors of talent: anaerobic capacity and aerobic capacity.

- **Anaerobic capacity** is your ability to work without oxygen, relying on your anaerobic energy systems to produce energy. This is important for sports that are shorter in duration, often involving extended sprints, for example the 200 metre sprint.

- **Aerobic capacity** (also known as maximal oxygen uptake or aerobic endurance) is the maximal capacity for oxygen consumption by the body. It is important in activities that are of longer duration, for example the triathlon.

Sociological predictors

Sociological factors associated with talent relate to the influence of parents, carers and coaches, opportunities for deliberate play and deliberate practice and education.

- **Parental support** has been shown to have both positive and negative effects on the performance of young athletes. When there is an optimal level of support from parents, young athletes tend to have higher levels of self-esteem and confidence. However, when there is *too* much support or involvement from parents, this can lead to the young athlete feeling pressured which can have a negative effect on performance.

- **Practice opportunities** – the opportunity to play and practise is fundamental to the development of young athletes. If there are more opportunities to play and practise, young athletes will have a greater chance of developing more general motor skills as well as more sport specific skills which will, in turn, give them more chance of being identified as a talented player.

- **Education** – some countries provide an education system that helps to identify talented young athletes. For example, in the UK Gifted and Talented Coordinators are employed in schools to identify talented young athletes so that they can be referred to the appropriate national governing body or sports organisation for further guidance.

Psychological factors

Have you ever heard the phrase 'the first five yards is in your head'? This is a saying often used in football to demonstrate the importance of psychological factors in sport. Psychological factors can often be the determining factors between a talented athlete being identified and being missed. Key psychological factors such as confidence, concentration, anticipation, decision-making and game intelligence are often qualities that can be spotted by an educated eye as they can change the way you act in different sports settings and can make you seem quicker than other players.

- **Confidence** is your belief that you can achieve a desired behaviour. In sport, the desired behaviours might be winning a race or kicking a football correctly, but generally speaking, if you *believe* you are able to do something, you are more likely to be able to do it. If you believe that you can do something, you are also more likely to be able to reduce the anxiety levels that can be associated with performance, which will in turn have added benefits for maintaining concentration.

Case study: Roger Bannister – the 4-minute mile man!

Roger Bannister was a medical student who, on 6 May 1954, broke the 4 minute mile by running a mile in a time of 3:59.4. Up until this time, many athletes had tried to beat the 4 minute mile but had only managed to reach times that were slightly over 4 minutes. Things had reached a pass where many athletes believed that it was physiologically impossible to run a mile in less than 4 minutes.

Roger Bannister, however, believed that, with appropriate running conditions, he could run a mile in less than 4 minutes. He achieved his goal. In the year after the 4-minute marker was broken, a number of athletes also ran sub 4 minute miles.

1. Why do you think that so many athletes were able to break the four minute mile after Roger Bannister did, when they had previously believed that it was impossible?
2. Do you think psychological factors are important for sport performance?

- **Concentration** is the ability to maintain attention and focus on relevant cues. When these cues change, it is important to be able to alter your attention to meet these changes.
  - Attentional focus has two main dimensions: width (broad or narrow) and direction (external or internal).
  - Broad attentional focus relates to concentrating on, and responding to, lots of different cues (such as team mates, opposition, ball position) all at the same time. It is important for athletes such as midfielders in football.
  - Narrow attentional focus relates to concentrating on, and responding to, one or two different cues. This is important for golfers when they are lining up a putt.
  - External attentional focus relates to directing attention toward an external object, such as an opponent or a ball. An example of this could be planning your return in tennis based on the flight of the ball and the position of the opposing player.
  - Internal attentional focus relates to internal thoughts and feelings, for example, a high jumper using mental rehearsal of their take off prior to their event to reduce anxiety.

Generally, more talented athletes will have higher levels of concentration. They will be able to shift between concentration styles and block out potential distracters more so than their less talented counterparts.

Remember

It is quite common for the terms 'concentration', 'attention' and 'attentional focus' to be used interchangeably, so don't get confused if you see these different terms.

- **Anticipation, decision-making and game intelligence** – have you ever watched a match on television and heard the commentator talking about good players having 'vision' or being able to 'read the game'? When you hear this, they are talking about anticipation, decision-making and game intelligence. These three factors are all interlinked and directly influence each other. Think about when you have watched a football game. You will have seen a player pass a ball into a space before their team mate has even set off running; this is because they have the game intelligence (knowledge of the game and how it works) to be able to anticipate (predict something that will happen and react to it before it starts happening) and make the correct decision based on all of the available information. In the example of the football player, the player with the ball will pass it into a space that their team mate can run into and continue to build play from there. This is important for talent identification as talented individuals in all sports will have higher levels of anticipation, faster and more accurate decision-making skills and higher levels of game intelligence than their less talented counter parts. This will be evident through the speed of play that they can adopt (generally faster), the number of errors they make (play will generally be more accurate with fewer errors) and the amount of energy they use up (at times, talented players have been said to play 'effortlessly').

Skills

There are two different types of skills that coaches look for when identifying talent in young athletes.

- **General motor skills** are fundamental movement skills such as running, jumping, throwing and catching. They are often dependent on components of fitness such as agility, balance and coordination. Coaches look for these as young people that demonstrate these motor skills from a young age tend to be better athletes later in life (although not always).

- **Technical and tactical skills** are sport specific skills that are learned through game play. Technical skills relate to different techniques that you will use during the game whereas tactical skills relate to different positional plays or phases of play during the game. Tactical skills are very closely related to game intelligence.

Assessment activity 20.1 — P1 P2 · BTEC

You are working at a sports coaching business and you have been asked by a local sports club to 'keep your eye open' for talented young players in their sport. As part of this task, the club has asked you to produce a leaflet for all of your coaches so that you are all looking for the same things. Your leaflet needs to educate your coaches on the different types of talent and the different predictors of talent.

1. In your leaflet describe the different types of talent. **P1**

2. Describe the five different predictors of talent for performers in sport. **P2**

Grading tips

- To attain **P1** you need to describe include unidimensional, multidimensional, unisport and multisport talent within your descriptions.

- To attain **P2** you need to include physical, physiological, sociological, psychological and skill-based predictors of talent.

PLTS

When you are looking at the different predictors of talent, if you ask questions to extend your own thinking about the importance of the different predictors, you will provide evidence of your skills as a **creative thinker**.

Functional skills

If your leaflet is fit for purpose, you could provide evidence of your **ICT** skills.

2. Be able to design a talent identification programme for a chosen sport

Talent identification programmes are used by organisations such as UK Sport and the Australian Institute for Sport to try to identify talented athletes in a range of sports.

2.1 Current talent identification programmes

London 2012 – It could be you

There are a number of talent identification programmes that are used within the UK. Following on from the success of Team GB in the Beijing 2008 Olympics, a number of talent identification programmes to help prepare for the 2012 and 2016 Olympics have been introduced including:

- Girls4Gold
- Pitch2Podium
- Talent Transfer
- Sporting Giants
- Talent 2012: Fighting Chance
- Talent 2012: Paralympic Potential
- Talent 2016: Tall and Talented.

The structure of each of the talent identification programmes used in preparation for London 2012 Olympics (and beyond) is broadly similar, following a series of phases.

- Phase 1 is a talent assessment event that measures different elements of fitness including speed, power, endurance, strength and stature.

- Phase 2 explores potential to develop as a world-class athlete in one or more of the targeted sports. It involves more sport specific testing, including the athlete's ability to learn new skills relevant to the sport for which they have been identified.

- Phase 3 is a talent confirmation training programme lasting for 3–6 months. It looks at the athletes' commitment to their development and their ability to develop as an elite athlete. People who show exceptional talent at the end of the talent confirmation programme are invited to an Olympic Development Programme. As the Olympic Development Programme is the final stage, only

a small number of athletes are present. However, athletes who do not reach the final stage are provided with information about how they could continue their sport through different clubs and societies.

Girls4Gold

Girls4Gold was a talent identification programme started by UK Sport and the English Institute of Sport (EIS). This was a search for competitive female athletes aged between 17 and 25, competing in any sport at county/regional level, and with the potential to become Olympic champions in targeted sports of cycling, bob skeleton, canoeing, modern pentathlon, rowing and sailing. Girls4Gold is the most extensive female sporting talent identification programme ever undertaken in Great Britain. The overall aim of Girls4Gold was to find talented female athletes capable of achieving medal success in London in 2012 and beyond.

Pitch2Podium

There are a number of athletes who have started playing one sport only to find that they are actually better at another; for example, Darren Campbell (former Olympic gold medallist), played football for Plymouth Argyle before becoming an Olympic

What do you think are the strengths and limitations of the Girls4Gold initiative?

athlete! Pitch2Podium is aimed at this type of athlete. Pitch2Podium was a talent identification programme run by UK Sport, the English and Scottish Institutes of Sport and their partners within football and rugby (Football Association, Professional Footballers' Association, Premier League, The Football League, League Football Education, Scottish PFA, Premier Rugby and the Rugby Football Union).

The aim of the programme was to provide young football and rugby players who have been unsuccessful in securing a professional contract with an opportunity to succeed in a new Olympic sport by filtering those with outstanding potential into targeted World Class programmes within British Cycling, GB Hockey, UK Athletics, Pentathlon GB, the British Canoe Union and British Bob Skeleton.

Talent Transfer

UK Sport analysed the records of 1200 athletes that had received World Class Programme funding from 1997 and selected 150 of these athletes. This was the start of the Talent Transfer programme. The Talent Transfer programme aimed to recruit athletes already retired, or nearing retirement, and provide them with an opportunity to switch sports and directly contribute to Team GB in London 2012. Even though an athlete may not have made it in their chosen sport, they could have transferable skills necessary to succeed in an alternative sport. Examples of talent transfer ideas have included taking artistic gymnasts and assessing their potential as Olympic divers, and the Talent 2012: Fighting Chance initiative that has looked at turning the country's best martial artists into medal contenders in tae kwon do.

Sporting Giants

Sporting Giants was an initiative run by UK Sport and the EIS and was aimed at tall men (over 6 feet 3 inches) and women (over 5 feet 11 inches) with good all round athletic ability. The overall aim of the programme was to unearth talented athletes who could contribute to sports such as rowing, handball and volleyball to help Team GB increase their medal tally at London 2012 and beyond. From the original 3854 applicants, 34 rowers, 11 handball players and seven volleyball players were successfully integrated into British squads.

Scouting programmes and criteria

A number of team sports have scouting programmes that aim to identify talented athletes. While the scouting programmes often have criteria that players need to achieve to be classed as talented, whether or not the player meets that criteria is often very subjective and is often decided by a coach or scout that has 'an eye' for a player. Examples of scouting criteria that are used in sports such as football include:

* TABS: technique, attitude, balance, speed
* SUPS: speed, understanding, personality, skill
* TIPS: technique, intelligence, personality, speed
* PAS: pace, attitude, skill.

Remember

A subjective assessment is an assessment based on the opinion of an individual whereas an objective assessment is based against established normative values.

Activity: Talent identification for London 2012

UK Sport, the EIS and a number of national governing bodies have played leading roles in identifying talented young athletes for a range of sports in preparation for London 2012 (and subsequent competitions). So that people are more aware of these programmes, produce a poster that summarises each of the key initiatives, including:

* Girls4Gold
* Pitch2Podium
* Talent Transfer

* Sporting Giants
* Talent 2012: Fighting Chance
* Talent 2012: Paralympic Potential
* Talent 2016: Tall and Talented.

You may want to use the UK Sport website (www.uksport.gov.uk) and the EIS website (www.eis2win.co.uk).

Complete this for pupils who demonstrate **talent in PE.** 5= excellent 4=very good 3=good 2= satisfactory 1=needs support	Rating
Pupil's name: School:	
Physical	
Explores and develops skills demonstrating control, fluency and quality in a range of activities	
Demonstrates a range of skills in different compositional and tactical situations	
Demonstrates good peripheral vision and uses this in a range of situations across activities	
Shows precision when executing movement skills with high levels of coordination and balance	
Sub-total	
Social	
Demonstrates the ability to take the lead when working with others	
Communicates clearly to others when describing their performances showing an understanding of tactics/strategies and compositional ideas	
Demonstrates the ability to make good decisions when working collaboratively	
Enables and empowers other pupils in participating effectively in activities	
Sub-total	
Personal	
Shows motivation, commitment and focus when working	
Demonstrates the ability to self-regulate learning in independent learning environments	
Demonstrates the ability to evaluate own performance effectively	
Handles feedback in a constructive way and uses this to develop levels of performance	
Sub-total	
Cognitive	
Demonstrates the ability to transfer skills effectively across a range of activities	
Demonstrates the ability to plan and utilise a range of strategies in a number of activities	
Identifies strengths and weaknesses, offering suggestions for improvement, across a range of performances	
Uses a broad analysis vocabulary when describing performances	
Sub-total	
Creative	
Consolidates and develops skills in a creative, inventive and innovative way	
Responds to stimulus in an innovative way	
Offers a range of productive and viable solutions to a problem	
Is confident in experimenting with acquired skills and ideas through application (e.g. within a gymnastic sequence, dance composition or game)	
Total	

© Youth Sport Trust

Figure 20.1: What do you think the differences would be between this type of checklist and a sport specific checklist?

Talent identification checklists

Talent identification checklists are used in a variety of settings ranging from school PE all the way through to professional sport to identify potentially talented athletes. They include a range of criteria (for example, the scouting criteria shown above), action to make an assessment of that criteria and a section for any comments relating to evidence of that criteria. An example of a talent identification checklist for school PE can be seen below. When using this checklist, it is suggested that any learner scoring greater than 70 per cent overall should be highlighted as potentially talented by their PE teacher.

2.2 Structure of talent identification programmes

When you are designing talent identification programmes, you will generally follow the same type of structure including: aims, purpose, structure and format, phases, timescales, use of test batteries and the resources required.

Aims and purpose

The aims of the talent identification programme are what you would like to have achieved at the end of it. These aims could be quite broad (for example, increase Team GB's medal tally at London 2012) or they could be more specific (for example, to develop handball players who can win medals at an Olympic level). Without a clear aim and purpose, it is unlikely that the programme will be successful.

Structure and format

Every talent identification programme has a clear structure and format. This will generally be split into different phases and stages that will be laid out in a format broadly similar to the one below.

- **Receive applications** – this stage involves the young people submitting an application for the particular talent development programme.

- **Screen applications** – at this stage the organisation looks through the applications that have been received and decides whether the athletes should be invited onto the talent development programme.

- **Invite applicants to trial/screening** – after the screening, successful applicants are invited to complete the general fitness testing that normally forms Phase 1 of a talent identification programme. The process of receiving applicants to inviting applicants to trial can take anywhere from one day to a number of weeks, depending on the volume of applications and the number of people screening the applications.

- **Phase 1: general fitness testing** – the general fitness testing phase involves measuring components of fitness such as speed, endurance and body composition. When the testing is completed, the results will be analysed and the people with the highest fitness levels will be invited back for the sport specific testing. Generally, those

in the top 10–20 per cent will be invited back for sport specific testing. At an elite level, this process from completing the testing to analysing all of the results can take up to three months depending on the number of applicants.

- **Phase 2: sport specific testing** – this phase follows the general fitness testing and can take anything up to five months in some programmes. Sport specific tests differ from general tests in that they assess sport specific components of fitness, or they measure components in a sport specific manner (for example, in the cycling Girls4Gold programme, the cycle based VO_2 max assessment would be more appropriate than the multi-stage fitness test because it is more specific to the sporting action). At an elite level, this overall process can take up to five months depending on the number of people in the programme.

- **Phase 3: talent confirmation** – the top 3–5 per cent of applicants will generally be invited to this phase. This phase involves introducing and assessing sport specific skills and can take up to six months. For example, in a cycling assessment, applicants would need to learn how to generate standing acceleration and would complete flying time trials over 100 and 200 metres.

Use of test batteries

A test battery is a range of fitness tests that are used as part of a talent identification programme. It is normal to use both general fitness tests and sport specific fitness tests at different stages of a talent identification programme. These fitness test results will then be interpreted by comparing them to normative data to see how the athlete compares to other athletes from the same type of population. For more information on the process of fitness testing, see Student Book 1, Unit 7 Fitness testing for sport and exercise.

Resources required

There are three main types of resources that you will need to consider when planning a talent identification programme.

- **Human resources** are the people who will need to be involved in the talent identification process. These could include sport specific roles such as coaches, sports scientists, sports therapists and more non-specific roles such as administrative assistants.

- **Physical resources** generally relate to the facilities and equipment that will be required to successfully run a talent identification programme.

- **Fiscal resources** relates to the money required to run your talent identification programme. The fiscal resources available will ultimately determine the quality and amount of human resources available.

Assessment activity 20.2

P3 P4 M1 M2 D1 BTEC

You are working as a scout for a sports club which has not been very successful at identifying talented athletes. The manager has asked you to review the overall process of talent identification in your club. As part of this review, you need to describe a current talent identification programme that is used in professional sport and then design a new proposed talent identification programme for your club.

1. Choose one successful talent identification programme used in professional sport and describe it. **P3**

2. For the same programme, produce a summary evaluation of how successful it has been. **M1**

3. Design a talent identification programme that uses a standard structure. **P4**

4. Explain the activities involved with each phase of your talent identification programme. **M2**

5. Justify why you have chosen your activities for each phase of your talent identification programme. **D1**

Grading tips

- To attain **P3** describe the aims, structure, content and facilities required for the programme.

- To attain **M1** you could look at the number of successful or unsuccessful athletes that have come out of the programme, the ratio of successful to unsuccessful athletes and case studies of successful athletes.

- To attain **P4** you could use the format of a current talent identification programme as the basis for your programme. Try discussing your ideas with your tutor or friends.

- To attain **M2** you could provide examples of the different activities through diagrams and detailed instructions.

- To attain **D1** you should say why you have chosen the particular activities for the programme, looking at how they could identify talented athletes.

PLTS

If you present a persuasive course of action for your talent identification programme, you could provide evidence of your skill as an **effective participator**.

Functional skills

If you write an appropriate extended document that describes one talent identification programme and shows the plan for your proposed talent identification programme, you could provide evidence of your skills in **English**.

3. Know key factors in talent development in sport

After you have identified a talented athlete, this does not mean that they are guaranteed high levels of success in sport. The process of talent *development* involves a detailed knowledge of lots of different positive factors as well as an understanding of some of the obstacles that can stand in the way of an athlete.

Just as with talent identification, there are a number of different factors associated with talent development. These factors include physical, physiological, sociological, psychological, skills and obstacles.

Physical

Earlier in this unit we discussed a number of physical factors such as height, weight, muscle girth and somatotype that are important for talent identification. These factors are also important for talent development, and for similar reasons. While factors such as height cannot be developed, other factors can be developed to suit the requirements of particular sports (for example, a boxer choosing the correct training methods to maintain weight, muscle girth and somatotype to be at the correct weight class). It is quite common for tall talented athletes to be chosen for sports such as volleyball, handball and rowing and then working on the other physical elements to meet the needs of the specific sport.

Physiological

You should demonstrate appropriate physiological characteristics, such as aerobic capacity or anaerobic endurance, to be identified as talented (see page 228). These characteristics also need to be developed. However, physiological characteristics can only be further developed to a certain point once they have been established. For example, a sprinter would struggle to be a top level marathon runner even if they completely changed their training to try to match that of the top level marathon runner.

Sociological

There are a number of key sociological factors that can influence the development of young athletes, both positively and negatively. These key factors include support from parents, education, opportunities for deliberate practice and deliberate play, and the roles, skills and techniques of coaches.

Parental support

This is one of the most influential factors in the development of young athletes. There are a number of famous athletes such as Tom Daley and Lewis Hamilton who have been very open about the importance of the support provided by their parents. Generally, there are two different types of support offered by parents: **tangible support** and **intangible support**.

- **Tangible support** – parents are often called the forgotten sponsors of sport because they are the ones that often provide the money for new kit, provide transport to training and matches and pay subscription fees for their children. These are all examples of tangible support by parents, and without these most young people would not be able to get involved in sport in the first place.

- **Intangible support** – have you ever had a really bad game or race and your parent has been the first person there to see you at the end? They will have probably put their arm around your shoulder or given you a hug just to try to make you feel better when you were feeling down. These are examples of intangible support; they are non-physical things (such as praise or consolation) that are given by your parents. For many developing athletes, having their parents there to support them at games is an important factor in their development.

Key terms

Tangible support – physical support, such as money and kit.

Intangible support – non-physical support, such as watching games and giving praise.

While parental support has many positive influences, it can sometimes have a negative influence on development. Sometimes, when large amounts of support are offered or when the parents' behaviour at the sporting events is inappropriate, the young athlete can feel under pressure or ashamed, both of which can lead to dropping out from sport. Imagine how you would feel if your parent stood on the sideline at one of your games, constantly shouting instructions at you. After a while, you would probably get annoyed and feel quite disempowered (and possibly feel that your parent didn't trust your ability). This is another factor that can negatively affect the development of young athletes as it can damage their confidence and decision-making skills.

On page 233 we saw how education systems are involved with talent identification.

Take it further

The influence of family

As well as looking at the role of parents in talent development, more recent research has started to look at the influence of other family members such as siblings. Using the Internet and books, try to find out what positive and negative influences other family members can have on talent development. You may even want to think about some of your own experiences when you are doing this.

Education

On page 233 we saw how education systems are involved with talent identification. Educational settings play an important part in talent development by offering opportunities to take part in a range of sports and increasing the standards of teaching and learning in physical education through School Sports Partnerships and Specialist Sports Colleges; and by offering talented learners the chance to fulfil their sporting and educational potential through the Gifted and Talented initiative.

Take it further

More research

Go to www.youthsporttrust.org and research the following areas, looking at how they can be used to develop young athletes:
- Gifted and Talented
- Talented in sport
- Gifted in PE
- National Talent Orientation Camp.

Opportunities for deliberate practice

Ericsson, Krampe and Tesch-Römer have researched how much practice it takes to become an expert in your area, for example, in sport or the arts. They defined **deliberate practice** as activities that:

- need a lot of effort and attention

- do not lead to any immediate social or financial rewards
- are completed so that you can become a better athlete rather than because you enjoy them.

Research into a number of sports including football and ice-hockey have found that, in order to reach an elite level, an average of 10,000 hours of deliberate practice is required. Being able to reach this level of deliberate practice is dependent upon the resources that you have available and your motivation to practise, even when you are not enjoying it.

Key term

Deliberate practice – practice activities that need a lot of effort, are not inherently enjoyable and do not lead to immediate social or financial rewards.

Take it further

Developmental Model of Sport Participation

As well as deliberate practice, people involved with talent development have looked at the importance of other activities and how they can influence development through different stages. One of the models that looks at different factors and how they influence development of young athletes is the Developmental Model of Sport Participation. Using books and the Internet, research the Developmental Model of Sport Participation and answer the following:

1. **Who devised the model?**
2. **What are the different stages within the model?**
3. **What does the theory say about the importance of playing other sports?**
4. **How does this theory compare to the idea of deliberate practice?**

Roles, skills and techniques of coaches

The coach is one of the most important factors in the development of young athletes. The diagram below shows the different roles, skills and techniques often adopted by coaches. For a coach to be working from a developmental viewpoint, he or she needs to be

237

working in the best long-term interests of the athlete, rather than adopting a more short-term, 'win at all costs' approach. The following factors have been cited by athletes as being important in their development:

- Communication styles (verbal and non-verbal)
- Equality
- Sport specific knowledge
- Level of coaching qualification
- Use of a range of coaching/leadership styles
- Working as part of a support team and knowing who you can refer athletes to for specialist advice (for example, sports scientists, sports therapists, personal trainers).

For more information relating to the roles, skills and techniques of coaches, see Student Book 1, Unit 5 Sports coaching.

Psychological factors

On page 229, we discussed how different psychological factors can influence young athletes being identified as talented in their sport. These same factors (confidence, concentration, anticipation, decision-making and game intelligence) are also important for talent development because, in order to progress to higher levels of performance, you should develop these qualities at an appropriate rate. This has implications for coaches and other professionals working with young athletes

Activity: The importance of coaching in talent development

You are working as an advisor to young trainee coaches. Your job is to help develop them and to help them to work with long-term athlete development in mind. To do this, you want them to reflect on the positive and negative experiences they have had as a young athlete and how this could influence their work as coaches; and you want to educate them on the work of Sports Coach UK.

1. Produce a list of all of the things that you have experienced from your coaches, for example,

different coaching styles. Place these under positive or negative experiences and justify your answers.

2. Research the UK Coaching Framework and the Sports Coach UK Code of Practice for Sports Coaches and produce a mind map that answers the following question: How can the UK Coaching Framework and the Sports Coach UK Code of Conduct for Sports Coaches ensure that coaches are working in the long-term interests of their athletes?

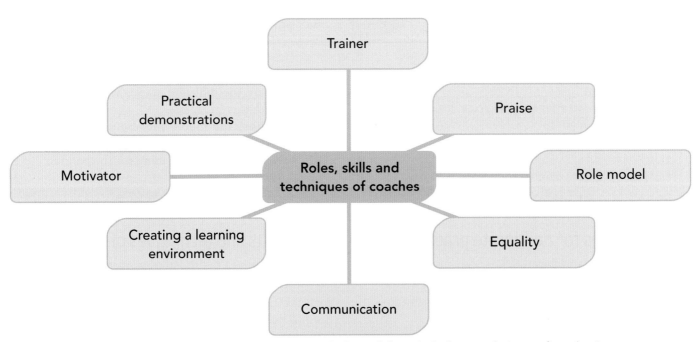

Figure 20.2: Which of the circles in the diagram are roles? Which are skills and which are techniques of coaches?

– they must devise appropriate ways to help their athletes develop these qualities. Research does provide suggestions for this and coaches should use these suggestions to help their athletes. For example, two ways of developing confidence are goal setting and highlighting achievements as these can help young athletes believe that they are capable of developing further. Concentration can be developed by helping young athletes to learn the difference between important environmental cues (for example, the position of the ball and opposition) and irrelevant environmental cues (for example, crowd noise). Opportunities for competition are often seen as one of the most important factors for developing decision-making and anticipatory skills, as well as developing game intelligence.

Obstacles

As well as a number of positive elements to talent development, there are also a number of obstacles that can negatively influence the development of young athletes, including injuries, peer pressure, role ambiguity, gender and age.

Injuries

Unfortunately, injuries are an inherent risk associated with sport participation. Any injury can have an influence on development to some degree as injuries inevitably lead to some time away from training and competition. For developing athletes, however, injuries (especially long-term or recurring injuries) can be particularly detrimental to development. Worryingly, a study in 2005 suggested that as many as 16 per cent of young talented athletes may have had their sporting career ended by injury.

Peer pressure

Peer pressure is one of the most common reasons for drop out from sport in young people. Quite often, sport can have very negative stereotypes attached to it that can discourage some young people from taking part (for example, sport is only for boys, girls shouldn't play sport). Thankfully, most of these stereotypes are disappearing although some are still evident. Young people can sometimes feel pressured into things that their friends feel are more socially acceptable and that can make it difficult for some young people to make the decision to play sport.

Role ambiguity

Role ambiguity is uncertainty or confusion over the role that you are supposed to be fulfilling. It is quite commonly experienced by student-athletes and athletes who are moving up levels within their sport (for example, progressing from county to a national squad). Student-athletes can sometimes feel this role ambiguity because they have multiple roles to fulfil within their school or college and because of this they can sometimes struggle with being both a good student and a good athlete. People who are moving up in levels of play (for example, from county squad to national squad) can suffer this role ambiguity because they have become used to being the best at a level – when they move up they could become one of the average payers within the team. This can lead to athletes questioning their worth and can have a harmful effect on development.

Gender differences

One of the key issues in talent development currently is that most of the research into talent development has examined how male athletes are developed in a number of sports and less attention has been paid to

What do you think are some of the developmental differences between male and female athletes?

the development of female athletes. As young male and female athletes have different developmental experiences, it is difficult to correctly develop female athletes as findings from research with male athletes cannot be applied directly to females. Thankfully, there has been an increased female involvement in a number of major sports which has stimulated greater interest in the development of female athletes. For example, football, which is the top female participation sport in England (there are now over 1 million registered female players).

Remember

Young male and female athletes have developmental differences so we need to make sure that the techniques we use are specific to the needs of each gender.

Age

Have you ever heard someone described as 'big for their age' or 'small for their age'? This is partly the basis for how age can become a barrier to development – it is not your age itself that can be a barrier, it is the maturational difference of people within your age group that can be the barrier. If you have two people in the same age group and one is born in January while the other is born in December, the first athlete has almost a full year's maturational advantage over the second athlete, which means they could be taller and have more muscle girth. This can be a barrier to development as, particularly at a younger age, the bigger athletes can appear to be better because they are faster, stronger and more dominant than smaller, younger athletes. This can be detrimental for the smaller, young athlete as they may not stand out as much as the bigger athlete, even though they may be technically more gifted.

Assessment activity 20.3 — P5 — BTEC

You are working as part of the youth academy at your local sports club. You want to get as much support from the key people around your young athletes as possible, so you have decided to produce an informational poster for parents of the young athletes to educate them on all of the different factors that can positively and negatively influence talent development.

Choose five different key factors that you think are the most important for your favourite sport and describe them. Provide examples of how these different factors can influence development. **P5**

Grading tip

- To attain **P5** you could research the different factors that are unique to your sport so that you are providing sport specific information.

PLTS

If you communicate your information in a manner that is appropriate for the parents of young athletes, you could provide evidence towards your skills as a **reflective learner**.

Functional skills

If your poster is fit for purpose, you could provide evidence of your **English** skills.

4. Be able to design a talent development programme for a chosen sport

Talent is a valuable commodity in the world of sport, so we need to make sure that we develop it in the best way possible so that young athletes get the greatest long-term benefits.

4.1 Current talent development programmes

There are a number of talent development programmes within the UK that are aimed at developing talent at all levels, ranging from long-term athlete development models that examine the development of athletes from childhood, all the way up to World Class Performance Plans that help elite athletes become even better.

World Class Performance Plans (WCPP)

At an elite level, sport is every bit as much a complex science as it is a competition. To be able to be the best, elite athletes need the best support team around them – this is where World Class Performance Plans (WCPP) come in. Each sport has its own WCPP, but they have the same broad content and format. A WCPP generally has:

- a four to eight year time frame to allow for long term development
- annual reviews to ensure progress towards targets
- performance directors and managers
- world-class coaches
- sports science support
- sports medicine support
- warm-weather training
- acclimatisation training
- international competition programmes (including travel and accommodation)
- athlete development programmes (including both sport and education)
- international standard training facilities
- athlete personal award (financial support towards living costs for athletes so that they don't have to work full time).

Take it further

WCPP for UK Athletics

Go to www.UKA.org.uk and research the WCPP for UK Athletics.

1. **What are the overall aims of the WCPP?**
2. **Using the bullet points above as a guide, produce a summary of the WCPP for UK Athletics.**
3. **How could you use this as a guide for developing your own talent development programme?**

Talented Athlete Scholarship Scheme (TASS)

The Talented Athlete Scholarship Scheme (TASS) is a government funded programme to support young talented athletes. It is designed to support athletes within the education system during higher and further education. The TASS programme is designed to help athletes fulfil their potential in sport and maintain a balance between academic life or employment while training and competing as an athlete.

One of the main aims of TASS is to reduce the drop out of talented athletes from sport due to academic and financial pressures. TASS athletes are awarded scholarships to sporting services (currently equivalent to £3000). TASS 2012 is an initiative for athletes that have the potential to win medals at the 2012 Olympics. Athletes awarded a TASS 2012 scholarship will receive sporting services up to the value of £10,000. TASS provides athletes with services including coaching, strength and conditioning, lifestyle support and sports medicine support, as well as support with competition and training expenses. You can find more information about TASS at www.tass.gov.uk.

World Class Start and Potential programmes

The aim of the World Class Start programme is to identify talented young performers and give them a basis from which to build future world-class success. The aim of the World Class Potential programme is to select performers with potential and develop their talents in order to give them the best chance of achieving international success.

Long Term Athlete Development (LTAD) models

Long Term Athlete Development (LTAD) models are used by coaches in different sports to try to ensure the appropriate development of young athletes through different stages. LTAD models are based on either **early specialisation sports** (such as gymnastics) which means that to be able to excel in that sport, you must start sport specific training from an early age, or **late specialisation sports** (such as football) where the emphasis of early training should be on fun and developing general motor skills before gauging later training around sport specific skills.

LTAD models have a series of phases which can be seen in table 20.1.

Table 20.1: Phases of Long Term Athlete Development models.

Phase	Description
Phase 1: FUNdamentals	The objective of this phase is to develop fundamental movement skills through structured, fun activities. This stage focuses on developing the ABCs (agility, balance, coordination and speed) to help develop general skills used in all sports (running, jumping and throwing). In this stage, young athletes should be physically active 5–6 times per week. If they have a favourite sport, they could play this sport once or twice per week, but involvement in a range of activities is important for future development.
Phase 2: learning to train	The objective of this phase is to learn fundamental sports skills. This phase concentrates on: • the range of fundamental sports skills, such as throwing, catching, jumping and running • an introduction to readiness (being mentally and physically prepared for competition) • fundamental tactics • cognitive and emotional development • practising skills in challenging formats. The frequency of activities in this phase is similar to phase 1 except, where there is a favoured sport, at least 50% of the time is allocated to other sports/activities to develop a range of skills.
Phase 3: training to train	The objective of this phase is to build fitness and sport specific skills. This phase focuses on sport specific skills, fitness training, mental preparation, perceptual skill development (e.g. tactical understanding) and decision-making skills This phase has approximately 75% training to 25% competition.
Phase 4: training to compete	The objective of this phase is to refine skills for a particular event or position. This phase focuses on: • individual sport/position/event specific training all year round • performing skill under pressure/competition • technical and tactical preparation • psychological preparation. This phase involves 50% competition and 50% training.
Phase 5: training to win	The objective of this phase is to attain peak performance in competition. This phase is characterised by fully establishing physical, technical, tactical and mental characteristics required for the sport/event or position. The training to competition ratio changes in this phase to 25% training and 75% competition.
Phase 6: retirement/ retraining/retaining	This stage relates to the activities performed after an athlete has retired from competition permanently. During this final stage, ex-athletes use their valuable experiences and move into sport-related careers including coaching, officiating, sport administration, masters competition and the media.

Foundation phase		Performance phase			Recreation phase
FUNdamentals Females aged 5–8 Males aged 6–9	**Learning to train** Females aged 8–11 Males aged 9–12	**Training to train** Females aged 11–15 Males aged 12–16	**Training to compete** Females aged 15–17 Males aged 16–18	**Training to win** Females aged 17+ Males aged 18+	**Retainment** All ages, through choice

Figure 20.3: Why do you think it is important to have different activities at different stages of talent development?

4.2 Structure of talent development programmes

Just as when you planned your talent identification programme earlier, you will need to make sure that your talent development programme has an appropriate structure.

Aims and purpose

Your talent development programme should have a clear aim and purpose. Talent development programmes have the broad aim of holistically developing young athletes, but can have more specific aims for different phases.

Structure and format

Most talent development programmes will follow either the whole structure of either early or late specialisation models that you learned about earlier; or the structure of a specific phase of the LTAD model. If your talent development programme follows a full LTAD model, you should make sure that athletes progress logically through the phases of the programme.

Use of test batteries, screening and norm values

A lot of talent development programmes use a series of fitness tests to measure the development of athletes. It is important to make sure that you select tests that are specific to your chosen sport when you are designing talent development programmes. These test batteries are used to screen athletes for their suitability for the sport. You will be able to judge how athletes are progressing through their chosen sports by comparing their test results against norm data for that test.

Goal setting

After you have completed your testing as part of your development programme, you should encourage athletes to set goals to help them progress. These goals should:

- follow the SMART principle
- include a range of short-term goals that will help the athlete progress through their medium- and long-term goals

- use a combination of outcome, performance and process goals (see Unit 17 Psychology for sport performance in Student Book 1).

You also need to make sure that the types of goals that you set are appropriate for the athlete's age and gender. For example, if you were to set goals for a 17-year-old female football player, you should make sure that the language use is appropriate for the age and that the comparison of the goal is made to female players rather than male players.

Timescales

Full LTAD programmes can take up to ten years for athletes to progress from FUNdamentals through to the Training to win stage. When designing your talent development programme, you should make sure that the timescale will allow the athlete to develop at an appropriate rate.

Resources

When you learned about talent identification programmes, you looked at the different human, physical and fiscal resources required to run a talent identification programme. You will also need to consider these when planning your talent development programme.

Considerations in talent development programmes

There are a number of other considerations that need to be taken into account when planning talent development programmes.

- **Creating a learning environment** – it is difficult to learn if you are not offered the chance to solve problems, cannot reflect on your progress and discuss your progress with others, such as the coach. Your talent development programme should include some problem-based learning so that athletes can develop perceptual, tactical and decision-making skills; and should include some form of log or diary where both athletes and coaches can record their targets and progress.
- **Feedback** – a really important part of creating a learning environment is ensuring that there is appropriate time for athletes and coaches to give feedback to each other. Feedback can be in the form of knowledge of results (did you win/lose/draw?)

and knowledge of performance (why did you win/lose/draw?). Without getting the correct type of feedback at regular intervals, it is very difficult for young athletes to learn.

- **Communication** – think about the times when you have discussed your performance with your coach or tutor. There will have been times when you repeatedly said 'yes' and nodded in agreement, but your posture will have been very slumped, you will have made very little eye contact and your mind will have been far away. While your verbal messages appear quite clear, your non-verbal communication tells a different story! In order to give and receive the appropriate feedback, decide on development plans and set or review targets; effective communication between coach and performer (and sometimes the support team) is essential. Effective communication involves being able to send and receive clear messages, both verbally and non-verbally.

- **Roles, skills and techniques of coaches** – earlier you looked at the different roles, skills and techniques that are important for talent development. You need to make sure that your talent development programme will allow the coach to fulfil their roles and use appropriate skills and techniques to be able to effectively develop their athletes. For example, if your coach is working with a group of under-10 football players, you would want your coach to use simple, clear terminology and provide short instructions. You would also want your coach to provide the players with simple problems to solve relating to different tactics and would want to allow players time to work together to solve problems.

- **Reasons for participation in sport** – one of the key considerations for your talent development programme is the reasons for taking part in sport. There are a number of benefits from taking part in sport including being healthy, increased self-esteem, developing team skills and having fun. However, for many people involved with competitive sport, they take part because they want to win. Your talent development programme must cater for the various reasons for participation.

- **People's perceptions of their own ability and the impact of sport on children and adolescents** – much of a young athlete's self-worth is attached to their ability in sport. This means that, when athletes feel that they are good at their sport or that they are improving, they are likely to feel better about themselves generally; your talent development programme should aim to support this positive perception. If you can produce a talent development programme that fosters this increased self-perception, young people are more likely to have a positive experience from their involvement in sport, making it more likely that they will gain important life skills such as socially acceptable behaviour, self-discipline and communication.

Remember

If you don't create the right type of learning environment within your talent development programme, your athletes will not be able to develop at an appropriate rate.

Assessment activity 20.4

You are working as a youth coach for a sports club which has not been very successful at developing young talented athletes. The manager has asked you to review the overall process of talent development in your club. As part of this review, you need to describe a current talent development programme that is used in your sport and then design a new proposed talent development programme for your club.

1. Choose and describe one successful talent development programme used in professional sport. **P6**

2. For the same programme, produce a summary evaluation of how successful it has been. **M3**

3. Design a talent development programme that follows a standard structure (such as the structure of a LTAD model). **P7**

4. Explain the activities involved with each phase of your talent development programme. **M4**

5. Justify why you have chosen your activities for each phase of your talent development programme. **D2**

Grading tips

- To attain **P6** describe the aims, structure, content and facilities required for the programme.

- To attain **M3** you could look at the number of successful or unsuccessful athletes that have come out of the programme, the ratio of successful to unsuccessful athletes and case studies of successful athletes.

- To attain **P7** you could use the format of a current talent development programme as the basis of your programme. You may want to discuss your ideas with your tutors or friends.

- To attain **M4** you could provide examples of activities through diagrams and detailed instructions.

- To attain **D2** you could discuss why you have included your chosen activities, saying how they will benefit the athlete.

PLTS

If you present a persuasive course of action for your talent development programme, you could provide evidence of your skill as an **effective participator**.

Functional skills

If you write an appropriate extended document that describes one talent development programme and shows the plan for your proposed talent identification programme, you could provide evidence of your skills in **English**.

Paul Jeffries
Football coach

Paul is 22 and a sports coach. He is employed by a multi-sports coaching firm that works with a range of different organisations including schools and sports teams.

He is responsible for producing and running age appropriate coaching sessions, conducting player reviews and providing feedback to parents and carers.

'Sports coaching is a great job. I get to work with lots of really keen young people which is great. Helping them to develop is really fufilling. It isn't all easy though and there are some difficult parts. One of the biggest problems that I face is when I am working with different age groups. I currently coach football teams for under-10s, under-12s and under-14s so there are lots of different things that I need to take into account when I am planning and running sessions.

At times it can get a little confusing, especially when I'm working with some of the older 10-year-olds who are maturationally more advanced than some of the younger 12-year-olds! I often think that working with people based on their age group is not the best way to work, especially between the ages of 10 and 14. This is where there are some of the biggest differences in growth and maturation and I'm always trying to find better ways of working with my players to meet their individual needs rather than the needs of their age group.'

Think about it!

- If you were Paul, how would you try to deal with the maturational differences within and between the different age groups?
- What differences could there be between people in the same age group and different age groups?
- What different roles, skills and techniques could you use to make sure that you are meeting the needs of your players?

Just checking

1. What are the different types of talent?
2. List five factors that people look for when trying to identify talented young athletes.
3. What is the Girls4Gold initiative?
4. List five factors that are associated with talent development in sport.
5. How can these different factors influence talent development in sport?
6. What is the World Class Performance Plan?
7. What are the different phases of a LTAD programme?
8. What are the objectives, content and training to competition ratio at each phase?
9. What is the difference between early and late specialisation sports?
10. List five different factors that you would need to consider when designing your own talent development programme.

edexcel

Assignment tips

- There are a number of websites that provide useful information for this unit, but you may find these websites useful:
  - UK Sport – www.uksport.gov.uk
  - English Institute for Sport – www.eis2win.co.uk
  - Sports Coach UK – www.sportscoachuk.org

- To get a better understanding of LTAD models, it will be useful for you to look at sport specific LTADs. You will be able to find an LTAD for different sports by searching the Internet or contacting national governing bodies directly.

- Try to complete the activities in your talent identification and talent development plans in as much detail as possible.

- If you know any sports coaches or people that work for national governing bodies, it could be useful to speak to them about the talent identification and development procedures that are used within that sport. This will help you to develop your sport specific knowledge.

- Looking at talent development from lots of different perspectives (for example, physical, physiological, psychological, sociological and skill-based) will help you to get a better picture of how to best develop talented athletes.

Credit value: 10

21 Sport and exercise massage

Think about when you have started an event and your legs have felt tired and heavy, or when you have finished a race and your legs felt sore shortly after. How many times have you immediately rubbed your legs to make them feel better? What you have started to do is some very basic massage.

Due to the increasingly competitive nature of sport, athletes are exploring every avenue to give themselves the best chance of success. In order to be successful, athletes need to use as many ways as possible to prepare for their competition and to recover from competitive schedules. As a result of this, sport and exercise massage has become more prominent and popular within the sporting world in recent years.

Throughout this unit, you will learn about the effects and benefits of sport and exercise massage before looking at the roles of sport and exercise massage professionals. You will then learn about the different practices involved with sport massage ranging from how to identify the massage requirements of different athletes all of the way through to being able to perform different massage techniques.

Learning outcomes

After completing this unit you should:

1. know the effects and benefits of sport and exercise massage
2. know the roles of sport and exercise massage professionals
3. be able to identify the sport and exercise requirements of athletes
4. be able to perform and review sport and exercise massage techniques.

Assessment and grading criteria

This table shows you what you must do in order to achieve a pass, merit or distinction grade, and where you can find activities in this book to help you.

To achieve a **pass** grade the evidence must show that you are able to:	To achieve a **merit** grade the evidence must show that, in addition to the pass criteria, you are able to:	To achieve a **distinction** grade the evidence must show that, in addition to the pass and merit criteria, you are able to:
P1 describe the effects and benefits of sport and exercise massage **See Assessment activity 21.1, page 255**	**M1** explain the beneficial effects of sport and exercise massage **See Assessment activity 21.1, page 255**	
P2 describe the roles of sport and exercise massage professionals **See Assessment activity 21.2, page 257**		
P3 carry out pre-treatment consultations on two different athletes **See Assessment activity 21.3, page 273**	**M2** explain the sport and exercise massage requirements of two different athletes **See Assessment activity 21.3, page 273**	**D1** compare and contrast the sport and exercise massage requirements of two athletes **See Assessment activity 21.3, page 273**
P4 describe six contraindications to massage treatment **See Assessment activity 21.3, page 273**		
P5 produce a treatment plan for two athletes **See Assessment activity 21.3, page 273**		
P6 demonstrate appropriate sport and exercise massage techniques on two athletes **See Assessment activity 21.4, page 276**		
P7 review the treatment plan for two athletes, describing future treatment opportunities **See Assessment activity 21.4, page 276**	**M3** explain the appropriate sport and exercise massage treatment for two athletes **See Assessment activity 21.4, page 276**	**D2** evaluate the appropriate sport and exercise massage treatment for two athletes **See Assessment activity 21.4, page 276**

How you will be assessed

This unit will be assessed by internal assignments that will be designed and marked by the tutors at your centre. Your assessments could be in the form of:

- written reports
- posters
- leaflets
- presentations
- practical sports and exercise massage routines.

Sophie, 19-year-old sport massage therapist

This unit was really useful for me as I always wanted to be a sport massage therapist. Until I started this unit, I thought a sport massage therapist was somebody who just knew how to give a massage treatment to people, but it is so much more than that! It was really good to get an understanding of the benefits of sport and exercise massage as well as learning about all of the different roles of a sport and exercise massage professional.

This unit also got me thinking about all of the different directions that I could take my work in, how it could link in with sports injuries and how important sport and exercise massage is within sporting environments.

The part of this unit that I enjoyed the most was learning the massage techniques. It was really hands on, practical work which suits how I learn and it helped me to develop the different massage techniques that I use every day with my clients.

Over to you!

1. **Which parts of the unit do you think you will find interesting?**
2. **Which other units do you think would help you throughout this unit?**
3. **How are you going to prepare yourself for this unit?**

1. Know the effects and benefits of sport and exercise massage

Warm-up

What are the benefits of sport and exercise massage?
The basic aim of sport and exercise massage is to maintain or restore normal functioning. The sport and exercise massage professional uses massage to help assist performance and reduce the risk of injury. Why do you think athletes are so keen to use sport and exercise massage professionals in sport?

Due to the effects and benefits of sport and exercise massage, it has become an integral part of the training programmes of many athletes and regular exercisers.

1.1 Effects

Physical and mechanical effects

There are a number of physical and mechanical effects of sport and exercise massage that can be seen in Figure 21.1 below. These include blood and lymphatic circulation, tissue permeability, stretching, reducing and remodelling scar tissue and opening micro-circulation.

- **Blood and lymphatic circulation** – localised blood circulation can be improved as a result of sport and exercise massage. Circulation can be stimulated because the pressure exerted by the massage technique compresses and releases blood vessels which supplements their normal pumping action. When you massage a limb, it stimulates blood flow to that limb and stimulates blood flow to the other limb which makes massage particularly useful for people that have had limb injuries that has left one limb immobilised (for example, a broken leg). Increased circulation as a result of massage has the benefit of increasing the supply of oxygen and nutrients to the area and aids **lymphatic drainage**.

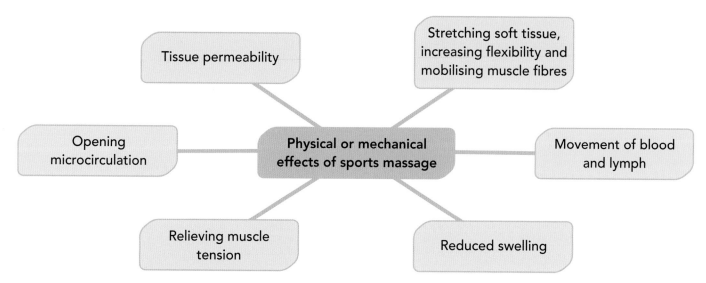

Figure 21.1: How will these effects help you to be a better athlete?

Lymphatic drainage is important because it helps to remove waste products and reduce swelling.

- **Tissue permeability** – massage improves the absorption of substances within the body tissues. It also affects **cell permeability**, which allows nutrients and other substances to enter the cell more readily and allows the removal of waste products from the cell.

- **Stretching** – most of the flexibility within a muscle comes from the surrounding connective tissues and the muscle fibres. With the forces that are applied through massage, muscle fibres can be separated, the connective tissues that surround the fibres can be stretched and the fibres can be stretched longitudinally. These three things, combined with the increased muscle temperature and circulation, make the tissue more pliable and reduces **adhesions**.

- **Reducing and remodelling scar tissue** – as muscle fibres start to heal after being damaged, they start to lose their elasticity and can become rigid – this causes scar tissue. If this is left untreated, it will cause permanent weakness and decreased flexibility in that area. Massage can help this as applying massage techniques across the direction of the muscle fibre can separate fibres that have adhered together and can break down scar tissue.

- **Opening micro-circulation** – massage opens the blood vessels by stretching them, enabling nutrients to pass through more easily.

Key terms

Lymphatic drainage – a massage treatment that uses light pressure and long, rhythmic strokes to increase lymphatic flow. Lymph, a fluid that contains white cells, is drained from tissue spaces by the vessels of the lymphatic system. It can transport bacteria, viruses and cancer cells. The lymphatic system is associated with the removal of excess fluid from the body. It is made up of lymphatic capillaries, lymphatic vessels, lymph nodes and lymph ducts.

Cell permeability – allowing or activating the passage of a substance through cells or from one cell to another.

Adhesions – pieces of scar tissue that attach to structures within the body, limiting movement and sometimes causing pain.

Physiological effects

There are a number of physiological effects of sport massage (see Figure 21.2 below). These will be due in some part to the effects of the massage technique on the autonomic nervous system, which is made up of the sympathetic and parasympathetic nervous systems.

The autonomic nerves are responsible for controlling the functioning of the vital organs in the body. Within this, the sympathetic nervous system stimulates activity within physiological systems, whereas the parasympathetic nervous system inhibits activity. Sport massage therapists use different massage techniques to stimulate the client's sense of touch, and by stimulating this sense of touch you can enhance the effects and benefits of sport massage.

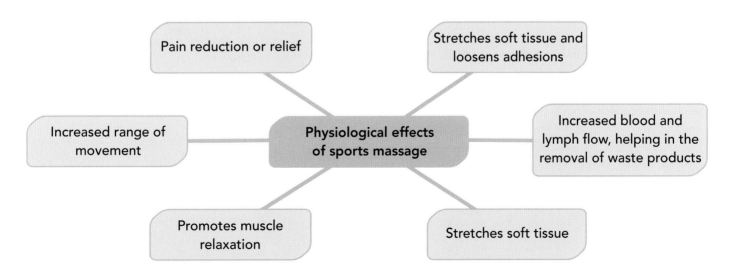

Figure 21.2: What physiological effects does sport massage have on sport and exercise performance?

Massage techniques that are deeper or more vigorous can stimulate the nervous system. Placing a small amount of pressure on the nervous system can also relieve pain by blocking nerve impulses, thus resulting in a numbing sensation in the area. Alternatively, slow, smooth massage techniques can produce a relaxing effect on the nerves. These effects are commonly accepted as the effects of massage on the nervous system, but some research has not found any sympathetic or parasympathetic responses to different massage techniques.

1.2 Benefits of sport and exercise massage

There are a number of physiological and psychological benefits of sport and exercise massage including stress reduction, enhanced wellbeing, improved body awareness, pain reduction and relaxation.

Stress reduction and enhanced wellbeing

Sport and exercise massage techniques can enhance a sense of wellbeing by stimulating the release of **endorphins** and by reducing levels of stress hormones such as **cortisol**.

Improved body awareness

Physiologically, massage can increase body awareness by enhancing nervous system function and giving you a greater awareness of your body. Psychologically, massage gives you an increased awareness of how your body actually looks, rather than how you think it looks, which can lead to a more positive body image.

Pain reduction

When pain occurs in an area, messages are sent to your brain via **afferent nerves**. By massaging the painful area, you stimulate **cutaneous mechanoreceptors** that block the signals before they reach your spinal cord. As your brain never receives the pain signals from the affected area, your perception of the pain is reduced.

Relaxation

Certain massage techniques can have relaxing effects on your nervous system and can release muscle tension, as well as stimulating the release of endorphins which can enhance your mood. This combination leads to a generally pleasant, relaxed feeling.

Key terms

Endorphins – morphine-like chemicals that can reduce pain and improve mood.

Cortisol – a hormone that is associated with stress, anxiety and depression.

Afferent nerves – sensory nerves that usually have receptors at the skin and joints.

Cutaneous mechanoreceptors – sensory nerve endings in the skin.

Remember

To understand the benefits of sport and exercise massage, you need to know how different body systems influence each other. For example, a sprinter may be worried about their performance because they cannot run as fast as normal and are starting to feel more stressed about their performance levels. They have very tight quadriceps and hamstrings which could be compressing the nerves passing through the muscles. When the nerve is compressed, the nerve impulse that travels down the nerve is slowed which will then slow down the overall muscle contraction. Using different massage techniques, the muscle tension is released, which increases the rate of the nerve impulse and the speed of contraction. Ultimately, this increases performance and reduces performance related stress.

2. Know the roles of sport and exercise massage professionals

Sport and exercise massage professionals work in a variety of settings including private practice, health and fitness clubs, spas and alongside other professionals such as physiotherapists. When working as a sport and exercise massage professional, you must have a detailed knowledge of the types of work you may do, the different treatments that you can apply and knowledge of your profession.

2.1 Roles

Types of work

When working as a sport and exercise massage professional, you must be confident in your ability to work with clients and be aware of your limitations of practice. Your limitations of practice are the things that you can and cannot do as a sport and exercise massage professional. As a sport and exercise massage professional, you are able to administer sport and exercise massage therapy for its intended purpose

and you will generally find yourself working with sport or exercise related athletes (although anybody can benefit from sport and exercise massage techniques). Therefore, you must understand the effects of massage on sport or exercise related performance. You are not trained to diagnose medical conditions, so you must always have a referral network of other professionals that you can work with and to whom you can send your clients if necessary.

Take it further

Sport Massage Association Code of Conduct

Using the Sport Massage Association Code of Conduct, find out more about the roles of a sport and exercise massage professional and their limitations of practice. Visit the association website (www.sportsmassageassociation.org).

Types of activities

There are a range of activities that you need to do to be an effective professional. Your activities will range from administrative tasks (such as checking and replying to emails, website maintenance, completing stock checks of materials and ordering stationery) to client assessments (such as biomechanical assessments) and treating clients.

Treatments applied

As a sport and exercise massage professional, you can apply several types of treatment dependent upon your experience and training. The main treatments that you could apply are massage, relaxation, strapping and taping, manipulation and electrotherapy treatments.

- **Massage** – the different massage techniques that you could use include effleurage, petrissage, frictions, tapotement and vibrations. These massage techniques involve the manipulation of soft tissue to assist in correcting problems and imbalances that can be caused by sport and exercise to help improve performance, prevent injury and enhance recovery.

- **Relaxation** – sport and exercise massage professionals are trained in different activities to aid relaxation, including massage techniques, stretching techniques and breathing techniques. One such advanced massage technique that combines the use of different strengthening, stretching, massage and breathing activities to elicit relaxation is known as Muscle Energy Technique (MET).

- **Strapping and taping** techniques are used by sport and exercise massage professionals to prevent injury and recurrence while returning to sport. The tape limits the movement in an injured area (such as a joint) to prevent excess or abnormal movement. Tape can also be used to protect unstable joints where repeated or severe ligament damage has resulted in stretching of the ligaments and joint instability. For example, if a taped ankle starts to over-invert (commonly known as 'going over on your ankle') after landing from a basketball jump shot, the tape will restrict excessive movement and inform the body that it needs to contract muscles to prevent too much movement at the ankle. Without this feedback the athlete may be unaware the ankle has started to invert and land on it thus

injuring it again. Tape should support the muscles surrounding the joint that may be under additional strain due to connective tissue injury.

- **Manipulation** – soft tissue manipulation is the stretching or lifting of tissues without lubrication; or the physical manipulation of joints to assist movement. This technique is used to help with the realignment of tissues and/or joint surfaces that have been misaligned as a result of injury. Manipulation should only be used by sport and exercise massage professionals after appropriate training.

- **Electrotherapy modalities** – electrotherapy is a technique that uses electrical currents at different frequencies to aid recovery from injury. Some common modalities of electrotherapy include ultrasound, Transcutaneous Electrical Nerve Stimulation (TENS) and interferential therapy. The use of these techniques requires specialist training.

Take it further

Muscle Energy Technique (MET)

Using books and the Internet, research MET.
1. **How can this technique benefit your massage clients?**
2. **What are some of the dangers of using MET?**

Knowledge

To maintain your reputation and work in the best interests of your client, you must make sure that your knowledge is up to date. You must have specific knowledge of your training requirements, career opportunities and the application of your treatments to sport and exercise.

- **Training** – sport and exercise massage is currently not regulated by law within the UK, but sport and exercise massage professionals do have professional bodies with which they associate themselves. These include the Sport Massage Association (www.sportsmassageassociation.org) and the Society of Sports Therapists (www.society-of-sports-therapists.org). Both of these professional bodies provide lists of accredited training courses on their websites and provide details of the training and experiential requirements to be accredited or be a member of the professional body. Once you are qualified as a sport and exercise massage professional, you need to make sure that you follow a programme of continued professional development (CPD) so that the professional body know that you are improving your knowledge and skills base.

- **Career opportunities** – there are a number of career opportunities for sport and exercise massage professionals which include working:
  - as a self-employed practitioner
  - in health and leisure clubs
  - for sports clubs
  - within the health services.

  Each will have their own training requirements and experience requirements, so it is a good idea to spend time researching what you will need to do to be able to progress into that career.

- **Application to sport** – when you work within sport and exercise massage, you will work mainly (although not exclusively) with athletes actively involved in sport or exercise. Massage can be an integral part of preparation for, and recovery from,

sport or exercise and can be used to increase training benefits, reduce or rehabilitate sports injuries and increase sport performance. You must understand how the different treatments can be applied specifically to sport and exercise.

Activity: Careers in sport and exercise massage

Imagine you want a career in sport and exercise massage but you don't really know how to get there. Spend time researching the different career opportunities so that you have a good idea of the requirements of the different careers. Using the Internet and books, research the different careers that are available in sport and exercise massage and find one that you are interested in. When you have done this, find out what qualifications and experience you will need to be able to progress into that career. Use the Sport Massage Association and the Society of Sports Therapists websites to help you.

Assessment activity 21.2   P2   BTEC

You have applied for a job working as a sport and exercise massage professional at a major health and fitness chain. As part of your application process, you must demonstrate that you fully understand the job.

Produce a presentation that describes the roles of sport and exercise massage professionals. **P2**

Grading tip

- To attain **P2** describe the types of work and activities undertaken by sport and exercise massage professionals, the treatments they apply and the knowledge they must have.

PLTS

If you communicate your information regarding the roles of sport and exercise massage professionals effectively, you could provide evidence of your skills as a **reflective learner**.

Functional skills

If your presentation is fit for purpose, you will provide evidence of your **English** skills.

3. Be able to identify the sport and exercise massage requirements of athletes

When you start to work with clients you must make sure that your massage is well planned and that you know why you are doing it. To do this, you need to conduct client assessments, keep appropriate documentation and be aware of the different contraindications to massage; and then use all of this information to propose an appropriate treatment plan.

3.1 Assessment

Your client assessment involves using initial consultations, making referrals to practitioners (if required), identifying the treatment area and having a knowledge of different simple injuries.

Initial consultation

During your initial consultation you should complete a client consultation form using questions and answers (a verbal assessment), an assessment of posture (a visual assessment) and an assessment of tension and movement (a physical assessment). Your questionnaire should include:

- key personal details of the client
- medical history history
- any current problems
- lifestyle details
- a diagram to identify areas and level of pain
- a section for therapist's comments
- a consent section where the patient and the therapist sign to show that the information is correct and that consent has been given by the client for treatment.

An example of a consultation form can be seen in Figure 21.4.

During the consultation you must visually assess a client's posture to see if there are any postural problems that could be a factor in injury. Figure 21.3 shows examples of good and bad posture; and the different warning signs to look for.

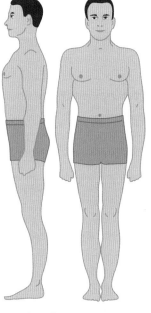
Good posture

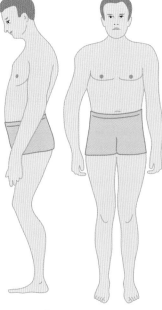
Poor posture

Figure 21.3: How does your posture compare to the images?

Client consultation form

Client name ....   Date of birth ....

Address ....   Occupation ....

....   Marital status ....

....   G.P. name ....

Home telephone ....   G.P. surgery address ....

Mobile telephone ....

Email ....

Medical history

Current general health status. (Circle as appropriate.)

Excellent   *Good*   *Average*   *Poor*   *Very Poor*

Any current or recent injuries? Yes / No (if yes, please specify)

....

Do you currently experience any problems with the following areas? (Circle as appropriate.)

Muscular   *Skeletal*   *Circulatory*   *Respiratory*

Are you currently undergoing any medical treatments? Yes / No (If yes, please specify.)

....

Are you currently taking any medication? Yes / No (If yes, please specify name and dosage.)

....

Do you have a family history of any medical conditions? Yes / No? (If yes, please specify.)

....

Lifestyle information

How would you describe your current diet? (please circle)

Excellent   *Good*   *Average*   *Poor*   *Very Poor*

Do you currently smoke? Yes / No (If yes, please specify)   ☐ Cigarettes per day

Do you drink alcohol? Yes / No (If yes, please specify)   ☐ Units per week

Do you currently use any other form of recreational drug? Yes / No (If yes, please specify.)

Do you currently take part in sport / exercise / physical activity? Yes / No (If yes, please specify.)

....

....

Other information

On the diagram, please indicate the site of pain and give it a level from 1–10.
(1 = not painful at all, 10 = extremely painful)

Is there anything that you can do that makes the pain ease?

....

....

....

....

....

Therapist notes (to include techniques to be used and justification of techniques)

Client signature ....   Date ....

Therapist signature ....   Date ....

Figure 21.4: Why is it important to have a detailed consultation form?

As well as a general assessment of posture, there are specific areas to look at while observing your client from behind. When you are assessing posture from behind, you should stand approximately 1 metre away (standing closer will prevent you from effectively comparing the left and right halves of the body).

Activity: Postural observation

Observe a friend from behind. Can you see any of the specific postural issues listed below?

- Are the ears level? If not, there could be spinal misalignment.

- Are the shoulders level at the acromio-clavicular joints and is the muscle bulk the same on both sides?

- Are the scapulae (shoulder blades) level? (See Figure 21.5.)

Figure 21.5: Uneven scapulae.

- How does the overall spine alignment look? Is there a straight or curved line between the neck and pelvis?

- Is the 'keyhole' (the gap between the arms and the body) even on both sides? If not, there could be spinal or shoulder misalignment (see Figure 21.6).

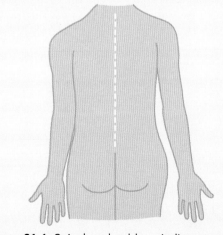

Figure 21.6: Spinal or shoulder misalignment.

- Are there any skin creases at the waist level? Are there more on one side than the other? This could indicate the person has a tendency to lean to one side.

- Is the pelvis level at both sides?

- Are the creases between the buttocks and the top of the hamstrings level? If not, there could be some pelvic misalignment (see Figure 21.7).

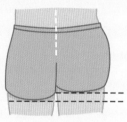

Figure 21.7: Pelvic misalignment.

- Check the number and angles of knee creases and check overall muscle bulk to assess any imbalances in the legs.

- Is the Achilles tendon vertically aligned or is it twisted? Is there any thickening of the tendon? Is the muscle bulk the same at the midline of the calf? These could indicate postural issues in the legs and feet.

- Are the feet pointing forwards when standing relaxed and barefoot? Are there any signs of hard skin? Does the client naturally invert or evert their feet when relaxed or walking?

Take it further

Researching postural terms

When you are conducting your postural assessments, it is good to have as much information as you can. Using books and the Internet, research the following terms and produce a description of each term with diagrams to accompany your description:

- plumb line
- head thrust
- flat back
- kyphosis (type 1)
- kyphosis (type 2)
- lordosis
- scoliosis
- bow legs
- knock knees
- back knees
- flat feet

The final part of your initial consultation is the physical consultation which involves the sport and exercise massage professional palpating (touching) the area to detect any tension in the area; and the client performing different movements so that the therapist can assess the range of movement at different joints and find out if there is any pain or discomfort when performing different activities. When you are assessing pain that is experienced through either palpation or movement, you should ask the client to rate the pain on a scale from 1 (minimal pain) to 10 (unbearable pain). Palpation is a key part of the initial physical consultation. When you examine your client using palpation, they could be standing, sitting or lying (prone and supine). This part of the consultation has two parts: a general assessment of the tissues within the area and precise palpation to try to find areas of tension, sensitivity or any trigger points. Some different activities that you could use to assess range of movement include:

- Forward bending from the waist with the legs straight. (How easy was it for the client? Are the vertebrae stiff or mobile? Are the hamstrings tight?)
- Side bending from the waist. (How easy was this? Was there any difference between sides?)
- Backward bending from the waist. (How easy was this for the client?)
- Turning head left and right. (Is the chin in line with the shoulders? Is there a difference between left and right?)
- Tilting head forwards and backwards. (Can the chin touch the chest? Can the back of the head touch the cervical/thoracic junction of the spine?)
- Gait analysis. (How does the client walk? Any limping/favouring? Any excessive inversion/eversion?)

Activity: Conducting initial consultations

The initial consultation is an important process as it will give you the information you need to be able to decide on your client's massage requirements. Working with a friend, complete an initial consultation that you could use to draw up a massage treatment plan. As part of your consultation, you need to:

- design and use your own client consultation form (you could use the one in Figure 21.4 as a guide)
- complete a visual assessment of your client, looking at their posture and noting down any areas of concern
- complete a physical assessment of your client including both palpation and range of movement. When you are palpating your client remember these points:
  - Look at the colour of the area that you are palpating and compare it with other parts of the body. Do you notice any differences in colour or any noticeable swelling?
  - Start by touching your client gently. Lay your hand on the area you are palpating and feel for the temperature (is it too hot/cold?) and moisture of the area (is it damp or dry?).
  - Progress by pressing a little deeper and move the skin over the underlying layers. Do the underlying layers feel connected or loose? Are they pliable? Are there any differences in temperature and moisture?
  - Palpate different areas of the muscle. Do they feel tense or can you feel any knots? Ask your client to let you know about any areas that feel different to normal, for example, ticklish or tender.
  - Pay attention to any non-verbal cues that your client may give you as you palpate including wincing, holding their breath, wriggling or spasms.
  - Palpate for any trigger points but make sure that you don't press too firmly as this could hurt too much.
- record all of the information that you have gained through your initial consultation and store it in a safe place.

Referral to practitioners

By working within the limitations of your practice, you need to know when, and to whom, you could refer your clients if the problem is something that you are not qualified or experienced enough to deal with. Other professionals to whom you could refer clients include GPs, physiotherapists, podiatrists, chiropractors, sports therapists or surgeons. To refer your clients, you may need to write a referral letter to the appropriate professional. An example is shown in Figure 21.8.

When making the decision to refer your client, consider the following points:

- Is the pain sudden and inexplicable (is there no traumatic or overuse cause)?
- Is the injury not responding to treatment?
- Is the injury severely swollen?

- In the case of a head injury, does the client have a headache or feel sick?
- Does the injury continue to hurt despite rest?
- Are there continual throbbing and shooting pains, numbness or tingling sensations?
- Is there anything that you do not recognise?

Treatment area

As a sport and exercise massage professional you should be able to identify the correct treatment area using appropriate anatomical terminology. The different anatomical reference terms can be seen in Table 21.1 and are illustrated in Figure 21.9.

Simple injuries

As a sport and exercise massage professional you need an understanding of some simple injuries including the different types of haematoma, muscle tears, tendon injuries, inflammation and ligament injuries. You also need an understanding of how massage can benefit them.

Merton College Sports Academy
Sports Injury Clinic
Merton College
Hurst St, Merton, MT3 1JF
Telephone 01897 336 6888

Mr T. Shap
Townhouse Chiropodist and Podiatrist
Argyll St
Merton

Dear Mr Shap,

Re: Jason Burns, Maple Way, Merton

Jason is a competitive footballer suffering from a recurring painful Achilles tendonitis. During recent consultation we discussed his history of stiffness and soreness in the area of the gastrocnemius. Following a biomedical assessment I was aware that he appeared to have a significant genu-varus of his knees that may be causing over-pronation.

In discussion with Jason we agreed that it would be advisable to make this referral for podiatrist assessment.

Yours sincerely

Andre Lee
Sport massage therapist

Figure 21.8: Why is it important to refer to other practitioners?

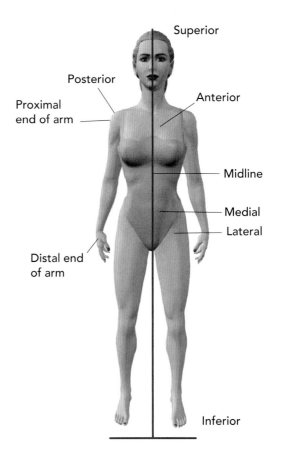

Figure 21.9: Why is it important for therapists to use correct anatomical terminology?

Table 21.1: Anatomical references.

Anatomical reference	Definition
Anterior	The front view of the client
Posterior	The rear view of the client
Midline	An imaginary vertical line that divides the body into symmetrical left and right halves
Superior	A body part that is higher in location
Inferior	A body part that is lower in location
Lateral	The part of the limb or body that is furthest from the midline
Medial	The part of the limb or body that is closest to the midline
Proximal	A body part nearer to the point of reference or to the centre of the body than something else is. For example, the elbow is proximal to the hand.
Distal	A body part further from the point of reference or to the centre of the body than something else is. For example, the elbow is distal to the shoulder.

- **Haematoma** – this is a mass of blood in the tissue caused by an injury when the muscle is squashed between the object of impact and the bone underlying the muscle. There are two types of haematoma:
  - **Inter-muscular haematomas** happen when the sheath surrounding the muscle fibre is ruptured and the blood is able to move into the surrounding tissue, causing bruising, swelling, a loss of power and a loss of range of movement.
  - **Intra-muscular haematomas** happen when the sheath surrounding the muscle fibres stays intact, causing bleeding within the muscle which results in a blood clot within the muscle. Intra-muscular haematomas result in inflammation and a great reduction in range of movement, usually because of the build-up of pressure within the muscle and the associated pain. Bruising is not always evident as the blood is contained within the muscle sheath. This type of haematoma takes much longer to recover. Remember that you should not massage an intra-muscular haematoma as this can worsen it and also worsen a condition called myositis ossifans, where bone cells grow within the haematoma and cause a severe loss of movement. If you suspect myositis ossifans is present, you must refer your client to their GP who will then refer them to a specialist.

- **Muscle tears or strains** – when a muscle is torn (strained), a number of the muscle fibres and their associated capillaries are torn. There are three different degrees of muscle tear, shown in Table 21.2.

Key terms

Inter-muscular haematoma – a haematoma that escapes the muscle sheath through a tear or rupture.

Intra-muscular haematoma – a haematoma that remains trapped inside the muscle sheath.

Table 21.2: Muscle tear classification.

Classification of tear	Fibres torn	Symptoms
Grade 1	Mild tear A few fibres torn	Minor inflammation Minimal pain
Grade 2	Moderate tear Up to 50% of fibres torn	Noticeable inflammation Noticeable pain
Grade 3	Severe tear Up to 100% of fibres torn	Major inflammation Severe pain

- **Tendon injuries** – tendons can become injured either by overuse or by trauma, such as being kicked. Overuse injuries of the tendon (or the paratendon) lead to pain, swelling and loss of mobility (commonly known as **tendonitis** or **paratendonitis**) or the deterioration of the tendon itself (known as **tendonosis**), whereas trauma related injuries can lead to partial or complete tears of the tendon.

- **Inflammation** is the body's response to an injury. The signs of inflammation are heat, redness, swelling, pain and loss of function. There are three different types of inflammation; **haemarthrosis**, **oedema** and **synovial effusion**.

- **Ligament injuries** – the most common injury that sport and exercise massage professionals assist in is the rehabilitation of a sprain. There are different degrees of sprain, shown in Table 21.3.

Key terms

Tendonitis – inflammation of the tendon.

Paratendonitis – inflammation of the paratendon (the tissue surrounding the tendon).

Tendonosis – deterioration of the tendon.

Haemarthrosis – a build-up of blood in the joint.

Oedema – a build-up of blood and tissue fluid within the tissue.

Synovial effusion – a build-up of synovial fluid within the joint.

3.2 Documentation

You must maintain the correct documentation when working with clients to monitor their progress across the treatment. This documentation should be kept in a safe place (such as a locked filing cabinet, or a password protected computer and within an encrypted file). The main documentation you will keep will be your record cards.

Record cards

Your record cards will include a range of information, including:

- the date of treatment
- the treatments proposed/completed (including the type, duration, responses to and effectiveness of treatment) and relevant health and safety information (including the medium used for treatment, such as oil, talc or cream)
- homecare and aftercare advice given to clients
- notes regarding future treatments
- dates of future appointments.

Treatments

Your record card should show details of the treatments that you plan to use with your client (or the treatments that you have used), the details about the treatments (highlighted above) and your justification for using those treatments (see pages 267–268 for details of the different massage techniques and when to use them).

Table 21.3: Classifying sprains.

Classification of sprain	Effects	Symptoms
Grade 1	Minor sprain with only a few fibres torn No joint instability	Minor inflammation Minimal pain
Grade 2	Moderate sprain 50% of fibres torn Minor joint instability	Noticeable inflammation Noticeable pain
Grade 3	Severe sprain Up to 100% of fibres torn Severe joint instability	Major inflammation Severe pain

Relevant health and safety information

Your record card should show details of the medium used for the massage and show that you have checked for any allergies that could prevent the use of a certain medium (for example, some oils are nut based so cannot be used with people with nut allergies). Other health and safety information that could be included on the record card could be a confirmation that you have given the client a basic fire safety induction on their first visit.

Aftercare advice

Your aftercare advice should be included in your treatment plan. The general aftercare advice that you give your client should be to drink plenty of fluids to rehydrate the body as massage can have a dehydrating effect as well as increasing circulation, so water will be needed to aid both of these. You may also need to advise your client to rest after the massage (where appropriate).

Homecare advice

As with aftercare advice, you should provide homecare advice for your client as they will have to manage the injury in between treatments. The homecare that you will provide will be dependent upon the individual, their treatments and their injury. However, some general advice that can be given to most clients is to try to eliminate the cause of the problem (for example, adjust your working position if the problem is lower back pain), attempt to reduce inflammation (for example, give advice regarding the use of ice) and provide home-based exercise (for example, stretching exercises to increase flexibility of muscles and connective tissues to prevent recurrence of the injury).

3.3 Contraindications to massage

A contraindication is a reason to avoid massage treatment. There are a number of contraindications to massage including the client history, the type of injury, the location of the injury, different skin conditions, circulatory conditions and other medical conditions.

Client history

There may be elements of the client's history that mean they should not receive certain massage treatments, for example, a negative reaction to a previous massage treatment. These contraindications could be local contraindications (a particular body part cannot receive massage treatment) or general contraindications (the client shouldn't receive massage treatment at all). Other factors that would contraindicate the client from massage would be feeling unwell or pregnancy.

Type of injury

There are numerous types of injuries that should not be massaged including:

- acute trauma injuries (24–72 hours post trauma)
- dislocations
- fractures
- swollen, hot, bruised or painful areas
- intra-muscular haematoma.

Location of injury

Massage can be applied to most areas of the body (other than directly to the eyes and genitalia) but you need to take care when massaging the injury site itself.

Skin conditions

Certain skin conditions mean that massage is contraindicated as it could worsen the condition and/or the condition could spread to the therapist. These conditions include:

- acne
- cuts and abrasions
- new scar tissue
- sunburn or windburn
- blisters
- warts
- moles
- infectious skin diseases, such as impetigo.

Circulatory conditions

There are some circulatory conditions that are contraindications to sport and exercise massage as they could increase the chance of blood clots travelling around the body. These include:

- varicose veins
- phlebitis (inflammation of the walls of the veins)
- high or low blood pressure
- thrombosis (blood clots) or deep vein thrombosis.

Table 21.4: Contraindications.

Contraindication	Reason
Multiple sclerosis	Although massage can be beneficial, it can also increase muscle spasm and cause more pain.
Cancer	Although more recent research demonstrates some contrasting viewpoints, it is widely believed that massage can cause the tumour to disintegrate and can influence circulation, causing the cancer to spread more quickly.
Uncontrolled epilepsy (epilepsy not controlled by medication)	Over-stimulation or deep relaxation may result in convulsions. Some types of epilepsy can be triggered by different smells so could react to your massage medium.
Diabetes	Blood sugars tend to drop during and after massage so the client and therapist need to be aware of this and make sure that they are appropriately prepared. Some diabetes patients also suffer from sensory impairment, so they will not be able to give you accurate feedback on the pressure.
Osteoporosis	Brittle bones could be further damaged by deep massage techniques.

Other medical conditions

Other medical conditions that can contraindicate sport and exercise massage can be seen in Table 21.4. If a client with any of these conditions approaches you for massage, you should always seek advice from their GP before starting treatments.

Remember

If you are in doubt about any contraindications, do not massage. Refer your client to the appropriate professional and wait for that professional's permission to commence any treatments.

Activity: Contraindications to sport massage

You are working as a sport and exercise massage professional and have just started marketing your services. You want to include some information on your website for potential clients so that they understand some of the different contraindications and can gain appropriate clearance from their GP before visiting you if necessary. You need to prepare the following information for your website:

* descriptions of the different contraindications

* reasons why they contraindicate massage.

3.4 Proposed treatment plan

Your proposed treatment plan should be based on all of the information that you will have gained through your verbal, visual and physical consultations, and your knowledge of any contraindications, and should be recorded on appropriate documentation. Throughout your treatments, you will use a range of techniques including effleurage, petrissage, frictions, tapotement and vibrations. These techniques will be used as part of overall massage treatments. Massage treatments will generally fall into the following categories:

* pre-event

* inter-event

* post-event.

Massage techniques and procedures

The different massage techniques, their aims and associated techniques are summarised in Table 21.5.

Take it further

Researching massage techniques

Using books and the Internet, find a detailed description and images or videos of each of the different techniques (and their associated techniques) highlighted in Table 21.5. Use the information to produce a booklet or electronic file of the different massage techniques.

Table 21.5: Massage techniques, aims and associated techniques.

Technique	Aims	Associated techniques
Effleurage	Introduces touch to the client Stimulates nerve endings Relaxes the muscles Increases circulation Stretches tissues	Stroking using palm of the hand, pads of the fingers and thumb, heel of the hand, forearm, elbow, ulna border, or clenched fist
Petrissage	Increases mobility Stretches muscle fibres Increases circulation (increases venous and lymphatic return)	Kneading Wringing Skin rolling Thumb sliding Knuckling Heel squeezing
Frictions	Separates adhesions Breaks down scar tissue Realigns scar tissue Stimulates blood flow Relieves pain	Circular frictions Transverse frictions
Tapotement	Warms muscle tissue Increases circulation Improves muscle tone Stimulates nerve endings	Cupping Hacking Slapping Pounding Beating
Vibrations	Relieves tension Provides relaxation Stimulates nerve endings Relieves pain Loosens connective tissue	Static vibrations Running vibrations

- **Effleurage** is usually the first technique used in a massage and is used in pre-event, inter-event and post-event massage. It can be either superficial (light stroking) or deep (pressured stroking). The speed and pressure of stroking can be altered, depending on whether you are performing pre-, inter-, or post-event massage. When you start effleurage, you should work with a light touch in a rhythmical and relaxed manner and progress through to a deeper pressure with slower movements that can help to increase circulation and stretch tissues.

The direction of the stroke is always in the direction of the heart to encourage venous return and lymphatic fluid drainage. When you use strokes which pass over bony prominences, you must ease the pressure but maintain contact. Effleurage movements can be performed using both hands simultaneously or by using alternate hands. On the return stroke, the hands should maintain light contact but avoid the path taken on the initial stroke.

- **Petrissage** is used to have a deeper effect on soft tissues than effleurage by compressing and releasing the tissue, either by picking up and squeezing the skin and muscle or by applying direct pressure. This technique can be used in pre-, inter- and post-event massage.

When using petrissage, the pressure is applied in the direction of the heart to encourage venous return, but the overall direction is from proximal to distal. This is achieved by you applying shorter strokes in the direction of the heart to push the blood out of the area followed by deliberately sliding the hands distally to push fresh blood back

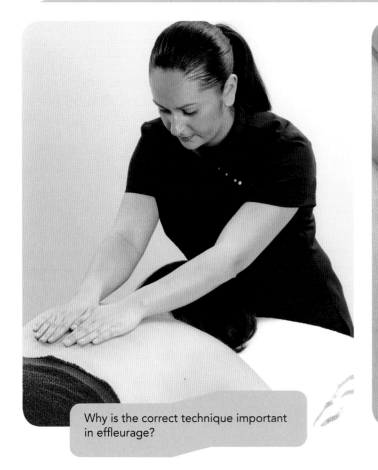

Why is the correct technique important in effleurage?

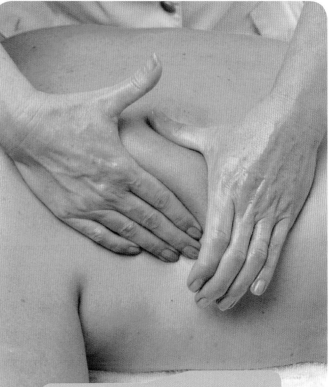

Why is the correct technique important in petrissage?

into the area before starting the technique again. During petrissage, your hands stay in constant contact with the client's skin while moving it over the underlying muscle.

- **Frictions** are techniques that use significantly more pressure than the two previous techniques, and the pressure is more localised to specific areas using the pads of the fingers or thumbs (or the elbow in some cases). Before you use frictions with the client, you must reassuringly warn them that the technique can be painful due to its aims and you may need to help them relax by taking them through some deep breathing activities prior to and during the treatment.

When you perform frictions, your thumb or finger pads must remain in constant contact with your client's skin while you move their subcutaneous tissue over deeper tissue. The thumb or finger pads move in either circular or transverse directions, depending on the technique you are applying and very firm pressure will need to be applied when you are trying to break down scar tissue or separating muscle fibres.

As frictions are classed as advanced massage techniques and can cause pain to your client, you must be sure of three things before you attempt to use them: that you can accurately locate the problem, that you can place the affected area in full stretch by using your knowledge of origins and insertions and that you are confident there will be an overall benefit. Your clients must also be aware that frictions may need to be used two to three times per week and may have to be applied for a period of minutes during the massage session to be effective.

- **Tapotement** techniques use rhythmic movements of the hands to stimulate muscle tissue and nerve endings. The tissue is struck with both hands alternately, but the tapotement technique that you will use will determine which part of the hand is used and the type of contact made. Tapotement techniques are often used in pre- and inter-event massage.

- **Vibrations** are performed using one or both hands and any number of fingers. The technique uses a moderate degree of pressure and involves the fingers being shaken in a fast action so that the vibrations pass through the body part.

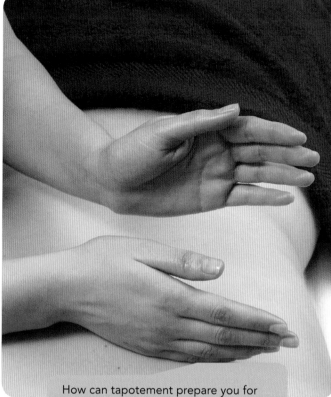

How can tapotement prepare you for competition?

Table 21.6: Massage routines.

Sample positions and sequences of body sections for planning treatments	
Position	**Sequencing of body sections**
Prone	Legs, back, neck, shoulder, lumbar
Supine	Legs, arms, front torso, neck, head
Side – lying	Legs, arms, back, obliques
Sitting	Back, arms, neck, head
Standing	Arms, shoulders, back, legs
Sample sequences for body sections for planning treatments	
Section	**Sequencing of sub-sections**
Arms	Shoulder, upper arm, forearm, hand
Legs	Hip, thigh, knee, lower leg, foot
Back	Sacroiliac joint, lumbar region, thoracic region, shoulder girdle, neck
Progressions in the quality of movements in massage	
Quality of movement	**Progression**
Pressure	Light to heavy
Rhythm	Even to uneven
Pace	Slow to fast
Continuity	Smooth to vigorous transitions
Specificity	General to specific

Massage routines

While the individual massage requirements of different people will vary, there are routines that can be used as a guide when providing massage treatments. The sequencing of routines relates to the sequencing of positions, the sequencing of sections and sub-sections for each position and the sequencing of steps within each section. These can be seen in Table 21.6.

Pre-event massage

Think back to when you have been getting ready to play your sport. You will have rubbed and shaken your legs to try to warm them a little more. If this has been of benefit, imagine how a massage before your event could have helped. A pre-event massage helps to prepare you physically and psychologically, and can be performed anywhere between a few minutes before the event to a few days before the event. Remember that pre-event massage should not take the place of a full warm-up.

Remember

Pre-event massage techniques are often used less deeply and more vigorously, and for a shorter period of time, so that you can be prepared for the demands of your sport quite quickly.

- **Aims** – while the aims of the pre-event massage and the techniques used will vary depending upon when you are performing the massage, pre-event massage has the following general aims of:
  - warming the muscles
  - stretching
  - increasing the range of movement, mobility and circulation
  - psychological preparation.
- **Massage procedures** – effleurage, petrissage and tapotement are the main techniques that you will use in pre-event massage.
- **Massage duration** – pre-event massages normally last for about 10–15 minutes.

Case study: 15-minute pre-event massage

The pre-event massage routine below can be used for a centre–midfielder in football.

Massage the front of the legs with the client lying supine:

- Effleurage with long strokes of the whole leg
- Effleurage on the thigh – fast, short, vigorous movements
- Palmar kneading on the thigh, checking depth and pressure to ensure no bruising occurs
- Wringing of the quadriceps
- Wringing of the adductors
- Palmar kneading of the iliotibial band, checking depth and pressure to ensure no bruising occurs
- Hacking, cupping or shaking of the thigh
- Thumb kneading around the knee joint
- Thumb kneading of the tibialis anterior
- Effleurage lower leg
- Thumb knead ankle around lateral and medial maleolus
- Effleurage the whole leg, finish with shaking

Massage the back of the legs with the client lying prone:

- Effleurage the whole leg
- Short, vigorous effleurage to the hamstrings
- Palmar kneading of the hamstrings
- Wringing of the hamstrings
- Hacking or cupping of the hamstrings
- Effleurage of the hamstrings
- Muscle rolling of the hamstrings
- Effleurage of the calf
- Wringing of the calf
- Hacking/cupping of the calf
- Thumb kneading of achilles tendon
- Effleurage to whole leg, finishing with shaking

1. **Do you think that this routine would be suitable for all sports?**
2. **How could you alter this treatment to meet the needs of different clients such as those with less or greater muscle bulk, younger athletes or older athletes?**

Inter-event massage

Think of a football game that has gone into extra time and penalties, and before the players go back out, somebody massages and shakes their legs – this is inter-event massage. Inter-event massage takes place during intervals in competition, for example at half time in football. You use this type of massage to keep your client physically and psychologically prepared for their sport.

Remember

Inter-event massage should work on the muscles that are going to be used as well as the muscles that have just been used, and may require both stimulating and relaxing massage techniques.

- **Aims** – the main aims of inter-event massage are to:
  - relieve muscle tension
  - maintain body temperature
  - remove waste products.
- **Massage procedures** – effleurage, petrissage and tapotement are the main techniques that you will use in inter-event massage.
- **Massage duration** – inter-event massage can last up to 25 minutes.

Post-event massage

Post-event massage helps the body recover from the stress of the activity and relaxes the client. This type of massage tends to be deeper and can be used to identify any issues that may have arisen during the game (for example, injuries, knots or tension). The massage should be performed at a depth that does not worsen any conditions that happen as a result of the activity (such as delayed onset of muscle soreness (DOMS)), and the depth of techniques should be increased as the muscles loosen and relax. There is some debate about whether a post-event massage can take the place of a cool down, so it is always best to complete a cool down after activity even if you will be having a post-event massage.

- **Aims** – the main aims of post-event massage are to:
  - accelerate the recovery process
  - reduce DOMS

  - remove waste products
  - stretch the muscle tissue.
- **Massage procedures** – effleurage, petrissage, vibrations and stretching activities are the common techniques used within post-event massage.
- **Massage duration** – post-event massage can take up to 60 minutes.

Case study: 5-minute inter-event massage

The inter-event massage routine below can be used for a point-guard in basketball.

Front of the legs:
- Effleurage of the whole leg
- Effleurage of the quadriceps
- Wringing of the quadriceps
- Hacking/cupping of quadriceps
- Effleurage of the whole leg
- Stretching

Back of the legs:
- Effleurage of the whole leg
- Effleurage of the hamstrings

- Wringing of the hamstrings
- Hacking/cupping of the hamstrings
- Effleurage of the whole leg
- Stretching

1. **Do you think that this routine would be suitable for all sports?**
2. **How could you alter this treatment to meet the needs of different clients such as those with less or greater muscle bulk, younger athletes or older athletes?**

Case study: 60-minute post-event massage

The post-event massage routine below can be used for the back, legs and arms of a rugby player.

Back
- Effleurage of the back
- Effleurage of the neck
- Thumb and finger kneading of the upper trapezius and cervical region of the neck
- Knead shoulder area towards axillary lymph node
- Circular frictions of the scapular region to release knots, adhesions or tightness
- Effleurage of the rhomboid region
- Effleurage of the trapezius and both shoulders
- Deep stroking of lateral regions of the back, using the ulna border if necessary
- Knead lateral regions of the back from waist to shoulder

- Transverse and circular frictions of the erector spinae (light pressure)
- Circular frictions of the lumbar region (around L5 and sacrum and into gluteus medius if necessary)
- Effleurage of the whole back, finish with shaking and stretching

Front of the upper legs (with client in supine position)
- Slow effleurage of the thigh (proximal to distal)
- Strong linear stroking of the thigh
- Kneading/ringing of the thigh
- Linear stroking of the tensor fascia latae
- Palmar linear stroking of the iliotibial band
- Effleurage to the adductors with the therapist supporting the knee
- Wringing of the adductors

- Gentle thumb stroking around the knee joint line
- Effleurage to the whole of the thigh, finish with shaking and stretching

Front of the lower legs (with the client in supine position)

- Effleurage to whole of lower leg
- Linear stroking of the tibialis anterior
- Linear stroking of the peroneus longus and peroneus brevis
- Stroking of the medial and lateral borders of the tibia
- Finger kneading of the medial and lateral malleolus and the ankle joint line
- Effleurage to the foot
- Kneading of the arch of the foot
- Effleurage to the whole of the front of the lower leg, finish with shaking and stretching

Back of the upper legs (with the client in a prone position)

- Effleurage to the hamstrings (proximal to distal)
- Linear stroking of the hamstrings
- Circular frictions to the origin of the hamstrings
- Kneading of the hamstrings
- Wringing of the origin and insertion of the hamstrings
- Effleurage to the whole of the hamstrings, finish with shaking and stretching

Back of the lower legs (with the client in a prone position)

- Effleurage to the whole of the back of the lower leg
- Deep linear stroking of the calf region
- Kneading of the calf region
- Wringing of the calf region
- Effleurage to calf region
- Effleurage to the Achilles tendon
- Finger kneading of the Achilles tendon
- Effleurage to the whole of the lower leg, finish with shaking and stretching

Arm

- Effleurage to the whole of the arm (distal to proximal)
- Petrissage to the upper arm, from the elbow to deltoid (including biceps and triceps)
- Shaking of the upper arm
- Effleurage to the lower arm
- Frictions to the tendon insertion at the elbow joint
- Effleurage to the whole of the arm, finish with shaking and stretching

1. **Do you think that this routine would be suitable for all sports?**
2. **How could you alter this treatment to meet the needs of different clients such as those with less or greater muscle bulk, younger athletes or older athletes?**

Assessment activity 21.3

P3 P4 P5 M2 D1 · BTEC

You are the sports therapist for a sports team that has male and female players. You are getting ready to massage one of the clients from a male squad and one of the players from a female squad and need to produce a treatment plan for these two different athletes.

1. Using a male and a female friend as your clients, produce a treatment plan for each of them that is based on pre-treatment consultations. **P3**

2. Explain the sport and exercise massage requirements of each client. **M2**

3. Compare and contrast the treatment requirements of the two clients. **D1**

4. Choose six contraindications to massage that are relevant to your clients and describe them. **P4**

5. Produce a treatment plan for each client based on the information that you have gathered through the consultation. **P5**

Grading tips

- To attain **P3** complete verbal, visual and physical aspects of the initial consultation with your two clients and record your findings on appropriate documentation.

- To attain **M2** include the area to be treated, the simple injuries that you have looked for and any referrals to practitioners that you may have to make.

- To attain **D1** justify why you have chosen the massage treatments for each client.

- To attain **P4** say why they contraindicate massage treatment.

- To attain **P5** say whether you need to use pre-, inter- or post-event massage and plan a massage treatment that includes the duration of the treatment and a description of the massage procedure (the routines and techniques) that you will use.

PLTS

When producing your client consultation form, identifying questions to ask and problems that need to be resolved will provide evidence of your skills as an **independent enquirer**.

Functional skills

If you make effective contributions to the discussion with your client during the verbal element of your initial consultations, you could provide evidence of your **English** skills.

4. Be able to perform and review sport and exercise massage techniques

Your major function as a sport and exercise massage professional is to provide massage treatments for different clients. In order to do this, you need to make sure that the environment in which you work, your client preparation and the different techniques that you use are all up to standard. As a professional, ensure that you review your work so that you can aim for the highest quality of service for your clients.

4.1 Client preparation

After the initial consultation, your client will need to undress and lie on the massage couch. You should leave the area before they undress and provide them with a towel so that when they lie on the couch, they can cover themselves before you return. You should place additional towels in appropriate places to further protect their modesty, for example when lying prone in place for a back massage, a female client may need additional rolled towels placing along the side of the torso so that her breasts are not exposed.

Health and safety

You need to consider health and safety and hygiene as part of your client preparation. Make sure they know where to find the fire exit and the toilet; provide them with water if they require it and make sure that they are positioned on the couch in a manner that will prevent them from falling.

Sport and exercise massage professionals must also be aware of appropriate health and safety legislation including the Health and Safety at Work Act, COSHH (Control of Substances Hazardous to Health) and PPE (Personal and Protective Equipment).

Hygiene

You must wash your hands before massaging your client. You may also need to clean parts of their body before you massage, for example their feet. This can be done with antibacterial wipes.

4.2 Demonstrate

Safe and effective massage

The massage treatment you use with your client needs to be safe and effective for both you and your client. To achieve this maintain the correct posture when massaging, position your client so that they won't fall off the couch, ensure that the correct technique is used and monitor your client throughout by checking levels of pain and pressure.

Different techniques

Earlier, when looking at your proposed treatment plan, you examined the different techniques that you can use when providing massage treatments, including effleurage, petrissage, frictions, tapotement and vibrations. You should refer back to these (see pages 267–268), the example routines and the work you did for the 'Take it further' activities when you are preparing to deliver your sport massage treatment. You need to ensure correct application of these techniques when you deliver your massage treatment.

Application of techniques

When you are delivering your sport massage treatments maintain the correct technique. Part of this is ensuring you have the correct posture. When delivering massage, you should stand with your feet comfortably apart to maintain good balance, have your back straight and stand close enough to the couch to deliver the massage. If you maintain the correct

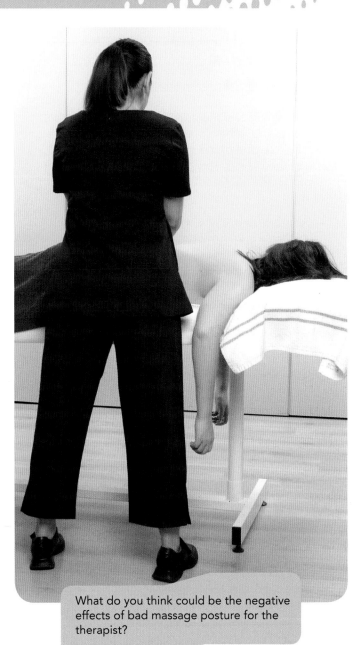

What do you think could be the negative effects of bad massage posture for the therapist?

posture, you will reduce the amount of effort that you need to put into your massage with the result that you will not be as tired and achy at the end of it. In addition to this, you must refer to pages 266–272 for details of the techniques, routines and durations of massage.

Try to develop a rapport with your client. He or she could be quite nervous when having a sport and exercise massage, especially if it is their first time. You need to make sure that you put your client at ease during the treatment by checking the pressure and pain levels resulting from the different techniques as well as chatting to the client about things like hobbies.

4.3 Mediums

The three mediums used during massage are oil, talc and creams.

> ## Activity: Conducting sport and exercise massage
>
> Under the supervision of your tutor, complete the different massage treatments with a partner on their legs, arms and back. Ask your tutor and your client to give you feedback about the quality of your massage.

4.4 Documentation

When you have finished your treatment with your client, complete a record card that shows:

- the date of the treatment
- the type of treatment
- the duration of the treatment
- the response of the client to the treatment
- the dates of any future appointments.

4.5 Review

After your massage treatment, review it against different criteria including speed, depth, rate of sport massage, effectiveness of treatment, liaison with the athlete, timing, adaptation of treatment and recommendations for future treatments.

Speed, depth and rate of massage

During your treatment, you will need to liaise with your client. Ask your client to rate the speed, depth and rate of treatment by asking questions such as 'How is the pressure for you?'. The responses you get will determine whether or not you need to alter your massage treatment for your client. You can use this feedback from your client to review your massage after the treatment has finished.

Effectiveness of treatment

The effectiveness of your treatment can be assessed by asking your client questions during the treatment and getting their feedback and by using the same visual and physical tests that you completed as part of your initial consultation. If there is more mobility in the area, or less tension, or less pain, you could say that your massage technique has been effective. When reviewing the effectiveness of your treatment, it is a good idea to ask your client to fill out a short questionnaire after their treatment so that they can give you some feedback regarding the treatment.

Timing

Different massage treatments have timings that you should try to adhere to. When assessing your massage, you should make a comment about whether you managed to stay on time.

Adaptation of treatment

During your session you may need to adapt your treatment to meet the needs of your client (for example, changing the speed, rate or depth of massage). If you have to do this, make a comment in your evaluation about the changes that you made, why you made them and how they benefited your client.

Table 21.7: Advantages and disadvantages of massage mediums.

Medium	Advantages	Disadvantages
Oil	Longer lasting Additives can be relaxing or stimulating	Quite expensive Can contain nut derivatives Not practical for people with a lot of body hair
Talc	Produces frictions	Can be quite messy Can only be used pre-event
Cream	Generally cheaper than oils Better for people with more body hair Tend to be hypo-allergenic	Can be absorbed quite quickly

Future treatment

After your massage, reflect on any adaptations to the treatment that you needed to make during the session. Think about any changes that you should make for future treatments, including any adaptations of the current treatments and additions to the treatments. Give your client a return date for their next appointment and subsequent appointments (if applicable). The final part of your future treatment section should include some aftercare and homecare advice for your client as they will need to manage the injury or the problem during their treatments (see page 265).

Assessment activity 21.4

P6 P7 M3 D2 **BTEC**

1. Using the treatment plan that you produced for Assessment activity 21.3, provide a sport and exercise massage treatment for your two clients. You should complete this treatment under the supervision of your tutor. **P6**

2. Explain the appropriate sport and exercise massage treatments for your two clients. **M3**

3. Evaluate the treatments. **D2**

4. Review the treatment plan for your two athletes and describe future treatment requirements. **P7**

Grading tips

- To attain **P6** prior to the massage, follow appropriate client preparation techniques. Make sure that you are using the correct technique as you go through your treatment, paying attention to the technique that you are using, the application of the technique, following a set routine, using an appropriate medium for your client, adhering to your time limit and talking to your client to make sure that they are OK.

- To attain **M3** explain to your tutor the techniques that you are using for each of your athletes as you are conducting the massage.

- To attain **D2** tell your tutor why you are using different massage techniques with each client.

- To attain **P7** comment on the effectiveness of the treatments you have provided.

PLTS

When reviewing your treatment and deciding on future treatment requirements, you could provide evidence of your skills as a **creative thinker**.

Functional skills

If you are able to make effective contributions to discussions with your tutor and clients regarding the treatment and the effectiveness of the treatment, you could provide evidence of your **English** skills.

Lucy Dureli
Sport massage therapist

Lucy is a self-employed sport massage therapist working for a number of sports teams. She is also employed at major sports events including football and rugby matches as well as massaging at the London Marathon and Great North Run every year.

She is responsible for planning and conducting sport massage treatments with a range of clients.

'Sport massage is a great job. I get to work with lots of different people who want to get the best out of their training and competition which is really fulfilling. The skills the course has given me help me to work with my clients as I have a greater understanding of the different massage techniques that can be used with clients, when to use them and what the benefits are. The course has also helped me to recognise the different contraindications to massage. Both of these aspects have helped me to give a higher quality of service to my clients, allowing them to recover from injuries and return to training at an appropriate rate.

Helping people to recover from injuries and get back to training gives me a great sense of satisfaction. It isn't all easy though and there are some difficult parts of the job. One of the biggest problems that I face is recognising and dealing with all of the different contraindications to massage when working within the field. I currently work in a variety of settings with a wide range of clients, so there are a number of different things that I need to take into account when I am planning and conducting massage sessions. One of the issues that I do face regularly at the different charity events is people who have different contraindications but who would still like to receive a sport massage.'

Think about it!

- If you were Lucy, what different contraindications to massage would you need to be aware of?
- How could you deal with these different contraindications?
- What advice would you give to clients who had different contraindications to sport massage?

Just checking

1. What are the physical and mechanical effects of massage?
2. What are the physiological effects of massage?
3. What are the benefits of massage?
4. What are the different treatments that can be applied by sport and exercise massage professionals?
5. What are the main elements of an initial consultation?
6. What information needs to be included on a record card?
7. Name five contraindications to sport and exercise massage and explain why massage is contraindicated.
8. Describe three massage techniques, including their aims and associated techniques.
9. What is meant by the terms pre-event massage, inter-event massage and post-event massage?
10. What are the different criteria that you can use to review your sport and exercise massage routine?

edexcel :::

Assignment tips

- Sport and exercise massage is very 'hands on', so it is always good to practise your techniques under the supervision of your tutor whenever possible so that you can learn the correct technique.

- To help extend your learning you may want to use some specific sport massage textbooks that give a detailed overview of all massage techniques.

- There are some good websites that you can use to help with this unit including physioroom.com (www.physioroom.com), sports injury clinic (www.sportsinjuryclinic.net) and the Sport Massage Association website (www.sportsmassageassociation.org).

- If you know any sports therapists, it could be good to discuss this unit with them. They can talk to you about the different roles that they fulfil and the different clients that they work with.

- If you are interested in sport and exercise massage therapy as a career, you may want to ask your college's work placement office to help you find work placements as this will help you to gain a greater understanding of the world of work in this area.

- Always check your work over with your tutor. Sometimes you may need to clarify the requirements of the higher level grading criteria to make sure that you are doing the right things and your tutor will be able to advise you on this.

Credit value: 10

22 Rules, regulations and officiating in sport

Officials are essential to the success of sports at all levels, from the international stage to a local Sunday league game. Officials apply rules and maintain health and safety. They need skills of self-management, empathy, communication and a passion for sport. For sport to develop people must be encouraged to referee or umpire competitive matches.

Sport is constantly evolving and rule and law changes are common in order to improve the safety of sport or the experience for participants, spectators and officials. Greater enjoyment and excitement levels increase a sport's popularity and provide the media with better drama. Governing bodies realise that the more exciting their sport is, the more marketable it is and more likely to gain greater media coverage. Officials must be up to date with changes which should be implemented professionally and clearly.

The aim of this unit is to examine the rules and regulations of a number of selected sports and to explain the roles and responsibilities of all the officials who participate in sport. The unit will further examine the performance of officials in selected sports and explain how to officiate in your chosen area.

Learning outcomes

After completing this unit you should:

1. know the rules, laws and regulations of a selected sport
2. know the roles and responsibilities of officials involved in a selected sport
3. understand the performance of officials in a selected sport
4. be able to officiate effectively in a selected sport.

Assessment and grading criteria

This table shows you what you must do in order to achieve a pass, merit or distinction grade, and where you can find activities in this book to help you.

To achieve a **pass** grade the evidence must show that you are able to:	To achieve a **merit** grade the evidence must show that, in addition to the pass criteria, you are able to:	To achieve a **distinction** grade the evidence must show that, in addition to the pass and merit criteria, you are able to:
P1 describe the rules, laws and regulations of a selected sport **See Assessment activity 22.1, page 289**		
P2 describe the roles and responsibilities of officials in a selected sport **See Assessment activity 22.2, page 294**		
P3 apply the rules, laws and regulations of a selected sport in three different situations **See Assessment activity 22.3, page 298**	**M1** explain the application of the rules, laws and regulations of a selected sport in three different situations **See Assessment activity 22.3, page 298**	
P4 devise suitable criteria to analyse the performance of officials in a selected sport **See Assessment activity 22.4, page 298**		
P5 analyse the performance of two officials in a selected sport, identifying strengths and areas for improvement **See Assessment activity 22.4, page 298**	**M2** explain the identified strengths and areas for improvement of two officials, and make suggestions relating to improvement **See Assessment activity 22.4, page 298**	**D1** justify suggestions made in relation to improving performance of two officials from a selected sport **See Assessment activity 22.4, page 298**
P6 officiate in a selected sport, with tutor support **See Assessment activity 22.5, page 302**	**M3** independently officiate in a selected sport **See Assessment activity 22.5, page 302**	
P7 review own performance in officiating in a selected sport, identifying strengths and areas for improvement **See Assessment activity 22.5, page 302**	**M4** explain the identified strengths and areas for improvement, and make suggestions in relation to improving own performance **See Assessment activity 22.5, page 302**	**D2** analyse own performance and justify suggestions made in relation to improving own performance **See Assessment activity 22.5, page 302**

How you will be assessed

This unit is assessed internally using a variety of methods designed by the tutors at your centre. Your assessments could be in the form of:

- presentations
- practical performance/officiating
- self evaluation
- observation
- case studies
- written reports

Gary, 18-year-old footballer

This unit gave me an invaluable insight into the role of officials in a number of different sports. It made me realise that officials are essential to sport and that without them competitive sport could not take place. The unit gave me an understanding of the detailed rules in my sport, football, as well as a wide variety of sports that I was less familiar with. I particularly enjoyed the challenge of officiating at a number of matches and this made me realise how demanding being an official can be.

I also enjoyed learning about a wide variety of different sports that I hadn't tried before and learning the rules and regulations for these. Officiating in these made me think about how my skills, for example, communication, could be transferred between sports.

The unit allowed me to be actively involved in sport and I felt that by officiating I gained an insight into how sport should be played and the responsibility that players and the officials have in following the rules and regulations.

Over to you!

1. Which section of the unit are you most looking forward to?

2. What areas of the unit might you find challenging?

3. How can you prepare for the unit assessments?

1. Know the rules, laws and regulations of a selected sport

Warm-up

Why are officials so important in sport?

Understanding the role of officials helps you to appreciate their importance for sport. Knowing the rules and regulations of a variety of sports, and how these should be implemented, will help you understand their roles. In groups, discuss the main roles of officials. Consider which skills make them successful and how you can develop them yourself.

1.1 Sport

Sport is a physical activity that is governed by rules and customs and may involve competition with other performers or teams. Because of its competitive nature, officials are essential in ensuring that the published rules, as set out by the governing bodies, are implemented fairly and objectively.

Football

The Football Association is responsible for ensuring that the international Laws of the Game are applied on the field, and that the rules and regulations concerned with running football in England are observed by officials, clubs and players. These rules are updated regularly and it is the responsibility of everybody involved in football to have a thorough knowledge of them. These rules and regulations cover matters ranging from the affiliation of clubs within a league (both grass roots and elite levels), dealing with misconduct of players and coaches, on field 'match' rules and defining specific competition regulations.

Football is played by two teams of 11 players and lasts 90 minutes with a break after 45 minutes. The purpose of the game is to kick or head the ball into the opposition's goal (only the goalkeeper may use his hands and only in the permitted area) and the team with the highest number of goals is declared the winner. If the scores are level or no goals are scored the match is considered a draw. Some competitions will use extra time or penalty kicks to decide a winner if the scores are level after 90 minutes.

Rugby union

The aim of the game is very simple – one team has to score more points than the other team. Points can be gained by scoring tries, conversions, drop goals and penalties in your opponent's goal area. If both teams score the same amount, or no points are scored, then the match is a draw.

- **A try** is scored when a player puts the ball on the ground with 'downward pressure' inside the opposition's in-goal area between the try line and dead-ball line and is worth five points.

- **Ruck** – if a tackled player goes to ground, they must release the ball immediately. However, the opposition will want to get their hands on the ball, while the team in possession will not want to give it away, so a ruck is formed when the ball is on the ground with at least one player in physical contact with a member of the opposition. To get hold of the ball, both sides will drive over to make it available for their nearest team mate. However, only players on their feet can handle the ball in a ruck. If a player joins a ruck, they can only do so from behind the line of the ball. This means they cannot come in from the sides of the ruck, otherwise the referee will award a penalty to the opposing team. Also, every player must be 'bound' in the ruck. This means they must have at least one arm round a team mate who is involved in the ruck. If the ball does not come out of the ruck quickly enough, the referee will award the team moving forward at the ruck the feed at the scrum. There are very strict rules for a ruck which every player must follow, otherwise they will give away needless penalties. These rules are designed to ensure that all the players remain safe.

- **A scrum** is a way of re-starting play after:
  - the ball has been knocked on
  - the ball has gone forward
  - accidental offside
  - the ball has not come out from a ruck.

  Not everyone can join a scrum – only eight players from each team can take part. The scrum is formed at the place where the infringement happened and all scrums must take place at least 5 metres from the touch or try lines.

- **Ball not released** – when the player holding the ball has been tackled to the ground, they have to let go of the ball. However it is common for players to purposely hold onto the ball when they have gone down in a tackle to stop the other team getting hold of it and starting a quick attack. If the referee sees a player holding onto the ball on the ground, he will immediately award a penalty to the opposing team.

Cricket

Cricket is a team sport for two teams of 11 players. A formal game of cricket can last anything from an afternoon to up to five days. Each team will bat in successive innings and attempt to score as many runs as possible within the over or allocated time limit. The opposing team then fields and attempts to bring an end to the batting team's innings by getting each of the opposition batsmen out. A batsman can be given out for the following reasons:

- caught
- bowled
- stumped
- run out
- handled the ball
- leg before wicket (LBW)
- timed out.

After each team has batted an equal number of innings (either one or two, depending on the rules of the competition), the team with the most runs wins. If scores are equal at the end of the match then the game is called a tie. If the game runs out with a team still batting then it is considered a draw.

Badminton

The aim of the game of badminton is to hit the shuttlecock back and forth over a net without permitting it to hit the floor in bounds on your side of the net.

Similarly to tennis, badminton can be played by singles and doubles both mixed and same sex. Matches are played to the best of three sets.

Recent rule changes mean that players play up to 21 points. If the score reaches 20–20, the winner is the player or team with a 2-point advantage. In addition to this, if the score goes up to 29–29, the winner is the first to reach 30 points. Under these changes points can be scored on your or the opposition's serve. Also a team now has only one serve in doubles, rather than two under the old rules.

In singles, players serve diagonally from one service box to another, alternating between the left and right side of the court as points are won. The server always serves from the right-hand box at the start of a game and when they have an even number of points. They serve from the left-hand court when they have an odd number of points.

In doubles, the player on the right always starts the serve and, when a point is won, the players switch sides and the server then serves from the left, continuing to alternate until a serve is lost.

The shuttlecock must be served underarm with the racquet below the waist and the racket head must stay below the server's wrist.

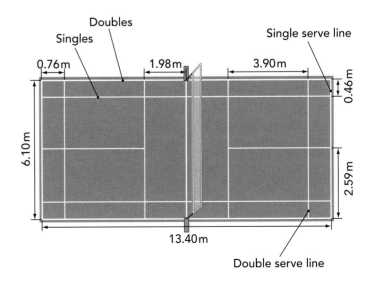

Figure 22.1: Which court markings are used when a singles match is played and which are used for a doubles match?

Rugby league

Like rugby union, the aim of the game is to score more points than the other team. Each team is given six tackles or chances to score. If, after six tackles, they have not scored, the ball is handed over to the other team who then get the chance to score with their six tackles.

A game of rugby league consists of two halves of 40 minutes, with injury time added on at the end of each half. In between the two halves, there is a 10-minute break after which both teams change ends and attack the half they were defending. A hooter or whistle will indicate the start and finish of the half. Play is only allowed to continue after the whistle or hooter sounds if the ball is still in play.

The half will immediately end once a tackle is made or the ball goes out to touch. However, time can be extended for a penalty kick or a kick at goal. In that case, the half will end when the next ball goes out of play or a tackle has been made. Rugby league is played on a pitch which is no more than 100 metres in length and 68 metres in width.

Basketball

Basketball is played by two teams who score points by throwing a ball into the opposing team's basket. The team who scores the most points are the winners. Each team has a squad of 12 players to choose from. Five of those players are allowed on the court at any one time, with unlimited substitutions. Players can move the ball around the court by passing, tapping, throwing, rolling or dribbling.

The game consists of four quarters of 10 minutes each, with a 15-minute break at half-time. There are also two-minute intervals between the first and second periods, and between the third and fourth periods. If the game is tied after the fourth period, it continues with an extra period of 5 minutes, then as many 5-minute periods as are necessary to break the tie.

The main officials include one referee and one umpire. The court is divided between them and they swap places after each foul involving a free throw penalty, as well as after each jump ball decision. They use whistles and hand signals to make and explain their decisions. Points are scored for shooting the basketball through the hoop: two points for a goal inside the three-point semicircle, and three points for goals scored from outside. Free throws, taken from the free-throw line and awarded after a foul, are worth one point.

Netball

Netball is a non-contact sport; players cannot make physical contact with one another on the court or run with the ball. The aim of the game is similar to basketball where a team has to shoot the ball into the opposing team's goal. There are seven players on a netball team and a match lasts 60 minutes and is divided into four 15-minute quarters. Netball can be played both indoors and outdoors. Defenders have to stand 0.9 metres (3 feet) away from the player with the ball. From this distance a player can try and win the ball back, but *only* when it has been thrown into the air. Players can defend a member of the other team who does not have the ball but they cannot touch them or snatch the ball from under their nose! If a player makes physical contact and disrupts play then a penalty pass is awarded.

Volleyball

The aim of volleyball is to get the ball into the opposing team's court area while preventing them getting the ball into your area. There are six players on court in each team with these divided into three at the front (nearest the net) and three at the back. The team who reaches 25 points first is the winner. The game starts with a serve from the backline of the court and, after serving, the server moves back onto the court to help their team. Once the ball has been served *any* player can move *anywhere* on court and even chase the ball out of court if needed.

- **Hitting the ball** – the ball can be hit with any part of the body. The exception to this rule is the serve which must be hit with the hand. The hit has to be clean – no scoops, catch-and-rethrows, dunks, etc. are allowed in volleyball. The team has up to three touches to return the ball over the net, although it can be returned by the first or second touch. A player cannot have two consecutive hits but hitting it first and third is permissible. During the rally, players cannot touch the net. However the ball *can* touch the net on the way over providing it does not touch the supporting posts. A team can win points in the following ways:
  - If the ball touches the court floor on the opposite side
  - If the ball touches one of the opposition players and then the floor/wall

o   If the other team hits the ball more than three times

- **Blocking** is the term used to describe jumping at the net with the arms up to stop the ball coming over it. However, players must not touch the net and they are not allowed to block a serve. Rotation is an important part of volleyball. This means that every time your team win the serve from the other team, all your players rotate their position on court clockwise. However, if you lose the serve your team does not rotate and if you keep the serve your team does not rotate.

The winner is the first to reach 25 points by 2 clear points. If you serve and get the point, you keep the serve; if you do not get the point, the other team gets the serve *and* also a point. In other words the score changes every time there is a serve.

Hockey

The aim of the game is to hit the ball into the opponent's goal. The team scoring the most goals wins. To score a goal the ball must pass between the goalposts and beneath the crossbar. If both teams score the same amount or no goals are scored, the match is a draw. The game is started with a pushback from the centre spot. A game is split into two halves lasting 35 minutes each. At the beginning of each half play begins with a pass from the centre of the halfway line. After a goal, the match is restarted in the same way. There is a 5 minute half-time interval, or longer if previously agreed. Each goal is worth 1 point. They can only be scored from inside the shooting circle – a semicircular area in front of the opponent's goal. Goals scored from outside this area are disallowed.

There are 11 players in a hockey team and up to five substitutes. Every team must have a goalkeeper. The other ten are field players. The field players can be attackers, defenders or midfielders. The exact line-up will depend on the team strategy and so the exact number of forwards, midfielders and backs will vary. Hockey is played with a hard ball and emphasis is placed on safety. Players must not play the ball dangerously or in a way which leads to dangerous play. It is the responsibility of officials and players to ensure that the laws are always followed. A ball is considered dangerous when it causes legitimate evasive action by players.

Tennis

Tennis is played on a rectangular court by two players (singles) or four (doubles). Players stand on opposite sides of a net and use a stringed racquet to hit a ball back and forth to each other. Each player has a maximum of one bounce after it has been hit by their opponent to return the ball over the net and within the boundaries of the court. The aim is to gain enough points to win a game, enough games to win a set and enough sets to win a match. The first person to win six games wins a set, but only if they are leading by two clear games. That means that if your opponent wins five games, you must win the set 7–5, or play a tiebreak if the game score reaches six all. Matches are usually the best of three (women) or the best of five sets (men), although some men's tournaments just play the best of three sets.

Wheelchair basketball

Wheelchair basketball is considered to be one of the major sports for disabled people. Based on basketball, wheelchair basketball uses the same court and rules

Wheelchair basketball has its own designated governing body. Why do you think this sport needs its own governing body?

as basketball although some are adapted to take into account the use of a wheelchair, for example the 'travelling rule' and players must pass, bounce or shoot the ball before they can touch their wheels again.

> **Take it further**
>
> **Wheelchair basketball**
>
> There are many active leagues that promote wheelchair basketball and the sport is represented at the Paralympics held every four years. The International Wheelchair Basketball Federation (IWBF) is the governing body for this sport (www.iwbf.org).

Wheelchair tennis

Wheelchair tennis uses the same rules and principles as tennis and is a sport for people who have a lower body disability. There are two main differences between tennis and wheelchair tennis, namely that the ball can bounce twice and that specially designed wheelchairs are used. Wheelchair tennis is part of the Paralympics and has a major following helped largely by media attention.

Boccia

Boccia is a recreational sport designed for people with disabilities. Originally played by people with cerebral palsy the sport has been adapted to include a wide range of motor skill disabilities. The aim of the sport is to throw leather balls as close as possible to a white target ball known as the jack (similar to bowls). Players take turns to throw their balls and the player who lands closest to the jack is awarded a point. Due to the nature of the sport, the balls can be thrown, kicked or in cases of severe disability, an assistive ramp can be used. Boccia can be played by individuals, pairs or groups of three.

1.2 Rules, laws and regulations

As published by governing body

The rules and regulations of any sport are usually written, enforced and amended by its **national governing body (NGB)**. Rules and regulations can also be set by an International Sports Federation (ISF). Rules are there to ensure that participants are safe

and that the sport is played fairly. They define how a team or player can win. It is common for national governing bodies or international sports federations to amend or change rules as they aim to improve their sports. For example, the Federation Internationale de Football (FIFA), the world governing body for football, amended the back pass rule to prevent teams from wasting time and to make the game more enjoyable. The national governing body, the Football Association (FA), ensured that all the players and officials were aware of this important rule change.

> **Key term**
>
> **National governing bodies (NGBs)** – responsible for the rules and organisation of competitions for their sports. They also select representative teams and deal with funding and disciplinary issues.

Court/pitch layout

One of the key regulations of any sport is to define the area in which the sport can be played. Sport can take place on pitches, courts, swimming pools, tables or rinks and most sports will define the size of these in order for a standard competitive game to take place. The dimensions of the playing surface are clearly stated by the governing body and a breach of these can invalidate the competition. For example, an Olympic size pool is defined as 50 metres in length and all international competitions will use this as a standard. Some sports are more flexible in their playing dimensions rules. For example, football can be played on pitches of slightly different sizes as long as they are between 90 and 120 metres long and 45 and 90 metres wide. However, the dimensions of the markings on the pitch will be of a standard size as will the size of the goals.

Playing surface

Different sports can be played on a number of different surfaces and this can affect the performance or the tactics used by the athlete. It can also affect the equipment that can be used (for example, footwear). A good example of this is tennis where the surface of the court can be grass, clay or a hard surface and can be played both outside and inside. As such it is important that officials and players are aware of any rules that exist that may take into account the different surfaces. Hockey is another example of a sport where

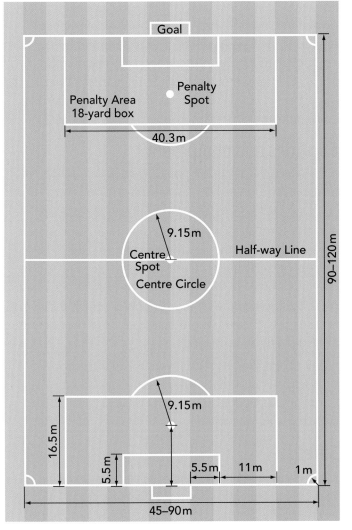

Figure 22.2: Although football pitches vary in size, their marking should be standardised.

Hockey is an example of a sport that uses a synthetic pitch. What are the advantages of using such surfaces in sport?

the surface is critical. Historically hockey has been played on grass pitches but, with the development of technology and the creation of synthetic pitches, hockey is now played on artificial water based surfaces. The advantage of this is that the pitch is even and the ball will not bobble. This in turn has made the game faster as the players no longer have to worry about pitch conditions. Artificial pitches also reduce the need for maintenance and can be used in all weathers.

Officials must also ensure that the surface of the pitch is suitable for sport before competition begins. An official will check that the surface is safe and free from dangers such as broken glass, damaged drinks cans and divots. Likewise, indoor courts must be free from water or dirt which may cause a player to slip or injure themselves. Outdoor pitches may become waterlogged or frozen and as such an official must decide whether the pitch is safe for play.

Fouls and sanctions

It is the responsibility of officials to ensure that the rules or laws of the sport are correctly applied. If the rules are broken then it is normal for the official to recognise foul play and punish the offending team or player. This punishment may include:

- awarding points to the opposition
- awarding possession to the opposition
- cautioning a player or team
- awarding a free kick or free throw
- removing a player from the field of play
- suspending a player from future matches
- fining a player or team.

Remember that rules are designed to ensure that the sport is played fairly and safely and it is the responsibility of the officials to make impartial and objective decisions that prevent the rules from being broken. Players also have a responsibility to ensure that sport is played fairly and safely.

Number of players

Different sports will have different numbers of players. Some sports such as golf and swimming are considered individual sports while others such as basketball or cricket are team sports. However some sports can be played as both. For example badminton can be played either individually or as part of a 'doubles' team.

Substitution

The officials must always check that each team has the correct number of players before competition starts. Most sports now allow for substitutions during a match for tactical reasons or to replace an injured player and officials must always know when a player leaves or enters the field of play to ensure that the correct number are always participating.

Time

Most team sports have time constraints and can be divided into different periods of play. For example, football is played for two periods (or halves) of 45 minutes while netball is played for four quarters of 15 minutes. The team with the most points or goals at the end of this time are declared the winners, while if the scores are tied then the game is normally declared a draw. Some sports will have a stop/start clock where the time is stopped every time the ball leaves the field of play or where the official stops play for infringements. This means that a 60-minute game, for example, will often last much longer. An example of this is basketball where tactics can be developed by the coach to use a 'time out' to reorganise his or her team. In many sports, if the scores are even at the end of the 'normal' period of play, then extra time is used to declare a winner. This is common for cup competitions where to progress to the next stage of the tournament a clear winner is needed. Where extra time is not used a replay between the teams is sometimes organised or even a penalty shootout.

Facilities and equipment

It is the responsibility of the officials to ensure that the facilities are suitable for competition prior to the sport starting. This is to make sure that both the players and the spectators are safe before, during and after a game. Likewise the equipment that is used by the players must be suitable and not pose any risk to the players or officials. For example, the players' footwear must be appropriate to the surface on which the sport is being played and where studs are used these must not be sharp or damaged.

Many sports require the players to wear the correct protective equipment to reduce the risk of injury. For example, in cricket, players will wear protective padding and helmets.

Safety

It is the responsibility of the officials to ensure that all participants are safe at all times before, during and after a game. Before a match officials should check that players have removed all jewellery and that long hair is tied back. Players who are wearing any form of jewellery or lack the necessary protective equipment should not be allowed to enter the field of play under any circumstances. It is also the responsibility of the officials to ensure that the laws of the game are correctly and impartially applied. Many rules are designed to protect players from injury and if foul play is witnessed this should be dealt with according to the laws of the game.

Scoring

Every sport has a different scoring system designed to identify the winning team or player. It is usual for the team with the highest number of points or goals to be declared the winner. However, the exception to this is golf where the winner is the player who has the lowest score or in other words has played the fewest number of shots. Scoring may involve placing or kicking a ball in the opponent's goal or shooting the ball through an object such as a hoop (for example, basketball or

Figure 22.3: Time is often displayed as well as the score so that players and spectators know how much longer a game will last. How can this be a benefit to players and spectators?

netball). Some sports will give different amounts of points dependent on where the ball goes or where the player took the shot from. In cricket, for example, it is possible for a player to score between one and six runs per ball.

Methods of victory

Victory in sport is normally awarded to the team or player with the highest score at the end of the match and can be measured in points or goals. However, extra time may be used if the scores are identical at the end of normal time or a penalty shoot out may be used to find a clear winner. Some sports such as marathon running will use time to decide a winner; the athlete who completes the course in the quickest time is the winner.

Assessment activity 22.1   P1   BTEC

The local sports development officer (SDO) has asked you to explain the rules, laws and regulations of one sport to a group of primary school children. To ensure they are interested and fully understand the chosen sport, the SDO has asked you to make a large and colourful poster that highlights all the key rules, laws and regulations for your chosen sport. **P1**

Grading tip

- To attain **P1** ensure that you describe the main rules of the sport and identify why these rules exist. For example, is a rule in place to protect the players or is it to ensure fair play?

PLTS

By working in a group you are able to produce evidence of your skills as a **team worker** and by considering why rules exist you are demonstrating your skills as a **reflective learner**.

Functional skills

By researching the rules, laws and regulations of your chosen sport, and by displaying them attractively and clearly, you could display your skills in **ICT** and **English**.

2.   Know the roles and responsibilities of officials involved in a selected sport

2.1 Officials

Different sports may use umpires, referees, line judges, third umpires, timekeepers, scorers or judges to control the game. Each of these will play a specific part in the management of play and competition and will ensure that teams and players follow the rules and laws of the game in question. These **officials** can be categorised in two ways:

- performance controllers – officials who regulate the sport within or close to the action, for example, in cricket, football or tennis

- performance managers – reassure and remind players against standards, for example, gymnasts, sprinters or snooker players.

• Key term

Officials – responsible for ensuring fair play and the welfare of players and spectators through the correct application of the rules, laws and regulations.

289

Umpire

Sports that use umpires include cricket, tennis, netball and hockey. The umpire (or official) is responsible for all on-field activity during a game. They will ensure that the laws of the game are followed and that the spirit of the game is maintained (sportsmanship). The umpire will also make key decisions such as whether a batsman is out in cricket or whether a serve is valid in tennis. To ensure that spectators, players and scorers understand the decisions that have been made, a series of hand signals are used. These will clearly demonstrate each decision.

Activity: Sports and their officials

Use the following table to identify the different sports that use different types of officials. Remember to include as many sports as possible for each category.

Official	Sport
Umpire	
Line judge	
Timekeeper	
Linesman/assistant referee	
Scorer	
Referee	
Fourth official	

Line judges

Line judges are required to indicate whether a ball is in play or has travelled outside of the court markings. These are primarily used in tennis and their signals will be used by the umpire to make a decision. A line judge will use a clear and easily recognised signal to indicate their decision. Recent developments have led to the use of automated computer systems that can judge whether a ball is in or out (an example is Hawkeye). The advantage of this technology is that it is not affected by human error and therefore the decisions made should be more accurate than those made by human line judges. Players can now refer to such technology to question the line judge's decision.

Timekeepers

Many sports will use official timekeepers to keep a record of how long the game has been played. The timekeeper is responsible for ensuring that the clock starts and stops during play and their use allows the on field match official to concentrate solely on making the correct decisions. One sport that uses timekeepers is basketball.

Scorers

The most important aspect of any sport is keeping a record of the score. This must be accurate at all times and as such many sports will use specific scorers. They will record not only the points or goals scored but also information such as the time of goals, the number of balls bowled and the number of conversions.

Linesmen

The role of the linesmen in sport is to assist the referee (and they are now often referred to as assistant referees). They may provide information on foul play or whether the ball has left the field of play or not. Linesmen will also determine whether a player is offside in football, for example, and are a valuable part of the game.

Referees

The role of the referee is to ensure that all the rules or laws of the game are followed. Normally the referee will be a part of the on field competition and has the authority to make decisions about play. However, some sports use match referees who are not an active part of the play. For example, cricket uses match referees to support the umpires and they will make judgements concerning the correct conduct of the game and hand out penalties for breaches of the laws of the game.

Fourth officials

It is now common in football to see a fourth official. Their role is to support the other officials such as the on field referee and linesmen (assistant referees). In the event of an injury to an on field official the fourth official will be called upon to replace him or her. Other duties the fourth official is responsible for include:

- assisting the referee in pre-match preparations such as collecting team sheets from each manager and ensuring the pitch is fit for play
- inspecting players' equipment, for example, the

condition of boots and studs. This may also include ensuring that protective equipment is worn

- organising substitutions during play and notifying the referee and spectators of the substitution
- indicating the amount of time to be played at the end of each period of play (injury time). This is done using a large electronic display board that is visible to players and spectators alike
- developing and maintaining relationships with managers, coaches and substitute players and intervening if these people become frustrated or aggressive
- ensuring that all non-participants such as managers and coaches remain in their technical areas.

The fourth official is a key member of the officiating team even though they are not on the field of play. The fourth official will also keep an extra set of records such as the score, scorers and players who have been booked for foul play. This is to ensure that the on field referee does not make any mistakes such as cautioning the wrong player.

Video referees

More and more sports are now using video referees to support the on field officials. The role of the video referee is to use television footage to adjudicate or make key decisions on a specific event that the on field

officials feel they are uncertain of. Video referees are used in many sports, including cricket (third umpire), rugby union, rugby league and ice hockey. However, because of the cost of the specialist equipment, the use of video referees is normally limited to professional or elite sport.

Judges

Sports such as boxing and athletics use judges to officiate. The role of the judge is to ensure that the rules and laws have been correctly followed and to make a judgement on performance. It is often the judge's decision that will determine whether a person has won or not.

2.2 Roles

An official will have many roles as part of their duties. These roles will have to be learned, understood and implemented if an official is to be successful.

Arbiter

An arbiter is a person who has the authority to make decisions and to decide on matters during sport. The decision should be viewed as final and should not be questioned by the players. As such it is vital that officials are completely neutral and do not display any bias towards a team or individual player. The laws of

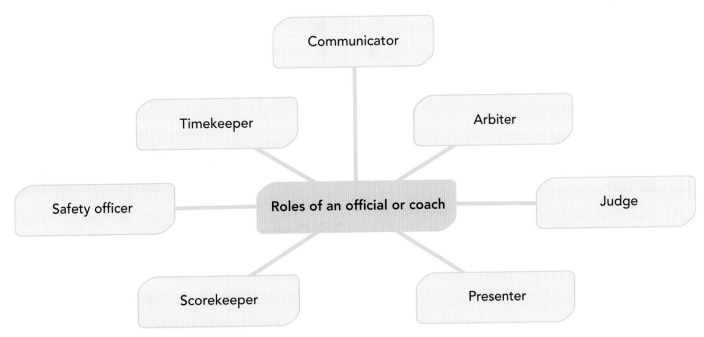

Figure 22.4: A coach will have many roles. Consider why each of these is so important.

the game must be enforced completely objectively and personal opinion or emotion must not be used to make a decision. The role of the official is to ensure that fair play is upheld at all times.

Judge

Sport requires officials to make judgements according to the rules/laws of the game and within the nature and spirit of the activity. Officials should also do their best to communicate their decisions to all concerned. This communication may be through discussion with the players and other officials on the field of play or it may involve using recognised signals so that spectators know what decision was made. The communication of decisions is just as important to the players as it is to the spectators. The judgement process must be fair and objective and must only judge the specific situation in accordance with governing body rules.

Communication

It is the role of the officials to ensure that their decisions are clearly and unambiguously communicated. An official will have to communicate with a wide variety of people including other officials, players or participants, coaches or managers, spectators and the media. New or inexperienced officials will need to develop their communication skills as part of their officiating practice and training.

Presentation

The way an official presents themselves to the players and spectators is very important. An official must be professional in terms of their conduct and their appearance. The conduct of an official must display confidence and authority so that decisions are understood and respected. This respect will be gained if a professional appearance and manner is established and maintained and rules are correctly interpreted and implemented.

Timekeeper

It is important to keep accurate track of the exact duration of play, and many sports use official timekeepers to keep a record of how long play has continued.

Scorekeeper

Many sports such as football and netball require the on field officials to keep a record of the score during play

(in addition to their other on field duties). Therefore it is essential that such records are accurate and up to date so that scores can be quickly relayed to others at any point during or after competition. It is useful to keep a written record of scores rather than trying to remember them – this will prevent confusion and inaccuracy.

Safety officer

There can be a risk of injury in most sports. Any sport that involves teams contesting over possession of an object will have a high risk of injury through collision with other players or the opposition. An official must therefore ensure that every step is taken to ensure that all participants are safe at all times. This will involve the correct interpretation of the rules and making clear and confident judgements. Players that deliberately break the laws should be subject to sanctions. Safety officers will also be responsible for the safety of spectators and make sure that the stadiums are suitable for the number of people watching the sport.

Activity: Safety rules in sport

For the following sports, identify specific rules that are designed to protect the participants from injury. Consider why the rules prevent injury and give reasons why this is important.

Sport	Law/rule	Reasons why this rule is important
Football	No tackles from behind	
Cricket		
Netball		
Rugby union		
Hockey		

2.3 Responsibilities

Application of the rules

To be a successful official you must have both an up to date and thorough knowledge of the rules and a clear understanding of how these rules should be applied during a game. It is the responsibility of the official to ensure that the rules are correctly implemented and that the decisions made are clear and without confusion. However, an official will need a degree of common sense when implementing the rules. Officials should allow a game to flow and only intervene when necessary. It is often suggested that a referee or official should enhance a game rather interfere with over-exuberant use of the whistle. Most officials are happy if the players and spectators are unaware they are there as this means the game is flowing well and their decisions are correct.

Health and safety

All sports officials have a duty of care to the participants. This means that they are expected to exercise a reasonable amount of care in ensuring that all participants remain safe and free from harm during sport. Therefore an official must ensure that health and safety is at the forefront of their minds when making decisions. Many sports such as netball and basketball specifically state that contact between participants is not allowed. If this rule is broken the official should correctly penalise the offender and award a free throw. Other sports such as football and rugby allow contact but within clear guidelines. This means that an official will have to judge whether contact is within the rules

or whether such contact is unfair or even dangerous. Again sanctions can be applied if the official feels that unfair contact has been made.

The official must also ensure that facilities and equipment are checked prior to participation for health and safety risks. For example, indoor courts must be free from water (including sweat) that may pose a risk of slipping to the competitors and outside pitches must be checked for divots, broken glass or other unsafe objects. The weather should also be considered, especially if pitches have become frozen or waterlogged. Remember, if you feel that the safety of participants is in question then you are within your rights to postpone a game.

Communicating information

It is the responsibility of officials to communicate with a wide variety of people involved in their sport including players, co officials, managers and spectators. However, because of the nature of sport it is important to communicate with a number of people by using clear non- verbal communications to indicate decisions. These signals are important to both the players and the spectators and must convey the correct information.

What image does this present to children? How might this prevent people from becoming officials?

Establishing and maintaining relationships

To be a successful official it is important that you establish and maintain a positive relationship with players, other officials and managers and coaches. Being able to deal with people in a variety of situations will aid the sport as conflict and aggression can be dealt with effectively. An official should use clear communication to explain decisions and must be confident in their judgements. This will develop with experience where an official will be subjected to a wide variety of situations.

Using these experiences and self analysis means that, should it recur, the official will be able to recount how they dealt with it on previous occasions.

Scoring

One of the key responsibilities of the officials in sports such as hockey, football and netball is to keep a track of the score during the game. It is essential that all officials involved in a competition also keep track of the scores and that they are accurate and consistent.

Assessment activity 22.2

P2 · **BTEC**

Following your work with the local school, a teacher has asked you to talk to the children about the roles and responsibilities of officials in sport. The teacher is concerned that the children do not understand the purpose of officials in sport and that they have been increasingly questioning officials' decisions.

Choose one sport and prepare a short presentation that describes the roles and responsibilities of the officials in your chosen sport. **P2**

Grading tip

- To attain **P2** you should use examples from sports that the children may be playing at the school. Consider the importance of these roles and describe what would happen if officials didn't exist in the sport.

PLTS

By completing this task you are able to demonstrate your skills as a **reflective learner**.

Functional skills

Preparing a presentation and handout will help you gain evidence of functional skills in **English** and **ICT**.

3. Understand the performance of officials in a selected sport

3.1 Situations

Player in illegal position

Many sports require players to remain in specific areas of the pitch or court. Examples of this include netball where players can only play in certain sections of the court depending on their given position in the team. It is normal for pitch or court markings to clearly define where boundaries exist to aid both the players and the officials. By leaving these designated areas,

an infringement will occur and a free kick or throw can be awarded to the opposing team. Some sports will require more than one official to oversee such infringements with assistant referees used to help match officials.

Player injured

By the nature of sport it is possible that players will become injured at some point during competition. Injuries may be caused by collision with other players or pulling muscles. However, the officials should try and help players avoid injuries if possible. This can be done by ensuring that the rules of the game that prevent foul or dangerous tackles are followed, that protective equipment such as shin pads is worn and that the facilities or pitch are suitable and free from hazards.

If injury does occur during play it is normal for the official to stop play so that the player can receive treatment. When this happens the official will stop the clock so that time cannot be wasted. If possible the injury should be treated off the pitch so that play can resume as quickly as possible. In more serious cases a player may have to be substituted if they can no longer continue and the official should allow this within the rules of the game. Both rugby league and rugby union use the 'blood' substitution rule. This means that a player has to leave the field of play if they have received a visible bleeding injury. While treatment is being received the team may temporarily replace the player with a substitute until the injured player is fit to return to the game.

Ball out of play

Most sports will have defined boundaries which outline to the players and officials whether the ball has left the field of play or the court. These lines are important as they influence who has possession of the ball when play resumes and this can have a direct

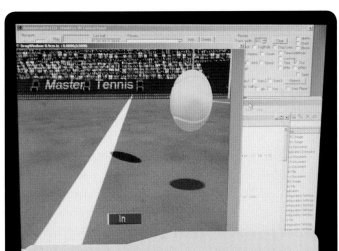

Technology is now used to aid officials in making the correct decisions. For example, Hawkeye is used in both cricket and tennis. Within your group discuss the positive and negative aspects of using technology in sport. Giving examples, how can such use aid officials?

effect on the scoring of the game. For example, in tennis if a ball is considered out of play a point will be awarded to the opposing player so it is essential that officials can see whether a ball is out of play or not. A recent development in sport is the use of technology to aid the officials to determine whether a ball is in or out of play. This video technology has recently been implemented in tennis to see whether an umpire has made the correct decision and is used in rugby to see whether a ball has crossed the line for a try.

Illegal challenge

It is the role of the officials to ensure that players conduct themselves appropriately and follow the rules or laws of the game. A player who is challenging another player outside of these rules will be penalised and a free kick is normally awarded to the opposing team. In more serious cases a player can be sent from the field of play as punishment for their actions. It is essential that officials deal with illegal challenges in accordance with the rules as allowing these to happen can result in serious injury to the players.

3.2 Officials

Anybody involved in sport will have a desire to improve. This is true of both players and officials and there are several ways they can do this. Recent research indicates that to improve in sport you must be able to analyse your performance objectively. This can be done as part of a self evaluation or it can be performed using other people to give advice and guidance. There are a number of considerations that an official must take into account when undertaking their duties. These are:

- consistency – making sure that the correct decision is made regardless of pressure from others such as players or spectators (being consistent will bring respect from players and build your own confidence)

- enjoyment – an important and often forgotten part of officiating is ensuring that you enjoy the experience. Often too much pressure is put on officials by players, media and spectators and this can have a negative effect on performance. In some sports such as football there is now a shortage of officials due to the unnecessary stress put on them.

The Football Association (FA) has recognised that there is a need for qualified and experienced officials. It is no longer a case of recruiting ex-players who wish to 'give something back to the game'. As such the FA is now looking to train and recruit 10 000 referees annually in order to officiate games at all levels. They estimate that at present, in some parts of the country, up to 20 per cent of games take place without officials. Without these officials the FA recognises that competitive football cannot take place.

The FA is also keen to recruit referees, both male and female, aged between 16 and 25 so that they have time to reach the top of the game.

- Consider why self-control is important for an official. What are the implications for the sport if officials did not demonstrate self-control?
- Knowledge of the rules is vital to sport. What would happen if an official did not have up to date knowledge of the game being played?
- Consider why control of players or individuals is important. How would you deal with confrontation or inappropriate behaviour?

3.3 Analysis

Observation checklist

A checklist is a simple and easy to use list that can be applied in real time by an observer or can be used as part of a video analysis and used to help provide you with feedback about your match performance. Checklists are also useful tools to assist you in self analysis after a performance. A suitable checklist may include:

- effective communication
- professional appearance and manner
- up to date knowledge of rules
- communication with co officials
- fitness for the sport and level
- manner
- correct interpretation of the rules/laws
- health and safety considerations (duty of care)
- use of common sense
- dealing with pressure from players, spectators and coaches/managers
- dealing with conflict and confrontation.

Method

There are many ways in which an official can analyse their skills in order to improve. The purpose of this is to recognise both strengths and weaknesses and to further develop their officiating skills.

- **Observation and video analysis** – an easy way in which to improve and develop officiating skills is to observe others. This is best done by watching an elite or experienced official and noting their strengths and weaknesses. You should be able to identify the key techniques required to improve. Another way of analysing performance is simply having your performance filmed. This will provide you with an objective record of what happened with the advantage of being able to analyse in slow motion or real time.

- **Notational analysis** studies movement patterns in team sports and is primarily concerned with strategy and tactics. However, it can be a useful method for officials to analyse their movement during a match as well as the number of decisions made. Patterns of play can then be identified and strengths and weaknesses highlighted and this information can then be used as a strategy in subsequent matches to improve performance.

- **Performance profiling** analysis can be used to document, assess and predict the ability of the official to meet the demands of performance, covering various aspects of technical skill, tactical awareness, physical capacity and psychological factors. Performance profiling is a way of giving an official information of what actually happened in their sport rather than what they *think* happened. This provides an insight into the official's state of mind. For example, there may be occasions when the official has underperformed due to nerves or lack of concentration. Therefore the purpose of performance profiling is to:
  - assist the official with their psychological needs
  - improve the official's motivation and performance.

Therefore, performance profiling will assess the official before and after the match and should address the following important psychological factors:

- confidence
- concentration
- commitment
- control
- refocusing of effort.

Understanding each of these will allow you to prepare a strategy that can address any issue that have been highlighted as part of the profiling.

Strengths

It is important that when analysing performance the official does not solely concentrate on weaknesses. Through observation and discussion the strengths of performance should also be highlighted. To further aid this it is useful for the coach to observe an experienced or elite official so that their strengths and skills can be identified.

Areas for improvement

The purpose of any performance analysis is to identify any strengths and weaknesses. Having identified these the official can choose strategies to develop areas that may need to be improved. Regular evaluation is needed to ensure that skills are up to date and suitable for a variety of match situations. Having identified areas for improvement the official should investigate how to alter these. This may involve enrolling on recognised courses or taking refresher sessions.

Take it further

Training courses

Most governing bodies will offer a range of courses designed to train officials or to update existing skills. Contact the governing body of your chosen sport for further information.

Development

- **Practice** – one of the easiest ways in which an official can improve is to practise in a variety of situations. By practising and evaluating performance an official will be able to understand their strengths and weaknesses and devise ways in which to further develop. For example, a football referee may wish to officiate in junior football and gain valuable experience and confidence before they progress on to adult football.

- **Training** – any successful official will regularly train. This means that they will update their skills regularly and practise using them in a variety of situations. The official will also undertake regular physical training similar to the players. Many sports will require the official to have a high level of fitness and as such they will need to be able to keep up with play during a competition. This is of particular importance for sports such as football, rugby and basketball which can be very fast moving. Being physically fit will also help the official to make the correct decision even if they are feeling the signs of fatigue.

Remember

In football the FA sets very clear guidelines for fitness levels for new referees. To qualify as a referee a standard fitness test must be passed. The standard FIFA fitness test involves:

- eyesight test (car number plate at 25 metres)
- two runs of 50 metres each in less than 7.5 seconds
- two runs of 200 metres each in less than 32 seconds
- a minimum distance run of at least 2700 metres in 12 minutes of continuous running.

- **Qualifications** – most officials will have gained a recognised qualification at some point in their career. It is generally accepted that to improve you should become qualified. For some sports this may be the only way of receiving any kind of training prior to gaining experience. Most national governing bodies will offer up to date qualifications that will not only train you but also keep you up to date with relevant rule changes and different scenarios. Gaining a recognised qualification will also allow you to achieve a certificate as well as introduce you to other officials so that you can share ideas and skills.

- **Self analysis** – there are a number of ways in which it is possible to analyse officiating. Each of the methods can be used in a variety of sports and at all levels and you should try each one to see which you prefer. It is important to point out that there is no correct or necessarily more accurate method. One method that can be used and is relatively easy to undertake is self reflection. This means that you consider your own performance after the event and think carefully about the strengths and weaknesses in order to suggest what you could do better in the future.

- **Buddy systems** are where an experienced official will mentor a new or inexperienced official and help them develop their skills and techniques. This system allows the new official to observe and learn from their colleague and ask questions and seek advice when needed. A buddy system can provide an official with invaluable information such as how to deal with a wide variety of situations or how to deal with conflict within the sport. Often as a new official it is easier for peers to relate to the kind of situations that you might be in, and offer you the benefit of their own experiences and ways in which they have dealt with challenging situations.

Assessment activity 22.3   P3 M1   :BTEC

Following on from Assessment activity 22.1, you feel that the best way to describe the rules of your sport is to show the local school children how they can be applied in a game situation.

1. Apply the rules, laws and regulations of your chosen sport in three different situations that are common to it. **P3**

2. Explain the purpose of these rules, laws and regulations in your three chosen game or match situations. **M1**

Grading tips

- To attain **P3** ensure that the situations are likely to occur in your sport so that the children can see how the rules and laws control the game.

- To attain **M1** consider why these rules, laws and regulations are important and consider what would happen if they did not exist.

PLTS

By applying the rules, laws and regulations of your chosen sport, you can demonstrate your skills as a **creative thinker** and an **effective participator**.

Assessment activity 22.4   P4 P5 M2 D1   :BTEC

Having outlined the roles and responsibilities of officials in Assessment activity 22.2, you feel it would be helpful for the children to analyse the performance of an elite official. To do this, however, you realise that the children will need some form of analysis checklist.

1. Prepare an analysis checklist that can be used to observe an official in your chosen sport. **P4**

2. Use this checklist to analyse the performances of **two** officials in your chosen sport. The analysis should identify the strengths of their performance as well as any weaknesses or areas for improvement. **P5**

3. Explain the strengths and weaknesses you have recognised and make suggestions relating to performance. **M2**

4. You should now justify your recommendations explaining why you have made these so that the officials' future performances can be improved. **D1**

Grading tips

- To attain **P4** ensure that the checklist is relevant to your chosen sport.

- To attain **P5** you may wish to consider communication (verbal and non-verbal), application of rules, relationships with the players and health and safety. Try to be objective – only analyse what you see!

- To attain **M2** consider both the good and bad parts of the officials' performance. What would you have done in a similar situation and what aspects would you use for your own performance?

- To attain **D1** explain your decisions and make clear suggestions on what you would change in the future.

4.   Be able to officiate effectively in a selected sport

4.1 Officiate

Application of the rules/laws

For a sport to be developed and well managed the application of the rules/laws is an essential part of any game. Even during childhood, games are bound by rules even though an official is very rarely present in the playground or park; children devise their own rules and as a result judge the boundaries of the activity.

The official has the authority to judge where indiscretions have occurred and is required to administer punishment for infringements, acts of over aggression or persistent rule breaking.

Control of the game

There are several ways in which an official can control the game to ensure safety and smooth running. Invasion games such as rugby league, rugby union, netball, football, basketball and hockey are controlled primarily by a referee/umpire and their assistants who will use a whistle to signify the beginning and stoppages in play. Sports such as golf, tennis, badminton and athletics, which are non-contact and rely more on technical development, still require an official but the control of situations is more passive and will normally be directed by verbal instruction in the form of score updates and clarification of rules and decisions.

Effectively using scoring systems

Any official who is in charge must understand the scoring system to ensure that the game is managed correctly. Not all sports carry the one point scoring system that is seen in football and in some areas there is no logical progression between scores. Tennis is an excellent example of this:

- winning your first point – 15
- winning your second point – 30
- winning your third point – 40.

Ensuring health and safety of all participants

There are many potential hazards when playing sports and the official is responsible for minimising the risk to the participants. For example, this can be achieved by:

- checking the playing surface is:
  - dry
  - flat
  - suitable for the sport
  - marked out correctly
  - free from debris
- ensuring participants:
  - have removed jewellery
  - are wearing correct footwear
  - have the required protective equipment.

As an official there is an ongoing responsibility to ensure that everyone participating behaves in a manner that will not cause harm to others. If you feel that there is cause to warn a player this can be done and in certain situations the player can be withdrawn from the game for a short period (at the official's discretion) or for the remaining time in the game. In sports such as boxing, judo, karate and long distance running the official has the responsibility to gauge the physical wellbeing of the participants; if they are in distress and cannot defend themselves or sustain normal physical activity the event should be stopped or the individual withdrawn.

Relationships with others

A good official should posses the relevant skills to develop positive relationships with the people involved in their sport. Unfortunately, officials can become the focal point of blame for many coaches, spectators and performers because their team or individual has not performed as they could/should have done. An official should remain impartial at all times and should act in a manner which is appropriate to a person in authority; there should be no bias shown and players should not expect special treatment during the game. Coaches and players need to understand that there are boundaries that must not be crossed (verbal abuse in particular is unacceptable as is the questioning of an official's decision).

Conflict management

Due to the competitive nature of sport it is likely that there will be occasions when frustration or conflict will develop between opponents and/or coaching staff of the opposing teams. The official has to ensure that these volatile situations are defused quickly and a balanced environment is restored. In situations where it is difficult to resolve the problems, the same control measures that are employed with players can be used and coaches can be removed from the playing area.

Remember

You role is to implement the rules fairly. Do not get involved in arguments and remember that you have the authority to control the players and the game.

Checking equipment

Before officiating in any event ensure that you are well prepared and have any equipment at your disposal to help you perform to the best of your ability. This may include: timekeeping instruments (normally two); pens, pencils and markers for run ups; score sheets; cards to enforce discipline; whistle or counting instruments. This is not a complete list and a good official will find different equipment to help them to be as efficient as possible. As part of the responsibility for safety a good official will check all equipment that is to be used by the players or athletes. This may mean checking that the tennis net is at the correct height, the football net is attached correctly and that the ball pressure is correct. Without these checks the official is endangering the participants and ultimately is failing to do everything within his or her power to prevent injury.

Use of signals

An official will use signals or gestures in order to signal a decision or action. This is seen in cricket when the umpire raises his finger to give a batsman out after an appeal, or when a line judge in tennis will raise their arm to the side to signal that the ball was 'out'. Signals are a useful form of communication, especially when players are too far away to hear the official's instructions but are near enough to see a signal or gesture. (This is important in professional sport when crowd noise may affect the message being heard by the players.)

Dealing with pressure

Like any performer, an official may be nervous before they take part, especially if it is an important game/ match or event. Coping with nerves is difficult as, unlike many of the participants, the officials are on their own with only the support of their assisting personnel. It is important to enjoy the performance – perform as well as you can and ensure that you provide a safe and enjoyable area for people to play in. Your overriding thought should be that you have faith in your own ability and that you will officiate in a way that shows no bias and will allow the match/event or game to flow.

Take it further

Ask the experts

The next time that you play organised sport, take time to speak to the officials after the game and ask them what they enjoy about their role, what they dislike and how they got involved in officiating your sport.

4.2 Review

Formative and summative

A formative review takes place during the performance and is ongoing. A summative review is a final summary review and normally takes place after the match or game is finished.

Feedback

With any performance, it is important that there is a desire to improve. The key factor is to find out how you performed through the eyes of the players, coaches, observers, supervisors and spectators. Their feedback must be honest and designed to improve performance. Constructive criticism will highlight any potential weaknesses and will help, not undermine. Players can often provide an official with good feedback as they work closely with them and can assess their ways of dealing with challenging or disruptive behaviour (coaches and spectators might be too far away to pick up on this). However, coaches and spectators can observe from a distance and see the bigger picture; they can focus on the way the official looks, the image they project and their body language in specific areas and situations.

Feedback is often given as part of an official assessment. For example, a referee may have their performance graded after a game by the teams or individuals involved. Reports are often sent to the national governing bodies and feedback is used to allow officials to gain promotion to higher levels.

Strengths and areas for improvement

When an official receives feedback it is good to take on board what has been said, especially if a number of people have picked up on the same points. The purpose of the feedback is to look at what is successful and what participants have liked about the performance and take positives away from this. The negative comments then highlight the areas for improvement. It is important to accept that there will always be areas to work on and if the weaknesses are identified and worked on quickly they will soon disappear. Being able to understand and accept feedback is an invaluable tool in the search for perfection.

Figure 22.5: Clear signals are important to both players and spectators. Why are signals used in sport rather than verbal communication?

Assessment activity 22.5

P6 M3 P7 M4 D2 ⬤ BTEC

Having worked closely with the school children on the roles of officials in sport, you feel that it would be beneficial if you officiated in a sport of your choice.

1. Select a sport, and with support, officiate within a game or match situation. **P6**

2. To achieve the **M3** grading criterion you should undertake the role of an official without support (i.e. independently).

3. Review your performance and identify your strengths and any areas for improvement. **P7**

4. Explain your performance and make recommendations on how you can improve. **M4**

5. Justify your own performance and explain why you behaved in certain ways. **D2**

Grading tips

- To attain **P6** you may wish to prepare a checklist prior to officiating or ask someone to video your performance so that you can review this objectively.

- To attain **M3** you should perform the above task without support.

- To attain **P7** your review should be honest and identify what went well and any areas that you feel you need to address to improve in future.

- To attain **M4** consider what went well and what areas of your performance were disappointing. Fully consider the good points as well as the bad points and make sure that you consider what you would change. Be specific.

- To attain **D2** justify how you can address any areas of weakness in order to improve in future. You should fully consider the decisions you have made and explain why you made these decisions. To help you with this, consider the difficult decisions and the responses you made.

PLTS

By officiating in a chosen sport you are able to produce evidence of your skills as a **self-manager**. By reviewing your performance you are a **reflective learner**.

Daniel Cotton
Part-time cricket umpire

Dan is a part-time cricket umpire. He must ensure that players adhere to the laws of the game and that he makes the correct decisions. His role requires a high level of concentration and patience.

'I have played cricket since I was young and achieved personal and team success at several clubs. But I suffered an injury but wanted to continue my involvement, I wanted to give something back. I decided to focus on umpiring and I now appreciate what a hard job it is! I am now a panel umpire operating within the county cricket league.

I arrive at the ground at 11 a.m. and take a slow walk around the facilities, checking for the normal things like appropriate boundary markings, the positioning of the sightscreens and fielding discs and the condition of the playing surface. We assist the captains with the coin toss and prior to the start we must have a list of all players for our match card. We pay particular attention to the young cricketers who have restrictions on the amount of overs they are allowed to bowl in a particular spell. Then we ring the bell to signal the start of the game. This is where the main bulk of the work begins for an umpire.

As an umpire, you have a high level of game interaction. We provide signals to the scorers, make decisions on dismissals, ensure the game is played in the correct spirit, deal with behaviour issues and keep on top of a counting process and timekeeping on a ball-by-ball case. We are always involved in every ball in one way or another. The role requires a high level of concentration.

When the game is over the administration work begins and a match report is completed by me and my colleague. Both captains have to sign and agree the result and they also complete a questionnaire on the umpires. This helps us to improve and we all find the feedback very useful.'

Think about it!

- What are the main demands on Dan as an umpire in cricket?
- What skills must Dan possess to be successful?
- Why is concentration so important for a cricket umpire?

Just checking

1. For a sport of your choice describe the roles and responsibilities of an official.
2. Who is responsible for devising and amending rules in sport?
3. Why is it important to analyse the performance of an official?
4. What can performance be measured against?
5. Using examples, describe how an official may deal with a conflict or confrontation.
6. Why is confidence important in officiating?
7. For a sport of your choice, explain how you can communicate with players and spectators.
8. How can an official ensure that health and safety is maintained?
9. Using a sport of your choice describe any recent rule changes and explain why these have been introduced.
10. What is meant by common sense and how can this be applied to the rules of a game?

edexcel **:::**

Assignment tips

- Remember that officiating is meant to be fun. Enjoy the experience and you are far more likely to see improvements in your skills and techniques as well as those that you are leading.
- When practising, use a sport that you are familiar with. Ensure that you have an up to date knowledge of the sport including all the rules.
- Do not be too hard on yourself if you do not achieve what you want first time. Making mistakes is part of learning.
- Support your peers and they will support you. Work together giving each other tips and encouragement.
- Learn from your tutors, instructors and officials. They will all be experienced and have plenty to teach you. Talk to them and gather information from them to assist with your assignments. Evaluate their performances.
- Make sure that you are fully prepared for practical officiating sessions including equipment that you may need.
- Use websites to help you gather research material. They contain plenty of useful information on how to gain recognised qualifications in officiating.
- Ensure that you properly read the assignment briefs. Take your time and ensure you are happy with the task set for you. If not, ask your tutor for additional assistance.

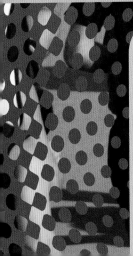

Credit value: 10

23 Organising sports events

Some of the most memorable events which happen are sporting events, from the Olympic Games to the Football World Cup and Wimbledon fortnight, drawing spectators, players and support teams from all over the globe. The events within the London Olympic Games were planned for many years. Each has its own set of requirements and complex logistics. All will be reviewed for their effectiveness before the next set of games in Rio de Janeiro are planned so that good practice can be rolled forward and the bad changed for the better.

In this unit, you will be learning to plan, deliver and review a sports event. Your event will not be on a large scale, but it will have a unique purpose or aim and set of objectives, which should guide you to a successful conclusion. For many people working in the sports industry, planning and running events is commonplace – so the knowledge, skills and challenges presented in this unit will be very valuable.

Learning outcomes

After completing this unit you should:

1. know about different types of sports events
2. know about the roles and responsibilities of people involved in planning and delivering sports events
3. be able to plan and promote a sports event
4. be able to deliver a sports event
5. be able to review the planning and delivery of a sports event.

Assessment and grading criteria

This table shows you what you must do in order to achieve a pass, merit or distinction grade, and where you can find activities in this book to help you.

To achieve a **pass** grade the evidence must show that you are able to:	To achieve a **merit** grade the evidence must show that, in addition to the pass criteria, you are able to:	To achieve a **distinction** grade the evidence must show that, in addition to the pass and merit criteria, you are able to:
P1 describe three different types of sports events, using examples **See Assessment activity 23.1, page 310**		
P2 describe roles and responsibilities of four individuals in planning and delivering sports events **See Assessment activity 23.2, page 313**	**M1** explain four roles and four responsibilities of individuals involved in planning and delivering sports events **See Assessment activity 23.2, page 313**	
P3 plan a sports event, with tutor support **See Assessment activity 23.3, page 319**	**M2** independently plan a sports event **See Assessment activity 23.3, page 319**	
P4 produce material suitable for promoting the sports event **See Assessment activity 23.4, page 321**	**M3** describe the impact of promotional materials on attendance at an event **See Assessment activity 23.4, page 321**	**D1** analyse the impact of promotional materials on an event **See Assessment activity 23.4, page 321**
P5 deliver a sports event, with tutor support, describing own roles and responsibilities **See Assessment activity 23.5, page 323**	**M4** independently deliver a sports event, describing own roles and responsibilities **See Assessment activity 23.5, page 323**	**D2** deliver a sports event, assessing own contribution **See Assessment activity 23.5, page 323**
P6 review the planning and delivery of sports event, identifying strengths and areas for improvement, and making suggestions relating to future personal development **See Assessment activity 23.6, page 326**	**M5** review the planning and delivery of a sports event, explaining identified strengths and areas for improvement and suggestions relating to future personal development **See Assessment activity 23.6, page 326**	**D3** evaluate own performance in the planning and delivery of the event, justifying suggestions relating to future personal development **See Assessment activity 23.6, page 326**

How you will be assessed

You will be assessed for this unit by planning, running and evaluating an event as a project. You could be assessed through:

- a written report or presentation
- evidence in the form of a portfolio
- witness statements, testimonies or observation records.

You may also have to make interim presentations on planning, progress and promotion.

Katarina, 18-year-old netball player

This was a challenging unit. We had to bring our skills and knowledge together to complete the event successfully – it was a girls' netball tournament.

Just getting our ideas into a manageable package was a challenge. I had to learn to listen more to others, while other team members had to learn to speak up and sometimes take charge. We had to remember to keep good records of what we agreed and our tasks and responsibilities. I learned that running an event is a task which needs different skills, attention to detail, handling money, logistics and promotion, being nice to customers and ensuring all goes smoothly. After it was all over we had to assess our contributions, and justify our decisions, especially those that did not go well. I felt that good communication was essential, along with staying calm. Looking back I enjoyed the event unit so much it motivated me to choose a degree in Event Management at university.

Over to you!

1. Can you think of two things that could have spoiled the netball tournament?
2. Katarina didn't mention a venue so what sort of venue do you think would suit a netball tournament best and what facilities would it need to have?

1. Know about different types of sports events

Will your event be a pain or a pleasure?

Planning and running an event can be painful as you plan every detail but pleasurable when people enjoy it. With a partner, create a flow chart to show how you think things should be tackled to stage a sportspersons' award dinner. Compare your flow charts with those of other groups.

1.1 Sports events

The sports industry offers a broad range of events. In this section you will learn about these. You will then explore the many different purposes or aims of events. These may give useful ideas for your event.

Types of event

- **Competition** – probably the most common type of sports event is competition based. This could take the form of a league in which teams compete. This competition is actually composed of many smaller events, i.e. matches. So this first type helps to show that an event can last over a period of time (a season) such as the Champions League.

- **Tournament** – this is a shorter type of competitive sports event, with a much shorter time span, i.e. a knockout tournament lasting a day or two or mini leagues played over a weekend with the top two teams going into a final.

- **Training camps** are also an event. They often have a time span of approximately five days to a week, which represents a medium time span. These types of events are targeted at talented players or athletes and are often residential, with participants staying at a specific centre suited to their sport.

- **Coaching courses** are linked to training camp events. They are run in a similar vein to teach skills and to help people qualify as coaches or match officials. There is a wide variety of coaching events such as level 1 certificates in coaching football, basketball or volleyball.

Why do you think people are so willing to run for charities?

- **Sponsored events** are very common as clubs try to raise funds through all sorts of sporting activities – swimathons, walks and fun runs. Perhaps the most memorable is the London Marathon with many competitors running for charities and generating hundreds of thousands of pounds in sponsorship. The scale of events can vary from a small local one to a very large national event.

- **Field trips** are events that you are probably familiar with. Schools and colleges regularly organise these for students so that they can learn about their subject in new locations. These types of events with children need safety checks and parental permission.

- **Outdoor education events** are one step up from a field visit. Your first introduction to the environment of rivers, countryside or forests might have been during an outdoor education trip. These types of events often involve outdoor activities such as introductions to sailing, climbing or canoeing. Some events can be challenging.

- **Expeditions** represent a much more serious outdoor event with a journey as the basis and extensive planning and logistics beforehand (with a longer term planning time span). There will be varied means of transport and the likelihood that you must be self-sufficient while on the move. Expeditions tend to be to more remote places with an element of challenge, for example, in the jungle or mountainous areas.

Take it further

Training camps

Carry out some online research to identify two types of training camps you could attend to improve your skills in a specific sport (for example, during half-term). What other benefits might come from these types of events?

Purpose

Events have a variety of purposes. They can:

- educate
- raise environmental awareness
- aid personal development
- foster **social inclusion**
- raise funds
- give enjoyment (participant focused).

Key term

Social inclusion – trying to involve those who are not really engaged with society (they are excluded to some extent).

Educational events for PE teachers are very common – such as one day conferences. It is likely that organisers will have to advertise what the aims and objectives are for the event in order to attract delegates. Typical objectives linked to sport might be:

- to introduce pupils to the safety procedures at sports stadiums
- to attract 50 pupils to a talk by a famous sports person
- to raise awareness of the dangers of drug taking in sport.

Environmental awareness events – the drive to raise our awareness of global warming and dwindling resources has brought many such events to the fore, for example, a clean up campaign for a local sports venue or park. There is pressure to make events sustainable and green in their nature by encouraging spectators to walk or cycle to an event or to use energy saving bulbs for lighting.

Developmental events can:

- foster physical benefits such as walking to health
- encourage socialisation, for example, making new friends at an over 60s bowling event
- boost personal skills and confidence amongst people who are trying an activity at an event for the first time.

Social inclusion events – many people do not have good access to sport facilities or resources. They may lack confidence or money to join a club so free or taster events encourage social inclusion.

Fundraising events – it is very likely that you have taken part in a fundraising event. The grass roots of sport in this country are small clubs playing week after week on low budgets and run by volunteers. Fundraisers are annual events to keep the club running, for example, a sponsored walk or car wash or a raffle.

Participant focused events are staged to give people a good time or for them to enjoy their sport with others. A good example of this would be a family orienteering event, so that each age group can take part. Another would be a school ski trip which gives the options of snowboarding or skiing and classes for each participant. Participants can gain a lot before their event by researching the location online and then keep it alive in their memories afterwards by taking lots of photographs and perhaps having a reunion night.

In order to help you understand the range of events that you might run, carry out some research into three different types of sports events and prepare a short report describing each of them. If each person in your group does this you will have a fair range to choose from. **P1**

Grading tip

- To attain **P1** try to give an insight into the planning of the events as well as what is needed to run them. You might observe an event in action or search online and in textbooks and magazines for likely examples.

PLTS

When you research and describe your three different types of sports events there will be opportunities to show your skills as an **independent enquirer**.

Functional skills

ICT opportunities exist to use graphics to display images or text. Use of written **English** will come through when you type or present your work and aspects of speaking and listening when you discuss issues with your team mates.

2. Know about the roles and responsibilities of people involved in planning and delivering sports events

2.1 Roles

Each person in your event team will have to take on tasks to ensure that the event runs smoothly. These tasks are usually grouped under headings, which in turn give the roles for people in the team. These roles are usually organised and presented in a structure diagram.

Some possible roles for your event team are summed up in Figure 23.1.

These roles usually have some specific aspects to them as shown below.

- **Coordinator** – this person coordinates the operational side of the event planning and preparation, i.e. specific tasks and responsibilities. It is best if they do not undertake too many tasks of their own so that they can take an overview of the project. They will be in charge on the day and coordinate evaluation and clear up.

- **Chairperson** – this person often has two roles: the first is internal, as they chair and organise meetings, and the second is external as they represent the team when dealing with outside organisations, for example, venues or other committees.

- **Secretary** – he or she heads up the administration of an event, taking notes at meetings and dealing with other types of communication such as emails or phone calls. They are often at the heart of communications.

- **Finance officer** – he or she will look after any money the team deals with. They control budgets, record income and spending and balance up at the end.

- **Marketing officer** – he or she looks after the trading and selling opportunities of the event, for example, tickets sales and sponsorship potential.

- **Publicity officer** – this person coordinates how the event is publicised. They work with the marketing person to decide how to attract people to the event.

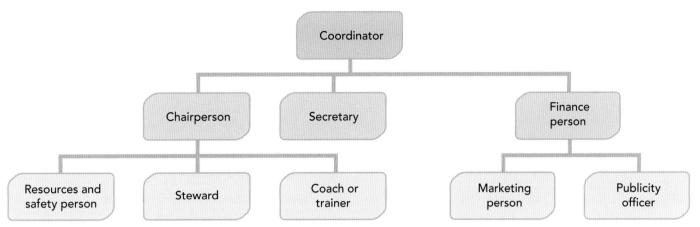

Figure 23.1: An event team structure. The lines connecting the roles show lines of authority and communication. Would this type of structure suit your plans? If not, how would you modify it?

- **Stewards** are often volunteers; they assist participants and/or spectators and direct cars or people as necessary ensuring crowd control and safety.

- **Specialist coaches or trainers** may come in to take sessions focusing on skills, training or tactics. Although a key part of the event, they are not really in the event team and may not know much about the organisational side of things so they will need briefing.

- **Resource and safety manager** – this person ensures the right kind of equipment is in place and that it is safe to use.

2.2 Responsibilities

From the explanation of the roles you can see that some key areas of responsibility can be highlighted. Although all event teams will not have the same roles there are certain aspects of event management that are always present as **responsibilities**.

- **Logistics** – looking after the flow of materials through and to the event (often called the supply chain). This responsibility needs a keen eye for detail and someone able to identify what is needed, when, where and in what quantity.

Key terms

Responsibilities – being accountable for certain tasks and related actions and decisions.

Logistics – establishing good communications and the delivery of resources on time (for example, finance, people or equipment).

- **Equipment** – these are resources such as chairs for spectators, any sports kit, or safety gear. The person responsible for this should be properly trained as there can be a lot of lifting and technical aspects.

- **Health and safety** – perhaps the most important responsibility. (This might even have to be left to an expert.) The team must comply with legislation and codes of practice otherwise, apart from injuring people, you may be accused of **negligence**. Thorough risk assessments are necessary for any event.

- **Liaison** – external and internal communication between the team and groups outside and members of the team. Information needs to be communicated effectively, especially when changes occur that affect others.

Key terms

Negligence – lacking due attention or duty of care which causes loss or injury.

Liaison – working between two parties or more as a communicator.

- **Marketing** – involves working closely with all of the team to devise a marketing plan. This should cover the 4Ps:
  - product (what kind of event)
  - price (of entry)
  - place (where it will be held)
  - promotion (what techniques will be used).

- **Publicity** – working closely with the marketing person (these two areas of responsibility could be combined) to promote the event. A range of techniques could be used – posters, talks, small advertisements, direct emails or texts – even radio and press releases.

- **Raising funds** – if you have no budget then you need to fundraise to provide money for resources and prizes. There are many ways to fundraise. A good sequence is shown in Figure 23.2.

After the event you must evaluate your contributions, i.e. roles and responsibilities. So it is useful at this stage to agree with your team what criteria you will use to do this. Evaluation criteria can be scores for each

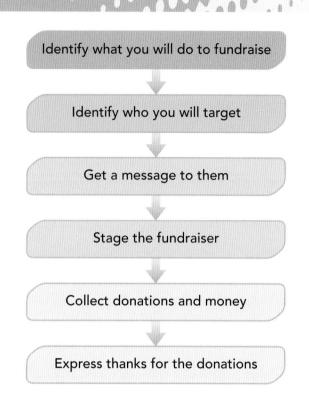

Figure 23.2: What problems might you need to overcome between the stages of the flow chart?

other, ratings against tasks allocated, effectiveness in the role (for example, good/fair/poor) and how well you dealt with your responsibilities.

It would also be very useful, once roles and responsibilities are allocated and agreed, if your team could create a clear job description for each role and its associated responsibilities relevant to your event. That way you will be able to make comparisons before and after the event more effectively.

Activity: Fundraising ideas

The table below shows a range of event fundraising ideas. Can you add two more of your own in each column? Which one do you need a licence for?

Small scale	Medium sized	Large scheme
Raffle	Raffle	Raffle
Table top sale	Fun run or walk	Seeking
Car wash	Donation	sponsorship
Quiz night	of prizes for	Supermarket
	auction	bag packing

Assessment activity 23.2

P2 M1   BTEC

1. Select and describe the roles and responsibilities of four people in an event team who are planning and running sports events. Prepare four slides of these roles with their responsibilities to show to the rest of your group. **P2**
2. Explain the roles and responsibilities of the four individuals. **M1**

Grading tips

- To attain **P2** you could choose four roles that are quite closely related so you can write about their links or four that are very different to show how diverse these can be. You might find some useful examples online. You should also consider relating these to your own forthcoming event.

- To attain **M1** you definitely need to draw together the roles and responsibilities and give much more explanatory detail. You should also consider relating these to your own forthcoming event.

PLTS

You can demonstrate your skills as an **independent enquirer** and **creative thinker** as you research and prepare your findings.

Functional skills

You can provide evidence of your **ICT** skills when you present or type up your findings for the four roles and their associated responsibilities. **English** skills might be generated through discussion and background reading.

3.   Be able to plan and promote a sports event

You could consider the planning and promoting of an event as about 75 per cent of the whole project – so the bulk of your efforts must be focused on preparation.

Remember

Fail to plan and you plan to fail!

3.1 Plan

Aims and objectives

Once you have your basic idea for your event you need to formulate this into an overall aim and its objectives.

The aim is the vision you have for the event (for example, to stage a successful seven-a-side hockey tournament). To gauge how successful you have been you set

objectives which are measurable (for example, attracting eight teams to your tournament). As objectives are key factors in judging your performance after the event, you need a good understanding of them.

- **Profit** – you may set a profit aim but you should set this as a clear objective, perhaps to raise £100 for charity, so you can judge your achievements.
- **Fundraising** may well be the aim, so again set a target for yourselves – maybe £250 to buy new sports kit for your college.
- **Bonding** – although you may not set this as an aim, bonding will inevitably happen as you work closely and, hopefully, in harmony with each other. Bonding usually takes place as people share common goals and build friendships through working together. Sometimes this can make a team stronger if times are tough. (Think of 'I'm a Celebrity Get Me Out Of Here' as an example.)

- **Education** – if you choose an educational aim to help improve people's understanding of something, perhaps small conferences on racism in sport or a drugs awareness campaign. You can set objectives for this by aiming to invite, for example, 30 participants.

- **Environmental awareness** sports events are not very common, but it would be possible to create this in conjunction with a sponsored country walk or cycle event with the objective of getting 50 youngsters to complete the course.

SMART targets

All targets should be quantifiable. There is an accepted way of keeping your objectives under control using the acronym SMART.

Specific: related to the tasks you are doing or the event

Measurable: something quantifiable, for example, tickets sold

Achievable: within the scope of the event (not too ambitious)

Realistic: suits your capabilities and skills

Timed: bound to a set date (you might have deadlines at each stage)

Activity: Setting targets

You should be very clear about targets by now but try this exercise as a test.

- Set three targets for an event team trying to plan a swimming gala.

- Is this an aim or an objective? *To stage a basketball free throw competition for charity.*

- How SMART are plans for a group to hold a training camp, over a weekend, in one month's time, with 80 players attending and sleeping over in the gym, paying £55 each?

Goals

Realistic event planners set several types of goals as targets which relate to the timed aspect of SMART. It is good practice to have goals that help you check that you are on track to achieve your objectives and overall aim. Goals can be:

- Short-term – probably just for a few weeks at most – goals might be set for securing the venue or getting posters made up.

- Medium-term – maybe a month or two – these goals would cover the promotional activities ahead of the event.

- Long-term – these goals would cover the actual event, but might run past in the wind up period as thanks are sent out and a review is undertaken. The best goal may be to run the event again next year!

Resources

One key aspect of planning is to identify what resources will be needed. There are three different types of resources as shown in Table 23.1. It is best to keep a record of these using checklists which can be easily ticked off or amended. Some tips are included in the table to guide you.

Table 23.1: Three different types of resources.

Physical	Relating to logistics and equipment; anything from chairs for spectators to scoreboards for results.
	Tip: hold a whole team meeting to think through these in detail.
Fiscal	Anything financial comes under this heading.
	Tip: put someone in this role who understands income, expenditure, profit, budgets, and how to keep records and spending under control.
Human	Four categories; yourself, staff and other professionals, participants and volunteers.
	Tip: choose people with good communication skills to look after this side of organisation.

Key terms

Fiscal – anything to do with finance or the money aspects of an event.

Feasibility – the act of assessing whether something can work or needs changing.

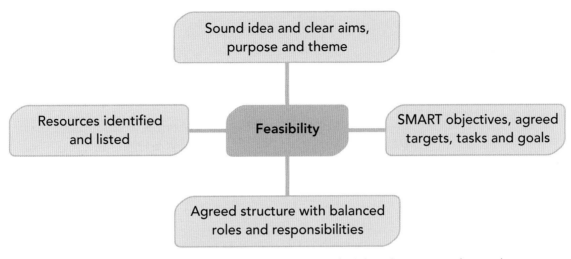

Figure 23.3: Feasibility tests – where any of these are not satisfied then the team needs to make adjustments or do more work to meet them. If, for example, your feasibility assessment found that some people were doing more than others, how could you re-balance this?

Feasibility

By the time you have formulated your aim and objectives, and identified the resources that you will need, you should be able to begin to judge how feasible your initial plans are. This is a key short-term goal. It is at this point that a meeting should be held to assess **feasibility** with all team members contributing their data, knowledge or research findings. The outcome might mean that you have to adjust your parameters, reduce your objectives or re-plan resources, so be flexible and make adjustments to the overall plan. The feasibility assessment should cover aspects shown in Figure 23.3 at this stage.

If your plans are sound then you can move on to the next phases of planning and add more detail.

Health and safety

Assessing health, safety and security for the event is an essential task. The basis for doing this is called risk assessment.

- **Risk assessment** can be done in six easy stages, as shown in the cycle in Figure 23.4. (You will find the Health & Safety Executive materials useful in Student Book 1, Unit 3 Assessing risk in sport.)

You need to understand some key terminology and processes attached to risk assessment at each stage.

- A hazard is anything that can cause harm (such as cables left un-taped on a floor).
- Groups at a sports event could be participants, parents, staff and helpers.
- 'Likelihood' means 'probability of it happening' – you can use a scale from 1 to 5 to judge this (1 being little chance and 5 being very likely). At sports events you could consider that an injury of some sort is very likely to happen and give it a 5. This would apply to participants.
- Severity can be rated in the same way using a scale from 1 to 5 (with 1 as minor, up to 5 as very serious). So for a sport event a broken limb would rate a 5. This would apply to participants.
- An overall assessment with two 5s would mean that rigorous safety measures needed to be in place at the event for participants.
- Safety measures for the injury could include having first-aiders on duty, an extensive first-aid kit and possibly an ambulance on standby (but at the very least emergency numbers should be known by all organisers so they can call for assistance).

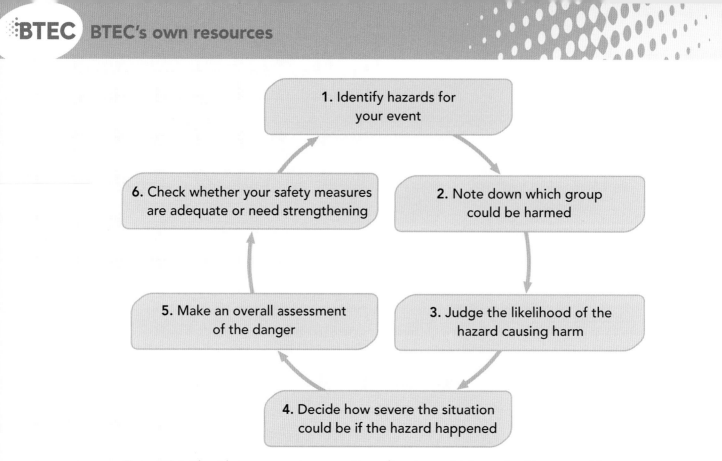

Figure 23.4: The risk management process. How often do you think you should reassess risk or hazards and review measures taken?

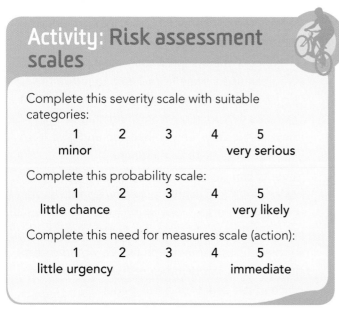

Activity: Risk assessment scales

Complete this severity scale with suitable categories:

1	2	3	4	5
minor				very serious

Complete this probability scale:

1	2	3	4	5
little chance				very likely

Complete this need for measures scale (action):

1	2	3	4	5
little urgency				immediate

- **First-aid cover** – you are required by law to provide first-aid cover at any event open to the public. You can consult a professional for advice on this or look up Health and Safety (First-aid) Regulations (1981). The basic requirements for any event would be that the equipment and facilities are adequate and appropriate for the circumstances, and that first-aid is readily available for anyone that is injured or becomes ill.

- **Informed consent** – if children under 18 are involved in your event then you will have to create a parental consent form like the one in Figure 23.5 (schools and colleges usually have a standard format for these). You should ask to see this and check that it will cover your planned event, i.e. for insurance, behaviour, emergency aid and possibly photography.

- **Other legislation** you may have to comply with will be determined by the type of event you are running. Here are a few examples you might need to be aware of and some of the contexts in which they might apply:

  o Management of Health & Safety at Work – any general contexts in or around a sports building

  o Control of Substances Hazardous to Health – for example, pool or cleaning chemicals

  o Reporting of Diseases and Dangerous Occurrences – contagious illnesses (e.g. swine flu) or accidents

  o Electrical regulations – to ensure power is safe and equipment is PAT tested

  o Safety at sports grounds including fire safety – for crowd and fire control

  o Personal protective clothing – if helmets, gloves or overalls are needed

---

Parental consent form

Roxham RFC *Fun Run*

To be signed by parent or guardian of all entrants under the age of 18

Please sign and return this form for the entry of every fun runner under 18 years of age taking part in the Fun Run event

I, _____, the parent or guardian of _____,

who was born on _____,

AGREE to his/her participation in the event and DECLARE that:
1. I understand and agree that my son/daughter participates in event, entirely at his/her own risk.
2. My son/daughter is able to take full responsibility for his/her own safety while taking part in this event.

Signed: _____   Date: _____

Figure 23.5: It is important that parents read the small print as the most important information lies there. What might be missing from this form in terms of medical care?

- Manual handling – to guide anyone who has to lift heavy kit or equipment
- Occupier's **liability** – if you rent premises
- Food hygiene – if you plan to serve food and soft drinks
- Licensing and gambling – if you will have a raffle or music
- Adventure activities – if your event is adventurous by nature
- Consumer protection – if you are selling goods.

This list clearly has links to other units and risk assessment, for example, Student Book 1, Unit 3 Assessing risk in sport. At this stage in your planning you will have a heightened awareness of things that could go wrong, so it is time to make some plans to cope with this.

The best way to try and identify problems that might occur is for each person to consider these under their roles and responsibilities and make a list. The whole team should then meet to discuss potential problems and then go on to agree what plans could be made to cope. This is called contingency planning.

Contingency plans

Contingency plans might be needed if, for example:

- **the weather** was bad (not just for participants but for spectators too)
- **an accident** occurred (if this happens at your event you will need measures to deal with it)
- **resources** prove to be a problem (there could be range of issues here such as a key performer not turning up, not enough equipment or maybe the financial problem of an overspent budget)

For bad weather you could consider having an indoor venue on standby or an alternative date lined up. First-aid must be on hand for accidents. Contingency plans for the resource issues outlined above could include having a backup performer on call, always having a spare set of equipment close by and not allowing anyone to spend without the treasurer's approval.

Key terms

Liability – being legally obliged or responsible for something.

Contingency – a possible, but not very likely, future occurrence.

Legal considerations

As well as the legislation highlighted above there are a number of other legal considerations which could apply and which all have implications, for example, being found negligent, having liability for something getting broken, **copyright infringement** by using images or text you don't own or not meeting **contractual obligations**. You need to ask someone to check these areas for your event as contravention of any of them can have serious outcomes.

Key terms

Copyright infringement – not having the right to use or publish something.

Contractual obligations – agreement to deliver or do something.

One other legal consideration which might affect your event could be child protection legislation. This is needed to ensure that adults working with children are checked for a criminal record (CRB checks). The Criminal Records Bureau is run by the Home Office and processes applications from people who wish to work with children or vulnerable young adults. The principle behind this legislation is to protect young people from being exploited or abused by adults whose care they are in. So, for example, if your event was targeted at young people, any adults involved would need to have a CRB check specifically for the event. This is called a vetting process.

Activity: Child protection

Carry out some research on the Sport England or NSPCC websites to find out what best practice is with regard to child protection from their points of view.

Other considerations

A range of other considerations may help you cover situations which might apply to your event.

- **Environment** – if your event makes particular use of the environment then you will need to ensure that you 'leave no trace', i.e. litter is picked up (and recycled), excessive noise is not created and traffic fumes or congestion are minimised.

- **Code of ethics** – it is important that you apply a **code of ethics** to your event so that:
  - no one is discriminated against
  - standards follow national governing body guidelines, for example, the FA charter standard
  - everyone attending respects the participants and coaches.

  You might consider having everyone sign a code of conduct. If you do, ensure this is part of their entry form.

- **Own organisational/institutional policies and guidelines** – your institution or organisation will have its own **policies** and guidelines that you should follow. Make sure that you familiarise yourself with these. If you are in doubt about anyone's conduct, invite some staff to oversee the event or to give a welcome talk that mentions these guidelines.

Key terms

Code of ethics – a set of principles for the fairest way of doing things, i.e. with respect.

Policies – a plan of action, usually from an authoritative source that must be followed.

Assessment activity 23.3

P3 M2 BTEC

Most professional event teams will create an event manual (portfolio) with appropriate sections for each of the planning elements. That is your task too.

1. Create a portfolio, with the support of your tutor, which clearly shows the components of planning you have agreed upon for your event. Sections are given below to guide you:

   - An overview giving theme, aims and objectives and any specific targets or goals.
   - A resources section specifying financial plans, physical resource lists and sources, people involved with roles and responsibilities (including your team).
   - Risk assessments for health, safety and security and notes of which legislation you need to comply with and measures/processes in place to cover these.
   - Contingency plans for predictable contingencies.

   - Other considerations specific to your event such as environmental, children, conduct guidelines and licences. **P3**

2. Carry out this task without the support of your tutor. **M2**

Grading tips

- To attain **P3** you could obtain guidance from guest speakers or event managers as well as your tutor. A workshop could help your team prepare. As well as the contents specified above the portfolio should contain notes or minutes from meetings, checklists, action points and verification of tasks done. This is a comprehensive document so pay attention to detail throughout.

- To attain **M2** you must tackle this independently.

PLTS

You will demonstrate your skills as an **independent enquirer** when you carry out research to assess feasibility and as a **reflective learner** when you make changes based on reflection. Prove your skills as a **team worker** as you collaborate with others.

Functional skills

Demonstrate your **ICT** skills as you prepare and type up your plans and your **English** skills as you draft lists and prepare documents and discuss plans with colleagues.

3.2 Promote

With plans in place you should be confident to launch your publicity for the event.

Table 23.2: Types of promotional material.

Material

Part of your planning will have been a marketing plan so you must decide on the materials and media you will use to publicise your event. There are some guidelines in Table 23.2.

Publicity	Purpose
Create a small advertisement	For a newspaper or school magazine Many small events teams create a Facebook site and use this to contact and attract their friends
Compose a poster	To go on college walls or noticeboards or at the venue you will use
Design some neat flyers (or leaflets)	To hand out to classes or your friends and family – these could be your tickets too
Prepare a press release	For your local paper to feature (free)
Write a script to use on local radio or television	Use this so you can be interviewed as an organiser. If you raise money for charity (for example, Children in Need) you might even feature on regional TV.

Purpose

You must always keep in mind the purpose of your promotion and ensure that it is accurate. It should inform your customers as shown below:

- the date of the event (for participants)
- the time it will start and in some cases when it will finish (for parents)
- the location of the venue – address, telephone number, perhaps a small map (for spectators, VIPs or the press)
- the cost – to enter, to spectate or if people can buy things.

Take it further

Flyer layout

Using an A4 sheet, sketch out a possible layout for your flyer, including the information above.

Theme

You should use your promotional material to reinforce the event's theme. This will link to the type of event you have chosen, perhaps raising awareness of a charity, or raising funds, or raising health and fitness levels, competitive elements or fun themes. These themes should be part of your aims and form part of your final review to ascertain if they were successfully achieved.

Remember

If you are promoting it, you need to put plans in place to achieve it and interim targets to show your progress – or lack of it.

Impact

The impact of your promotional work and materials is crucial to the success of your event. It needs to be effective enough to bring the benefits you want for your event such as an attractive image. It will have to be enticing enough to attract participants, especially if there is something else on at the same time that they might go to instead or if you are charging for entry (which could represent a barrier for some). The material will have to sell benefits to the potential participants (for example, a chance to improve their skills). Above all, you want people to leave the event saying things like 'It was great! It really lived up to my expectations. When are you doing the next one?' Sure signs that you did a great job! Real event organisers would hope to be asked back – this is called repeat business.

Hopefully, your event will have a positive impact on all who are concerned. It might help your event if you can promote these impacts in your materials and proposals. Some ideas are shown in Figure 23.6.

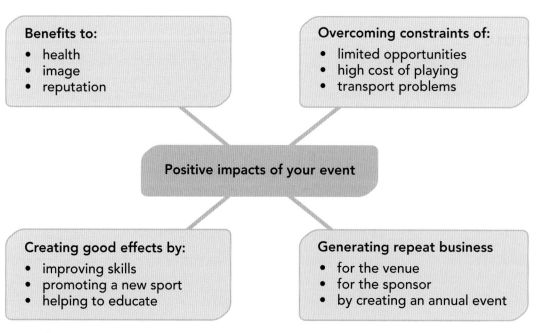

Figure 23.6: Can you think of two more positive impacts?

Activity: Professional practice

Before you finalise your plans, visit a few of these event management company websites to learn how they tackle their large scale events. There might be some themes and style factors in there for you to pick up on. Several include case studies which you might be able to adopt or adapt.

- www.europeanevents.co.uk
- www.fire-events.com
- www.eco.co.uk
- www.sxsevents.co.uk
- www.redlolly.co.uk
- www.revolution-events.com
- www.eclipseglobalevents.com

Assessment activity 23.4

P4 M3 D1 **BTEC**

1. Produce a portfolio of materials suitable for promoting your sports event. **P4**

2. Describe the impact of your promotional materials on attendance at the event. You could use a report format. **M3**

3. Produce a report to analyse the impacts of your promotional materials on the event. **D1**

Grading tips

- To attain **P4** design a small flyer which has the essential information for your customers (date, time, venue and cost), a larger poster to attract customers, an advertisement to go in the college newspaper/website and a press release describing the event.

- To attain **M3** describe the likely benefits to those attending, any constraints the event might help to overcome or which it might have itself, what effect the promotion might have on the target group and the impacts for the institution or host organisation.

- To help attain **D1** remember that the impact analysis could be both positive and negative.

PLTS

As you devise the content of your promotional materials you can display your skills as a **creative thinker**, as a **reflective learner** as you reflect and make changes, as a **team worker** as you collaborate with your team, as a **self-manager** when you meet deadlines, and as an **effective participator** throughout.

Functional skills

You have the opportunity to display your **ICT** skills as you compile the marketing materials and your skills in **English** as you discuss your plans.

4. Be able to deliver a sports event

With all your planning time over, in the last few days before the event you and your team need to mentally rehearse or practice (have a dry run) any aspects you can to ensure everyone knows their part. One technique to help with this is visualisation – try to think/imagine the whole event as you hope it would run, from start to finish in your mind. Make notes of things that you do not think are ready yet. Make sure you have some methods in place to assess what your participants thought of the event, for example, customer surveys, to help with your reviewing.

4.1 Delivery

Take it further

Arrange a talk

Ask your tutor to invite an event organiser in to talk your through delivery or arrange a visit to an event venue and receive a talk from an organiser there.

Table 23.3: A checklist of reminders for the day.

On the day of the event

✓ Make sure you have a note of your **roles and responsibilities** to refer to in case things get very busy and you get stretched. You can use this for reviewing later too.

✓ It is a good idea to have a flip chart in your base room or at reception where the whole team can see it restating your **aims and objectives** as a reminder and motivator. At some point before people arrive get everyone together for a pep talk and to wish each other good luck. Build on your bonding.

✓ Keep in mind your **targets and goals**. Know how close you are to achieving them – they might also go on your reminder sheets. Keep records of numbers for all the categories, for example, tickets sold, entries, participants, spectators.

✓ You should make a final check on **resources** the day before the event, to give you some time if there is a shortfall. Always have some spares, especially if something is crucial to the event such as a scoreboard or a laptop or a referee.

✓ Carry out a final **risk assessment** in the hours before the event and make sure nothing changes to affect this and the measures in place.

During the event

✓ Keep considering **health and safety** and security as the event takes place. Observation is key here – if you see a hazard, fix it or find someone who can. (That's a legal requirement.)

✓ If a **contingency** arises, use the plans you have made to deal with a number of scenarios that could occur when delivering your event. Be decisive and take control – it reassures people that you know what you are doing.

✓ The glue that will hold your event together is **communication**. Keep everyone informed. You could even consider using radios, texts or other means to stay in touch if you are likely to be far apart or isolated or if it is noisy.

✓ Keep in mind **legal considerations** – you must stay within the law. Remind yourselves of your duty of care for participants, the policies you have to follow or codes of practice. You, your tutor or your institution can be found negligent – be safe, not sorry.

✓ Good coordination and **decision-making** will mean that your team deals decisively with any issues. Quick decision-making means you will need to rapidly evaluate the situation, assess what alternatives you could choose and settle on a decision that suits the situation best.

✓ Above all try to show **competence and care** in what you do. If you have practised, and if your planning has been effective, this will shine through. Shaky plans and poor problem solving will lead to disaster.

✓ Ensure that you look after the **wellbeing** of your team, yourself, and your visitors using good customer care principles.

Case study: When things go wrong

A group of five university students planned to stage an event for rag week on their campus. They thought up the idea of holding a rodeo night in the bar. They quickly booked the bar for six weeks ahead, booked a rodeo machine from a supplier who said they would set it all up and have an engineer there all night. It all sounded good. They paid a printer to make them some tickets and promoted the night by going round the campus and classes dressed up as cowboys and cowgirls.

Most people they spoke to said they would come (but none bought tickets at £5). Meanwhile the group went round local shops to ask for donations of prizes for the night's raffle.

One week before the event the bar said it had forgotten it had another function already booked and asked if they could change the night. The group agreed.

On the rearranged day the engineer came and tried to fit up the apparatus, but it was too big for the bar and had to be squeezed in close to some seating.

On the night it rained heavily, so few people came. The group made a loss. They couldn't sell their raffle tickets as they had forgotten to get a licence.

1. **Troubleshoot the event and say what the students could have done better in terms of bookings, set up, pricing, ticketing and legality.**

Assessment activity 23.5   P5 M4 D2   BTEC

1. Using tutor support, deliver a sports event. Describe the tasks, roles and responsibilities allocated. **P5**

2. Independently deliver a sports event, describing tasks, roles and responsibilities. **M4**

3. Deliver a sports event, assessing your own contribution. **D2**

Grading tips

- To attain **P5** complete a log or diary which describes or assesses your completion of roles, responsibilities and contributions from the planning through to the delivery of the event. (If you created some feedback sheets earlier you can use this material too.)

- To attain **M4** ensure you deliver the event without support (though plans might need approval).

- To attain **D2** you could evaluate how you coped with logistics, use of equipment, health and safety, communication, finance, targets, contingencies, ethics, sticking to plans and policies, dealing with customers and colleagues or others.

PLTS

You can hone your skills as a **self-manager** as you prepare your log and as an **independent enquirer** when you carry out research to assess feedback. Your skill as a **reflective learner** will grow as you make judgements based on reflection and notes and you can demonstrate your skills as an **effective participator** throughout.

Functional skills

You will use your **ICT** skills when you prepare and type up your logbook and your **English** skills when you discuss outcomes and feedback.

5. Be able to review the planning and delivery of a sports event

Being able to review your planning and delivery is crucial. It is called being a reflective practitioner and shows that you can analyse what went well and what could be improved. This needs to be an honest process that you and your team do thoroughly. The reviewing process should be objective and will draw mainly from the factual evidence for which evidence can be provided. This is preferable to drawing on personal opinions or anecdotes which can be rather subjective.

Now that your event is over (and let's hope it was successful) you need to review your performance, as all professional teams do. If you have been really well organised, you will have collected a range of feedback before, during and after the event. On pages 311 and 312 guidance was given on to how to collate this and what to assess. These are sometimes called key performance indicators or **KPIs**. This section will take you through the review process.

Key term

KPIs – key performance indicators – criteria showing how well something has performed.

5.1 Review

Event teams want customers to take away great memories and to say how good the company was that organised it. It could mean a repeat booking or a recommendation to other clients – those are the plusses. On the negative side, if things went wrong they need to be picked up and changes made so that the problem is not repeated. In this case it may be important to follow up the problems quickly with apologies or refunds so that clients can be satisfied in some way.

'Strike while the iron is hot' is the phrase to remember at this stage.

Reviewing the planning of the event

The review process requires you to evaluate how effective the planning process was in reality. In other words – were the actual outcomes those that your team planned?

To guide this evaluation here is a reminder of what your planning should have covered and some guidance on how to evaluate the outcomes. It is important to assess why results came out as they did throughout this process.

- Aims and objectives – were these met, not met or exceeded?
- Achievement of targets – if your team had short-, medium- or long-term planning goals, were these met, not met or exceeded? You might also evaluate if the group worked in harmony all the time towards these, identifying highs and lows.
- Resource needs – were these adequate or inadequate? Where a shortfall occurred, why was this? Subheadings could be used under this category to help you pinpoint some other important aspects such as equipment or budgets. Did you also have enough resources to ensure the wellbeing of others?
- Feasibility – which estimates were correct and worked well, which came out as underestimates or overestimates and what did you not cover at all? Subheadings could be used under this category to help you pinpoint some other important aspects such as considerations of health, safety and security.
- Contingency plans – were these needed? If so, did they work and how well or were they failures for your event? Subheadings could be used under this category to help you pinpoint some other important aspects such as decision-making and problem solving.
- Legal considerations – did you comply with all legislation effectively or was something missed and did this have an impact?
- Other considerations – did you meet environmental targets and follow guidelines or codes? Did you communicate effectively?

Reviewing the delivery of the event

The second area for review is your performance, i.e. what you delivered in terms of your roles and responsibilities. It was suggested earlier that you keep accurate records so that you can carry this out by rating or scoring yourself against targets and goals. Use your logbook or diary for this. Professional events organisers would use this review process to guide their personal and staff development, as it may give material for discussion at an appraisal or show gaps in knowledge and skills that require training or upgrading.

There are three key areas to focus on for your review: attainment of goals, development opportunities and potential barriers to development.

- **Attainment of goals** – from a personal point of view (and for assessment purposes) you can review these aspects from a few angles. First of all for personal satisfaction, second to identify what you were good at for future reference (or maybe your CV) and third so that others can judge your capabilities.

- **Development opportunities** – out of this process will come some useful feedback which you can use to help you develop. The positives will give you opportunities to develop your potential and the negatives (hopefully few) will help you understand what you need to work on and what the main barriers could be.

- Professional teams will give each other candid feedback about their roles and responsibilities, as well as using customer feedback. All of this makes them a stronger team as they share their views and assessments.

  The feedback you and your team mates gathered needs to be reviewed. This can be **formative**, which means it was taken early and allowed you time to improve, or **summative** feedback which is taken after the event. Both can be based on questionnaires, witness statements, peer comments or customer surveys. Your group should work through this material and data to extract points for the team, the event and individuals where possible.

Based on the findings you should be able to identify your strengths, where attainment was good or excellent and areas for improvement, where attainment was poor or just satisfactory. This process should then lead on to you as an individual and your team mates identifying development opportunities and issues. This can be formulated into a SWOT analysis.

You could represent these quite easily in tables, such as Table 23.5 shown below.

- **Barriers to development** – some simple barriers are given in Table 23.5 but many others could exist (not all in one person). You might consider some of the following would apply to yourself or others in your team (you will of course need evidence for your claim): lack of confidence when speaking to customers, not very well organised, untidy and often late, not a good leader, not a good follower, weak IT skills, needs things explaining a lot. Perhaps by now you will have noticed that many of these barriers relate to the personal, learning and thinking skills, and also the functional skills, that feature in all units. This would give you good source for comparison. Remember weaknesses need remedies so don't forget to suggest these in your review later.

Key terms

Formative – in this case gathering of data as you learn, to help you improve.

Summative – in this case gathering of data at the end of the process, to see how well you have done or how much you have improved.

Table 23.4: Identifying strengths and areas for improvement.

Strengths	Evidence	Areas for improvement	Evidence
Positive attitude	Customer comments	Concern for health and safety	Tutor observation
Met deadlines	Team feedback	Poor communications	Self evidence from log (felt quite shy with participants)

Table 23.5: Identifying development opportunities and barriers to development.

Development opportunities	How to action	Barriers to development	How to overcome
Improve knowledge of safety factors in sport	Background reading or take a short course	Shyness	Do some activities to build confidence with new people
Good with marketing ideas	Think of this as a career option	Need to develop listening skills	Practise in group situations

If you wish to check the quality and depth of your review of planning and delivery, you can use the reminders in this checklist.

- Aim(s) – was it/they achieved? What evidence do you have?
- Objectives – were they achieved fully or just partially? Give some statistics.
- Health and safety – did the event go smoothly or did accidents happen and were these recorded?

- Legalisation and policy guidelines – did your team follow these and if not why not?
- Were you required to initiate any contingency plans – did they work?
- Did any other considerations spoil the event and could they have been avoided?

Conclude your review with some recommendations for the future for you, your team and event delivery.

Assessment activity 23.6   P6 M5 D3   BTEC

Carry out a review of your event to cover the following in report or presentation format.

1. Review the planning and delivery of your sports event, identifying strengths and areas for improvement, and making suggestions relating to future personal development. **P6**

2. Review the planning and delivery of your sports event, explaining identified strengths and areas for improvement and suggestions relating to future personal development. **M5**

3. Evaluate your own performance in the planning and delivery of the event, justifying suggestions relating to future personal development. **D3**

Grading tips

- To attain **P6** use factual evidence as much as possible to assess the strengths and weaknesses in the requirements of the planning and delivery sections. Use feedback evidence to assess whether the event was delivered well. Ensure your suggestions for future personal development are realistic.

- To attain **M5** where possible supplement your explanations of strengths and weaknesses with charts or tables showing supporting evidence for your assertions or evaluation. Photographic evidence of the event might also be of value. Ensure your suggestions for future personal development are achievable.

- To attain **D3**, if you have created an effective portfolio for your event and log for yourself, there should be plenty of raw data for you to evaluate your own performance. Ensure that the suggestions you make for future personal development are SMART and justify each proposal you make.

PLTS

Demonstrate your skills as an **independent enquirer** as you seek feedback about performance to identify strengths and areas for improvement. You will be an **effective team worker** as you work with your team to review the event. Finally, you will show your skills as a **reflective learner** when you make recommendations for future performance.

Functional skills

You will be using your **ICT** skills as you draw up your SWOT charts and your **English** skills when you discuss evaluations of your performance.

James Hall
Event manager

James Hall is an event manager at a rugby club in Scarborough. In the run up to Christmas he will often manage several events simultaneously on the pitches and in the halls of the venue. In 2009 these included a 7-a-side floodlit tournament, a children's nativity play with the players acting the roles, corporate Christmas parties in the function suite, a sponsored rowing night in the gym for players' wives, a junior disco and a New Year's day first team fixture, followed by a huge party.

'Although I've built up my planning and personal skills over the years as an event manager, I still need the support of a group of other professionals who bring technical, marketing and customer care skills to the team, to manage such a diverse programme. Together we can then ensure that everything is in place, everyone is briefed and all goes smoothly. That includes guiding all the casual staff needed to support the various events, such as caterers and stewards, plus VIP guests, other visitors and visiting players.

I am usually the overall coordinator and have to make sure that logistics and equipment are ordered in time, all health and safety issues are covered, promotional materials go out on time and ticket sales are on target. I also have to be chief troubleshooter for each event, so my problem-solving and decision-making powers are tested regularly as every audience brings its own challenges and contingencies.

With such a busy and diverse schedule I usually take a bit of break after this peak part of the season, but not before the team sits down and reviews their performance, picking up on what went well and what needs improving for next year's events.

For me the cycle of events will begin again in late January as we plan for the Six Nations international rugby which is shown on television, a popular Valentine's night dance, the regular fixtures for five teams and the fast approaching Easter 7s events. There is rarely a dull moment in sports event management!'

Think about it!

- How many aspects can you pick out that would be common to any sports event?
- Discuss whether it is more important to have a good leader or be in a great team.
- What aspects/criteria do you think James and his team use when they review an event? Can you list five?

Just checking

1. Name three outdoor types of events which have three different purposes.
2. Who is most likely to look after the money for an event?
3. What is the main role of the coordinator?
4. List three possible promotional techniques for a sports event.
5. What is the difference between an aim and an objective?
6. What does feasibility test?
7. What do contingency plans help with?
8. Explain what legislation means.
9. Give three ways in which you could gather feedback.
10. What is the main point of a review?

edexcel

Assignment tips

- Try at some stage to get a guest speaker to give an input to help your planning and running plans.
- Don't forget to keep a detailed portfolio containing as much evidence as possible for each stage – planning, running and evaluation – this will help your assignment work enormously.
- If you are aiming for the merit and distinction grades you will have to work independently, so be very clear about your objectives and capabilities.
- Some knowledge from other units is likely to come into this one so think of other units you have completed that might help.
- Structure your notes carefully as you can bring in a lot of evidence, not just for the unit, but towards personal, learning and thinking skills and functional skills as this unit has an applied approach.
- Keep everything SMART throughout the planning, running and evaluation!

24 Physical education and the care of children and young people

Have you ever heard the phrase 'a healthy mind in a healthy body'? This has been the foundation for the development of Physical Education (PE) and provides you with a basic understanding of how PE can benefit young people, both throughout school and in later life. PE helps children learn about their capabilities, their potential and their limitations and forms the foundation of all sports participation. PE helps children understand themselves and learn how to work with, and to respect, others. PE is now recognised as having important implications for wider society as well as for academic achievement.

Throughout this unit, you will learn about the structure of PE within the curriculum and will develop an understanding of the importance of PE within society. You will then progress to learning about lesson planning in PE and will finish the unit looking at key information relating to safeguarding yourself and children/young people in sport.

Learning outcomes

After completing this unit you should:

1. know the structure of physical education within the curriculum
2. understand the importance of physical education in society
3. be able to structure a lesson of physical education
4. know the responsibilities of those who work with children to safeguard and promote their welfare, and strategies for safeguarding children, young people and self.

Assessment and grading criteria

This table shows you what you must do in order to achieve a pass, merit or distinction grade, and where you can find activities in this book to help you.

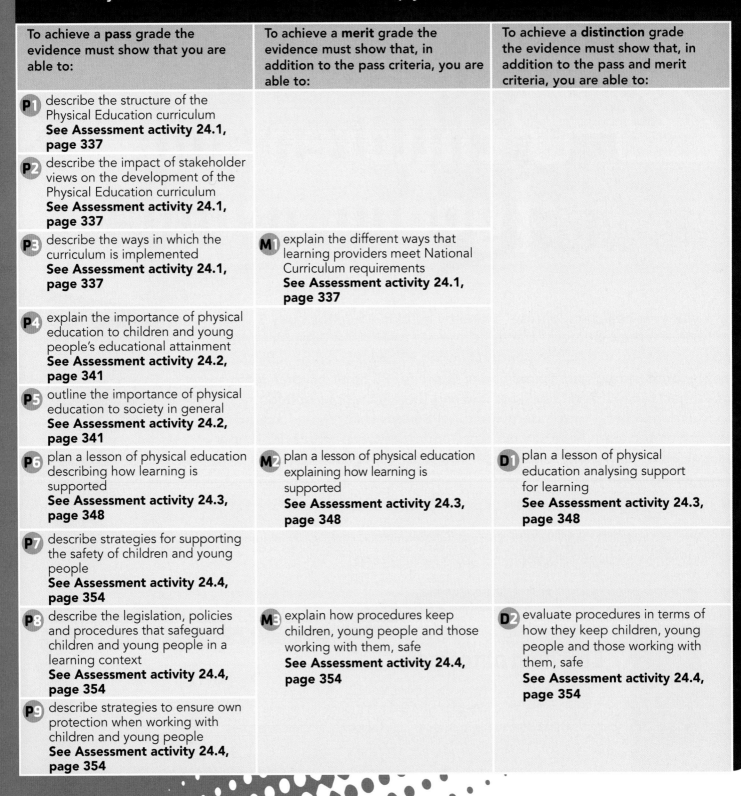

To achieve a **pass** grade the evidence must show that you are able to:	To achieve a **merit** grade the evidence must show that, in addition to the pass criteria, you are able to:	To achieve a **distinction** grade the evidence must show that, in addition to the pass and merit criteria, you are able to:
P1 describe the structure of the Physical Education curriculum **See Assessment activity 24.1, page 337**		
P2 describe the impact of stakeholder views on the development of the Physical Education curriculum **See Assessment activity 24.1, page 337**		
P3 describe the ways in which the curriculum is implemented **See Assessment activity 24.1, page 337**	**M1** explain the different ways that learning providers meet National Curriculum requirements **See Assessment activity 24.1, page 337**	
P4 explain the importance of physical education to children and young people's educational attainment **See Assessment activity 24.2, page 341**		
P5 outline the importance of physical education to society in general **See Assessment activity 24.2, page 341**		
P6 plan a lesson of physical education describing how learning is supported **See Assessment activity 24.3, page 348**	**M2** plan a lesson of physical education explaining how learning is supported **See Assessment activity 24.3, page 348**	**D1** plan a lesson of physical education analysing support for learning **See Assessment activity 24.3, page 348**
P7 describe strategies for supporting the safety of children and young people **See Assessment activity 24.4, page 354**		
P8 describe the legislation, policies and procedures that safeguard children and young people in a learning context **See Assessment activity 24.4, page 354**	**M3** explain how procedures keep children, young people and those working with them, safe **See Assessment activity 24.4, page 354**	**D2** evaluate procedures in terms of how they keep children, young people and those working with them, safe **See Assessment activity 24.4, page 354**
P9 describe strategies to ensure own protection when working with children and young people **See Assessment activity 24.4, page 354**		

How you will be assessed

This unit will be assessed by internal assignments that will be designed and marked by the tutors at your centre. Your assessments could be in the form of:

- written reports
- posters
- presentations
- lesson plans
- information leaflets.

Sophie, 17-year-old sport student

I found this unit really valuable as I want to become a PE teacher when I'm older. This has given me a really good insight into how you can run PE lessons at different levels and what are the best ways of running different lessons with different groups.

The part that I have enjoyed the most was the PE lessons. It was really good planning and taking part in lots of different lessons – I think that it will have been good practice for me. I'm hoping to go to university to study PE so this will be really useful for me if I have to do anything like this as part of my interview. I also really enjoyed looking at the different learning styles as it helped me to appreciate my preferred learning style and this has helped me to change the way I work a little bit.

Over to you!

1. What are you looking forward to learning about in this unit?
2. How do you think this unit will benefit you?
3. What do you think you will need to do to prepare for this unit?

1. Know the structure of physical education within the curriculum

1.1 Structure

Early Years Foundation Stage

The Early Years Foundation Stage (EYFS) is the framework that covers the learning, development and care for children from birth to five years old in England. The principles of the EYFS are grouped into four themes that contextualise the requirements of the EYFS framework and describe how people working with young children within this stage should support their learning, development and care. The four main themes are:

- A unique child: every child is a competent learner from birth who can be resilient, capable, confident and self-assured. The main commitments in this stage are development, inclusion, safety and health and wellbeing.

- Positive relationships: describes how children learn to be strong and independent from a base of secure and loving relationships with significant others (for example, parents). The key commitments in this stage are respect, partnerships with parents, supporting learning and the roles of the key person (such as a carer).

- Enabling environments: recognises how environment can shape the child's development and learning. The commitments of this stage are observation, assessment and planning, support for every child and the learning environment.

- Learning development: recognises that children learn and develop in different ways and at different rates. It recognises that all areas of learning and development are equally important and are related.

The learning and development requirements of the EYFS are laid out by the Childcare Act (2006). These contain three elements:

- the early learning goals: the knowledge, skills and understanding that young children should have acquired by the end of the academic year in which they reach five years old

- the educational programmes: the matters, skills and processes that are to be taught to young children

- the assessment arrangements: the arrangements for assessing young children to measure their achievements. The assessment arrangements are broken down into assessment during the EYFS, assessment at the end of the EYFS and the assessment requirements.

The early learning goals and the educational programmes are separated into six areas shown in Figure 24.1. They are equally important and related, so must be delivered through planned and purposeful play with a balance of adult-led and child-initiated activities to support a rounded approach to child development.

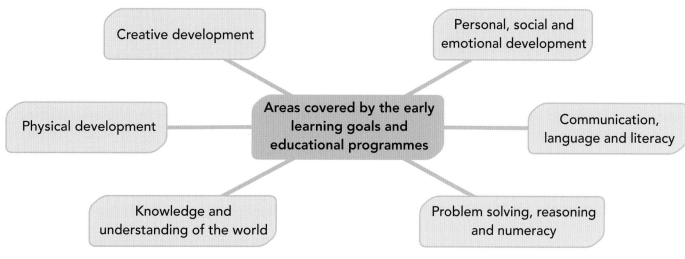

Figure 24.1: Early learning goals and educational programmes.

National Curriculum Key Stages 1–4

The National Curriculum in England is structured into four key stages that cover 5–16-year-olds. These are:

- Key Stage 1 – ages 5–7 (school years 1–2)
- Key Stage 2 – ages 7–11 (school years 3–6)
- Key Stage 3 – ages 11–14 (school years 7– 9)
- Key Stage 4 – ages 14–16 (school years 10–11)

The structure and mandatory and optional content of the key stages can be seen at curriculum.qcda.gov.uk.

Knowledge, skills and understanding

The knowledge, skills and understanding taught at Key Stages 1 and 2 are separated into four areas:

- acquiring and developing skills
- selecting and applying skills, tactics and compositional ideas
- evaluating and improving performance
- knowledge and understanding of fitness and health

Key Stage 1

During Key Stage 1, children build on their natural enthusiasm for movement. They use it to explore and learn about their world. Children start to work and play with other children in pairs or groups. By watching, listening and experimenting they develop movement and coordination skills. During this stage, children get the opportunity to enjoy expressing and testing themselves in a variety of situations.

Knowledge, skills and understanding at Key Stage 1

Knowledge, skills and understanding should be taught through dance, games and gymnastics activities (mandatory) and swimming activities and water safety (optional).

Key Stage 2

During Key Stage 2 children enjoy being active and using their creativity and imagination during physical activity. Through Key Stage 2, children learn new skills, discover how to use them in different ways, linking them to make actions, phrases and sequences of movement. They will enjoy communicating, collaborating and competing with each other. Children develop an understanding of how to succeed in different activities and learn how to identify and evaluate their own success.

Knowledge, skills and understanding at Key Stage 2

The knowledge, skills and understanding should be taught through five activities including dance, games and gymnastics activities (mandatory) and two activities to be chosen from swimming activities and water safety, athletic activities and outdoor and adventurous activities. Swimming activities and water safety must be chosen as one of these areas of activity unless children have completed the full Key Stage 2 teaching requirements during Key Stage 1.

Structure of Key Stages 3 and 4

Key Stages 3 and 4 were reviewed in 2007 and came into effect in September 2008. The programme of study at Key Stages 3 and 4 is now separated into four areas: **key concepts**, **key processes**, **range and content** and **curriculum opportunities**.

Key terms

Key concepts – concepts that children need to understand in order to deepen and broaden their knowledge, skills and understanding. The key concepts at Key Stages 3 and 4 are competence, performance, creativity and health, active lifestyles.

Key processes – essential skills and processes that children need to learn in order to progress in PE. The key processes at Key stages 3 and 4 are developing skills in physical activity; making and applying decisions; developing physical and mental capacity; evaluating and improving; and making informed decisions about healthy, active lifestyles.

Range and content – the breadth of the subject on which teachers should draw when teaching the key concepts and key processes.

Curriculum opportunities – the opportunities that should be offered to children to enhance their engagement with the concepts, processes and content of PE.

Key Stage 3 – range and content

At Key Stage 3, PE should include activities that cover at least four of the following areas:

- outwitting opponents, as in games activities
- accurate replication of actions, phrases and sequences, as in gymnastic activities

- exploring and communicating ideas, concepts and emotions, as in dance activities
- performing at maximum levels in relation to speed, height, distance, strength or accuracy, as in athletic activities
- identifying and solving problems to overcome challenges of an adventurous nature, as in lifesaving and personal survival in swimming and outdoor activities
- exercising safely and effectively to improve health and wellbeing, as in fitness and health activities.

Key Stage 3 – curriculum opportunities

At Key Stage 3, the curriculum should provide opportunities for children to:

- get involved in a range of different activities that develop the whole body
- experience a range of roles within a physical activity
- specialise in specific activities and roles
- follow pathways to other activities in and beyond school
- perform as an individual, in a group or as part of a team in formal competitions or performances to audiences beyond the class
- use ICT as an aid to improving performance and tracking progress
- make links between PE and other subjects and areas of the curriculum.

Key Stage 4 – range and content

At Key Stage 4, PE should include activities that cover at least two of these areas:

- outwitting opponents, as in games activities
- accurate replication of actions, phrases and sequences, as in gymnastic activities
- exploring and communicating ideas, concepts and emotions, as in dance activities
- performing at maximum levels in relation to speed, height, distance, strength or accuracy, as in athletic activities
- identifying and solving problems to overcome challenges of an adventurous nature, as in lifesaving and personal survival in swimming and outdoor activities
- exercising safely and effectively to improve health and wellbeing, as in fitness and health activities.

Key Stage 4 – curriculum opportunities

At Key Stage 4, the curriculum should provide opportunities for young people to:

- get involved in a range of different activities that develop the whole body
- experience a range of roles within a physical activity
- specialise in specific activities and roles, taking accredited courses and qualifications where appropriate
- follow pathways to other activities in and beyond school and, where possible, work with sportsmen and women, coaches and other specialists
- perform as an individual, in a group or as part of a team in formal competitions or performances to audiences beyond the class
- make links between PE and other subjects and areas of the curriculum
- use ICT to assist in planning for improvement and involvement in physical activity
- work with others to organise, manage, officiate and run festivals, tournaments, competitions and events, both in school and in the local community.

Take it further

Programmes of study

Go to curriculum.qcda.gov.uk and download the programmes of study for each of the different key stages. Summarise the examples that are included in the programmes of study and keep them – they could be useful when you are planning the PE lesson later!

Differences in home countries

The provision of PE in schools varies between each of the home countries. To find out and compare the differences in sport and PE in schools in England, Scotland, Northern Ireland and Wales you can visit each country's educational department website and look at PE in the curriculum.

1.2 Stakeholders

Sector Skills Councils

SkillsActive is the Sector Skills Council for Active Leisure and Learning. It works with employers to lead the skills and productivity drive across sport and recreation, health and fitness, outdoors and playwork. SkillsActive works in the UK with representatives in all four home countries. In England there are nine regional managers, with other home country managers based in Northern Ireland, Scotland and Wales. SkillsActive has a role in increasing the number of industry recognised qualifications for the active leisure and learning sector. It works with industry and higher education experts, partners and employers to develop qualifications which will assist the growth of the workforce. In doing so, SkillsActive aims to professionalise and upskill the active learning and leisure sector in the run up to, and beyond, the London 2012 Olympic Games and Paralympic Games. This involves developing different types of apprenticeships and qualifications related to National Occupational Standards.

National Occupational Standards (NOS) define the knowledge, understanding, skills and level of competence required to carry out tasks at work. They can be used to create job descriptions, develop training plans, identify skills shortages and create performance standards. They play an important role in curriculum development providing the framework against which vocational qualifications can be designed and form the structure of the Scottish National Vocational Qualifications (S/NVQs).

National governing bodies and their work with children and young people

The work of sport governing bodies may not directly influence the PE curriculum, but it can play an important role in PE in schools. Governing bodies may work with local sports clubs to foster school and community links. They may also promote participation in their sports which may influence children and young people to take up sport in school.

Government initiatives

As PE and sport has a beneficial effect on education, health, confidence and interpersonal skills, there are different initiatives in place to increase the amount and quality of PE available to young people.

PE and Sport Strategy for Young People (PESSYP) replaces the government's previous initiative, the PE School Sport and Club Links (PESSCL). This new initiative has been developed and implemented by Department for Children, Schools and Families (DCSF), the Department for Culture, Media and Sport (DCMS), the Youth Sports Trust and Sport England. They aim to use the legacy of the London 2012 Olympics to get more children and young people taking part in quality PE and sport. The central aspect of this strategy is the five hour offer. The five hour offer is made up of two hours of curriculum PE per week, one hour of sport organised by schools on school sites and two hours of a mixture of school and community/club organised sport, either on school sites or in community/club sites. Achievement of the five hour offer will be measured against these targets:

- 40 per cent of young people to take part in five hours per week of PE and sport (three hours for 16–19-year-olds) by the end of the academic year 2010–2011
- 80 per cent of 5–16 year olds in every School Sport Partnership to take part in three hours per week of PE and sport (three hours for 16–19-year-olds) by the end of the academic year 2010–2011
- 60 per cent of young people to take part in five hours per week PE and sport (three hours for 16–19-year-olds) by the end of the academic year 2012–2013.

The PESSYP has ten key work strands, each of which maximises opportunities for children and young people to access quality PE. These strands are shown in Figure 24.2.

The PESSYP targets three groups of children and young people: those engaged, partially engaged, and not engaged in PE and sport. Here is a model for working towards the five hour offer with these groups.

The overall ambitions for delivering the five hour offer are to:

- deliver a successful Olympic and Paralympic Games with a legacy of more children and young people participating in PE and sport
- create a world-class system of PE and sport for young people
- give every young person aged 5–16 in England access to five hours of PE and sport every week (three hours for 16–19-year-olds).

1.3 Implementation of curriculum in different contexts

Key Stages 1 and 2 of the PE curriculum are implemented in primary schools and Key Stages 3 and 4 are implemented in secondary schools. Look back at section 1.1, pages 333–334 for more information.

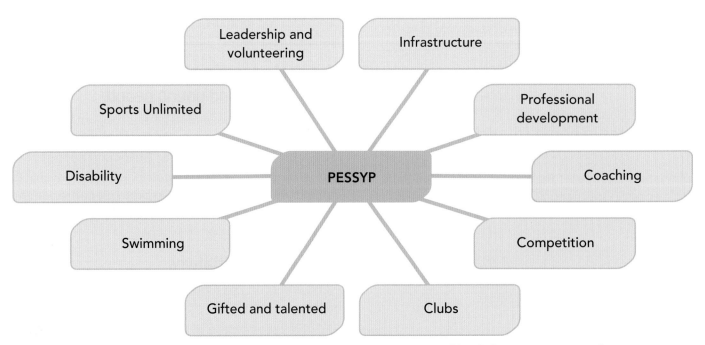

Figure 24.2: How effective do you think the PESSYP will be at developing sport at all levels from grass roots to elite?

	1	2	3	4	5	5+
Sustaining and challenging those already engaged			Appropriate competitive sport, access to quality coaching and progression to quality clubs			Quality clubs, competition and coaching linked to the school
Fully engaging those partially engaged	Two hours per week of high quality physical education for all young people		Alternative activities and traditional sports presented differently, linked to quality community provision	Easily accessible menu of sporting provision available in a range of community settings		
Engaging those not yet engaged			Encouraging active lifestyles	Supporting active lifestyles		

KEY

School Sports Partnership	Health providers and Primary Care Trusts	Transition between the two sectors	County Sports Partnership, National Governing Bodies and other Community providers	Transition between the two sectors

Figure 24.3: Why do you think that the structure of the programmes differs in how it targets the different groups? (Diagram adapted from *The PE and Sport Strategy for Young People. A guide to delivering the five hour offer*, courtesy of Sport England).

Assessment activity 24.1   P1 P2 P3 M1   BTEC

You have just started your job as a PE teacher. You want to develop the PE provision at your school by drawing in more community links and by providing learners with a greater understanding of the links between PE and the world of work. Before you get the go ahead, your manager has asked for a report that demonstrates how all of these different areas can link together.

1. Describe the structure of the PE curriculum. **P1**

2. Describe the impact of stakeholder views on the development of the PE curriculum. **P2**

3. Describe the ways in which the curriculum is implemented. **P3**

4. Explain the different ways that learning providers meet National Curriculum requirements. **M1**

Grading tips

- To attain **P1** look at the different levels and differences in home countries.

- To attain **P2** describe how sector skills councils (such as Skills Active), National Occupational Standards, national governing bodies and different government initiatives impact on the development of the PE curriculum.

- To attain **P3** describe which elements of the curriculum are delivered through primary and which are delivered through secondary schools.

- To attain **M1** explain the optional and mandatory elements of the National Curriculum and suggest why and how learning providers may meet the curriculum in different ways.

PLTS

Thinking about the different ways that learning providers may meet the curriculum could provide evidence of your skills as a **creative thinker**.

Functional skills

If your report is fit for purpose, you will provide evidence towards your **English** skills.

2. Understand the importance of physical education in society

2.1 PE and educational attainment

PE and sport benefits young people and can help to improve academic success.

Physical activity and academic success

People think that physically active children are more likely to have greater academic success for a number of reasons including increased cognitive functioning, improved behaviour and increased self-esteem. Although research is contradictory on the effects of physical activity on academic achievement, there is enough evidence to show that there is a link between physical activity and academic success.

Improved cognitive function

One reason why physical activity improves academic success is improved cognitive function. During the school day, breaks for physical activity help children to concentrate and improve behaviour; this helps them achieve higher test scores and increases academic performance. Children involved in moderate to vigorous physical activity have increased memory and recall, increased observational skills, increased problem-solving skills and increased decision-making skills. We don't fully understand this relationship but suggestions include increased blood flow to the brain, increased arousal and brain stimulation, increased energy production and physical activity as a break from lesson time which gives your brain time to recover.

Physical literacy

Physical literacy is the motivation, confidence, physical competence, knowledge and understanding to maintain physical activity throughout life with the aim of improving quality of life. During the foundation years and primary school years, PE develops physical literacy as movement skills and an understanding of the importance of physical activity are developed. During secondary school, PE develops physical literacy because it provides an opportunity to contextualise physical literacy through a range of sport and exercise activities; you also develop your physical literacy through sport outside school. When you are researching physical literacy, you may find some useful articles at www.physical-literacy.org.uk.

Importance of high quality teaching establishing lifelong activity

Think about the subjects at school and college that you have enjoyed and those you haven't. Quality of teaching affects enjoyment. This is important as a child's experiences in PE affect lifelong participation in physical activity. Inactive adults cite bad experiences during their school PE lessons as a reason for being inactive, whereas more active adults have had positive experiences through school PE.

After school clubs

An after school club is a place for children to go from around 3.30 p.m. to 6 p.m. (after the school day has finished but normal office working hours haven't). The club could be in the child's school, but also in other settings such as community centres. Activities such as games, sports or art and crafts are provided for children under the care of playworkers and are designed to help children fulfil their potential through positive, social, emotional, physical and intellectual experiences.

Sport or physical activity

Have you ever heard somebody say 'Because I'm not into sport' as a reason for disliking PE? PE teachers should emphasise that PE is about learning about your body and the benefits of **physical activity**. Young people should understand that they can succeed in PE by being physically active and that they can get long-term health benefits from having active hobbies or daily activities. For more information about the benefits of physical activity, see Unit 14 Exercise, health and lifestyle.

Key terms

Physical activity – any force exerted by skeletal muscle that results in energy expenditure above resting level.

Take it further

PE – the wider benefits

For each of the aspects below, produce a mind map of how you think PE can benefit each area. You may wish to use books, the Internet and discussion with your friends or family to help.

- Team work
- Sense and understanding of competition
- How to deal with conflict
- Cooperating with others
- Community engagement

Take it further

Parents and family

To what extent do you think parents and family can influence a young person's involvement in sport? Think also about the implications of family finances.

2.2 PE in society

The benefits that PE brings to society stem from benefits to an individual. These affect society when an individual makes positive contributions to society.

Impacts on general health and physical fitness

PE plays an important role in society because it increases overall health and fitness. It reduces the prevalence of negative health factors such as obesity and mental health problems.

Emotional stability

PE develops self-confidence, self-esteem and feelings of peer acceptance in children and young people. Young people can develop better decision-making skills and are better equipped to deal with minor setbacks if they are involved in sport. PE can help them produce solutions to problems. This influences society as young people are less likely to suffer from mental health problems in later life.

Social cohesion

Social cohesion means how well you get on with other people in your group. Through PE, children and young people have an opportunity to develop social cohesion through play activities which can further help them to develop relationships in later life.

Social inclusion

The four elements that make up social inclusion include:

- spatial – being in close proximity to others and closing gaps between people of different social and economic status
- relational – feeling accepted or feeling as if you belong
- functional – improving knowledge, skills and understanding
- power – feeling more in control or empowered.

PE and sport increases social inclusion by bringing together young people from different social and economic backgrounds and providing a shared goal or activity that they feel is valuable (spatial) and offers young people the opportunity to be a part of a team, club or society (relational). PE helps young people to develop a range of appropriate knowledge, understanding and skills (functional) and involvement in games and activities that help them to develop decision-making skills or place them in positions of responsibility (power).

Crime reduction

Evidence shows a link between involvement in PE and sport and a reduction in crime. One UK-based project showed a reduction in drug taking and associated crime following a project involving sport. The project showed a 15 per cent reduction in overall crime and a 43 per cent reduction in youth crime.

Impacts on economy

As PE increases physical fitness it has a beneficial effect on different conditions associated with being unfit (for example, obesity). The cost of obesity to the NHS and the economy has been calculated at billions of pounds each year, so if we reduce the levels of obesity by helping children get active through PE, and instill positive lifestyle behaviours through the educational programme associated with PE, the financial cost of these conditions will be reduced.

Benefits

There many benefits of PE but three general areas are intellectual, ethical and aesthetic.

- **Intellectual** – a person's intellect relates to their ability to learn and reason, their capacity for knowledge and understanding, and their ability to think abstractly (in depth about or around a problem or event). PE develops a number of intellectual skills that are important for life such as decision-making and problem-solving.

- **Ethical** relates to understanding right from wrong, and morals, principles or standards. PE helps young people to learn about the rules that govern different sports, the spirit of fair play and how to work in everybody's best interests. When taking on the different roles of leader, coach and officials through PE, young people learn about the importance of adopting these roles responsibly.

- **Aesthetic** means the way something looks, especially in terms of its beauty or artistic worth. In some activities such as gymnastics and dance, movements must be aesthetically pleasing to score more points, whereas other activities simply have aesthetic benefits. Being physically active has many health-related benefits such as weight management, developing healthy bones, increased musculature and assisting correct posture. Young people can feel better about their appearance and enjoy being healthy as a result of school PE.

Case study: Sky Sports Living for Sport Project

The Sky Sports Living for Sport Project is a programme run by the Youth Sport Trust and funded by BSkyB. It is intended for 11–16-year-olds who are struggling with aspects of school life (for example, social exclusion, learning needs and behavioural problems) and who may have become disaffected. The project recognises that sport helps young people overcome these issues.

Schools apply to take part in the project and receive support to run it. Within the project, young people work with their teachers, support staff and other young people to set personal targets and goals, identify activities to take part in and to organise sport events for other children and young people. There is normally an annual celebration event at the end of each project.

Research the Sky Sports Living for Sport Project and answer these questions.

1. **What are the benefits of the Sky Sports Living for Sport Project?**
2. **How does the project link in with PE?**
3. **How effective is the project?**

Assessment activity 24.2

You are working as an outreach worker with a group of disaffected young people who have been missing their PE lessons. You want to help them discover the benefits of PE to try to reintroduce them to it so have decided to produce an information leaflet to try to stimulate their interest.

1. Explain the importance of PE to children and young people's educational attainment. **P4**

2. Outline the importance of PE to society in general. **P5**

Grading tips

*   To attain **P4** provide examples of how the link is explained (for example, cognitive functioning).
*   To attain **P5** discuss issues such as crime prevention.

PLTS

If you analyse and evaluate the information available that relates to the benefits of PE, you could provide evidence of your skills as an **independent enquirer**.

Functional skills

If your leaflet is fit for purpose, you could provide evidence of your skills in **English**.

3.   Be able to structure a lesson of physical education

3.1 Plan

To be effective lessons should be planned and reviewed. A lesson plan consists of different elements including learning outcomes, activities, opportunities for assessment, links to the curriculum and health and safety considerations.

Learning outcomes

Learning outcomes should be written so that they indicate what the person will know (for example, know the structure of the heart), or what they will understand (for example, understand how muscles and bones produce movement), or what skills they will have developed (for example, be able to safely and effectively run a sit and reach test with a client) by the end of the activity or lesson.

Remember

The learning outcomes are the knowledge, understanding and/or skills the young person should have by the end of the activity or class.

Activities

The activities that you include in the lesson should enable your students to achieve the learning outcomes. Activities should be varied and progressive so that you provide learners with an opportunity to learn in different ways that suit them and so that you are helping them to build on their skills and techniques as they progress through the individual classes and a series of lessons. For example, if you were to run a dance class with a group of Key Stage 1 learners, your activities could progress in this order:

*   Learners copy the dance movements performed by the teacher.
*   Observe, copy and repeat a short sequence of movements performed by the teacher.
*   Work in pairs to produce short sequence to music.
*   Work in pairs to alter the sequences to fit different music.

Assessment

The assessment that you use should be ongoing throughout the lesson and linked to assessing the learners against the tasks set in the class. Your lesson plan should detail how you will assess this learning, through questioning or observation. For example, if you were to assess the activities suggested for the dance class, you could include the following assessment strategies:

- Observation of learner's ability to copy teacher-led movements
- Observation of ability to move in space, altering movements
- Observation of ability to work cooperatively with a partner
- Questioning of ideas
- Ability to choose appropriate movements to fit a range of stimuli (different types of music).

Links to curriculum

When planning lessons in PE ensure that direct links are made to specific elements of the curriculum by showing which key stage the lesson is associated with, which part of the key stage content you are working on and any additional details associated with that key stage. For example, if you were to run a dance session with a group of Key Stage 1 learners, you could make these links to the knowledge, skills and understanding:

- Acquiring and developing skills:
  - To copy and explore movement ideas and respond imaginatively to a range of stimuli
- Selecting and applying skills and tactics
  - To move confidently using gesture and changes of movement, direction, speed and level
- Knowledge of health and fitness:
  - To recognise why our hearts beat faster when we 'warm-up'
- Evaluating and improving performance.
  - To describe basic body actions and recognise dynamic qualities of movement.

Health and safety considerations

- **Risk assessment** – a school will complete a risk assessment for the areas that you will be working in. However, you are responsible for ongoing health and safety throughout a session. In PE different

health and safety considerations include ensuring that learners are injury free, that they understand the instructions for the session or activity, that they understand the rules of any games you are playing and that all the equipment is appropriate for the groups that you are working with. For more information about health and safety considerations and risk assessment in sport settings, see Student Book 1, Unit 3 Assessing risk in sport.

- **Informed consent** is needed for some activities in PE. This is permission from the learner and their parent or carer to say that the learner may participate.

3.2 Learning

Different factors can affect an individual's learning. You should consider these when planning your lesson so that you can give your students the best learning experience.

Child or young person-centred learning

Child-centred learning allows children and young people to initiate their own learning. Teachers in a child-centred learning environment act as facilitators assisting children and young people in their learning without providing direct instruction. The teacher's role in child-centred learning is to provide structure within the class while allowing the learner to explore their potential. This type of learning focuses on the whole child and emphasises physical, psychological and emotional development. In child-centred learning, children choose activities that interest them. They work independently to discover their potential in unique ways. Child-centred learning allows students to work in ways that benefit their different learning styles. A child-centred learning environment will include a lot of learning through play (hence it is more common to see this form of education in early childhood). By learning through play with friends, social and emotional development happens more rapidly.

Adult-initiated experiences

This refers to how a teacher's experiences outside the classroom affect their teaching. For example, if a teacher has a range of industry experience, they are more likely to be able to bring their teaching to life using industry-related examples.

Why is it important to create the correct learning environment?

Adult-directed learning

This refers to teachers and other members of staff (for example, coaches and teaching assistants) leading classes.

Importance of the learning environment

The teacher should create the learning environment that suits the needs of their learners, groups and topics. You will be able to think of teachers that created the same learning environment by using the same teaching methods, the same layout and having the same people working together. You will probably remember times when the teaching environment was really effective and you got a lot out of it, but you will also be able to remember when you wished they would change things. Without the correct learning environment, children and young people won't learn much, so get to know your groups so that you can create the most appropriate learning environment.

3.3 Methods

There are numerous teaching methods that are used within PE lessons. Often they are used together to give children and young people the best learning experience.

Facilitating

When you are facilitating, you are assisting others in their learning process but not acting as the primary source of knowledge. Facilitating is often used during individual or group learning activities in PE and can be beneficial when trying to help your group of learners develop ways of working with each other on a task. One of the issues with facilitating as a teaching and learning method is that if the teacher cannot control the group effectively, less learning is likely to take place.

Leading

As the teacher, you are the leader of the group. You take responsibility for starting tasks and are responsible for maintaining progress on those tasks. Leading takes many forms, including: initiating discussions so learners can gauge the direction of the discussion and feel confident to join in; providing demonstrations of different activities so that learners can copy your movements and learn; you stopping and starting activities at different times.

There are a number of leadership styles used in teaching. There is no *best* style of leadership for every situation. The style you choose will affect how learners feel about their lesson and how motivated they are to learn. The most common styles of leadership used in teaching are coercive, pace-setting, authoritative, affiliative, democratic and coaching.

Encouraging

Think about when you were in a PE class at school. Was there a time when you did something well, for example, you managed to score a goal from a

Table 24.1: Styles of leadership.

Style	Description	When does it work?	Overall impact
Coercive	You use lots of directives, expect compliance and control things tightly. This is the 'Do what I tell you – now!' style of leadership	When splitting up your class for different activities or when you need to regain control of the class	Can be quite negative if overused as the learners feel that they don't have any control over learning
Pace-setting	You use this style when you want to get results quickly from higher level learners or when you feel that the lesson is going off track and you need to bring it back into line. This is very much the 'Come, get on with it!' style of leading	When you have got a class that is enjoying the lesson but might not be doing as well as they can	Can be positive in short spells to re-focus attention but can be negative if done for long periods of time as learners can become reliant on the teacher to get them out of trouble
Authoritative	You use this to provide a long-term direction for learning and to explain the importance of that direction. This is almost like the teacher saying 'Come with me, I'm going to lead you through this journey'	When introducing a new topic, such as at the start of a lesson in a new section of the curriculum	Generally positive as it gives clear direction to learning
Affiliative	You would use this style to help build relationships within the group. This is very much a 'person is more important than a learner' approach to leading the group	When the group are struggling to get to know each other or when they are becoming worried about a task	Very positive. Peer and teacher relationships, and having regard for a learner's overall welfare, are very important for learning
Democratic	You use this style to generate long-term commitment from learners by giving them an input in decision-making and generating ideas. This is very much the 'What do you think?' style of leading	When you want to get learners more involved with a topic or when you want to help learners develop thinking and decision- making skills	Very positive. Learners feel more in control of their learning and feel that their opinion is more valued, both of which increase motivation to learn
Coaching	You use this style to help learners plan for their long-term development in PE, helping them to identify their specific strengths and areas for improvement, and helping them to produce methods of reaching their goals. This is very much the 'Why don't you try this?' style of leadership	When you want to help learners develop their decision-making and problem-solving skills so that they can work both with and without the teacher	Very positive. It tends to lead to long-term development of the learner as it helps them to find ways of highlighting strengths and areas for improvement. It also helps them develop decision-making processes to aid improvements

Do you think everybody will respond in the same way to encouragement?

difficult angle in football or beat your personal best in athletics? You will probably remember your teacher saying 'Well done – I liked that shot!' Or 'Well done – that was great technique!'. They probably then helped you to realise *how* you managed to achieve the successful performance ('You kept your head over the ball and struck it with the right part of your foot') and how you could develop your performance even more ('What do you think would have happened if you had used different parts of your foot?'). This is an example of encouraging your learner.

When this teaching method is used correctly, it can have a strong motivational effect on the learner which means that they are more likely to try to replicate the behaviour that led to the encouragement. Through their efforts to replicate or improve the behaviour, learners are more likely to learn new things. When this teaching method is used incorrectly, it can have detrimental effects because the learner may not value the encouragement. It may also be the case that the learner cannot execute the performance straightaway and may worry that the encouragement will not come, both of which can affect learning negatively.

Questioning

Questioning is an important and effective method of teaching PE and is one of the most common teaching methods. There are three types of questioning that you use in a PE lesson:

- Questions that learners ask themselves that allow them to engage in and reflect on the tasks or activities (for example, how are the skills that I am learning helping me?).

- Questions that you use to help guide and direct learners to learn new things. These questions will get progressively harder as the learner begins to understand more. This method is often known as one part of an overall method of guided discovery.

- Summary questions that assess the learning that has taken place during the lesson. These can be in the form of open questions (questions that are asked to the group in general) or directed questions (questions that are asked to specific learners).

Questioning is also used as part of a problem-solving approach to teaching in PE. This approach encourages learners to improve their individual performance by developing decision-making skills, broadening learners' thinking patterns making them more creative in their work and helps develop group interaction if used in a group based setting.

There are a number of different settings in which questioning can be used. Teacher-to-child questioning assesses the learning of the child by the teacher; child-to-teacher questioning is used when the child wants to develop their ideas and clarify their knowledge or understanding; child-to-child questioning is used during peer learning, group work and peer assessment activities.

3.4 Designing learner focused activities

How many times have you been in a class and been struck by how much the teacher was trying to show off their knowledge? They may have used lots of words that you didn't understand – they talked, you listened and you didn't get involved... How much do you think you learned from that experience? What you will have experienced is the exact opposite of learner focused activities. Learner focused activities are designed around the needs of groups or individual learners. They cater for the needs of different learning styles and take into account individual or additional needs of learners within the group. The lesson plan should show evidence of a concept called differentiation (see page 346 for more details).

Learning styles

Think about how you like to learn. Sometimes you may like to be hands-on while at other times you might want to be reflective. While everybody has a mix of four learning styles, generally your favoured learning style will fall into one of four types: activist, reflector, theorist or pragmatist. When you are planning PE lessons, you should understand the preferred learning styles of your students to provide the best learning setting for them.

- **Activists** prefer to have new experiences and are eager when faced with new ideas. They like to do things and have a tendency to act first and think later. Activist learners are unlikely to prepare for their learning experience or reflect on their learning afterwards. Activists have better learning experiences when they are involved in new experiences, problems and opportunities, working with others in team tasks or role playing and when thrown in the deep end with a difficult task to solve. Activist learners learn little from sitting and listening to lectures, or when reading, writing or thinking alone, or following long sets of precise instructions or absorbing lots of information quickly.

- **Reflectors** think about problems or tasks from different perspectives. They prefer collecting information, reflecting on it and thinking carefully about a task or problem before coming to conclusions. Reflectors enjoy observing others and listening to the views of others before offering their own. Reflectors have better learning experiences when observing individuals or groups at work, reflecting on what has happened and thinking about what they have learned and completing tasks without strict deadlines. Reflectors tend to learn little when in leadership roles or role playing in front of others, completing tasks with no time to prepare or rushing to meet deadlines.

- **Theorists** like to transfer what they have seen into theories. They tend to think problems through logically and can often be perfectionists who like to fit things into a rational scheme. Theorists have better learning experiences when they are put into complex situations where they have to use their knowledge and skills, when they are in a structured situation that has a clear purpose and when they are posed ideas or questions that, although they may not be immediately relevant, allow the learner to ask questions and probe the topic so that they can gain a greater understanding. Theorists tend to learn little when taking part in unstructured activities or where the instructions are unclear, when they have to participate in activities which emphasise emotion and feelings and when completing

activities without knowing the principles, ideas, concepts or theory underpinning the activity.

- **Pragmatists** like to try things out and are practical. They like activities that can be applied to the real world. Pragmatists will often become impatient with long discussions. Pragmatists have better learning experiences when there is a link between the topic and the real world, when they have the chance to try out new skills or techniques and when shown a model skill or technique that will work on in their chosen setting and that they can copy. Pragmatists learn little when there is no obvious/immediate benefit to what they are doing, when what they are learning is 'theory based' work and not practical or when there are no clear guidelines to follow.

Individual or additional needs

You may work with some learners with individual or additional needs. These could be learning needs such as dyslexia or dyspraxia, physical disabilities or religious needs. For example, the British Muslim Council and the Association for Physical Education (2007) have guided schools on the needs of Muslim learners and the Qualifications and Curriculum Development Agency (QCDA) have produced guidelines for planning, teaching and assessing the PE curriculum for people with learning difficulties. Use the Internet to research guidance to help prepare you for planning different types of lessons.

Differentiation

Differentiation involves the teacher using a flexible approach to teaching and learning through the use of a range of activities and assessment methods. In this way they can meet the learning needs and styles of all the learners in their class. Differentiation can be as simple as making activities harder for advanced learners, or making activities easier for those who are struggling. However, differentiation can also mean:

- altering your classroom structure to allow learners to use different learning styles
- allowing learners to work in pairs or groups so that peer mentoring, peer assessment and shared learning can take place
- assessing learners throughout the class and at the end of the class so that they can demonstrate their knowledge, skills and understanding in the way that best suits them.

Activity: What is your learning style?

Complete this questionnaire to understand your preferred learning style. When you have finished, add up your scores using the guide at the bottom of this activity. No = 0, Yes = 1, Always = 2. There are no correct answers and you should choose the response that best applies to you. Try not to spend too much time on any one question.

Statement	No	Yes	Always	Score
1 Do you get bored easily?	No	Yes	Always	
2 Are you cautious and thoughtful?	No	Yes	Always	
3 Do you like being the centre of attention?	No	Yes	Always	
4 Do you like to 'get on with things' rather than talk about doing things?	No	Yes	Always	
5 Do you like the challenge of problem-solving?	No	Yes	Always	
6 Do you like to think things through before starting them?	No	Yes	Always	
7 Do you have clear ideas about the best way to do things?	No	Yes	Always	
8 Do you act first then think about the consequences later?	No	Yes	Always	
9 Do you daydream?	No	Yes	Always	
10 Do you keep lists of things to do?	No	Yes	Always	
11 Do you like more 'hands on' activities?	No	Yes	Always	
12 Do you ask lots of questions?	No	Yes	Always	
13 Do you prefer to focus on one thing at a time?	No	Yes	Always	
14 Do people think you are shy or quiet?	No	Yes	Always	
15 Do you see yourself as a perfectionist?	No	Yes	Always	
16 Do you have an enthusiasm for life?	No	Yes	Always	
17 Do you like to experiment to find the best way of doing things?	No	Yes	Always	
18 Do you often notice things that other people miss?	No	Yes	Always	
19 Do you find it easy to meet new people and make new friends?	No	Yes	Always	
20 Do you like to have everything in its place 'just as it should be'?	No	Yes	Always	
21 Do you prefer to think things through step–by–step?	No	Yes	Always	
22 Do people think you are a good listener?	No	Yes	Always	
23 Do you like trying out new things?	No	Yes	Always	
24 Do you like to try things out?	No	Yes	Always	

(Adapted from the Brainboxx 'Rough & Ready Reckoner', www.brainboxx.co.uk)

Activist questions 1, 3, 8, 16, 19 and 23 Total score =
Reflector questions 2, 6, 9, 14, 18 and 22 Total score =
Pragmatist questions 4, 5, 11, 13, 17, 24 Total score =
Theorist questions 7, 10, 12, 15, 20 and 21 Total score =

• Which is your dominant learning style?
• Based on the descriptions of the learning styles, would you have expected this to be your dominant style?

Importance of observation

Observation of children is crucial for the understanding and planning of PE classes. By observing children, you can:

- discover different influences on their participation
- monitor equality and inclusivity
- examine which aspects of the session worked well and which need to change
- identify any further areas of learning that need extending or supporting.

Observations can be conducted live during classes, completed retrospectively using videos or through using observation forms.

Involvement of children and young people

Involving children and young people allows you to:

- gain their perspective on what is happening
- find out if they are enjoying what they are doing, providing them with a sense of control over the planning process
- find out what children are finding beneficial.

Availability and use of resources

Before going to your lesson check the availability of resources for your class. This should be done well in advance of the class. Your lesson plan should detail the resources required and how you are going to use them.

Assessment activity 24.3
P6 M2 D1 · **BTEC**

You are preparing for an interview as a PE teacher. As part of your interview, you have to produce a lesson plan for the lesson that you are going to deliver.

1. Plan a PE lesson describing how learning is supported. **P6**
2. Now you need to explain how the learning is supported in your lesson. **M2**
3. Finally, you should analyse the support for learning. **D1**

Grading tips

- To attain **P6** produce a lesson plan using a standard format and describe how you will support learning within the lesson. This could be achieved by saying how different activities will help the learner.
- To attain **M2** provide specific examples of things that you will do in your lesson so that you can explain how learning will be supported.
- To attain **D1** expand your information further, analysing how the examples that you have given will support learning, for example, why have they been beneficial for supporting learning and how have they developed learning?

PLTS

If you ask questions to extend your thinking about how your plan will support learning, you could provide evidence of your skills as a **creative thinker**.

Functional skills

If you present your completed lesson plan using correct text and tables, you could provide evidence of **ICT** skills.

4. Know the responsibilities of those who work with children to safeguard and promote their welfare, and strategies for safeguarding children, young people and self

4.1 Safeguarding children and young people

The government produced a document called 'Working Together to Safeguard Children' (2006) and this outlines how organisations and individuals should work together to safeguard children and young people and promote their welfare. The following components are key elements:

- Protecting children and young people from abuse and neglect
- Preventing impairment of children's health or development
- Ensuring that children are growing up in circumstances and conditions that are classed as effective care
- Giving children and young people the best chances in life to develop as a person and become an adult.

There are a number of different strategies that ensure that children and young people are safeguarded. The following sections introduce you to these strategies but be aware that legislation, policies and procedures change regularly so ensure that you are using the version that is most relevant to your work.

Awareness of disclosure procedures

The Criminal Records Bureau (CRB) was set up to improve access to criminal records for employment and voluntary work purposes. The CRB provides this access through a process called disclosure. Disclosure is a process whereby individuals are checked for their suitability to work with children or young people. There were originally three levels of disclosure: basic, standard and enhanced (see Table 24.2) although the basic level was never introduced.

When a disclosure is issued, a copy will be given to the applicant and the organisation/employer. The organisation must ensure that all information is kept confidential. For more information regarding the CRB check, visit www.crb.homeoffice.gov.uk.

Empowering children and young people

When in your care, children and young people should feel empowered. This means that they should feel confident in their ability to come and speak to you

Table 24.2: The three levels of disclosure.

Level of disclosure	What happens?	Who is it suitable for?
Basic	Check of unspent convictions	Those working in a position that will bring them into indirect contact with children or young people
Standard	Check of all convictions, cautions or warnings held on the police national computer, plus information held by Department for Children, Schools and Families under section 142 of the Education Act on those considered unsuitable for, and banned from, working with children. Check of information from the Protection of Children Act list and information from the Protection of Vulnerable Adults list.	Those working in direct contact with children and young people that are always under direct supervision of a senior member of staff
Enhanced	Everything included above, plus local police force records (including non-conviction information considered relevant by chief police officers)	Any individuals in significant direct contact with children or young people

about anything without feeling that they will be judged. Having empowered children and young people is vital for developing a good working relationship and can help if you suspect cases of neglect or abuse as they are more likely to tell you.

Unconditional acceptance of the child/young person

All children and young people should be treated equally, regardless of race, gender, socio-economic background, sexual orientation, religious opinion or disabilities. When working with young children, you must accept them unconditionally and offer them opportunities to develop through sport. You should challenge any form of discrimination.

Building self-esteem, assertiveness, self-confidence and reliance

Participation in sport helps children and young people to develop key aspects of their character. Importantly, sport and physical activity has been shown to positively benefit the mental health of children and young people. To help children to develop you could:

- provide children and young people with choices about the types of activities in the session
- treat children and young people as individuals
- encourage children and young people to talk with teachers and coaches about their performance
- help children and young people to develop a well-balanced lifestyle
- encourage children and young people to make their own decisions.

Ensuring children and young people are aware of procedures in case of accidents, illness and emergency

Make sure that all children or young people are aware of any procedures in case of accidents, illness or emergency. These could be particularly important if you are the person that has been injured and a child or young person has to find help for you.

Injuries, illness and other emergencies

If a child or young person is accidentally hurt, is injured or becomes ill while they are under your supervision or care, you should report the incident as soon as possible to your senior member of staff.

4.2 Legislation, policies and procedures

Key legislation can influence, in some way, who can work with children and young people and how they can work with them. The acts are listed below.

- The Children Act (1989)
- The Protection of Children Act (1999)
- Care Standards Act (2000)
- Every Child Matters and the Children Act (2004)
- The Childcare Act (2006)
- Safeguarding Vulnerable Groups Act (2006)

The NSPCC Child Protection in Sport Unit has published standards for safeguarding and protecting children in sport. In addition, they have also published a guidance document entitled 'Roles, Skills, Knowledge and Competencies for Safeguarding and Protecting Children in the Sport Sector'; it is designed to be used by everybody working with children and young people in sport. These documents will be useful for you when understanding the different requirements as they are based on good practice, legislation and research from different sports settings and can be downloaded from www.nspcc.org.uk.

National and local

Safeguarding children is the responsibility of everybody who works with them. The 'Working Together to Safeguard Children' (2006) document is a key national initiative in place to safeguard children and young people (you can find this document at www.dcsf.gov.uk/everychildmatters). This programme is controlled on a local level by Local Safeguarding Children Boards (LSCB). A LSCB is made up of Local Authorities (LA), health bodies, the police and other bodies such as schools and colleges.

Relating to lines of reporting

While there is a grey area relating to reporting child protection issues in the UK, the Children Act 1989 and 'Working Together to Safeguard Children' (2006) do have recommendations relating to the responsibility of adults working with children or young people. If you are working with children or young people, it is your responsibility to report your concerns to the child protection officer in your organisation. A lot of sports clubs have child protection officers, so they should be your first point of contact.

Whistle blowing

If you suspect that a colleague is acting inappropriately with a child or young person with whom they are working, you should report this to the appropriate individual in the organisation (for example, your manager or the child protection officer).

Child protection

Child protection is used to protect children and young people who are suffering, or who are at risk from, harm. There is legislation relating to child protection. The current child protection system for the UK is based on the Children Act (1989). This act introduced the paramount principle which means that a child's welfare is of paramount importance, and it introduced parental responsibility into legislation which sets out the rights, duties, powers and responsibilities of the parent or carer of the child. After the Children Act, the Education Act (2002) was introduced which requires school governing bodies, local education authorities and further education institutions to ensure that they safeguard and promote the welfare of children.

Health, safety, security and hygiene

There is important legislation that governs health, safety, security and hygiene when working in sports environments including Health and Safety at Work Act (1974), Reporting of Injuries, Diseases and Dangerous Occurrences Regulations (RIDDOR) and Personal Protective Equipment (2002). You should look at the work you have done in Student Book 1, Unit 3 Assessing risk in sport for more details about the different legislation.

4.3 Safeguarding self

When you are working with young people, you need to think about safeguarding yourself. In this section you will look at what you need to understand to make sure you work appropriately with young people, which will mean that you safeguard yourself.

Take it further

NSPCC

Organisations such as the NSPCC have resources that will help you to understand what constitutes working appropriately to safeguard young people. Go to the NSPCC website and watch their videos on working appropriately with young people.

Guidelines

Guidelines have been produced by different bodies focusing on safeguarding children. These guidelines are available through the 'Working Together to Safeguard Children' document, and through specialist workshops offered through bodies such as Sports Coach UK, the Football Association and the Rugby Football Union.

Local authority guidelines for working with children and young people

Local authorities have legal duties underpinned by the Children Act (1989 and 2004) and the Protection of Children Act (1999). To protect yourself when working with children and young people, you must be aware of, and follow, your local authority's guidelines on working with children and young people. Your Local Safeguarding Children Board will provide you with guidelines that are specific to your local area.

Staff behaviour in a relevant context

You should work appropriately with children and young people and not use behaviour that could be misinterpreted by them. If you were to behave in a manner that could be misunderstood or misinterpreted, you could be accused of engaging in behaviour that could constitute abuse. Things that you should never do when working with children and young people include:

- allow or engage in any form of inappropriate touching
- allow children or young people to use inappropriate language without challenging it
- enter into a adult relationship (physical/sexual) with a person under 18 to whom you are in a position of trust, even if they consent to or suggest the relationship
- allow allegations to go unchallenged, unrecorded or not acted on.

Police screening of staff

CRB checking is an essential screening process that must be done prior to a member of staff working with children or young people.

Limits and boundaries and why these are important

As a teacher or coach, you should develop relationships with children and young people based

Why is it important to ensure appropriate behaviour and boundaries at all times?

on honesty, trust and respect; both you and the young people must understand the boundaries. Once you have set these boundaries, do what you say you are going to do. This means that there will not be any confusion about the relationship between you and the young person, which will in turn mean that you are less likely to be at risk from allegations.

Understanding neglect and abuse

Child abuse takes many forms, but it can be put into the five main categories of:

- neglect
- physical abuse
- sexual abuse
- emotional abuse
- bullying and harassment.

- **Neglect** occurs when adults do not meet the basic physical and/or psychological needs of the child; not meeting these needs could result in impairing the child's health or development. An example of neglect in PE could be the teacher using activities that lead to an unnecessary risk of injury to the child.

- **Physical abuse** occurs when somebody deliberately physically harms a child. An example of physical abuse in PE could be the teacher hitting a child.

- **Sexual abuse** occurs when adults or other children use children to meet their sexual needs. An obvious example of this type of abuse is a teacher having sexual intercourse with a child, but other signs of sexual abuse that could be more difficult to detect could be not following correct guidelines for physical contact with children or taking inappropriate photographs or videos of children.

- **Emotional abuse** is the emotional mistreatment of children that negatively influences their development; and often accompanies neglect, physical abuse or sexual abuse. An example of emotional abuse in PE could be a teacher frightening a child by threatening them; but it could also be at the other end of the spectrum where a teacher does not allow a child to emotionally develop because the teacher is overprotective.

- **Bullying and harassment** – bullying is deliberately hurtful behaviour that is usually experienced over a period of time. Harassment is often linked to bullying as this occurs when an individual feels that they have been subjected to unacceptable behaviour. An example of bullying and harassment in PE could be a teacher repeatedly calling a child a name because they are overweight.

Activity: What is abuse?

Imagine that you are working for a national training organisation as part of their child protection training network. You regularly run training events for teachers and sports coaches about child abuse and are in the process of developing some new materials. For your next training event, produce a poster that includes a mind map for each type of abuse. Include as many different examples of each type of abuse as you can think of.

Recognising the signs of neglect and abuse

Recognising the signs of abuse is difficult, even for those who have worked with children for a long time. When children play, they may have accidents that result in cuts and bruises; or they may not be enjoying a game because they are losing which may make them seem uncharacteristically low. There are, however, some signs that you must look out for including: significant changes in the child's behaviour, unexplained bruising, cuts or other marks, deterioration in the child's general wellbeing and comments that cause concern.

Other examples of things that you should report:

- There is a chance that a relationship is developing which could be an abuse of trust.

- You worry that a child or young person is attracted to you or a colleague who is in a position of power or influence over them.

- You have been required to physically restrain a child or young person to prevent them from harming themselves or another person, or from causing significant damage to property.
- A child or young person tells you they are being abused or describes experiences you believe may constitute abuse.

Procedures and policies for expressing concerns about children's welfare

There are set procedures and policies in place for expressing concerns about a child's welfare. These are laid out in the publication 'What to do if you are worried a child is being abused – Summary' that is published by the DCSF, so download and save this document. Figure 24.4 gives you an overview of how to deal with concerns about abuse.

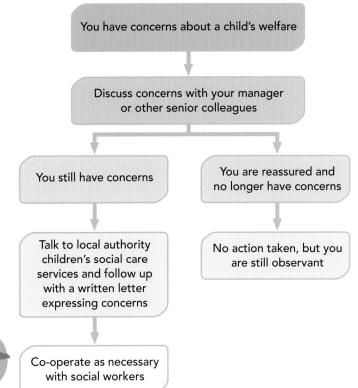

Figure 24.4: How should you deal with any concerns of child abuse?

Case study: What should you do?

You work at a local leisure centre that offers swimming lessons in the pool for children and young people of different ages. You are one of three swimming teachers working with different groups and the leisure centre manager is the appointed child protection and welfare officer.

Jack is five years old. He has swimming lessons at the local leisure centre during the week and during the holidays. He comes from a very respectable family – his father is a local businessman and his mother is a teacher. With their jobs, Jack's parents are often busy and are in a hurry when they come to collect Jack. Jack is generally a very happy boy – he always joins in with lessons and gets on well with the other children in the group.

Last week, Jack's father came to pick him up from swimming lessons and appeared unusually rushed. Before Jack had finished getting changed, his father put him in the car and drove off at speed. This week, Jack has arrived at the lesson as normal, his father seems much less rushed and Jack is his usual happy self. When Jack comes out to the pool, you notice that he has five straight red marks across the back of his thigh.

1. Is there anything strange about the nature of the marks on Jack's legs?
2. Do you have any reason to be concerned and why?
3. What should you do in this situation?

Roles and responsibilities of those involved in safeguarding children and promoting their welfare, health, safety and security

Everybody who works with a child or young person is responsible for safeguarding them. When working with children you are in a position of trust. This means that you have power and influence over them. You must have transparency in your work and have the highest standards of ethics and behaviour. Some examples include:

- If any of your teaching involves necessary physical contact, you should inform children, young people, parents or carers of this. For example, it may be necessary in gymnastics to support a child for health and safety reasons.
- Make sure that you use age-appropriate language and clarify anything you say.
- Provide all relevant health and safety information.
- Do not leave children or young people unattended.
- Pay attention to any signs of abuse.
- Report concerns that you have to the welfare officer, your manager or child protection officer.
- Maintain confidentiality on a 'need to know' basis.

There are job roles and organisations with specific responsibilities which deal with concerns over child abuse including:

- welfare officer
- social services
- child protection officer
- police.

Sources of information and support

There are lots of sources of information and support when working with children or young people. Details of a number of organisations can be found in Table 24.3.

Table 24.3: Sources of information and support when working with children and young people.

Name	Website
Child Protection in Sport Unit	www.nspcc.org.uk
Criminal Records Bureau	www.crb.homeoffice.gov.uk
NSPCC	www.nspcc.org.uk
Sport England	www.sportengland.org
UK Sport	www.uksport.gov.uk
Youth Sport Trust	www.youthsporttrust.org

Assessment activity 24.4

 P7 P8 P9 M3 D2 :BTEC

You are working as a welfare officer for your local sports club. You have taken on board some new sports coaches and you are responsible for delivering the information relating to safeguarding the children and young people that they are working with and ensuring their own protection. You have been asked to deliver this information as a presentation to the staff.

1. Describe strategies for supporting the safety of children and young people. **P7**

2. Describe the legislation, policies and procedures that safeguard children and young people. **P8**

3. Explain how these procedures keep children, young people and those working with them safe. **M3**

4. Evaluate these procedures in terms of how they keep everyone concerned safe. **D2**

5. Describe strategies to ensure your own protection when working with children and young people. **P9**

Grading tips

- To attain **P7** describe a range of strategies, for example, empowering children and young people.

- To attain **P8** select a range of relevant legislation (for example, the Children Act), procedures and policies (for example, CRB checks) that are used to safeguard children and young people and describe the parts that are relevant to a learning environment.

- To attain **M3**, for the procedures that you selected, explain (for example, by providing examples) how they keep children, young people and those working with them, safe.

- To attain **D2**, for the procedures that you selected, evaluate their effectiveness by looking at strengths or areas for improvement within the procedures.

- To attain **P9** describe a range of strategies that are used to ensure your own protection (for example, using appropriate behaviour).

PLTS

When you are researching, compiling and making your presentation you can demonstrate your **self-manager**, **independent enquirer** and **creative thinker** skills.

Functional skills

When you are accessing and assessing safeguarding policies for your presentation you can demonstrate your **ICT** and **English** skills.

Carmelle Brinton
PE teacher

Carmelle is a PE teacher who works in a secondary school. Her job involves planning and designing lessons, teaching PE lessons, observing peers teaching their lessons, running sports teams and assessing children and young people's progress through the National Curriculum.

'School PE presents opportunities for children and young people to be physically active or get involved in sport at a level that is appropriate for them. PE also gives children and young people the chance to stay fit and healthy, to gain a range of personal and social skills and it is something that they really enjoy. All of this gives me a great sense of satisfaction and it's a big part of why I do this job. It is really satisfying seeing young people develop as they go through school and the sense of achievement that you get from knowing that you have helped them is amazing.

Like all jobs though, it has its ups and downs. There is a lot of work to do on the planning and administration side of things and you are often presented with a number of different issues that you need to control. One of the biggest problems that I face is when individuals or small groups of learners become disruptive in class. This is really unfair on those learners who are trying to learn so it's normally quite a big part of my job when I'm teaching to make sure that all groups stay on track and progress towards their learning outcomes as they should. To be able to do this, I need to make sure that I use the most appropriate teaching, learning and leadership styles with the right groups.

Think about it!

- What are the different factors that you would need to consider when trying to control groups in PE?
- How do you think that different teaching styles and different types of activities can influence the learning of different children and young people?
- Do you think you would enjoy a career in PE teaching?

Just checking

1. What are the different stages of the National Curriculum for PE within the UK?
2. What does the term National Occupational Standards mean and how do they influence the development of the curriculum?
3. How is the PE curriculum implemented within the UK?
4. How can PE influence educational attainment?
5. How can PE positively benefit society in general?
6. Name four different methods of teaching in PE and describe their benefits.
7. What factors should you consider when designing learner focused activities in PE?
8. What are the different levels of disclosure and what information do they provide?
9. Name three pieces of legislation that are important for child protection and discuss how they influence child protection policies and procedures.
10. What are the different types of abuse?

edexcel

Assignment tips

- There are lots of government papers, policies and procedures that will be very useful when you are completing the assessments for this unit so it would be worthwhile downloading and saving copies of each.
- Make sure you use key websites to help you get a deeper understanding of organisational and safeguarding children topics. Some useful websites include:
  - Youth Sport Trust (www.youthsporttrust.org)
  - Sport England (www.sportengland.org)
  - Department for Children, Schools and Families (www.dcsf.gov.uk)
  - NSPCC (www.nspcc.org.uk)
- There are lots of ideas for different teaching resources available so you may want to look at the following websites for different ideas and tips for planning lessons.
  - www.teachpe.com
  - www.tes.co.uk
  - www.afpe.org.uk
  - www.teachernet.gov.uk

25 Sport as a business

Sport is big business. We are familiar with the products and services on sale from global retailers of sports equipment and clothing, media organisations, premiership clubs, stadia and arenas and the many private gyms that have sprung up on the back of the health and fitness boom. However, many sports businesses are small, employing just a few people – often the manager has to have all the business skills. Most fitness instructors are self-employed. There is also a need for amateur clubs to be run in a businesslike way to survive. Business skills are important for anybody who wants to work in the sports industry.

This unit will introduce you to the core skills used by sports businesses and the key aspects of business and management including organisation, structure, finance, legislation and marketing. Getting these aspects in balance for a sports business is crucial for success. Sports businesses can only survive and thrive if they make a profit, have a customer-focused approach and adjust to changes in the market; to do this they must be proactive in their business methods. These are key themes emphasised in this unit.

Learning outcomes

After completing this unit you should:

1. know how businesses in sport are organised
2. know what makes a successful sports business
3. know the legal and financial influences on sport as a business
4. be able to use market research and marketing for a sports business.

Assessment and grading criteria

This table shows you what you must do in order to achieve a pass, merit or distinction grade, and where you can find activities in this book to help you.

To achieve a **pass** grade the evidence must show that you are able to:	To achieve a **merit** grade the evidence must show that, in addition to the pass criteria, you are able to:	To achieve a **distinction** grade the evidence must show that, in addition to the pass and merit criteria, you are able to:
P1 describe the organisation of two different sports businesses **See Assessment activity 25.1, page 365**	**M1** compare and contrast the organisation of two different sports businesses **See Assessment activity 25.1, page 365**	
P2 describe what makes a successful sports business **See Assessment activity 25.2, page 368**	**M2** explain what makes a successful sports business **See Assessment activity 25.2, page 368**	
P3 describe three legal influences on a sports business **See Assessment activity 25.3, page 374**	**M3** explain three legal influences on businesses in sport **See Assessment activity 25.3, page 374**	
P4 describe a basic cash flow for a selected business **See Assessment activity 25.3, page 374**		
P5 plan market research related to, and appropriate for, a selected sports business **See Assessment activity 25.4, page 382**		
P6 conduct market research related to, and appropriate for, a selected sports business, recording and interpreting results **See Assessment activity 25.4, page 382**	**M4** conduct market research related to, and appropriate for, a selected sports business, explaining the results **See Assessment activity 25.4, page 382**	**D1** analyse the results of the market research, drawing valid conclusions **See Assessment activity 25.4, page 382**
P7 describe the marketing activities of a selected sports business **See Assessment activity 25.4, page 382**		
P8 produce a promotional plan for a selected sports product or service, drawing on market research **See Assessment activity 25.4, page 382**	**M5** justify a promotional plan for a selected sports product or service **See Assessment activity 25.4, page 382**	**D2** evaluate the promotional plan identifying areas for improvement **See Assessment activity 25.4, page 382**

How you will be assessed

There will be a range of assessment styles possible in this unit including:

- reports with supplements such as posters or wall charts
- tables with supporting summaries
- presentations with leaflets
- promotional plans and booklets.

Tom, 16-year-old keen cricketer

When I was considering taking this unit I knew it would be a challenge to cover all the skills and knowledge. However, I had an idea I could use the sports shop my brother works in on a Saturday to give me a start at researching a sports business. My brother got me an interview with the owner so I could learn more and he was very helpful telling me about the structure of the business (which was a limited company) and the legal and financial side of a sports business.

After I spoke to the owner he passed me onto the marketing person who took me through all that he has to do to research and promote sports products. I enjoyed learning more about how that aspect of the business worked because it gave me a chance to understand what goes on behind the scenes. It made me think I might study marketing later. This was great experience for me and helped me to see how some of the classroom stuff we did is applied in real life.

Over to you!

1. Can you identify which sector the sports shop operated in?
2. Tom learned a lot about marketing, finance and the legal side of sports businesses. Which do you think is the most important?
3. What do you think is the secret of small sports businesses who can survive against the bigger sports shop chains?

1. Know how businesses in sport are organised

There is a diverse range of organisations and people operating in the sports industry to provide products and services. Some are in the public sector providing opportunities for local communities; others exist in the private sector seeking to make a profit, while even more are amateur clubs run by volunteers. Many are individuals offering professional services. This leads to different philosophies and approaches to delivery, but all have to adopt efficient business processes to be successful. This section will help you learn about all the different types of business and how they are organised.

1.1 Sports businesses

Public sports and leisure clubs

These are usually based at local authority centres such as a swimming club or karate club. Managers of these centres have to operate professionally, following a strategy to meet targets and working to a budget. Any club arrangement will have to comply with their requirements and pay the going rate for hiring space. Prices are usually set as low as possible to help make it easy for people to join, but at a level that keeps the organisation sustainable. They often have to stage some additional fundraising activities to boost income.

Private sports and leisure clubs

These types of club are businesses with membership fees set at the market rate or above and members enjoy good benefits. A good example is a golf club where members have a bar, restaurant and good quality changing rooms. The club will try to develop

the sport and make a profit. Some larger corporations with large headquarters often have this type of private club for staff (for example, The Royal Bank of Scotland). Members can enjoy not just sports, but also health and wellbeing programmes. This type of membership is a business perk.

Professional sports clubs

These are the types of sports clubs which you may support or even play for at junior level. They are set up to predominantly compete in leagues and tournaments at the highest level they can. Many have long histories dating back to their creation over 100 years ago, such as the most famous rugby, football and cricket clubs. Their operations are diverse and are businesses with staff such as marketers, a commercial manager, a human resources manager, and business activities such as a merchandising shop for fans, function suites for events and corporate boxes for match days. These are focused on making income for the club away from the turnstiles. The largest and best known are the Premiership Clubs such as Arsenal and Liverpool, Manchester Utd and Chelsea who all have a range of business activities at their grounds as well as the playing area including function suites and conference facilities.

Amateur sports clubs

These types of clubs are smaller than professional clubs, but represent the bulk of British sport. They are sometimes described as the grass roots of sport. Sport England estimate there may be as many as 8 million people involved in sport at some level, through the amateur club system. The essence of these clubs is that they are often run by enthusiasts with not much business knowledge, who give their time freely and reflect the ideals of volunteerism. They survive on fundraising, fees, donations and maybe a little sponsorship.

Remember

The key issues for many amateur clubs is finding people who will volunteer to run them and keeping a flow of younger players coming into the club to maintain its teams.

Coaching services

This sector has grown in recent years, as the national governing bodies (NGBs) of sport have developed awards schemes for youngsters, which require qualified coaches to run them. This has given individual coaches a chance to create a career for themselves working with schools, academies, colleges and clubs locally offering their coaching services. Many are ex-players. Despite this growth, the UK is not as advanced as other countries in creating and valuing coaches. The opportunities for coaches can be limited in certain sports areas, and often the hourly pay rate is not enough to live on. Most coaches are self-employed and require governing body qualifications for approval to coach (and CRB checks if they work with children).

Health and fitness facilities

This sector is typified by gyms, spas and health resorts, often in one complex or attached to another leisure facility. Some experts think this business sector has peaked after rapid growth in the early 2000s as many organisations have to work hard to retain and gain members especially in times of recession. However, growth has been attributable to our increased awareness of the need for healthier lifestyles and exercise and our willingness to pay for it. Several well-known British entrepreneurs traded on this awareness and, in the last decade, created very successful fitness chains which are now household names (for example, Duncan Bannatyne, Richard Branson and David Lloyd).

Not all gyms are part of a chain and many local private gyms have been created; some are family businesses and are successful. They may not be in purpose-built premises but they offer a personal service which some people prefer.

Health and fitness facilities are well established and are often found as features in holiday brochures to attract people to hotels, cruise ships, holiday camps and caravan parks. Large organisations often offer gyms and facilities as part of their wellbeing programmes for staff.

Case study: Sports directors

Some of the larger sports bodies have created the post of director, which could be seen as the pinnacle of a coach's career. These posts are well paid. In the UK, the Director of English Cricket is reputed to earn £300,000 per annum. In the USA this type of post is common and according to a recent study carried out by the Chronicle of Higher Education, the average annual salary for a Division I sports director is now $158,200, a near 100 per cent increase from 1990. With that level of attainment, however, comes accountability and the need for success. If you consider the changes in the post of England rugby director since they won the World Cup in 2006, it has not been a very secure job.

1. **Do you think these high salaries have an impact on other aspects of sport? Where does the money come from to pay these salaries?**

2. **Compare these salaries with what a head coach at a large club in your area earns and draw some conclusions. Should there be a cap on what players and coaches can earn?**

1.2 Organisation

People on the commercial side of sport organise their companies to suit the products or services they will offer, the way they wish to operate and to comply with the law.

Types of business

- **Sole trader** – this is an individual, such as a personal fitness coach (offering a service) or a small sports shop run by an individual (selling products). They will be the decision-maker and run the business as they wish, will enjoy all the profits, and are responsible for all the debts. Those wishing to set themselves up as **sole traders** can get advice from HM Revenue & Customs and a bank to ensure they are properly informed and have a sensible business plan.

- **Partnerships** – this business arrangement is used when a few people wish to form a company. They all have to share responsibilities which are written into a deed of partnership. Advice for setting up this sort of business can be obtained from Companies House, where registrations are logged to make them legal. Partners are liable for any debts.

- **Private limited companies** – these are generally smaller businesses organised with shareholders who invest and take a share of the company. The shares cannot be traded on the stock market and often the shareholders will appoint a board of directors to make the business decisions, while a managing director deals with the every day running. There are sometimes tax advantages for a private limited company operating in the sports industry. If the company does not succeed, shareholders will only lose their investment and they will not be liable for any company debts. Perhaps the best known company of this type in sport is the London Organising Committee of the Olympic Games and Paralympic Games Ltd.

- **Public limited companies** – plcs, as they tend to be known, are larger businesses with shares offered for sale to the general pubic on the stock market. Shareholders can vote on general policies, but the organisation is run by a board of directors who are very experienced. Shareholders are paid a **dividend** from profits if they are made, but if the organisation makes a loss they are not likely to get a payment.

They are not liable for debts; however, directors may be liable. One example of a plc in the sports industry is shown in the case study below.

Case study: Sports Direct International

Sports Direct International plc is a sporting goods retailer that sells sports equipment and clothing through Exsports, Lillywhites, McGurks, Gilesports, Hargreaves and Streetwise and via the website sportsdirect.com.

It also owns other sports and leisure brands, including Antigua, Dunlop, Kangol, Karrimor, Lonsdale and Slazenger.

Sports Direct was floated on the London Stock Exchange making £929 million for majority stakeholder and founder Mike Ashley.

1. Where do you think the owner borrowed his capital from in the beginning? Why was he so successful?
2. Can you find out what the share price is worth now?
3. Do you think they almost have a monopoly?

- **Franchises** – are when someone (the franchisee) buys a business format, product or the right to use the trademark from another firm (the franchisor). A capital sum is paid to the franchisor for the rights and usually the franchisee is able to keep all profits after interest on loans, fees and other overheads are paid off. This can be a low risk way of starting a business as the franchisee is guided by the franchisor to follow a proven trading method with a proven product or service, for example, golf breaks, or health and fitness products. However, the most common form of **franchise** is a retail business. Franchises can be granted to retailers to sell imported sports products or clothing, for example, surf goods from California.

- **Public bodies** – these organisations (sometimes called quangos) have been set up and are funded by the government. Examples include the Youth Sport Trust, Sport England, UK Sport and the English Institute of Sport. They are intended to function 'at arms length' from the government, running their respective areas semi-autonomously, but with funding guaranteed, usually drawn from Lottery sources. They are not-for-profit organisations and work in a businesslike manner to fulfil their role.

Key terms

Sole trader – a one person business.

Dividend – a payment made to shareholders (usually once a year) in proportion to the numbers of shares they hold.

Franchise – a business bought from a bigger company specifically to sell their products or services.

Chief executive officer –the most senior person responsible for the day to day running of a company (but responsible to the board if it is a plc).

Operations – the everyday working of a business.

Structure

All sports businesses need a structure. This gives a clear definition of titles (posts), roles and responsibilities, lines of communication, and who is in authority. The type of structure adopted by a sports business will depend on a number of factors, such as the nature of the operation, types of products and services they offer, locations and number of employees. To enable you to gain a fuller insight this section covers management roles, different functions in a company and staffing.

- **Senior management** – a senior manager is next in line down from the board of directors or **chief executive officer**. They tend to be put in charge of a large facility, or maybe several for split-site operations. Their role is to take an overview of all **operations** and steer them towards the company's aims and goals.

- **Management** – working at management level means making many decisions, keeping staff motivated, ensuring standards are met, dealing with complaints, and interpreting and applying new instructions. You have to be a good leader, organised and knowledgeable to be effective. A manager is the link between senior staff who decide on directions for the business and the staff who

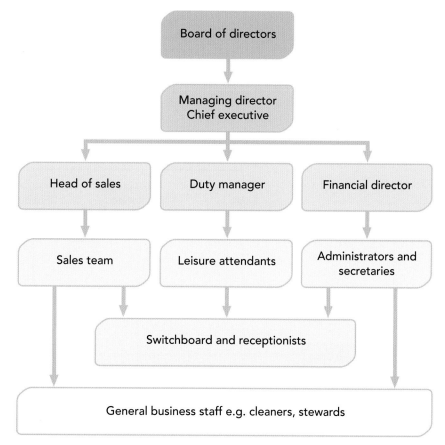

Figure 25.1: One example of sports business structure. What type of organisation do you think this represents?

apply working practices to meet the targets set. Typical titles include:

- ○ leisure operations manager – for a sport and leisure complex
- ○ development manager – for a professional club
- ○ customer services manager – for a retail outlet
- ○ project manager – for a series of sports events

- **Functional departments** – are used where a number of similar tasks and roles can be grouped together for efficiency, for example, marketing or finance functions. This can lead to a matrix of functions supporting the business such as in a stadium with an admin and security team, groundsmen, and maintenance teams all working across the business to support other dimensions as shown in Figure 25.2.

- **Regional structures** – these are used when the organisation is spread over a large area with many outlets such as a national company like Sports Direct. This can be described as a decentralised structure. To make it easier to coordinate, managers are usually appointed to run a region but have to report back to a senior manager at a central office.

Staff

Staff are often described as the key element in any business. Most are organised into teams or departments.

You can use the structure diagram on page 363 to identify the position of different types of staff in the hierarchy of an organisation. Their titles will also help you to understand roles and the flow of responsibilities, for example:

- the chief executive will decide on the organisation's **strategy**
- the duty manager(s) will have to implement this by adopting good tactics in day to day activities
- the sales manager will need to meet targets to achieve the operation's aims
- the receptionists and leisure attendants need to deliver the service and keep the customers happy and loyal to the business.

Key terms

Strategy – how a business plan is implemented.

Remember

Although there is a hierarchy and different needs everyone has to work as a team with a clear strategy, appropriate tactics, smooth operations and great delivery.

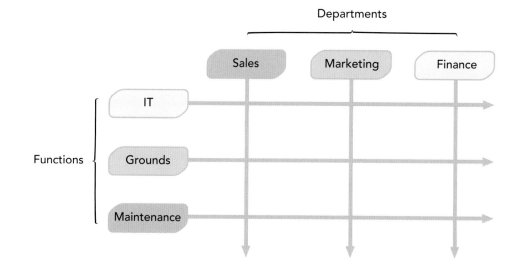

Figure 25.2: A matrix structure. Can you add two other departments and functions that you think might exist in the structure of stadium business?

Assessment activity 25.1 (P1)(M1) BTEC

You are preparing for two interviews for which you have been shortlisted by two different sports companies. By investigating both companies you can give yourself a better picture of their organisation, structure, staffing and operations, so that you are well prepared for the interviews.

1. Your task is to describe the organisation of the two different sports businesses. (P1)

2. Your challenge is to compare and contrast the organisation of the two different sports businesses. (M1)

Grading tips

- To attain (P1) study the types of businesses and select two which you feel have plenty of information for you to work with. Ensure that you identify what type of businesses they are, perhaps who their main customers are, what products or services they trade in and how they are set up to operate and their staff base. Research could be done as part of a visit, online, by contacting the organisations or using company reports.

- To attain (M1) you need to decide what criteria you will use to compare and contrast effectively. Comparing dissimilar organisations can be more difficult. The level of detail will be important as will the range of coverage and quality of your explanations.

PLTS

You will be able to evidence your skills as an **independent enquirer** as you research.

Functional skills

You can evidence your **ICT** skills when you find and select information, develop and present your findings.

2.   Know what makes a successful sports business

There are certain key elements that have to come together for success to be achieved – a well thought out strategy, adequate resources to deliver this strategy and a willing team of staff. Add to this good products and/or services and income from satisfied customers and the recipe for success is complete. This section will investigate these elements in detail.

Success

You can measure success in two ways:

- The tangible way is to count its measurable indicators such as profit, income or turnover, growth and size.

- The less tangible way to judge finds success in more subjective indicators such as image, levels of customer and staff satisfaction and sustainability.

This section will explain the importance of measuring success in both ways.

Income

This is the amount of money coming into an organisation. The amount of money going out of the organisation is called expenditure. To be successful, **income** needs to exceed **expenditure** and generate **profit**. Costs include:

- rent of premises
- raw goods and materials

Key terms

Income – an amount of money coming into an organisation over a period of time.

Expenditure – money used up by an organisation over a period of time.

Profit – excess of revenue over outlays and expenses for an organisation over a period of time.

- interest payable on loans
- utilities (heat, light and water) bills
- taxes (such as VAT and business rates) and national insurance
- staff wages.

Sources of income vary according to the type of business, but common sources include sales of products, membership charges, tickets sold and fees for services. Can you add one more?

Profit

Successful companies will end their year with a gross profit figure, which is income from sales less any costs of creating the goods or services they have sold. However, a better figure to use in judging success is that of net profit as that is the amount which is left over after deducting all costs of supplying the goods and also all other business costs such as rent and rates. So a company which used £800 to produce a trampoline to be sold for £1000 is not very efficient, because that would leave gross profit of only £200 to pay for all costs such as materials, wages and marketing. This would probably mean a very low net profit – if any!

You can roughly judge the profitability of a company by measuring the difference between its costs of producing something and how much profit it has produced.

Company owners require high net profit as this will not only define the success of their company, but it determines how much:

- can be taken as earnings
- will go to shareholders as dividends
- will be reinvested in the business.

In a climate of recession, firms may have much lower profit margins – indeed if no profit is made they will have to restructure (**downsize**) to try and stay in business, as Blacks did in 2009, or be liquidated as with Diadora in 2009.

Growth

Business growth comes through increased revenue allowing expansion (as with Sport Direct). Companies who show year on year growth can be considered successful. However, if growth is not resourced properly, staff can be overstretched. Many sports businesses have experienced growth during the past decade as demand for their products has soared – this

has been most apparent with franchises. However, it is less apparent during recession as survival or consolidation is the aim. Most market reports say that many sports industry businesses stalled at the beginning of 2010 and may not revive until the London Olympics.

Sustainability

This concept has three pillars; in modern terms, **sustainability** means not just the continuation of the business (the economic pillar), but it must also exhibit social responsibility (the ethical pillar) and environmental sustainability (the sustainable pillar), so that local communities and habitats are maintained. Many sports businesses now emphasise their fair trading and green practices to show customers they are sustainable and ethical.

Take it further

Sports organisations and sustainability

Carry out research to identify what sustainable approaches major sports organisations are carrying out such as recycling and energy saving schemes or supporting their local area.

Customer satisfaction

To achieve customer satisfaction you must ensure the business is customer-facing. This is achieved by having good policies and procedures for staff to follow and a customer charter. Top companies have a **quality system** aimed at customer satisfaction, which is applied throughout the business. Customer service is a team effort and must come from everyone in the organisation. There are many business advantages which come from good customer service (see Figure 25.3). Companies work hard to retain loyal customers.

Key terms

Downsize – to restructure, making an organisation smaller, usually to ensure its continued existence.

Sustainability – capable of providing steady support without becoming exhausted.

Quality system – plans, policies, processes and procedures which all come together in a systematic way to ensure the organisation works to a high standard.

Figure 25.3: Advantages of good customer care. Could you add two more advantages that sports businesses could gain?

Staff satisfaction

Creating successful and satisfied staff can be one of the biggest challenges for managers in sports businesses. Many of the principles outlined above for external customers also apply here: being polite, having a good attitude, establishing a good rapport and being consistent. Perhaps this is best summed up by the phrase 'being professional'. Table 25.1 shows you some good pointers and what a good company will do. From an organisation's point of view, keeping staff happy needs a blend of motivation and fulfilment.

Table 25.1: Being professional.

Individuals	Applied examples
Meet deadlines	For colleagues and customers and be on time
Stick to procedures	Follow rules and best practice
Do your share	Don't be a team loafer
Attention to detail	Dress appropriately
Listen to explanations and complaints	Show good eye contact and concentration
Be supportive	Show support for the team you are in
A company	**Applied examples**
Provide good working conditions	Clean and safe
Foster career progression	Create a structure in which staff can gain promotion
Praise and reward good work	Have an incentive scheme
Give a sense of value and belonging	Managers trust and respect staff
Operate anti-discriminatory and equal opportunities policies	Ensure these are applied throughout the organisation
Create good relationships with external suppliers	Have honest and transparent relationships

Achieving aims and targets

Aims are what a business is working towards – its vision or mission statement shows its overall strategic direction. Here are two examples of aims of sports businesses:

- Pitch, a public relations consultancy for sportspeople and businesses aims to be 'The No. 1 communications consultancy in sponsorship and sport' for the 2012 Olympics in London
- The British Olympic Association aims for Britain to achieve at least fourth place in the medal tables.

Smaller businesses might aim to make a profit in order to stay in business. Within a business, staff may have personal aims (for example, to gain promotion). These are discussed during their annual appraisal so that managers can know what staff want to aim for. Targets are measurable objectives (SMART). For a sports business, targets might be:

- increased sales by a set amount, e.g. 10%
- increased **customer base**, e.g. 800 new customers within six months
- greater profits, for example, £3000 per month
- growth in market share, e.g. 1% per year
- an improvement in staff productivity, e.g. 3 % .

Individuals may have personal targets such as sales per month or retention rates of members. Meeting or exceeding targets can bring bonuses.

Fulfilling the remit

This means reaching targets, meeting aims, and using resources well, to give good returns. It is doing all you are asked to do, on time, within budget and professionally. To achieve this, all aspects of the business have to be managed effectively and efficiently – the finance, the human resources, the physical resources used – all coming together to fulfil a remit. This is sometimes called **goal congruency**, when everyone's goals are reached at the same time. Many companies reward their staff if their **remit** is fulfilled with an end-of-year bonus or a special trip or event.

Key terms

Customer base – the number of customers a company regularly has.

Goal congruency – individual, organisational and team goals all going in the same direction at the right time to give maximum results.

Remit – the area or responsibility of a person or organisation.

Assessment activity 25.2

You have inherited some money, which you have decided to invest by buying shares in a sports business. You need to carry out some research to assess which one will give you the best prospects of success and some future dividends.

1. Describe what makes a successful sports business. **P2**
2. Explain what makes a successful sports business **M2**

Grading tips

- To attain **P2** identify the factors you feel are important to include when you are judging success and write about these clearly, showing you can also use business terminology effectively. Be accurate and give as much detail as possible. If one of the organisations you selected for Assessment activity 25.1 was a successful organisation you could perhaps use this again for this focus. Be sure you select a suitable organisation which has some depth of material about it.

- To attain **M2** your explanation must illustrate not just that you know about the factors which contribute to success for sports business, but that you can also evaluate and explain them as they apply to your selected sports business case study. You might consider discussing what makes business unsuccessful too.

PLTS

You can evidence skills as an **independent enquirer** as you research successful sports businesses.

Functional skills

You can evidence your **ICT** skills when you find and select information and present your findings.

3. Know the legal and financial influences on sport as a business

Research done by the former DTI and Barclays (even before the recession) estimated that as many as 65 per cent of small companies fail within three years because they do not plan well, especially for the cost of trading within the law. This figure may be higher in a recession. Legal and financial factors have to be managed efficiently.

3.1 Legal influences

Four key Acts of Parliament have been in place for some time which influence how companies must set themselves up and run. You need to know the legislation, what its influences are and their likely impacts.

The Companies Act (1989)

Under this act, large companies (plcs and those limited by guarantee) are required to register themselves at Companies House in Cardiff, and put in place procedures and systems to comply with aspects of business such as accounting records for each year, and a directors' report, which are checked by auditors. Smaller businesses (SMEs) do not have such strict regulations to follow, but must still produce accounts for the tax inspector. Failing to do so, or providing misleading information in these accounts, can mean an offence is committed. The act also defines what is permitted in terms of trading, share dealing and inspections for wrongdoing.

The Partnership Act (1890)

On page 362 you learned something of partnerships. This act regulates and guides how partnerships must operate in terms of responsibilities, liabilities and to ensure problems can be dealt with. (Learn more at www. hmrc.gov.uk.)

The Fair Trading Act (1973)

This act was updated and modernised to become the Enterprise Act in 2002, which along with the Competition Act (1998) governs how companies trade, merge with each other and generally compete for business. The act controls business practice, makes companies follow fair trading methods and prevents larger ones from dominating the market. (Learn more at www.competition-commission.org.uk.)

Health & Safety at Work Act (1974)

This act ensures that all companies have health and safety policies and provide training for their staff. As you will have learned in Student Book 1, Unit 3 Assessing risk in sport, the basis of safety is assessing risk and this act sets out the aspects that must be covered in a working environment. It is enforced by the Health and Safety Executive (HSE) which has powers to fine or close down companies or imprison individuals if standards are unsafe. (Learn more at www.hse.gov.uk.)

> **Remember**
>
> There are several EU regulations which must be adhered to such as Working Time , Manual Handling and Personal Protective Clothing which can influence how some sports businesses have to operate (for example, those with long shift systems, equipment to move and adventurous activities). (See Table 25.3, page 370.)

The benefits of complying with legislation are shown in Table 25.2.

Table 25.2: The benefits of compliance with legislation – can you add two more actions and their outcomes?

Action	Outcome
The business is safe for staff, customers and visitors.	Builds the organisation's reputation for quality
All transactions are transparent and fair.	Gives a good company image
The organisation avoids fines for bad practice and negligence claims.	Equality – people want to work for an organisation that is anti-discriminatory
Accidents, incidents and complaints are dealt with following recommended codes of practice and procedures.	Protects the company from legal action

Statutory requirements

A statutory piece of legislation is something which comes from government and prescribes what must be done or complied with, i.e. what is required in certain situations to keep people safe or protected generally. This makes it a legal document and part of the law of the land. In essence, any EU regulations or directives or UK Acts of Parliament must be followed by all businesses, as statutory requirements (for example, The Health and Safety at Work Act). Because of the diversity of sports businesses, managers and owners have to be well versed in appropriate legislation. Some examples are shown in Table 25.3 of legislation, applications and how they influence the way sports businesses operate.

From these examples you can see the breadth and range of regulations with which sports businesses must comply. In addition to these regulations, there are a range of recommended codes of practice, which it is wise to follow.

Table 25.3: Legislation, applications and influence on sports businesses. Can you list some differing sports businesses that would have to comply with the legislation for each example?

Legislation	Applications	Influences
Personal Protective Equipment (Clothing) (EU 1992)	Crash hats, gloves, glasses	Investment in safety gear
Manual Handling Operations (EU 1992)	Lifting gear	Training staff in the safest techniques
Working Time regulations (EU 1998)	Governs the hours staff can work and their breaks	Adjusting shifts and breaks to suit the legislation
Control of Substances Hazardous to Health (UK 1994)	Chemicals and cleaning fluid	Creating safe storage systems/ locations
Occupiers Liability (Duty of Care) (UK 1984)	Requires premises to be safe for customers	Buildings and rooms for hire must comply
Data Protection Act (UK 1984)	Requires information held on clients to be confidential	Secure IT systems
Disability Discrimination (UK 1995 & 2002)	Adaptation of premises and working practices	Investment in disabled friendly fittings and access routes – an equality policy
The Safety at Sports Grounds Act (UK 1975) Fire Safety and Safety of Places of Sport Act (UK 1987)	Safety inspections and certificates needed	Investment, time to train staff and equipment
Consumer Protection Acts	Goods must be fit for purpose	A returns and complaints procedure

Health and safety (and security)

Staff must be aware of customers' health, safety and security at all times (this is a duty of care). All staff must take responsibility for reporting hazards (they cannot regard this as someone else's job) and they cannot plead ignorance – in the eyes of the law this is negligence. Failure to comply with legislation can have some serious consequences such as:

- loss of possessions, injury or death
- an individual or manager being sued, fined or imprisoned
- bad publicity and damage to company reputation and image
- higher costs of putting things right and insurance premiums.

Learn more at www.hse.gov.uk.

Employment laws

These cover recruitment, working conditions and termination of contract and redundancy. They are meant to ensure fairness and equality and prevent discrimination on the grounds of age, gender, religion or ethnicity. Some examples cover discipline and grievance procedures. Employment laws are meant to help both employees and employers. (Learn more at www.direct.gov.uk.)

Licensing

Sports businesses often have additional functions in their premises which need licensing, for example, to sell alcohol or hold a fundraising evening which includes gambling.

> ## Take it further
>
> ### Licences
>
> Write an example of a real business next to each of the activities below.
> - Serving alcohol
> - Gaming or gambling
> - Running adventure activities
> - Staging sports events with large crowds
> - Motor racing
> - Selling goods
> - Operating boats or planes
>
> Who grants the licences for these activities? Start your research by visiting your local council's website.

Insurance

This is necessary for sports businesses. Premiums may be high, but being sued for negligence could be a much higher price to pay. Insurance gives everyone peace of mind. Examples of insurance policies include:

- when providing advice or services as a professional
- 'all-risks' cover for office contents and computers, including portable equipment
- cover for accidents to the public while on your premises
- product **liability**, in case products are faulty or break
- employers' liability
- business interruption (for example, not being able to use premises)
- buildings and grounds
- legal expenses.

Public liability is probably the most essential type of insurance for most organisations. It ensures that they can compensate any member of the public who is injured as a result of the business or its staff failing to exercise reasonable care.

Planning permission

Planning permission is required when, for example, you alter a building in any way or erect a fence or hoarding. The local authority planning office needs to be contacted. This is a formal process and can take months to complete, so needs to be done before any work begins. The planning office will require you to submit accurate drawings to show what the business is planning, for example, an extension, new shop front, gym or indoor pool.

Local bye-laws

These are formulated to suit local conditions, for example, **bye-laws** for a beach or a sports event, or access to and use of a park for sports. They are set by the local authority and periodically reviewed. A sports business would need to contact the local council to see what might apply.

> ## Key terms
>
> **Liability** – legal responsibility for something.
> **Bye-laws** – a rule made by the local authority.

Fast Sport

Profit and loss account
for the year ended 05.04.10

	£	£
Sales		47,500
Less cost of sales		
Opening stock	9,000	
Purchase of materials	15,000	
	24,000	
Less closing stock	3,750	
	20,250	
Gross profit		27,250
Less expenses		
Loan repayment	1,000	
Utilities	410	
Office expenses	100	
Tax	125	
Advertising	745	
Insurance	545	
	2,925	
Net profit		24,325

Figure 25.4: What can you tell about their profit for the year?

3.2 Projected cash flow

Cash flow is important for a sports business – it is what accountants call '**liquidity**'. It allows the organisation to buy in goods and services, to support its own activities, pay its debts and save for contingencies or future developments. A sports business must plan its cash flow to ensure it has enough money to carry out its plans and meet needs such as wages, loan repayments and utility bills. Planning involves making forecasts before the start of the business year, based on likely income in the approaching business period. That is then set against outgoings (payments) which will have to be made in the same period. Data must be gathered regularly in the same period to ensure that the actual flow matches the predicted one. Often new sports businesses don't keep a proper check of this or are too optimistic in their initial forecasts – a sudden change can find them short of cash and in need of an **overdraft** to bail them out, which can be costly. The following section examines factors which need to

be calculated into the cash flow projections or have an influence on how a company operates. Forecasts are usually done on a six monthly basis so that any exceptions can be quickly seen.

Cash inflow forecasts

Cash inflow is what the company expects to come in. This will help set targets and identify peaks and troughs of income.

Capital

This can have a dual meaning, but in this context it would be cash or raw materials used to generate income (**working capital**). This allows the business to know how much they will be operating with at least initially. But it can vary with the in and outflow of cash.

Key terms

Cash flow – the movement of money in and out of an organisation.

Liquidity – money (or assets that can be quickly turned into cash).

Overdraft – additional credit or borrowing from a bank.

Working capital – the amount of money available for a business to work with. (In accountancy terms, the amount that current assets exceed current liabilities.)

Sales

For the forecast, the business should calculate the monthly sales projections, perhaps based on previous years or predicted trends. This will give one income figure. Sales might be broken down into different units such as fees, merchandise and hires to give a more accurate picture.

Loans

This is money borrowed (usually from a bank) to help finance an aspect of the business (but a loan must be repaid so that creates an outflow of cash).

Timing of inflows

It is better for a business if there is a steady inflow of cash, but many sports business are affected by seasonality, which brings peaks, troughs and changes. They must plan for these periods and also allow extra time for late payers, so that they are not short of cash when their own bills need paying.

Cash outflows

Linking to the point above, cash outflows should be planned so that capital is not run down below a safe level, creating an over-reliance on income to meet bills. This could, at worst, cause the company to fold. Credit such as a bank overdraft might be arranged to help here.

Purchases

The organisation needs to project what purchases it will make in the year. This could be raw materials to make goods or equipment for the business (for example, new computers). This could be influenced by the timing of cash inflow.

Repayment of loans

The repayment of a loan will also have interest added, so in the long-term a company will always pay back more than they borrowed – hence the need to keep an eye on interest rates. Sometimes banks can call in loans at short notice.

Wages

All businesses need to calculate salary and wage payments for each month, which includes national insurance amounts and often pension contributions too, for the year. Wage rates may also fluctuate if staff are asked to work a lot of overtime. The more of this that can be predicted the better.

Rent

Many sports businesses do not own their premises but rent them, taking on a lease. Monthly rentals rate are usually a steady figure to project, but rent reviews may occur and this can change the rate.

Promotion costs

The cost of materials a company uses to promote itself and the media in which these are used will have to be budgeted for in the projected cash flow.

Purpose of the cash flow projection

There are many categories of costs and sources of income which need to be in parallel to give a picture of the cash flow position at various points in the year. This gives the business managers the best chance of smoothing the flows to suit the business.

Determination of working capital

Accurate cash flow projections help a sports business know how much cash it has to work with for the year –

its working capital. This in turn will help it predict other financial dimensions such as likely profit, pricing and borrowing needs.

Make business decisions

Sound cash flow projections will help other business decisions such as whether a new store could be opened, if new equipment can be bought or levels of staffing should be adjusted.

Use of projected cash flow software

Nowadays computer programs can be used to execute the calculations part of projections. Managers can feed in different values or expectations and run the program to see what outcomes would be. These programs can also deal with lots of variables that might crop up. Examples include Exl-Plan, Cashflow Plan and Cashflow Plan Ultra.

Interpretation of results

Whatever the figures show, there will always be a human element required to interpret the data. This leaves interpretation open to error. However, a systematic approach should be the basis for decision-making over instinct.

Activity: Planning a cash flow

With the information you have on cash flows, try to create a checklist or action plan for someone operating a small sports business who is about to plan their cash flow for the next six months. Try to say why they should carry out the actions you recommend. The following headings might be used:

Aspect to be calculated	Influence on the business

Remember

Projected cash flow is only one part of business planning and needs regular monitoring as the year progresses.

Assessment activity 25.3

P3 P4 M3

You have been asked to give a talk to a group of new staff who have just joined a sports business as part of their induction process. Your boss has asked you to cover three legal influences on the business in the first session.

1. Describe three legal influences on a sports business. **P3**

2. Explain three legal influences on businesses in sport. **M3**

3. Describe a basic cash flow for a selected business. **P4**

Grading tips

- To attain **P3** and **M3** you should do some further research into the legal influences to deepen your understanding before you tackle the description or explanation. It may help your understanding if your tutor could organise a visit or guest speaker to cover the legal and financial aspects in a little more detail. Make sure you use the correct legal terminology.

- To attain **P4** think of the risks a business might face if cash flow is not properly maintained. Make sure you use the correct financial terminology.

PLTS

You might generate evidence of your skills as an **independent enquirer** when you are conducting your research on the legal and financial aspects.

Functional skills

If you use an IT system to gather your data or present your work you can demonstrate your **ICT** skills.

4. Be able to use market research and marketing for a sports business

The marketing process for a sports product or service starts with the identification of customers and their needs. This requires research. The research contributes to a plan for the promotion of the goods or service. This could be anything from a tennis racket or sweat band to a pilates class or coaching course, so the methods of research have to be reliable, the marketing activities appropriate and the promotional plan flexible. This section examines this process and equips you to carry out market research, promotional planning and marketing activities.

4.1 Plan

Sports businesses have good reasons for planning their marketing – they need to build up knowledge of customers, competitors, their market, demand and **trends**, opportunities and pricing. We'll look at these in more detail.

Key terms

Trends – the general direction or tendency in the market.
ACORN classification – a neighbourhood classification system used to categorise social groups base on income and lifestyle and demographic group.

Customer knowledge

You need to understand the characteristics of customers and the segments they fall into, as this helps sports businesses match their products to customers' types and needs. Sports businesses may use a consumer classification system to help them, such as the **ACORN** one shown in Table 25.4, or a lifestyle model to show interests. Analysing preferences and sporting habits for each category can help a company know what is likely to sell, and at what price.

Table 25.4: The ACORN classification system table.

Category	% of UK population	Group
Wealthy achievers	25%	Executives/rich families
Urban prosperity	10%	Professionals/educated urbanites/aspiring singles
Comfortably off	25%	Starting out/secure families/settled suburbia/prudent pensioners
Moderate means	15%	Asian communities/post-industrial families/blue collar roots
Hard pressed	25%	Struggling families/burdened singles/high-rise hardship/inner city adversity/unemployed

Source: adapted from CACI (2004)

Activity: Classifying consumers

Table 25.4 classifies residential neighbourhoods into which a business might promote itself, for example, a new local gym. Which category would you target? Can you add a fourth column listing the sporting interests you think each group might have?

Competitors

Knowing what your competitors are doing in the short-term, and what their strengths and weaknesses are, is important to sports businesses. Making comparisons, or **benchmarking**, is one method of doing this. For large sports organisations, this is important for pricing decisions; for smaller operators, price may be less of an issue, but quality of goods or services will be key. Research may show that there are gaps in the market which represent an opportunity.

The market

Compare the market – you need an awareness of what is going on in the market for the particular goods or services, but also the general business environment, especially in times of recession. Normally marketers would use a **PESTLE analysis** to help with this, which you can see in Table 25.5.

Key terms

Benchmarking – judging performance against a competitor.
PESTLE analysis – a method for analysing factors which might affect a market.

Table 25.5: A PESTLE analysis helps businesses to note what is going on in their market or business environment. Can you add a new trend or change to each of the headings?

P	Political	Changes in government policy
		New taxation laws
E	Economic	An increase in interest rates
		Recession
S	Social	Health and fitness boom
		Changes in age groups
T	Technological	New materials
		New equipment
L	Legal	Change in import laws
		New consumer rules
E	Environmental	More recycling required
		New outdoor locations

Demand and trends

Demand is the quantity of goods or services that a customer will buy at a given price. Some research is needed to determine the volume, price and quality of a product before it is launched. Trends can often offer business opportunities or give an early warning that something is going out of fashion (for example, playing squash, which has become less fashionable in the last decade).

Opportunities for development

A PESTLE analysis will indicate opportunities as well as new trends. Try the activity on page 376 to see if you can spot opportunities. Make a list of these.

Activity: Analysing sports business trends

Sports business trends are regularly analysed to help businesses keep pace with changes. Two organisations active in this area in the last decade were www.plunkettresearch.com and www.smallbiztrends.com, who noted the following:

Trend

- Improvements in 'smart' sports fabrics
- Expansion in team merchandising
- Changes in population balance towards older customers
- Growth in sports media and electronic games.
- Growth in adventure sports and short breaks
- An increase in use of sports agents by professional players
- Growth in women's soccer

For each trend, try to identify which type of sports businesses might benefit.

Pricing strategies

Three broad approaches should be considered:

1. Low price to try and penetrate the market – this can produce a price war with rivals
2. Prices set at the market rate – usually for frequent purchases
3. A high price strategy – usually for upmarket goods or services

The final price might also be governed by factors such as: how much profit the sports business needs to make; if they want to drive out rivals; if it's a short term promotion rate.

Methods of market research

A great deal of research needs to be carried out to ensure that the maximum information can be gathered about the potential customers and product or service. A number of research methods can be used. They are classified as primary (information gathered directly from the public) or secondary (based on reports and studies that others have completed and published). It is important to select the appropriate methods of gathering data. Whatever combination is used, sports businesses must ensure that data is current, accurate, reliable and easy to understand.

Appropriate market research methods

- **Surveys** – there are two types:
  - a census which means testing everyone in the market
  - a sample where a selection of respondents are surveyed as being representative of the likely market
- **Questionnaires** – these are often the basis of surveys, but need careful design to be effective – too many open-ended answers will give too many varied responses to be of real use. Closed questions, where people answer yes or no, or state their preference, are much easier to analyse. Multiple choice answers are popular as are **Likert scales** shown below:

  1 = Strongly disagree

  2 = Disagree

  3 = Not sure

  4 = Agree

  5 = Strongly agree

- **Product testing** – is carried out once a product has passed through the research stage and is nearly ready to be launched. Can you think how you might test a new tennis racquet?
- **Recording** – means how the information is collected. It will have to suit time, budget, expertise and the type of information being gathered. Speedy methods are questionnaires being optically scanned, or data being collected from focus groups electronically. Presentation is important too – a range of different ways is commonly used, including pie charts, graphs, tables, bar graphs and comparative scales.
- **Interpreting** – this is the final but most crucial stage. It must be done carefully and by experts as the outcome will inform product and selling strategy.

Key term

Likert scales – a sequence of grades (in responses).

Areas of research

There are six main areas that need to be researched which are shown in Figure 25.5.

4.2 Conduct

Conducting research is a scientific process. This section will examine the essentials in preparation for your own activities.

Sampling

- **Size** – choose the size of your sample population. This can be random people, clusters of typical customers or a quota who seem to fit the typical type.

- **Location** – decide on the location for the sampling, for example, where there is a large footfall or on a suitable website.

- **Timing** – assess the importance of the timing of the sampling – morning, midday or evening, midweek or weekend? (This might be guided by lifestyle habits and customer types.)

- **Implications of different samples** – how do they complement each other, and can you cross-reference data?

- **Cost of gathering** – a large survey and team will be costly as will the interpretation.

- **Accuracy of sample** – the answers must be truthful and from the right customer type.

Survey design

- **Questions** – decide what to ask to get the data you need and whether it will be face to face or home based, for example.

- **Survey length** – decide how long your survey will be (no more than a few minutes is best).

- **Type of questions** – what type you will use – in a sequence, dichotomous (opposite choices) open-ended, closed, multiple-choice, scaled, and how these will be laid out.

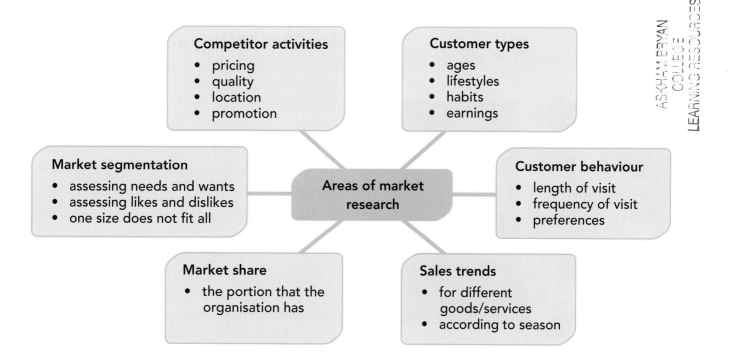

Figure 25.5: Areas for market research. For each part of the model write a short description or explanation of why you would cover these areas and what analysis of the data would tell you.

Table 25.6: Types of question.

Type of question	Example and layout
Sequenced	Respondents move through the questionnaire in a logical sequence guided by their previous reply such as 'if you answered yes to Q2 now go to Q5'.
Dichotomous	These would give two opposite opinions, such as recycling is good versus recycling is a waste of time.
Open-ended	This invites any sort of response such as 'What do you think about …?' This is more difficult to analyse.
Closed	Usually a yes or no reply is used here – this is much easier to analyse.
Multiple-choice	Respondents are given several responses – they choose the most appropriate one.
Scaled	There is a choice of responses here on a scale of, for example, 1 to 5 where 1 is 'strongly disagree' and 5 is 'strongly agree'.

Other aspects of surveys

- **Bias** – you must avoid bias in the interviewer's technique (maybe use a prompt card to ensure consistency).
- **Relevant** – make sure the questions sound relevant and are relevant to your required outcomes.
- **Responses** – decide how you will deal with responses, particularly the awkward or unexpected.
- **Record** – think about how you will record the response data, i.e. capturing the data and processing it before interpretation.
- **Presentation** – decide how you will present the outcomes – verbally, in a report with charts, tables and graphs?

Market research is sometimes carried out in the street. What problems could you identify with this technique?

4.3 Marketing activities

The results of the market research give the business its basis for marketing activities. For sports businesses this will be governed by:

- the budget available
- which medium their target audience mostly use
- the dates and timescale for getting the message out.

See the sequence below.

1. Select the main type of promotion medium to be used:
   - magazine (expensive if a glossy)
   - television (very expensive – local radio can be cheaper)
   - newspapers (national are expensive – local and free trade press are cheaper).

2. Develop the advertising messages:
   - Invent catchy phrases or product descriptions and benefits – sometimes images work too.

Retailers are particularly good at using their shop windows to promote offers. Why do you think they run these types of deals?

4.4 Promotional plan

Armed with the marketing materials and with the plans ready, there are just a few more pieces of the promotional jigsaw to put in place.

The steps that follow can be summed up as pre-launch management.

1. Development of promotional objectives

Set some promotional plan objectives. Any plan must have objectives so that the people implementing it know where they are aiming and when they achieved it. Remember all objectives must be SMART. Some examples might be:

- Setting a budget limit of £25
- Selecting a target audience (16–19-year-olds)
- Setting pricing bands for entry fees (£1–£3)
- Giving timescales for research feedback (within 1 week)
- Setting sample sizes (100 people)
- Identifying outlets (10)
- Having three practices for promotional communications.

2. Assess promotional opportunities, resources and policies

Assess the promotional **opportunities** – that could be following trends such as the Olympic boom or emphasising sustainable approaches. You may find that some of the outlets you would like to use for your promotions will not cooperate, so have some reserves.

Networking and using personal or family contacts is good way to develop the range of opportunities.

If you are involved in promoting a product, try to stage a demonstration or live promotion, maybe in a shopping mall, which attracts the public and may attract television and radio coverage.

All plans need **resources** to make them work – the promotional plan will need:

- people – such as a team leader, helpers to create and design posters and researchers
- finance, e.g. a budget for raw materials, printing and advertising costs and maybe expenses for people to deliver, or postage costs
- equipment such as paper, card, pens, access to computers, etc.

3. Train sales staff – they need good product or service knowledge so that they can describe it, demonstrate it and sell it confidently.

4. Plan sales promotional materials – leaflets, taster sessions, open days, special offers and promotional prices.

   Note: while this is going on someone in the team will assess competitors' prices which will help with formulating the final pricing plan.

5. Create an implementation plan for promotions to cover aspects such as: budget, timescale, quantity needed, locations, number of sessions, staffing and how long offers will last.

6. Formulate the pricing plan – this needs to involve setting prices, establishing who will get discounts and for how long, what the conditions of membership might be and fees or entry fees.

   Note: the content will of course depend on the type of sports business. You will have to think of other considerations that might apply to your selected organisation.

- venue(s) – as outlets for your promotional activities, for example, large stores or centres.

These all need to be identified, budgeted for, bought and put in your plan. You should also establish **policies** for each category so that people do not

- overspend
- go off at a tangent
- ignore instructions.

Regular team meetings will help to reinforce these.

3. Characteristics of target market

The promotions team should keep an eye on the characteristics of the target market, so that if people's preferences change or the whole market takes a downturn, adjustments can be made to the plan quickly. You might have to adjust to winter conditions. For example, consider the big freeze in 2009/10 when fewer people were able get around to see promotions or come to events or sales. Plans should never be set in stone, but reasonably flexible. Don't forget which part of the sports season you are in and promote accordingly.

4. Availability of promotional methods

Constraints which might affect the plan need to be identified, for example, the availability of promotional methods, i.e. lack of space in a newspaper or no airtime on the radio, or no slots for a product demonstration. You may not have the skills to create the materials you would really like or the budget to afford a professional version. This aspect needs careful consideration – again you can use SMART to guide you.

5. Formulate the promotional plan

At this stage it should be possible to formulate the final plan to include any revisions that have been necessary and go ahead with implementation. You might wish to write down all the details (in a manual) to ensure that people know what is planned and can refer to it at a glance if they forget or stray from the plan. As a reminder (checklist) the plan should contain:

- details of the market, its customers trends and typical pricing
- the methods you are going to use for research, analysis and marketing
- the activities which will be carried out

- an implementation section – showing how activities and tasks will be carried out, by whom and when (you could maybe use a **Gantt chart** here).

Writing it all out will make your evaluation much easier. Even better, if you do this electronically you can quickly make any revisions such as research updates, price changes or training needs.

Key term

Gantt chart – a planner-like calendar to show when things start and finish in a project.

Moving on, the steps that follow below can be classed as post-launch management. Managing and controlling activities and outcomes is the key aim.

1. Coordinate and control promotional activities

Hopefully only minor changes might be needed. Refer to your manual or written plan to check progress and manage exceptions and contingencies, i.e. things that crop up that are 'off target' or which you had not anticipated (such as poor personal communications or selling skills).

You may wish to appoint a coordinator for this stage to take an overview.

2. Advertising

Manage the advertising. This involves:

- keeping a close eye on the budget – appoint someone to do this
- monitoring the reactions of the target audience – through your research analysis, comments and observations
- ensuring that deliverers are using effective communication. For example, there are no spelling errors in written communications, verbal communication is clear with no slang or wrong terminology and visual communication 'images' are clear and not contravening copyright laws. Body language should be upbeat and appropriate – make some observations and give interim feedback.

3. Publicity

Exploit publicity opportunities. Examples are given on page 381.

- Press releases – these represent free publicity. They are simply a story about what you are doing. Send them to newspapers, television and radio companies.
- Feature articles – try for these in target market periodicals. Try to write an article which has features in it that are unique to you (these are called unique selling points or **USPs**).
- Magazines – use appropriate ones for the product or service. This might be your college magazine or a local publication, for example, a newsletter about events in the neighbourhood.
- Radio – try for an interview with your local DJ.
- Television – your regional station may be looking for human interest stories.
- Captioned photographs – contact the local press for a photo opportunity. If you have plenty of USPs they will usually be happy do this. Maybe invite them to photograph you at the business you are working with to give them some publicity too.

Key term

USPs – unique selling points for product or service (features to be promoted).

---

4. Public relations

This is usually shortened to PR and is best described as plans and actions used by an organisation to create and maintain good relations with not only its customers, but also suppliers, the media, investors and the public; in other words, to have a good reputation and relationship with everyone. This is usually achieved through marketing communications which are delivered in many dimensions as shown above. Managing and controlling these communications and the information they carry is a key aspect of business and is achieved in several ways by successful sports businesses:

- Targeting the message towards likely buyers by placing information (advertisements) in the media that they watch or read.
- Relationships and goodwill can be built through loyalty schemes, sponsorship and support for community events. Can you identify a local company that does this?

5. Sales promotion

These are usually short-term activities aimed at raising awareness or to compete with other similar products and services. They follow the model acronym AIDA by raising awareness, interest, desire and action to buy. The activities typically involve seasonal promotions such as sales and special offers, gifts and incentives, competitions or offering the product at a very attractive introductory price. Personal, or face to face, selling can also work with some customers through in-store demonstrations and parties.

With any of these techniques you need to adopt a managed and controlled approach, targeting the messages and activities, so that later you can identify which was the most successful.

As with any other programme or plan, you should judge each aspect's effectiveness in promoting the product, service or business against the objectives set. This way you can make recommendations of how to do it better next time – just like the professionals.

Remember

For any of these methods, timing is of the essence, i.e. getting the right message, to the right people, at the right time.

Local radio is a great way to promote – but make sure you go on at a time when your target audience will be listening and prepare your facts. What do you think would be the biggest challenge of talking on local radio?

Assessment activity 25.4

P5 P6 P7 P8 M4 M5 D1 D2 | BTEC

You are a consultant and have been commissioned by a local sports centre to review their marketing activities, carry out some research for them, analyse the outcomes, then make some proposals based on the research for promotion of an aspect of their business.

1. Plan market research related to, and appropriate for, the sports business. **P5**

2. Conduct market research related to, and appropriate for, the sports business, recording and interpreting results. **P6**

3. Conduct market research related to, and appropriate, for the sports business explaining the results. **M4**

4. Analyse the results of the market research, drawing valid conclusions. **D1**

5. Describe the marketing activities of the sports business. **P7**

6. Produce a promotional plan for the sports business, drawing on market research. **P8**

7. Justify the promotional plan for the sports business. **M5**

8. Evaluate the promotional plan for the sports business identifying areas for improvement. **D2**

Grading tips

- To attain **P5**, **P6**, **P7** and **P8** make sure you consider the range of techniques and activities carefully before selecting and also ensure there is a good fit between your methods, the product or service, the customers and the business. The strength of your work should be the detail of the description. Some tutor and peer discussion might help you clarify your plans.

- To attain **M4** and **M5**, as well as the points above, ensure you select an appropriate sample size. You might also choose a product or service with which you are familiar. Remember to include an implementation plan for your promotional plans.

- To attain **D1** and **D2** you will need to produce clear analysis, draw realistic conclusions and bring out areas for improvement, as well as noting the previous guidance.

PLTS

A range of PLTS skills evidence can come out in this piece of work – **independent enquirer** as you plan, conduct your research and activities and produce your findings. You will also find **creative thinker** opportunities especially as you record and interpret results. Where discussion is present you can provide evidence of your skills as a **team worker**. Depending on how you manage your time, **self-manager** evidence may exist as would **reflective learner** for those making recommendations.

Functional skills

Depending on how you present your work, evidence of your **ICT** skills might be found if you use IT systems or graphics. You can also provide evidence of your **English** skills when you carry out any survey work or discuss results with others.

Ben Jones
Membership and promotions assistant

Ben Jones has recently left college and now works as a membership and promotions assistant at a gym in Wolverhampton.

'The gym is planning a big promotions campaign to try and increase its market share in the city. The Managing Director (MD) has put me in charge of the promotions part of the marketing plan. I've got to plan how I will do some market research in the area. That means conducting surveys and analysing the responses to see what people would like us to have in the gym. I'm not sure if that will be more classes or a bigger range of equipment.

I have to give this most of my time at the moment, but I must also not forget about the current member needs. Based on the outcomes I have to let my boss know the results so that he can select what activities they should put on, what messages to send out and how best to price the opening rate for new members. The MD trusts me and has let me do most of the work so there is bit of pressure on me to deliver a good piece of work.

Here are my ideas at the moment… The gym is a budget one so they could try to undercut the price of other clubs in Wolverhampton. The market reports I've read suggest that it will be lower income people who are more likely to use the gym, so I thought the promotional message needs to be something like 'great value for money'. I think that some half-price taster sessions would be good and a leaflet drop would work best in those streets within a 10-minute walk or drive of the gym. With two months to go, I want to get some publicity in the Wolverhampton Press, maybe even in some of the free papers around town too. I might also suggest a radio advert if the MD feels the budget can stretch to that. But I'm off to carry out some surveys first to be sure my ideas are right.'

Think about it!

- What skills is Ben using on this project?
- Do you think he should spread the publicity range even wider?
- Do you think his assumptions are correct and what other suggestions could you make for Ben's project?

Just checking

1. How do you distinguish between a public, a private and a voluntary organisation?
2. Which of the above three types is truly a sports business and which use businesslike methods to run themselves?
3. Explain what a franchise is and give an example. (It does not have to be real.)
4. How does a duty manager differ from a chief executive?
5. Describe two factors you feel are important in making a sports business successful and two that can cause them problems.
6. What are statutory requirements? Give one example.
7. What are the common sources of cash inflow and outflow for a sports business?
8. List three different ways of setting out survey questions.
9. List three different types of promotion methods.
10. What is a press release and how can it help the promotion of a new sports service?

edexcel

Assignment tips

- There are a range of sports businesses you could select, but before you do make sure you have good access to data on them or some good contacts.

- Legal influences are quite diverse so stay focused on what their main purpose is, perhaps using an organisation you are familiar with.

- Current cash flow accounts are not easy to obtain, but if you go back a couple of years you should be able to get some good examples. Even better, you could get a company owner to explain them to you during a visit.

- Keep your sample size modest for your market research so that you have time to collect and analyse the data.

- Make sure any questions are clear and give you the answers the business needs (perhaps pilot a few to see if they work).

- Take note of what similar organisations to your selected one do as marketing. This may help with recommendations.

26 Work experience in sport

This is your chance to discover what it is like to work in the sports and leisure industry. The aim of the unit is to provide you with the skills to complete a work experience placement for a minimum of ten days. There are many career opportunities related to sport including management positions, coaching and fitness, sports development, sports science jobs, teaching, sports attendants and lifeguards. Sport and leisure is a growth industry with diverse opportunities. Work experience gives you the chance to progress your career. It looks great on your CV – it is an opportunity for somebody to give you a glowing reference and it will help you make career decisions.

In this unit you will look at different jobs in the industry and reflect on your key aims, objectives and targets for your career and your potential placements. You will look at different ways of applying for a job and interview skills. You will complete your work experience and reflect on your aims, objectives and targets and review them in relation to your career.

Learning outcomes

After completing this unit you should:

1. know about the opportunities for work-based experience in sport
2. be able to prepare for a work-based experience in sport
3. be able to undertake a work-based experience in sport
4. be able to review a work-based experience in sport.

Assessment and grading criteria

This table shows you what you must do in order to achieve a pass, merit or distinction grade, and where you can find activities in this book to help you.

To achieve a **pass** grade the evidence must show that you are able to:	To achieve a **merit** grade the evidence must show that, in addition to the pass criteria, you are able to:	To achieve a **distinction** grade the evidence must show that, in addition to the pass and merit criteria, you are able to:
P1 describe four realistic opportunities for appropriate work-based experience in sport **See Assessment activity 26.1, page 392**	**M1** explain four realistic opportunities for appropriate work-based experience in sport **See Assessment activity 26.1, page 392**	**D1** evaluate the opportunities for appropriate work-based experience in sport **See Assessment activity 26.1, page 392**
P2 select an appropriate work-based experience in sport and complete the application process **See Assessment activity 26.2, page 399**		
P3 demonstrate interview skills as an interviewee **See Assessment activity 26.2, page 399**		
P4 prepare for a work-based experience in sport, identifying targets, aims and objectives **See Assessment activity 26.2, page 399**	**M2** justify identified targets, aims and objectives of work-based experience in sport, suggesting how they can be achieved **See Assessment activity 26.2, page 399**	
P5 undertake a selected appropriate work-based experience in sport **See Assessment activity 26.3, page 402**		
P6 maintain a record of activities and achievements during a work-based experience **See Assessment activity 26.3, page 402**		
P7 present evidence of activities and achievements during work-based experience **See Assessment activity 26.4, page 404**		
P8 review a work-based experience in sport, identifying strengths and areas for improvements **See Assessment activity 26.4, page 404**	**M3** explain identified strengths and areas for improvements and make suggestions relating to own further development **See Assessment activity 26.4, page 404**	**D2** justify identified strengths, areas for improvement and suggestions relating to further development **See Assessment activity 26.4, page 404**

How you will be assessed

You will be assessed through:

- presentations which could be oral, multimedia, ICT- or video-based
- interview demonstration and practice
- a log of your placement which could be a diary, observation record and witness statements
- your application for a job (to include, for example, an application form, covering letter and CV)
- video evidence of your work and written assessments.

Jacob, 16-year-old enthusiastic sport student

I like all sports. I love keeping fit, working out, running, cycling and swimming. I knew I wanted to work in sports so decided to do my work experience in a secondary school and really enjoyed it. I am now working hard to get a good grade so I can go to university to study to become a PE teacher.

During my placement I cleaned out the cupboard, helped with team practices, took warm-ups, ran skills sessions, helped with lessons, compiled my own noticeboard, sorted out the kit and was generally helpful. The hardest thing was finding the placement; I had to find and approach the contact and attend an interview. I kept a record of my placement by making a video diary each day.

My placement made me realise how much work teachers do apart from teaching. They have to do practices, prepping, report writing, marking, planning, organising trips, washing kit and of course making tea! The atmosphere in the PE office was excellent! The best bit was teaching a non-swimmer to swim – it made me feel really good.

Over to you!

1. **What areas of this unit might you find challenging and what are you most looking forward to?**

2. **What preparations can you make in readiness for the unit assessment(s)?**

1. Know about the opportunities for work-based experience in sport

Warm-up

Work placements

Think about work experience from the point of view of the different people involved. How much time will the management at the placement have to invest? What will they worry about? How many work experience students will they have? What will the staff at the placement have to do?

1.1 Opportunities

The sports industry is a growth industry with many exciting opportunities for employment. The BTEC Level 3 National Diploma in Sport is a vocational qualification and so work experience is a vital part of your course.

Sectors

There are many different sectors in the sports industry, most will involve irregular hours. Many people have their leisure time in the evening and at the weekends; therefore these are the times you might be most likely to work.

- **The health and fitness** sector has a holistic approach to the mind and body. Many people go to centres where they can go to the gym, swim, eat a healthy meal, have their hair cut, enjoy a massage, take a class of their choice and read the papers. There are many health and fitness centres varying in size, with a range of jobs available.

- **The sport and recreation** sector includes coaching jobs in a range of specialist sports such as football and ice skating. This sector includes general leisure centre work, physical education teaching and sports development officers. The government have realised that sport and recreation has not been emphasised enough in recent years and now there is more investment in sports opportunities.

- **Outdoor education** is a growth area in the sports industry. There are many centres around the country where you can take part in activities such as sailing, surfing and rock climbing. These centres are run by a team of staff with specialist skills, knowledge

and qualifications in their chosen sports. Many large companies send their staff on training days to develop their teamwork. More people now take exercise classes outside such as British Military Fitness.

- **Sport and exercise science** is a specialist area of sports provision which works on:
  - the psychology of the game
  - analysis of how the body works
  - suggesting and refining small areas of technique to improve performance
  - injuries
  - improving and changing nutritional habits
  - muscle function (tests would be performed by a physiologist).

Remember

If the hours and the idea of shift patterns do not appeal, you must think very carefully about whether or not you are selecting the right industry for your future employment.

Providers

Sport and leisure in the UK is mainly organised into three sectors providing this service. These are the **public**, **private** and **voluntary** sectors. Dual use and partnership centres are also growing sectors of provision.

- **The public sector** is one of the largest providers of sport in this country. The facilities are usually owned by the local council or local authority (your borough). They can be run by organisations that the councils have selected or run by the council. They are open to the public and are not usually membership only – you can usually pay per visit. They will have a policy of making sport accessible to all sections of the community, particularly those who traditionally have not taken part in sport. Providing a service to the local community will be their primary aim.

- **The private sector** has enjoyed the largest growth over the last few years. Private centres are usually for the use of members only. They aim to provide an excellent service to members who may pay an initial joining fee followed by monthly membership fees. Members are normally tied to a minimum one year contract. Sometimes the centres will be specialist, such as a tennis, snooker or squash centre, but in the main they will provide a wider service. They aim to make a profit for the owners and most of the management team will have a performance-related pay agreement. They also reward their investors through dividends. They improve the service for their customers and employees will also enjoy enhanced conditions. Private sector organisations are usually owned either by individuals or shareholders (for example, David Lloyd Leisure Centres and Fitness First). Some centres are owned and run on a franchise basis; this allows for corporate marketing and branding and the benefit of a personal service.

- **The voluntary sector** provides a lot of sport in this country. It is run by volunteers who enjoy sport and want to develop their club or team. Examples include local football teams who play at weekends, swimming clubs, basketball teams, etc. They welcome all ages and usually cover their costs by collecting subscriptions (subs) each week. They do not normally own their facilities but rent them from local councils or local private facilities. The largest voluntary organisations are the scouts and the guides.

- **Partnerships** usually arise when more than one organisation is involved in the funding, operation or use of a facility. This can be beneficial as it might mean that a new facility can be built when there was no opportunity in the past; it can also be fraught with difficulties because more than one organisation (management committee) has a say in how it operates.

Sometimes, when local authorities grant planning permission for a large shopping centre, they do so on the condition that the organisation makes a contribution to a community facility, such as a leisure centre – this is called a 'planning gain'. It can lead to a partnership between the public and private sectors.

- **Dual use centres** are often schools that close their 'educational' service at 6 p.m. and open as a public facility during early mornings, evenings, weekends and holidays. This provides an excellent local service and maximises the investment in the school. It also provides opportunities for community links.

Key terms

Public – owned by the public sector, local councils providing a 'sport for all'.

Private – owned and run for profit (members usually pay on a monthly basis to belong).

Voluntary – run by volunteers for the good of the club.

1.2 Types of occupation

There are many different opportunities for employment in sport. Here are a few ideas for jobs in the different sectors.

Activity: Jobs in sport and leisure

List the careers or jobs you might want to do in the sports industry. Where can you do these locally? Search the Internet or the Yellow Pages and make a list of the name, number, address and contact at each placement you are interested in.

Record six different possibilities.

Health and fitness

Table 26.1: Examples of jobs in the health and fitness sector.

Job	Outline of role
Sports masseur	Gives massages to sports people – pre-performance massage, post-performance massage and injury rehabilitation.
Personal trainer	Normally works one-to-one with a client encouraging and motivating them through their personal workout and exercise plan.
Sports therapist	Works with individuals helping to rehabilitate them from injury.

What skills apart from massage do you think you need to be a sports masseur?

Sport and recreation

Table 26.2: Examples of jobs in the sport and recreation sector.

Job	Outline of role
Sports attendant/ recreation assistant	Puts out equipment and tidies it away. They keep the centre clean, deal with customers and have a good awareness of health and safety. They may work on poolside.
Fitness instructor	Most centres have a fitness instructor based at their gym to advise clients about their training programmes and progression.
Sports centre management	Runs the centre on a day to day basis. They will open and close the building, deal with any problems, organise the staffing, be responsible for cashing up and developing the centre.
Sports development officer	Responsible for the development of sport in a local area. They will try and improve sports participation. They may specialise in a particular sport such as netball and provide the opportunities to participate in that sport.
PE teacher	Will have been to university and completed a degree. They will have QTS (Qualified Teacher Status) and may have completed a PGCE (Post Graduate Certificate in Education). They will have a range of knowledge and abilities in a wide variety of sports that they will be expected to teach in a secondary school. There are now PE specialists in some junior schools who are responsible for PE across the whole school.
Sports coach	Usually specialises in one sport such as football or rugby. They will coach it to a range of different age groups and at a range of different levels. Professional football teams will have a coach for their first team and will also have another coach for the reserves, the under 18s, etc.
Coaching and fitness instructor	Works with a team or individual to improve the team's performance with drills and fitness tests specifically designed for that sport.
Professional sports performer	Will have a talent for a particular sport such as cycling and will train, usually full time, in that sport to achieve the highest standard possible. They will set their goal on reaching a particular event, such as the 2012 Olympics.
Sports promoter	Could represent a particular performer or team and arrange the team sponsorship deal. They may represent an event to raise its profile, such as the rugby world cup.

Sport and exercise science

Table 26.3: Examples of jobs in sport and exercise science.

Job	Outline of role
Exercise physiologist	May provide scientific support to sportsmen and women in a club or team setting or might work with cardiac rehabilitation patients and chronic diseases, providing expert advice.
Bio-mechanist	Uses the scientific principles of mechanics to study the effects of forces on sports performance. They will use this information to improve, refine and develop techniques for sports.
Sports psychologist	Helps with the mental/ cognitive components of the performance of sports performers.
Sports dietician	Devises nutritional programmes to help the sports performer to reach their potential by adapting their diet.
Sports scientist	Helps to maximise the performance of an individual, working on small areas of technique or fitness and devising programmes to improve performance.
Sports medicine	A qualified doctor who has decided to specialise in sport. They will diagnose, make recommendations and prescribe and refer.

Outdoor education

Table 26.4: Examples of jobs in the outdoor education centre

Job	Outline of role
Specialist sports instructor	Specialises in a sport such as canoeing. They could teach children, people with disabilities and adults on a range of courses.
Ground facility worker	Has a specialist knowledge of the physics of the ground. All sports grounds need to be maintained.

This person loves their job as a water sports instructor. Do you think you would like to work outside all day?

Considerations

- **Location** – when planning your work-based placement it is advisable that you go there before your first day. Find out where it is and familiarise yourself with the required transport.
- **Travel** – once you have found the venue you will then need to consider how you are going to arrive on time for your first day of the placement (and all subsequent days). You will need to consider the transport options available to you and be aware of how long it will take to get there. If you start work in the morning you may have to consider rush hour traffic. This can add a lot of time to the journey.

Prior to your first day, plan your bus, train, bicycle or car journey. Have a few trial runs to ensure that your journey is achievable in the time you have allocated.

- **Cost** – you will also have to consider the cost of transport to and from the venue for the duration of your placement and other expenses which you may be faced with. For example, equipment and the cost of refreshments.
- **Hours** – you will also have to consider the hours of work (these may be different to your hours at college/school). The hours you work may affect the transport on offer to you and the options you have. Prior to your placement you should agree the hours

which you can work with your placement provider and ensure that you can get to and from the venue of the placement on time and get home safely.

- **Regulations** – you will be subject to the regulations (rules) of the place where you are on work experience. If you have been given a uniform and told to wear it, then you will be obliged to do so. You will be told about various regulations of the placement very early on and you must abide by them.

- **Health and safety** – there are many laws controlling health and safety in the workplace (see Student Book 1, Unit 3 Assessing risk in sport). When you are on work experience you will be subject to them. You will told about some of them on your arrival. When you are on placement you could make a list of all the different laws that are mentioned.

- **Role and responsibilities** – your roles and responsibilities as a student on placement are to do as asked by the management and to be punctual, reliable, trustworthy, willing, helpful, honest and enthusiastic. If you are all these things you will be trusted to take on more roles and responsibilities.

- **Progression** – there are opportunities for progression in the industry. The roles and responsibilities are varied but most work in sport involves working with people so you must be a good communicator. All sections of the industry are subject to statutory regulations and laws; more information can be found in Student Book 1, Unit 3 Assessing risk in sport. NVQs provide the chance for staff in the industry to upgrade their qualifications while working within the job. Short courses and additional qualifications such as the governing body coaching and officiating awards form part of what is known as Continued Professional Development (CPD). Most organisations ensure that staff have plenty of opportunity for CPD. Staff must be kept up to date with changes in industry practice and in the law.

Take it further

Placements and jobs

Visit www.leisureopportunities.com for ideas about placements.

Research on the Internet about different jobs and the opportunities they offer for CPD.

Assessment activity 26.1   (P1) (M1) (D1)   BTEC

Imagine yourself in five years' time in the workplace. What sport-related job are you doing?

1. Make a table and describe four realistic opportunities for appropriate work-based experience where you could get a taste of that job. **P1**

2. Explain these four work placement opportunities. **M1**

3. Evaluate these opportunities. **D1**

Grading tips

- To attain **P1** select four quite different opportunities to evaluate as it is easier if they are very dissimilar.

- To attain **M1** you need to explain each of the four placement opportunities in detail discussing what you think it will offer you.

- To attain **D1** you need to think about what could be good as well as what could be bad about your selected work-based experiences.

PLTS

Describing the four opportunities for placement will help you demonstrate **independent enquirer** and **creative thinker** skills.

Functional skills

Researching the four placements will give you the opportunity to use your **ICT** skills.

2. Be able to prepare for a work-based experience in sport

In this section you will examine different ways of applying for work experience and jobs. To help you do this you will look at the process of applications and study how to reach the interview stage.

2.1 Application process

The application process for jobs in the sport and active leisure industry is much the same as with any job. You will need to make sure that you have carefully researched the jobs you would like to apply for and understand what the job would entail and how you can convince the employer that you are the best person for that role.

Job specifications

A **job specification (or description)** describes the duties and responsibilities of a particular job. You may find a job specification is contained in the advert for the vacancy or it may be sent to you when you apply for a job along with the **person specification** and the application form.

Key terms

Job specification/description – lists the duties of a particular job.

Person specification – based on the job description, it describes the best person for the job.

Freetown FC

Employer	Freetown FC
Job Title	Strength and Conditioning Coach
Sector	Coaching, Training & Medical
Sub-Sectors	Fitness Coach
Salary	£35,000 per annum
Benefits	plus football success-related bonus of up to 50%
Town/City	Freetown
Contract Type	Permanent
Passport/Visa Required	Must be eligible to live and work in the UK

Job Description

JOB TITLE: Strength and Conditioning Coach

REPORTS TO: Club Doctor

JOB FUNCTION:

- To provide fitness conditioning services to the first team squad as required.
- To assist in the preparation of players prior to first team matches as required.
- To take responsibility for the monitoring of the progress of all players' body strength with the use of weights and body weight exercises.
- To assist as required in carrying out fitness testing.
- To explain correct use of gym equipment to players.
- To liaise with and assist in the conditioning of reserve and youth players as required.
- To provide advice and guidance to the Head of Youth and Development Coaches in respect of the conditioning and fitness of under age players involved in the Club's development system.
- Generally to provide such conditioning and fitness services as required by the Doctor, Manager and coaches.
- To liaise with all members of the sports medical and sports science team to assist in the multi-disciplinary approach.

Qualifications required   Must have relevant experience in a professional sporting environment, ideally in football.

Figure 26.1: An example of a job description.

A job description is likely to include:

- the job title
- location
- who you would report to, for example, an assistant manager
- who you would be responsible for
- a brief summary of the job.

A person specification is based on the personal skills, knowledge, qualities, attributes and qualifications needed to do the job described in the job description. Subheadings might include:

- Personal attributes
- Personal qualities
- Vocational qualifications
- Academic qualifications
- Competence and experience
- Duties.

These will be listed as essential or desirable and it will indicate on the person specification whether or not the interviewer is going to find that information from the application form, the interview or the reference. The main reason for using job descriptions and person specifications as part of the recruitment and selection process is to ensure that the interviewer has a clear and objective basis on which to assess each candidate. Personal opinions and preferences are minimised.

Take it further

Job descriptions and specifications

Research the Internet for job descriptions and person specifications. Compare them and see if you match the criteria they are asking for.

Activity: Job descriptions and person specifications

Write a job description and a person specification for a job of your choice. Prepare 12 questions for mock interview practice. Work in groups with three on the interview panel. Plan the introduction and the completion of the interview. Carry out and feed back to each other how well you each did.

Preparing required application documents

There are three main ways to apply for a job or work experience:

1. curriculum vitae (CV)
2. application form
3. letter of application.

- A CV should be typed on a single side of A4, although as you gain more experience this will extend. There are no strict rules about layout but it must be neat, logical and look pleasing and distinctive. It should be easy for the prospective employer to find the information and you should use subheadings in bold. The content of the CV is your decision but as a rule it should contain:
  - name
  - address
  - date of birth
  - phone numbers including mobiles
  - email address
  - personal statement including your skills, qualities and attributes and your ambitions
  - employment record, most recent first with dates and a summary of your duties
  - education to date, most recent first with dates including short courses
  - other achievements, hobbies and interests
  - referees (check with your referees that they will write you a reference before you put their name down).

Adapt your CV to suit the job you are interested in; emphasise the relevant experience and skills that you have for that job. Leave out information that is irrelevant or reflects badly on you. This is your CV and there are no definitive rules about its content as long as what you write is true.

Remember

Your CV is a reflection of you. How it is presented will show your prospective employer many things about you. Make sure the spelling and grammar are accurate, present your work with pride and put the most recent education and employment first.

Your name
Your address
Your telephone number
Your email address
Your date of birth

Personal statement
In a short paragraph descried your best qualities and abilities. Use words such as **reliable**, **enthusiastic** and **responsible** and mention your skills, for instance that you have good communication skills, and work well in a team.

Education
List the most recent first, give the name of the school or college, the dates you were there, the qualifications you took and the grades you got.

School/college	Date	Qualifications
Endsley College of Further Education	2009-2011	BTEC National Diploma Sport Development, Coaching and Fitness
All Saints High School	2002- 2009	GCSEs English C Maths B PE A* Geography C Food tech B

Awards
List the most recent first, where you got them, the qualification and dates.

From	Date	Award
All Saints High School	2009	First-aid at Work
All Saints High School	2008	FA Level 1

Employment
List the most recent first. Include work experience if you have not had a job.

Position	Organisation	Dates	Responsibilities
Football coach	Hampton Soccer School	2008–present	Coach under-11s team Mentor young players
Waiter	Chino's Grill	2007–2009	Taking orders Providing good customer service

Other interests
Include information about yourself. For instance you mention that you play for a team. Highlight achievements like being made captain. Outline an occasion where you have taken responsibility, and include any voluntary work you may do or have done.

Referees
You should give your most recent employer and college tutor. Choose people who will say positive things about you.

Figure 26.2: You can adapt this CV template to suit you. Remember, your CV should take up one side of A4 paper.

- **An application form** is a set form you may be asked to complete for work experience and you must answer all questions fully and accurately. Application forms are the most common way of applying for a job so it is good practice. They are fair because all candidates complete the same form.

When completing an application form:
- write with a black pen
- check to see if they ask for block capitals
- write legibly or type if you have it electronically
- read the question carefully first before answering the question

- have a personal statement prepared (see below) that you can adapt to the job (most jobs will ask for one – you can adapt from your CV
- use the job description or person specification as a guide to what you should include in the statement (if one or both of these have been sent to you)
- sell yourself but do not waffle
- identify key statements from the advertisement, job description or person specification and talk about them on your form (you will be shortlisted based on these)
- if you make a mistake cross it out neatly and carry on
- do not lie – you are signing it as a true and accurate reflection of yourself
- try not to leave it until the last minute
- post in plenty of time or deliver by hand

Your address
Your phone numbers
Your email address

Name of contact
Company name and address

Date

Dear Sir or Madam (or Mr/Ms X)

Subheading in bold to show the position being applied for (e.g. Recreation Assistant, Emily Leisure Centre, Work Experience Placement)

Body of letter...
- Introduce yourself; mention what course you are doing, where you are doing it and why you have to do work experience as part of your course.
- Give reasons why you are interested in the work experience with their company.
- Give details of the skills, qualifications and experience you can offer.
- Please find enclosed my… (CV or application form).
- I look forward to hearing from you.

Yours faithfully (if you started with Dear Sir or Madam)

Yours sincerely (if you started with their name)

Your signature

Your name (typed)

Figure 26.3: What skills and qualifications would you talk about in your covering letter?

- make sure you have the right name on the envelope – this is especially important in a large organisation.
- **A letter of application** sets out all the information found on a CV but in letter style. Some employers ask for this method of application to see if a candidate is committed enough to write a letter. These will normally be completed on computer but some will ask for them to be handwritten. When you send your CV or your application form you need to send a short letter to accompany it (this is sometimes called a covering letter). It is set out in business style (see Figure 26.3 below). The letter needs to be accurate and well presented.
- **Personal statements** – most application forms will give you a full side to complete your personal statement; this will be similar to the information you wrote for your CV or put in your application letter. A personal statement must outline your strengths, skills, attributes, achievements and any other relevant information for that particular job that you have not put on the form for another question. They might want you to handwrite it. Prepare one in advance in rough to minimise the amount of mistakes.
- **Letters of acceptance/decline** – when you have been made a job/work experience offer you may be asked to reply in writing. This letter should be short and well presented thanking them for their offer and accepting or declining the job. It should be set out in business style.

Interviews

An interview will be based on the job description and the person specification. The interview panel will interview you using these two documents and (if appropriate) the answers you gave on your application form.

Prepare well for an interview. Make sure you know your route so that you know where you are going and how long it will take. Arrive early and dress smartly – be outgoing, confident and enthusiastic.

2.2 Interview skills

We can all improve at interviews; the more you practise, the better you will become. Mock interviews are good practice to ensure that you are relaxed and at ease. During mock interviews you can go through the job description and the person specification and try and work out questions that you might be asked based on these documents. When you practise, go through the whole process from beginning to end to become accustomed to the introduction process. Practise 'active listening'; this is when you look at the person talking to you and follow what they are saying while looking interested throughout.

Verbal communication

Your verbal communication skills need to be good in an interview – you need to be clear and you must not use slang or jargon. You need to be confident and use appropriate language for the industry. If you are not sure what the question is you can ask for clarification from the interviewer. Asking questions that are relevant is very important as it shows that you have given thought to what is expected of you. The interview should have a prepared format and will probably be carried out by more than one person. The format and questions should remain similar for all candidates as the panel will compare the answers.

There are a number of different types of questions you can be asked during an interview and some are easier to answer than others. Table 26.5 lists some of the different styles of questions you might be asked.

How do you cope with the pressure of an interview?

Table 26.5: Interview question types.

Question type	Description
Closed	To find out specific information (requires yes/no answers) For example: Have you worked shifts before?
Open	To encourage the interviewee to open up on a topic For example: Why do you carry out fitness tests?
Probing	To find out more on a particular point For example: Could you explain to me why you would use a Eurofit step test?
Clarifying	To check understanding For example: What do you mean by equal opportunities?
Scenario	To test the interviewee's ability to apply their knowledge For example: A child breaks their arm in your session. What do you do?
Rambling	Rambling questions are bad practice but they are often asked! You have to listen carefully to the long question and try to work out what they are asking. For example: When you have been at work, or not at work, what customer service or customer care skills and tips have you developed to help you in and out of work?
Multiple	Asking more than one question in the same question For example: What do you see yourself doing in three years' time – what do you hope to achieve and how are you going to achieve it?

Non-verbal communication

Non-verbal communication is very important. Sit forward and sit up straight – don't cross your arms and make sure you smile. Look as though you are interested. Your body language, facial expressions and posture will indicate your interest to the interviewer. Dress sensibly, smartly and appropriately.

Appropriate presentation

When you are going for an interview you need to dress in a suitable manner – don't wear jeans and opt for smart/casual. For an interview a tracksuit would be inappropriate – avoid large logos and pictures – low cut tops are also inappropriate.

Take it further

Interview questions

Research the type of interviews and questions the staff at your college and at the local leisure centre have been asked. Practise answering them.

Case study: Work experience interview

Siân Griffiths is outgoing and enthusiastic. She went for a work experience interview to work with a personal trainer. It is what she wants to do for a career but she was so nervous in the interview that she answered the questions much too briefly and didn't represent herself well.

1. **What could Siân do to overcome her nerves in interview?**
2. **How can she 'sell' herself more?**

2.3 Prepare

After you have completed your work experience search, telephone, write or email the places you have identified. Be very careful how you speak to staff on the 'phone. Begin the conversation by saying 'good morning/ good afternoon', introduce yourself and ask

to speak to the person who deals with work experience. If they are not there, ask what their name is and when it will be convenient to call again. They probably have a lot of enquiries for work experience so remember to 'phone back and if possible leave a message (although do not rely on them returning your call). When you ring again, ask for them by name, make sure you introduce yourself, what course you are doing, where you are doing it, what the work experience requirement is and what the dates are. Have a pen ready to take down any information you may need. Always be polite, enthusiastic and interested in the organisation.

Aims and objectives

Aims are 'large' in size and relate to your career and life aims. They are usually challenging such as 'I want to be a PE teacher and I am going to find a work experience placement in a school to find out what it is like to teach'. Objectives are 'medium' in size and are related to how you will achieve your aims. They are medium-term and achievable, such as 'I am going to contact three schools by the end of the week and send my CV with a covering letter' or 'I want to be able to run a whole session by myself'. You will usually have more objectives than aims.

SMART (specific, measurable, achievable, realistic, timed) targets

Targets are short-term, realistic and achievable; as they relate to your work experience they could be 'I am going to ring and follow up my letter' or 'I am going to ask what I am expected to wear on my placement' or 'I am going to ask to help with extra curricular practices and go to matches'. They will relate to your objectives. Your targets must be set against the SMART principles.

Personal

What personal targets are you setting yourself?

- **Knowledge development** – how do you want to increase and improve your knowledge?
- **Skills development** – what new skills do you want to learn?
- **Personal improvement** – how do you want to improve?

Table 26.6: SMART targets.

S	Specific	Your targets should relate to something you want to achieve.	I want a work experience placement in a leisure centre.
M	Measurable	They should be able to be measured.	I want to find ten contacts for work experience placements.
A	Achievable	They have to be achievable for you to reach.	I am going to set myself a task and a date that are real so that they will be met and not ignored.
R	Realistic	You must set your sights on something you can achieve otherwise you will be put off.	I must be realistic – will I be able to find myself a placement with a PE teacher in a secondary school?
T	Timed	You must set deadlines that can be met.	I want a placement by 3 January.

- **Qualifications** – find out what qualifications the staff at your placement have achieved. Many people move into the industry through a variety of routes. Decide what might help you the most.
- **Organisational** – how can I develop my organisational skills to prepare for work?
- **Relating to qualification/study** – what information can I gather while on work experience that will help me on my course?
- **Supplementary evidence** – what evidence can I gather that will support my work?

Assessment activity 26.2

P2 P3 P4 M2   BTEC

1. Select an appropriate work experience placement and complete the application process. **P2**
2. Demonstrate your interview skills as an interviewee. **P3**
3. Prepare for a work experience placement, identifying targets, aims and objectives. **P4**
4. Justify your identified targets, aims and objectives suggesting how they can be achieved. **M2**

Grading tips

- To attain **P2** decide on the job you are applying for when you complete your application form, CV and covering letter. This will help you to remain focused on the application.
- To attain **P3** film yourself being interviewed in your groups that you formed for your panel interviews and reflect on your performance.
- To attain **P4** create a table for your aims, objectives and targets of work experience.
- To attain **M2** add a column to your table; justify them and suggest ways in which they can be achieved.

PLTS

Independent enquirers, **reflective learners** and **creative thinkers** will be able to complete the aims, objectives and targets well. Writing CVs, letters and application forms will help you demonstrate **reflective learner** skills.

Functional skills

Letter writing, CV writing and filling in application forms will demonstrate **ICT** and **English** skills.

3. Be able to undertake a work-based experience in sport

This is it – you are now going to start your work experience! This could be a life changing time. Make sure you know how you are going to the placement and how long the journey takes. Be early! Take a diary with you to make notes about what you have done during the day.

3.1 Carry out

Before you start your placement you need to check what time you start, who you report to and what you are expected to wear. It is always better to ask than to arrive in the wrong kit, in the wrong place and at the wrong time!

Planned activities

Ask your placement supervisor what they want you to do. Be enthusiastic, reliable and helpful and use your initiative. If, for example, you are on work experience in a school with a PE teacher, ask if you can take warm-ups. Plan them, show your plans beforehand, discuss them and refine them. Build on this and by the end of your placement you might be allowed to run a whole session.

Case study: Rhianna's work experience

Rhianna Mair managed to find a placement in her local leisure centre. She was given a rota of general duties around the centre. Whenever she was in reception she sat in the receptionist's seat and the receptionist had to ask her to move out of her chair every time. This upset the receptionist and she complained to the manager.

1. **What should Rhianna have done?**
2. **Why should she move out of the chair?**
3. **Rhianna held her FA level 1 Coaching badge and offered to do an after school club at the centre. Who could she approach? What could she do to convince the management team that this was a good idea?**

Considerations

Always remember you are a visitor in the workplace; act in a mature manner as you are now a member of staff. Staff might need privacy to speak to management so

use your initiative and leave the room. Be sensitive to other people's needs and you will fit in well.

- **Codes of practice** – some organisations will require that the staff employed within the organisation adhere to certain behaviours in specific situations. As a temporary employee of the organisation you will also be expected to adhere to such codes. If this is the case, you should request copies of the codes prior to your placement to familiarise yourself with the provider's behaviour expectations.

- **Customer care** – in some instances your placement may involve you working with customers. When this is the case you must make sure you deal with customers appropriately. When dealing with customers you should always:
  - greet the customer politely
  - listen to the customer
  - respond politely
  - deal with a customer's complaint (or find someone who can)
  - be helpful.

- **Health and safety, legislation and regulation** – when you start your placement you will have to undertake a health and safety induction. This induction process will show you the health and safety procedures which are followed within the centre. The staff will show you what to do in the event of a number of incidents, for example, a fire alarm or major or minor injury to an employee or customer, etc. If you are required to set up equipment you should be shown how to do this in a safe and effective manner prior to having to do this independently. If you ever feel at risk of injury, or causing injury, you should must seek support and advice from the staff at the centre.

- **Equal opportunities** – by law all employers should treat their employees equally regardless of gender, race, religion, sexual orientation and ability. If an employer failed to treat all employers equally then they would be subject to criminal proceedings. It is important that, as an employee of an organisation, you also treat everyone within the organisation equally. Failure to comply with this could result in you being asked to leave the placement instantly.

- **Quality assurance** is the process of verifying or determining whether products or services meet or exceed customer expectations. As an employee of a company who carries out quality assurance of the services provided it is important that you follow the required guidelines and procedures effectively. It is possible that the employer will assess your ability to meet their expectations – this is also a measure of assuring quality of the service provided by you.

- **Specific skills** – when working within some organisations it may be a requirement that you possess specific skills, qualifications or experiences. If this is the case, prior to starting the work experience, you will need to ensure that you have obtained the required skills, qualifications or experiences so that you are not out of your depth and can carry out the requirements of the position while you are there. For example, prior to working for a coach in the community, he or she may request that you obtain a Level 1 coaching award in a specific sport to ensure that you are insured to support coaching sessions and that you have the required skills to support the delivery of such sessions. Failure to obtain the qualification could mean that you are not insured to work alongside children and the coach will not be able let you start your placement.

Take it further

Risk assessments

How does the risk assessment at your work experience compare to the risk assessment you use at college or one you have found in your research?

3.2 Record

Diary of daily activities

When on placement, record your experiences in the form of a daily log book. You should record the achievements which you have attained for each day of the placement and the areas which you could improve upon. You should identify in your diary what you have learned and exactly what you did during each day.

Achievement of goals, aims and objectives (personal, organisational, relating to qualification/study)

When you are on work experience, remember to learn as much as you can about as many different aspects of the sports industry as possible. You will be asked to review the aims, objectives and targets you set before you went on your placement. Have you achieved them? Set yourself new ones for your work experience. Relate them to your personal and organisational targets and those relating to your course and other qualifications you may be taking.

Activity: Diary of daily activities

While you are on your work placement, find out some information.
1. What does the organisation do and who are its customers?
2. What is the organisation's customer service policy?
3. Apart from those that you are studying, find out what other qualifications would be useful to the organisation.
4. Give six examples of the organisation's rules and regulations (Code of Practice).
5. What is the organisation's health and safety policy?
6. What is the emergency evacuation procedure? Where are the fire alarms and muster points?
7. Who is the first-aid officer and where is the first-aid kit?
8. What is a risk assessment and why would you carry one out?

Assessment activity 26.3

P5 **P6** · BTEC

You are now on work placement – enjoy it and keep a record of everything you have done. Reflect on your performance each day in your diary; this could be kept in a variety of formats including MP3, video diary, by email or in writing.

1. Undertake a selected appropriate work-based experience. **P5**

2. Maintain a record of activities and achievements during your work-based experience. **P6**

Grading tips

- To attain **P5** enjoy your experience and make the most of all the opportunities you are given.

- To attain **P6** report your experiences for the day every day, as you will soon forget the details of each day if you leave it until later.

PLTS

Team workers, **effective participators** and **self-managers** will do well at maintaining a record of their work experience.

Functional skills

Maintaining your record will utilise your **English** and **ICT** skills.

4. Be able to review a work-based experience in sport

This is your time to reflect on your work experience. Be honest with yourself about where you performed well and where there are areas for improvement. Include photographs that you have taken of yourself at work.

4.1 Present

You will need to make a presentation to your group about work experience.

Activities

Introduce the placement by explaining what the organisation does, where it is located and by giving general information. Explain the activities you did and expand on the points individually. You could write each point on a postcard to help you.

Achievements

What did you achieve when you were on work experience? What did you do that you were pleased with? What was a personal achievement for you? It may appear to have been a small achievement such as dealing with a complaint, helping a customer or motivating a reluctant 13-year-old girl to participate in a sports session. Remember you were only there for

a short time so any achievements are good. List your new experiences and at the end of your placement evaluate your performance and analyse what you have learned. The final question you need to ask yourself is 'Do I want to do this as a full-time career?'. If so, what do you need to do to achieve your aim?

Formats

You can deliver a presentation in a variety of formats. An oral presentation is perhaps the most traditional and straightforward format. You could make a written presentation with handouts and you can use your computer skills. The most common and popular method of computerised presentation is PowerPoint®. This consists of a sequence of slides that you can animate. You can include special effects and you can import pictures either taken by you on work experience or imported from the Internet (make sure you cite where you found the photos with the website address in your presentation). During your presentation handouts are very useful. Exhibits, work and leaflets from your placement all add interest. You can also use a whiteboard or flipchart which you can write on as you go along.

4.2 Review

You need to evaluate your performance during work experience. When you are doing this you need to critically analyse what you have done, what you can learn from the situation and how this will be useful in terms of building your skills and knowledge of the industry.

Remember

If you find it difficult to evaluate, imagine you will have to do your work experience placement again. What could you do differently to improve your performance and your opportunity to learn new things?

Activity: Work placement evaluation

1. List ten duties that you carried out.
2. What elements of the work did you enjoy and why? List three.
3. What aspects did you not enjoy and why? List three.
4. What new skills have you learned? List three.
5. Would this type of work interest you as a career? Why?
6. What advice would you give to a student who is about to start their work experience at your placement?
7. Is there anything that could have made the placement more useful than it was?
8. Were you prepared for this placement?
9. Was there anything extra that you needed to know before you started?

Activities

Review the activities that you did on work experience – were they what you expected? Did you do what you hoped to do? Were you given more responsibility than you expected? Did you feel as if you were an unpaid member of staff? Did you feel challenged, but not abandoned?

Achievements

What did you achieve? Were you pleased with what you achieved?

Achievement of goals

Before you went on work experience you listed your goals. Now you should analyse your achievements against your goals. Did you achieve them all? How many did you achieve? Did you achieve them fully or partially?

Aims and objectives

Review the aims and objectives you set for yourself for your work experience – did you achieve them? Has your placement changed your mind about what you want to achieve?

Strengths and areas for improvement

After having completed your work experience, what do you consider to be your strengths and what are your areas for improvement? Here is a list of competencies to help you:

- Communications
- Organisation
- Customer service
- Using initiative
- Dealing with problems
- Teamwork
- Coaching and teaching.

Evidence and techniques

When reviewing your work experience placement, reflect on how you could use evidence to support your work, such as photographs or video footage of you at work.

Interviews and use of witness testimony

Take the opportunity to interview staff about your placement and about your performance. A witness testimony is a statement of what you did, written by your supervisor. This should outline briefly what you did and it should be signed both by the supervising member of staff and by you. Interview the staff – how did they reach that position? What qualifications have they got? What is their biggest achievement to date?

Further development

On completion of the work-based placement you should complete a personal development plan which will reflect upon the attainment of the aims and objectives which you set at the start of the placement. The development plan should support the development of your overall career ambitions as well as those aims and objectives set prior to the work-based placement.

At the end of the placement you should consider what you could do next to support your development and attain your overall goal. To do this you will need to consider what else you could have done to achieve the aims and objectives that you set for yourself prior to the placement. This could include further time at the placement or seeking part-time employment

- **Experiences** – you should consider what other experiences you could pursue in order to fully meet your career ambitions or aims and objectives previously set.

- **Training** – after the work experience you may have been made aware of specific training courses which you could undertake to support your development and achievement of your aims and objectives. These could be included in your personal development plan.

- **Qualifications** – as well as specific training courses there may also be specific qualifications which you have to obtain in order to pursue the job or career of your dreams. In your development plan you should highlight these qualifications and provide yourself with targets of how and when you wish to attain these qualifications and where.

Assessment activity 26.4   P7 P8 M3 D2   BTEC

1. Having completed your work experience you now have to present the information to your group telling them about your activities and achievements. **P7**

2. Now you need to review your work experience, identifying strengths and areas for improvement. **P8**

3. Explain the strengths and areas for improvement you have identified, making suggestions relating to your further development. **M3**

4. Justify everything you explained for M3. **D2**

Grading tips

- To attain **P7** you must present evidence, such as photographs, of the placement.

- To attain **P8** go back to the aims, objectives and targets you set in the first assignment and review them.

- To attain **M3** make suggestions relating to your own further development, such as attending a level 2 FA coaching course (aim) as you want to develop your coaching skills (objective) and you are going to contact someone to organise your course by May (target).

- To attain **D2** remember to reflect on your achievements and areas for improvement and justify them in detail. What did you learn from your work experience? Relate it to what you want to go on to do now.

PLTS

Reflecting on and presenting your work experience will show evidence of your skills as an **independent enquirer**, a **reflective learner**, an **effective participator** and a **self-manager**.

Functional skills

When you make your presentation and reflect on your placement, you will demonstrate your skills in **English**.

Jordan Evans
Leisure centre duty manager

Jordan completed ten days' work experience at his local leisure centre. He had just passed his NPLQ at college and was offered a job as a lifeguard and sports attendant. He finished his National Diploma and now works full-time as duty manager.

Jordan has worked hard and taken every opportunity that was presented to him. He arrives at the centre at 6 a.m. to open up at 6.30 and closes it late at night – the centre shuts at 11 p.m. and he aims to leave at 11.30 p.m. depending on his shift. He cashes up and has very good customer service skills. He has completed his Pool Plant course, a management development course and managed to complete four governing body awards. He is 19 and wants to apply for the job as manager. The shifts he does are either an early or a late and he has one weekend in three off (but he does have time off during the week to make up for it). The skills he uses most are customer service skills, organisation and management techniques.

'I love being in contact with the public and being responsible for the smooth running of the centre. I particularly enjoy it when we have events like wedding receptions.

I really enjoy managing and organising the staff – it's like a complex game of chess! And it's great when it all comes together – I thrive on the challenge of working to a deadline and getting the set-up perfect. I have some training but now I want to learn about how to manage.'

Think about it!

- What does Jordan need to do to prove he is suitable for the manager position?
- What will he need to prepare for the interview?
- How can he make himself stand out from the other candidates?
- How can he persuade the interview panel that, at 19, he is ready for the manager's position?

Just checking

1. Who are the customers in public sector facilities? Who funds them?
2. Who are the customers in private sector facilities? Who funds them?
3. Who are the customers in voluntary sector facilities? Who funds them?
4. What is a dual use centre and what is a partnership centre?
5. What is the difference between a job description and a person specification?
6. What is a covering letter used for?
7. What is a letter of application?
8. What is the difference between aims, objectives and targets?
9. Have you reviewed your work experience?
10. What do you understand by evaluation?

edexcel

Assignment tips

- Set your aims, objectives and targets clearly — this will help in Assessment activity 26.4 when you have to review them after your work experience.
- Remember that work experience is meant to be fun. Enjoy the experience and be open to trying new things and working hard.
- Record what you do every day as you will soon forget. It also reminds the people you are now working with that you are there for a college course and you have to do work. It also gives you something to do when you have a few minutes to yourself.
- Be helpful and take some initiative on your placement. This will help you to enjoy it more and, if you enjoy it, you are more likely to perform better.
- Learn from the staff at the placement. Watch them carefully. They will all be experienced and have plenty to teach you. Talk to them and gather information from them to assist with your assignments.
- Ensure that you properly read the assignment briefs. Take your time and ensure you are happy with the task set for you. If not ask your tutor for additional assistance.

Glossary

ACORN classification – a neighbourhood classification system used to categorise social groups base on income and lifestyle and demographic group.

Adhesions – pieces of scar tissue that attach to structures within the body, limiting movement and sometimes causing pain.

Afferent nerves – sensory nerves that usually have receptors at the skin and joints.

Aim – something you want to achieve – a goal.

Antenatal – relating to pregnancy, this is the period from conception to birth.

Arousal – the psychological state of alertness that prepares the body for action.

Attribution – the reason you give to explain the outcome of an event.

Benchmarking – judging performance against competitor.

Broadcasting rights – having the contract to televise an event.

Burnout – when an athlete strives to meet training and competition demands despite repeated unsuccessful attempts, and so tries harder. Can lead to the athlete no longer wishing to participate in activities they used to enjoy.

Bye-laws – a rule made by the local authority.

Cardiac output – the amount of blood pushed out of the heart in one minute. This is the equivalent to stroke volume × heart rate.

Cash flow – the movement of money in and out of an organisation.

Cell permeability – allowing or activating the passage of a substance through cells or from one cell to another.

Chief executive officer – the most senior person responsible for the day to day running of a company (but responsible to the board if it is a plc).

Choking – the whole process that leads to decreased performance, not just the decreased performance itself.

Code of ethics – a set of principles for the fairest way of doing things, i.e. with respect.

Cognitive anxiety – the thought component of anxiety that most people refer to as 'worrying about something'.

Cohesion – the tendency for a group to stick together and remain united in the pursuit of its goals and objectives.

Connective tissue – (tendon) is used to attach muscles to bones, and is used for structure and support of the skeleton.

Contingency – a possible, but not very likely, future occurrence.

Contractual obligations – agreement to deliver or do something.

Contraindication – a physical or mental condition or factor that increases the risk involved when engaging in a particular activity. Contra means 'against'.

Coordination faults/losses – occur when players do not connect with their play, the team interacts poorly or ineffective strategies are used. Generally, sports that require more interaction or cooperation between players are more susceptible to coordination faults or losses.

Copyright infringement – not having the right to use or publish something.

Cortisol – a hormone that is associated with stress, anxiety and depression.

Curriculum opportunities – the opportunities that should be offered to children to enhance their engagement with the concepts, processes and content of PE.

Customer base – the number of customers a company regularly has.

Cutaneous mechanoreceptors – sensory nerve endings in the skin.

Delayed-onset muscle soreness (DOMS) – the pain or discomfort often felt 24–72 hours after exercising. It subsides generally within 2–3 days.

Deliberate practice – practice activities that need a lot of effort, are not inherently enjoyable and do not lead to immediate social or financial rewards.

Deviance – cheating or bad behaviour.

Dislocation – a displacement of the position of bones, often caused by a sudden impact.

Distress – extreme anxiety related to performance.

Dividend – a payment made to shareholders (usually once a year) in proportion to the numbers of shares they hold.

Downsize – to restructure, making an organisation smaller, usually to ensure its continued existence.

Early specialisation sports – sports that require sport specific training from an early age (such as gymnastics).

Endorphins – morphine-like chemicals that can reduce pain and improve mood.

Ethnicity – a group of people who identify themselves as from one nationality or culture.

Eustress – 'beneficial' stress that helps an athlete to perform.

Expenditure – money used up by an organisation over a period of time.

External imagery – imagining yourself doing something as though you are watching it on a film so that you can develop an awareness of how the activity looks.

Extrinsic – a risk or force from outside the body. These are external forces, such as from objects or other individuals making contact with someone

Extrinsic motivation – external rewards such as trophies, external praise and money.

Feasibility – the act of assessing whether something can work or needs changing.

Fiscal – anything to do with finance or the money aspects of an event.

FITT – frequency (how often), intensity (how hard), time (how long) and type (how appropriate).

Formative assessment – takes place informally and should support the development of a sports coach.

Fracture – a partial or complete break in a bone.

Franchise – a business bought from a bigger company specifically to sell their products.

Gamesmanship – when dubious tactics are employed in a sport to gain an advantage over the opposition, e.g. intimidation (this can be psychological and/or physical) or an attempt to disrupt concentration.

Gantt charts – a planner-like calendar to show when things start and finish in a project.

Goal congruency – individual, organisational and team goals all going in the same direction at the right time to give maximum results.

Hard tissue injury – injury to bones, joints and cartilage.

Haemarthrosis – a build-up of blood in the joint.

Haematoma – a collection of clotted blood due to bleeding in a specific area of the body.

Hazard – anything that has the potential to cause a person harm.

Health – as defined by the World Health Organization, is a state of complete physical, mental and social wellbeing and not merely the absence of disease and infirmity.

Income – an amount of money coming into an organisation over a period of time.

Intangible support – non-physical support offered by parents, such as watching games and giving praise.

Internal imagery – imagining yourself doing something and concentrating on how the activity feels.

Inter-muscular haematoma – a haematoma that escapes the muscle sheath through a tear or rupture.

Intra-muscular haematoma – a haematoma that remains trapped inside the muscle sheath.

Intrinsic – a risk or force from within the body. These are internal forces, which are stresses from within the body.

Intrinsic motivation – internal rewards such as love of the game and health benefits.

Job specification/description – lists the duties of a particular job.

Key concepts – concepts that children need to understand in order to deepen and broaden their knowledge, skills and understanding. The key concepts at Key Stages 3 and 4 are competence, performance, creativity and health, active lifestyles.

Key processes – essential skills and processes that children need to learn in order to progress in PE. The key processes at Key Stages 3 and 4 are developing skills in physical activity; making and applying decisions; developing physical and mental capacity; evaluating and improving; and making informed decisions about healthy, active lifestyles.

KPIs – key performance indicators – criteria showing how well something has performed.

Late specialisation sports – sports that require a generalised early approach to training followed by later, sport-specific training (such as football).

Liability – being legally obliged or responsible for something.

Liaison – working between two parties or more as a communicator.

Likert scales – a sequence of grades (in responses).

Liquidity – money or assets that can be quickly turned into cash.

Logistics – establishing good communications and the delivery of resources on time (for example, finance, people or equipment).

Lymphatic drainage – a massage treatment that uses light pressure and long, rhythmic strokes to increase lymphatic flow. Lymph, a fluid that contains white cells, is drained from tissue spaces by the vessels of the lymphatic system. It can transport bacteria, viruses and cancer cells. The lymphatic system is associated with the removal of excess fluid from the body. It is made up of lymphatic capillaries, lymphatic vessels, lymph nodes and lymph ducts.

Motivation – the direction and intensity of your effort is critical to sporting success.

Motivational faults/losses – occur when some members of the team do not give 100 per cent effort.

Narrative technique – the style of making a commentary.

National governing bodies (NGBs) – responsible for the rules and organisation of competitions for their sports. They also select representative teams and deal with funding and disciplinary issues.

Negligence – lacking due attention or duty of care which causes loss or injury.

Notational analysis – the collection of data either by using a computer or by hand. This process normally involves counting the frequency of an event, such as a shot on target.

Objective – how you are going to achieve your aim.

Oedema – a build-up of blood and tissue fluid within the tissue.

Officials – responsible for ensuring fair play and the welfare of players and spectators through the correct application of the rules, laws and regulations.

Operations – the everyday working of a business.

Overdraft – additional credit or borrowing from a bank.

Overtraining – the athlete trains under an excessive training load, which they cannot cope with.

Outdoor and adventurous activity – physical activity that stimulates and challenges participants and is done outside, often in a hostel environment.

Parasympathetic nervous system – part of the system that helps you to relax.

Paratendonitis – inflammation of the paratendon (the tissue surrounding the tendon).

Pedometer – a portable electronic device usually worn all day on the belt which counts each step taken.

Performance analysis – the provision of objective feedback to performers trying to achieve a positive change in performance.

Personality – the sum of the characteristics that make a person unique.

Person specification – based on the job description, it describes the best person for the job.

PESTLE analysis – a method for analysing factors which might affect a market.

Physical activity – any force exerted by skeletal muscle that results in energy expenditure above resting level.

Physiological response – the body's physical mechanisms that respond when an injury takes place. These are initiated to repair and protect the damaged tissue.

Policies – a plan of action, usually from an authoritative source that must be followed.

Post-natal – this relates to the period after childbirth.

PRICED – procedure for the treatment of acute injuries – protect, rest, ice, compression, elevation, diagnosis.

Private – owned and run for profit (members usually pay on a monthly basis to belong).

Profit – excess of revenue over outlays and expenses for an organisation over a period of time.

Psychological core – the part of you that contains your beliefs, values, attitudes and interests.

Psychological response – the mental aspect of how an athlete copes and comes to terms with their injury and treatment.

Psychological skills – qualities that the athlete needs to obtain through the PST programme.

Psychologist – an expert in the field of psychology (the science of mental life).

Public – owned by the public sector, local councils providing a 'sport for all'.

Punditry – so called expert opinion.

Qualitative analysis – uses descriptions and words to describe sporting performance.

Quality system – plans, policies, processes and procedures which all come together in a systematic way to ensure the organisation works to a high standard.

Quantitative analysis – uses numerical data or statistics to describe sporting performance.

Range and content – the breadth of the subject on which teachers should draw when teaching the key concepts and key processes.

Rationalisation – more organised and structured sport.

Regulation – following rules.

Rehabilitation – the process of restoring a person's physical functionality to a normal state, or as near as physically possible.

Remit – the area or responsibility of a person or organisation.

Responsibilities – being accountable for certain tasks and related actions and decisions.

Risk – the chance that a hazard may cause harm to someone.

Role-related behaviour – behaviour determined by the circumstances you find yourself in.

SALTAPS – procedure for the assessment of an injured person – stop, ask, look, touch, active movement, passive movement, strength testing.

Skill – an ability that can be learned or developed to allow an activity to be completed.

Social exclusion – feeling as though you are outside normal society.

Social inclusion – trying to involve those who are not really engaged with society (they are excluded to some extent).

Socio-economic groups – ways of grouping people according to income and job.

Soft tissue injury – injury to muscles, tendons, ligaments, internal organs and skin.

Sole trader – a one person business.

Sport – physical activity that is governed by a set of rules or customs and is engaged in competitively.

Sprain – a stretch or tear of ligaments.

Staleness – inability to maintain a previous performance level.

State anxiety – a temporary, ever-changing mood state that is an emotional response to any situation considered to be threatening.

Strain – an injury to muscle or tendon.

Strategy – how a business plan is implemented.

Stroke volume – the amount of blood pushed out of the heart in one contraction.

Summative assessment – takes place formally to assess the performance of a sports coach. This form of assessment is often used to assess a coach's ability (for example, when trying to gain a coaching qualification).

Sustainability – capable of providing steady support without becoming exhausted.

Sympathetic nervous system – part of the system responsible for the 'fight or flight' response.

Synovial effusion – a build-up of synovial fluid within the joint.

Synovial joints – freely movable joints that allow movement. A synovial capsule between the bones prevents bones rubbing together and lubricates the joint cavity.

Talent – a natural ability to be good at something that can be developed through appropriate training.

Tangible support – physical support offered by parents, such as money and kit.

Technique – techniques are always specific to an activity. They are how we perform movements, use equipment and ensure we get the best out of ourselves and our team.

Tendonitis – inflammation of the tendon.

Tendonosis – deterioration of the tendon.

The Ringelmann Effect – the tendency for individuals to lessen their effort when working as part of a group.

Trait – a relatively stable and enduring characteristic that is part of your personality.

Trait anxiety – a behavioural tendency to feel threatened even in situations that are not really threatening, and then to respond to this with high levels of state anxiety.

Trends – the general direction or tendency in the market.

USPs – unique selling points for product or service (features to be promoted).

Voluntary – run by volunteers for the good of the club.

VO$_2$ max – the maximum capacity to transport and utilise oxygen during incremental exercise.

Wellness – can be viewed as our approach to personal health that emphasises individual responsibility for wellbeing through the practice of health promoting lifestyle behaviours.

Working capital – the amount of money available for a business to work with. (In accountancy terms, the amount that current assets exceed current liabilities.)

Index

Index